GEORGE FARQUHAR

GEORGE FARQUHAR

EDITED, WITH AN INTRODUCTION AND NOTES,

BY

WILLIAM ARCHER

WILDSIDE PRESS

www.wildsidepress.com

CONTENTS

PREFATORY NOTE

THERE was little difficulty in selecting the four comedies to be reprinted in this edition. *Love and a Bottle* was excluded by reason of its youthful crudity, *The Inconstant* as a mere adaptation of a Jacobean play. The only question lay between *Sir Harry Wildair* and *The Twin-Rivals;* and it did not take long to decide in favour of the latter. *Sir Harry Wildair* is little more than a weak copy of *The Constant Couple*, whereas *The Twin-Rivals* marks a turning-point in Farquhar's career, and, indeed, in the history of English comedy.

The text of *The Constant Couple* has been collated with that of the second quarto, which was no doubt revised by the author ; but I have added in an appendix the original ending of Act V. Sc. 1, from the first quarto in the Bodleian Library (dated 1700 but published in December 1699). The text of *The Twin-Rivals* and *The Beaux' Stratagem* has been collated with the first quartos ; while in *The Recruiting Officer* the considerable differences between the first and second quartos have been noted. I have to thank Mr Edmund Gosse for placing at my disposal his fine set of Farquhar quartos, and Mr W. J. Lawrence for invaluable assistance in annotation.

I have been able to make one or two quite obvious emendations in the text of Leigh Hunt, which was too closely followed by the late Mr Ewald in his otherwise excellent edition (1892). In most cases I have reverted to the stage directions of the early editions, which are often curious and interesting, but I have not felt bound to do so where they were manifestly inadequate. In the matter of punctuation I have used a perfectly free hand. That of the early editions is rudimentary and haphazard ; that of later editions is but slightly amended. I have not hesitated to repunctuate wherever it seemed necessary in order to make clear the true phrasing of a speech or rhythm of a phrase.

W. A.

INTRODUCTION

I.—Biographical

IT appears from the matriculation-register of Trinity College, Dublin, that "Georgius Farquhare, Sizator, filius Gulielmi Farquhare Clerici," entered that seat of learning on July 17th, 1694. This is the earliest document we possess concerning him. It further records that he was born at Londonderry, and "ibidem educatus sub magistro Walker."[1] Under the rubric of age, we find the entry "Annos 17," whence the year of his birth is usually given as 1678 ; but Dr D. Schmid[2] argues that in all probability it really points to the year 1677. His father held a poor living somewhere in the North of Ireland, but not in Londonderry. He is said to have had only £150 a year, on which to bring up seven children ; but these traditions are very vague. It is further reported that the Farquhars were a family "of no mean rank," and that George's mother was a relative of "Dr Wiseman, Bishop of Dromore, a Baronet's son, of Essex." If this be true, he would be of mingled Irish and English strain. George is said to have written moral verses at the age of ten or thereabouts ; and at the age of thirteen or fourteen he composed a "Pindarick" *On the Death of General Schomberg, kill'd at the Boyn.*

[1] The temptation to identify this pedagogue with the heroic defender of Londonderry must, I fear, be resisted.
[2] *George Farquhar, Sein Leben und seine Original-Dramen.* Wien und Leipzig, 1904.

When he entered Trinity College, it was with a view to studying for the Church, in which he would have had good chances of preferment, through his relationship to the Bishop of Dromore. But that prelate died in 1695, and in the same year Farquhar's academic career came to an end. He is said to have "acquired a considerable reputation" at college; but other traditions represent him as "dull." According to one account, he was expelled for having answered a question as to Christ's walking on the water by some flippant allusion to the proverb about "a man born to be hanged." On leaving college, he is said to have become a corrector of the press : a tradition which receives some colour from the fact that a (presumably elder) brother of his is known to have been a bookseller in Dublin.[1] What is certain is that he "began very early to apply himself to the stage" and became an actor at the Smock Alley Theatre, where he is said to have made his first appearance as Othello !

It was probably the friendship of Robert Wilks, then in the first flush of popularity, that secured him this engagement. Friends they became, at any rate ; and throughout the remaining ten years of Farquhar's life, Wilks was his constant ally. It is recorded that, as an actor, Farquhar "never met with the least repulse from the audience in any of his performances." This modest panegyric does not conflict with the further assertion that he never overcame his tendency to stage-fright. The parts he is said to have played are, in comedy : Young Bellair in Etherege's *Man of Mode*, Careless in Howard's *Committee*, and Young Loveless in Beaumont and Fletcher's *Scornful Lady* ; in tragedy : Lenox in *Macbeth*, Dion in *Philaster*, Rochford in Banks's *Virtue Betrayed*, and Guyomar in Dryden's *Indian Emperor.* It was while playing the last-named character that he, by misadventure, stabbed and seriously injured a fellow-actor. This accident gave him such a disgust for the stage that he forthwith renounced it. By Wilks's advice, he determined to try his fortune as a comedy-writer, and to that end set forth for London, probably in 1697. It is said that Ashbury, the Smock Alley manager, gave him "a free benefit," and that

[1] At a somewhat later date (1704) ; but he may probably have been either established in, or apprenticed to, the trade as early as 1695.

Wilks lent him ten guineas. The statement that they came to London together is incorrect.

His first play, *Love and a Bottle*, was not produced until December 1698 ; and we do not know what he did, or how he supported himself, in the interval. Dr Schmid thinks that, having brought the scheme of his comedy ready-made from Dublin, he completed it soon after his arrival in London, but found no immediate opening for it, firstly because Vanbrugh's *Relapse* (produced early in December 1696)[1] blocked the way; secondly, because the appearance of Jeremy Collier's *Short View*, in March 1697-98, rendered the production of so licentious a play inadvisable. Neither the alleged fact nor the method of accounting for it is convincing. The probability is that *Love and a Bottle* was not completed very long before it appeared, since we can scarcely imagine that a young provincial, freshly arrived from Dublin, would be able instantly to produce a play which shows a familiar, if not an intimate, knowledge of London life.

Love and a Bottle was well received, and was acted nine times in its first season. It is obviously a youthful production, and we can scarcely be wrong in regarding it as, consciously or unconsciously, autobiographical. Roebuck, the hero, is a young Irishman, overflowing with animal spirits and animal passions, who finds himself landed in London without a penny, falls in with a friend who supplies him with clothes and money, and at once plunges with irrepressible zest into a whirl of amatory adventures. We need not go so far as to imagine that the adventures are those which actually befel the author. He was probably not followed from Ireland by a cast-off mistress (Trudge) with her bastard child, certainly not by a virtuous young lady of property (Leanthe) masquerading, for love of him, in male attire. It is evident that the astounding and inextricable imbroglio of disguises

[1] Genest gives the date as 1697, but this is almost certainly wrong. *The Post Boy* of December 26-29, 1696, advertises the quarto of *The Relapse* " as acted at the Theatre Royal, Drury Lane " ; and play-books were usually published about a fortnight after the production of the play. Similarly, the date of *Love and a Bottle* is fixed by an advertisement in *The Post Man* of December 27-29, 1698 : " This day is published the last new comedy called *Love and a Bottle*, wrote by Mr George Farguhar (*sic*.). The Epilogue made and spoke by Jo. Haynes."

and surprises in which the comedy ends never happened on this planet, to Farquhar or anyone else. But though the incidents are fantastic and extravagant, the character of Roebuck is only too probably a piece of idealised self-portraiture. A modern reader may wonder where the idealisation comes in ; but it is manifest that the author warmly admired his hero. "Wild as wind, and unconfin'd as air," says Leanthe, "yet I may reclaim him. His follies are weakly founded, upon the principles of honour, where the very foundation helps to undermine the structure.' How charming wou'd virtue look in him, whose behaviour can add a grace to the unseemliness of vice !" It is true that a certain rollicking good-nature distinguishes this Irish adventurer from the fine-gentleman libertines of Wycherley or Congreve. Thus early does Farquhar's individuality manifest itself. Except for his brutality to his cast-off mistress in the last scene, Roebuck is no more cruel than every reckless debauchee must necessarily be. But this is the utmost that can possibly be said for him. His unbridled licentiousness verges upon insanity ; and for the rest he is an accomplished model of the type known in latter-day slang as the " bounder."

It appears from Joe Haynes's prologue to *Love and a Bottle* that the author had shortly before its production been granted a commission in the army.[2] This clashes with the statement of Thomas Wilkes in the biographical sketch prefixed to the Dublin edition of Farquhar's works (1775), that the Earl of Orrery in 1702 gave him a lieutenant's commission. Probably Wilkes's date is wrong ; possibly he was transferred in 1702 from another regiment to the Earl of Orrery's. At any rate, his military duties seem to have lain very lightly on him. *The Recruiting Officer* was founded on personal experience ; but he seems never to have been on active service.

It was soon after the production of *Love and a Bottle* had given him a standing in the theatrical world that Farquhar, going one day to the Mitre Tavern in St James's Market, heard the niece of the hostess, Mrs Voss, reading

---

[1] Leanthe, like her creator, is Irish.
[2] " Foot to foot be set,
And our young Author's new Commission wet."

some passages from *The Scornful Lady* of Beaumont and
Fletcher with so much spirit that he divined in her a talent
for the theatre. The girl's name was Anne Oldfield. She
was brought to Vanbrugh's notice, and by him recommended
to Christopher Rich, the manager of Drury Lane. For
several seasons she attracted little attention, but came to the
front in 1704, and "created" two of Farquhar's heroines—
Silvia in *The Recruiting Officer*, and Mrs Sullen in
The Beaux' Stratagem.

In 1699 appeared a little book of 58 pp. entitled *The
Adventures of Covent Garden, in Imitation of Scarron's City
Romance*, the authorship of which Leigh Hunt claimed for
Farquhar. Schmid contests the attribution, on inadequate
grounds as it seems to me. It is clear, at any rate, that
Farquhar had some hand in the production, since one of his
poems, afterwards included in *Love and Business*, first appears
in it. Here, too, we find the outline of several incidents
which Farquhar was soon to use in *The Constant Couple*—
notably of the exchange of clothes between Beau Clincher
and Tim Errand. The probability is that in reproducing
these incidents Farquhar was simply plagiarizing from himself.

His second play, *The Constant Couple, or a Trip to the
Jubilee*, was produced in November or early December
1699. It was published, according to an advertisement in
The Post Man, on December 9th. This discovery (due to
Mr W. J. Lawrence) confirms the date given by Genest and
ingeniously defended by Dr Schmid. Other authorities
would place the production in 1700, a date which seems to
be supported by a passage in Farquhar's preface to *The
Inconstant:* "I remember that, about two years ago, I had
a gentleman from France that brought the playhouse some
fifty audiences in five months." There is no doubt that the
"gentleman from France" was Sir Harry Wildair in *The
Constant Couple;* and as we know (see p. 39) that the last
performance of the play occurred on July 13th, 1700,
Farquhar's "five months" would place the first performance
about the middle of February in the same year. His statement, though apparently precise, must have been only
approximate, for it cannot possibly be supposed that the
play was published in December 1699 and not acted till
the following February.

At all events, the comedy made an unprecedented success. Wilks's Sir Harry Wildair became instantly famous ; Norris's performance of the quaint part of young Clincher's servant so took the fancy of the town that he was thenceforth known as "Jubilee Dicky ; " and all the other parts were filled with more or less distinction by the "excellent and complete set of comedians" then assembled at Drury Lane. In the preface to *Love's Contrivance* (1703) Mrs Centlivre wrote : "I believe Mr Rich will own that he got more by *The Trip to the Jubilee* with all its irregularities than by the most uniform piece the stage could boast of ever since." "It was performed," says Thomas Wilkes (Dublin edition, 1775), "fifty-three nights the first season in London, and the manager gave the author four third nights." Farquhar's own statement, in the preface to *The Inconstant*, gives "some fifty" as the number of performances, and so corroborates Wilkes. Malone, however, will not have it so. He alleges that if *The Constant Couple* had been such a great success, there would have been no need for certain revivals of Jonson and Fletcher which took place in the spring at 1700. This reasoning is wholly baseless. Fifty-three performances in seven months gives an average of from seven to eight performances a month, leaving ample room for half-a-dozen revivals in addition. "Never did anything such wonders," said Gildon, a contemporary, and hostile, witness. He could not possibly have used such an expression had the play been acted, as Malone would have us think, only eighteen or twenty times.

On May 13th, 1700, Farquhar attended Dryden's funeral, and was but little impressed by it. From the early part of August to the end of October he was in Holland, but probably not (as Theophilus Cibber suggested) "upon military duty." To this year, too, belong most, if not all, of his extant letters, which relate partly to his travels, but mainly—in obscure and often unedifying terms—to his amorous adventures with two or three different ladies whom it is impossible, and fortunately unimportant, to identify. The tradition, reported by Theo. Cibber, that Mrs Oldfield was the "Penelope" of his most serious attachment, is not in itself improbable ; but Schmid has given several reasons for doubting it. One thing is clear—namely, that his lack of success in this amour was a serious blow to Farquhar.

Some of the letters referring to these transactions were printed in 1702, in a little book named *Love and Business : in a collection of occasionary verse and epistolary prose.* . . . *A Discourse likewise upon Comedy in reference to the English Stage.*[1] Other letters did not appear until 1718, in a compilation entitled *Familiar Letters of Love, Gallantry and several Occasions, by Wits of the last and present Age, together with Mr T. Brown's Remains.*

In the spring of 1701, Farquhar produced his third comedy, *Sir Harry Wildair : being the sequel of The Trip to the Jubilee.* It was fairly successful, being acted for nine nights to good houses ; but neither then nor afterwards did it rival *The Constant Couple* in popularity. It does not seem to have been revived until 1737. In truth, it shares the usual fate of continuations, and is a distinctly inferior play to its predecessor. Schmid suggests that it was written as task-work at a time when Farquhar was depressed by his unsuccessful love-affair, and by the after-effects of a severe illness which overtook him during his visit to Holland.

The year 1702 brought Farquhar twice before the public. Shortly before Lent he produced *The Inconstant; or the Way to Win Him*, an adaptation of Fletcher's *Wild-Goose Chase.* "As to the success of it," he says in the preface, "I think 'tis but a kind of Cremona business, I have neither lost nor won. I pushed fairly, but the French were prepossessed ; and the charms of Gallic heels were too hard for an English brain." Though performed six times, the play was a decided failure. Whether the fault lay in its intermixture of comedy and melodrama, or, (as the author will have it) in a foolish preference on the part of the public for foreign frivolities, it is impossible now to determine.

No better fortune attended the second production of 1702 : *The Twin-Rivals*, first acted on December 14th.[2] Farquhar

[1] For a charming essay on this work, with a study of Farquhar's character, see Edmund Gosse's *Gossip in a Library*.
[2] *See* Latreille's MS. transcripts of bills and advertisements, 1700-1750. B.M. Add. MSS., 32274: "December 14, 1702, never acted a new comedy call'd The Twin Rivals. A rencontre happened this evening on the stage between Mr Fielding and Mr Goodyer, in which the former was wounded." This was the notorious Beau Fielding. Curll, in his *Life of Ann Oldfield*, gives a different account of the affair.

himself tells us that "the galleries were thin during the run of this play," and the run was not a long one. It is hard to understand this failure, for the play is both strong and lively. Its significance as a symptom of the reaction against the brazen cynicism of Wycherley and Congreve will be discussed on a later page. Possibly the public resented the obtrusion of "poetical justice " in the scheme. Possibly the performance of Mrs Mandrake by the male comedian, Bullock, was more than even an eighteenth-century audience could stomach. Possibly, or rather probably, the play suffered from the rivalry of two excellent comedies—Steele's *Funeral* and Cibber's *She Wou'd and She Wou'd Not*—which were in possession of the field when it appeared. Eighteenth-century critics found it the most " regular " of Farquhar's pieces, and praised it for that reason ; but it never took a firm hold on the stage.

The next year, 1703, was probably the date of Farquhar's unfortunate marriage. An apparently trustworthy legend tells us that a young lady from Yorkshire fell in love with him, and " knowing that he was too much dissipated to think of matrimony unless advantage was annexed to it, " gave out that she possessed a fortune of £700 a year. The unwary poet fell into the trap ; and, says Wilkes, " to his honour be it spoken, though he found himself deceived, and his circumstances embarrassed, yet he never once upbraided her for the cheat, but behaved to her with all the delicacy and tenderness of an indulgent husband." The suspicious circumstance about this story is the neatness of the irony it involves. It may have been invented by someone who thought it pleasant to imagine that a writer of comedies should himself fall a victim to one of the classic ruses of comedy. On the other hand, the strong views on divorce expressed by several characters in *The Beaux' Stratagem* do not indicate that the writer's experience of marriage had been altogether fortunate. All we know for certain is that Farquhar did marry, that his wife's name was Margaret, and that he was no richer after his marriage than before it.

At one time in 1704 (the year of Blenheim) he seems to have expected orders to join Marlborough's army ; but he almost certainly did not do so. A farce, *The Stage Coach*, which (in collaboration with Peter Anthony Motteux) he adapted from *Les Carosses d'Orléans*, by Jean de la Chapelle, was produced at Lincoln's Inn Fields in February 1704, with moderate success. To this year, too, belongs a visit to Dublin, in the course of which he played Sir Harry Wildair in a performance given for his own benefit. He "failed greatly" as an actor, says Wilkes, but his profits from the benefit amounted to £100.

At the end of April 1705, occurred the relief of Barcelona, the news of which stirred England to perhaps disproportionate enthusiasm. It was doubtless in the heat of this emotion that Farquhar composed his one "epic": *Barcellona, a Poem; or The Spanish Expedition under the Command of Charles, Earl of Peterborough*. Divided into six cantos, this effusion runs to some fifteen hundred lines; but fifteen hundred worse lines it would be difficult to find even in the panegyric literature of that day. One or two specimens are perhaps worth quoting. A digression upon the victory at Vigo contains the following couplets :—

> This was Great *Ormond's* valiant Feat of Arms,
> Whose martial Presence *animates* and *charms*,
> *Mars*, the great God of War frowns in his Eye,
> And *Cupid*, God of Love, sits smiling by.

From a description of Gibraltar I cull these verses :—

> Along the Western Side the Hill decays,
> In Hills alternate, and rough abrupt Ways;
> And where so e'er the Interspaces fill,
> *Botanick Nature* shews her utmost Skill,
> Here *Æsculapius* trac'd the simpling Path,
> And *here* Instructed left his Art to *Garth*.

The opening lines of Canto V. thus depict the perplexities of the hero :—

> Now *Mordaunt*, walking in his Tent cou'd find
> No Rest amidst the Hurries of his Mind :
> His present *Crosses* met his *Troubles* past ;
> And all Misfortunes center in the last,
> Then striving to expectorate his Grief,
> In this Soliloquy he sought Relief.

The poem was not published until after Farquhar's death, when his widow prefixed to it an apology for its uncorrected state ; but, alas ! no mere correction could have infused any merit into it. Verse was never Farquhar's medium.

It was doubtless in 1705 that Farquhar's military duty took

him to Shrewsbury, in search of recruits for Marlborough's army. He was well received, he tells us, by the local magnates, whose kindness made recruiting, "which is the greatest fatigue upon earth to others," the greatest pleasure in the world to him. He seems to have returned in good spirits : for the comedy which he founded on his experiences abounds more than any of his other plays in the joy of life. *The Recruiting Officer* was produced at Drury Lane on April 8th, 1706.[1] With it Farquhar's luck revived, so far as the theatre was concerned. "The Duke of Ormond," he writes, "encouraged the author, and the Earl of Orrery approved the play. My recruits were reviewed by my general and my colonel and could not fail to pass muster." Genest says the play was "acted ten times," but its success was far greater than this figure would indicate. It at once became one of the stock comedies of the English theatre. When, in the autumn of 1706, the leading members of Rich's company went over to Swiney at the new Haymarket Theatre, the two houses played it against other. Most of the original cast were now at the Haymarket ; but Rich advertised that "the true Serjeant Kite"—that is Estcourt, whom Steele so warmly praises in the part—was to be seen at Drury Lane alone. Genest mentions fifteen notable revivals of the play, the last taking place at Covent Garden in 1829 ; but as a matter of fact the comedy was constantly being revived, whether in London or the provinces, throughout the eighteenth century. Contemporary gossip identified the leading characters of the play with local notabilities of Shropshire ; but their names mean nothing to the modern reader.

The success of *The Recruiting Officer*, unfortunately, did

---

[1] From the Latreille MSS. as above cited :—Drury Lane, Monday, April 8th, 1706, never acted before *The Recruiting Officer*. Repeated on 9th, 10th, 12th, 13th. On the last-mentioned date it was announced "by particular desire of some persons of quality." April 15th (sixth time), it was played for the benefit of the author. Again in bill on 17th. April 20th (eighth time), again played for benefit of author. June 11th, ninth time, and June 20th the tenth. For some reason or other the Drury Lane company began their next season at Dorset Gardens, opening on October 24th in *The Recruiting Officer*. Played it again on November 1st, and finished acting at Dorset Gardens on the following 28th. They then removed to Drury Lane, and on November 30th again put up *The Recruiting Officer*.

not fill Farquhar's exchequer. A "pretended patron," said to have been the Duke of Ormond, advised him to supply his present wants by selling his commission, and promised "to provide for him"—that is, to give him another commission—in a very short time. Farquhar acted on this advice and paid his creditors; but the patron was so dilatory in carrying out his part of the arrangement, that the poet sank into dire poverty. The sequel may be given in the words of Thomas Wilkes, who professed to have had the account from Colley Cibber :—[1]

"Mr Farquhar was a constant attendant on the theatre; but Mr Wilks, having missed him there for upwards of two months, went to the house where he lodged in York Buildings to enquire for him, and was informed that he had left it, but could not learn where he lived. Mr Wilks a few days after received a letter from Farquhar desiring to see him at his lodgings in St Martin's Lane. Wilks went there and found him in a most miserable situation, lodged in a back garret, and under the greatest agitation of mind. Wilks enquired the reason of his distress, and Farquhar acquainted him with the whole affair [of the commission]. . . . Wilks advised him to write a play, and that it should be brought on the stage with all expedition. 'Write!' says Farquhar, 'it is impossible that a man can write common sense who is heartless, and has not a shilling in his pocket.' 'Come, George,' replied Wilks, 'banish melancholy, draw your drama, and I will call on you this day week to see it; but as an empty pocket may cramp your genius, I desire you will accept of my mite,'—and gave him twenty guineas. Mr Farquhar immediately drew up the drama of *The Beaux' Stratagem*, which he delivered to Mr Wilks, and it was approved by him and the managers, and finished in six weeks. Mr Farquhar, during his writing this play, had a settled sickness on him, and most part of it he wrote in his bed, and before he had finished the second act he perceived the approaches of death. The first night that it was performed, his good friend Mr Wilks came to give him an account of its great success. . . . On the third night of its being performed, which was for his benefit, he died, which was the last week in April 1707. Among his papers was found the following note directed to Mr Wilks, viz. :—

"'DEAR BOB,—I have not anything to leave thee to perpetuate my memory, but two helpless girls; look upon them sometimes, and think on him that was to the last moment of his life thine,

'G. FARQUHAR.'

"He was buried in the church of St Martin's in the Fields, at the expense of Mr Wilks."

[1] In reality, however, he seems to have got most of his information from the account of Farquhar in Chetwood's *General History of the Stage* (1749). Chetwood says he had all his details from Robert Wilks, "who approved of them before they went to the publisher."

There is no reason to doubt the substantial accuracy of this account, though the death of the author on the very night of his benefit is probably a concession to the common taste for apt coincidences. Genest gives March 8th as the date of the first performance, and although we do not know his authority, it was probably trustworthy. The statement that Farquhar died in the last week of April is borne out by the register of St Martin's in the Fields which records the burial, on May 3rd, of " Mr George Falkwere." Thus there would be a good seven weeks between the production and the author's death ; and this is all the more probable as there was certainly time for him to write a prefatory note to the first edition of the play, speaking of its established success, and praising its representation (" which cannot be matched ") in such terms as to suggest that the writer had actually seen it.   It is well-nigh impossible, at any rate, that this " advertisement " should have been written between the first representation and the third.

Wilks, it is said, secured a benefit for Farquhar's family, and apprenticed the two daughters to mantua-makers. But the widow seems to have died in great poverty, and the daughters to have sunk rather than risen in the social scale. One of them married a tradesman and died soon afterwards ; the other was living so late as 1764, in the capacity, says Leigh Hunt, of a domestic servant. During the sixty and odd years of her life, how many managers and actors must her father's plays have helped to enrich ?

II.—CRITICAL [1]

N superstitious moments, one is some-
times apt to imagine that the destinies
bear a peculiar grudge against the
English theatre. They gave us
Shakespeare, indeed; but how dearly
have they made us pay for him!
Developing too early, ere yet the
nation had emerged from barbarism,
the drama of the seventeenth century remains, in all
essentials, a barbarous product; and when, with the opening
of the eighteenth century, our manners begin to show a
tincture of civilisation, the springs of dramatic genius
suddenly run dry. In later years one can point to many
cross accidents which seem almost to indicate a peculiar
malevolence on the part of the Sisters Three. Goldsmith
dies immediately after he has proved that his exquisite
genius is thoroughly at home on the stage. Sheridan lives
on, but his lack of character sterilises his talent. For a
century the drama sinks into abject dependency on France.
Then, when a revival sets in with T. W. Robertson, it appears as though a decree had gone forth that the power to
think and the power to write should scarcely ever co-exist in
the same person. In one person, indeed, they do co-exist;
but before he has done anything worthy of his talent, his
career is cut short by the most hideous of tragedies. Thus,
throughout the history of the English drama, it seems that
the gifts of the gods have always come at the wrong time, or
have been wrongly distributed, or cancelled by sheer misadventure. Fate seems to have repented of the favouritism
shown us at Stratford-on-Avon in 1564, and relentlessly set
itself to re-establish the balance.

Among the cross accidents above alluded to, not the
least, I think, was the death, in his thirtieth year, of Captain
George Farquhar. As this is not the view commonly taken
by literary historians, I will try to give my reasons for it.

First, let us get the dates clear. Of all the dramatists of
his group, Farquhar was the latest born and the earliest to

[1] Reprinted, by permission, from the *Fortnightly Review.*

die. Wycherley might almost have been Farquhar's grand-
father, yet outlived him by twelve pitiable years. Vanbrugh
was born in 1664, Congreve in 1670, Cibber in 1671, Steele
in 1672, Farquhar not till 1677 or 1678. Yet Vanbrugh outlived Farquhar by nineteen years, Congreve and Steele
outlived him by twenty-two, and Cibber by fifty. I state
these facts merely to remind the reader that all Farquhar's
work was produced in a few years of comparative immaturity,
between the ages of twenty-one and twenty-nine, and that
he was in the full flush of production when his life was cut
short. More justly than any of his contemporaries, he could
claim the excuse of youth for his faults ; and I shall try to
show that, more clearly than any of his contemporaries, he
was progressing towards a sane and humane form of
comedy when the pen fell from his hand.

Farquhar has been, if not damned, at any rate gravely
depreciated, by a single line of Pope's : "What pert, low
dialogue has Farquhar writ ! " This casual remark has struck
the keynote of criticism for more than a century and a half.
It echoes in Professor Ward's assertion that " He is happy
in the description of manners in a wider range than that
commanded by Vanbrugh ; but his dialogue is in general
less gay and sparkling, and while his morality is no better
than that of the most reckless of his contemporaries, he has
a coarseness of fibre which renders him less endurable than
some of these are to a refined taste." We have here an
indictment in three counts, which I shall attempt to meet
one by one, but in inverse order. I submit, first, that
Farquhar was much less nauseous in his coarseness than
Wycherley, Congreve, or Vanbrugh ; second, that he
showed clear traces of an advance in moral sensibility, nowhere discernible in the other three; third, that the alleged
lack of "sparkle " in his dialogue in reality means a return
to nature, an instinctive revolt against the sterilising convention of "wit." "Gaiety" Professor Ward must surely
have denied him by inadvertence. His severest critics have
contested the merit of his gaiety, but not the fact.

If there is any play of Farquhar's which lends colour to
the accusation of exceptional grossness, it is his earliest
comedy, *Love and a Bottle*, written when he was about
twenty. This is, indeed, an unfortunate effort, in which we

see a raw provincial youth, without any real knowledge either of the town or of the world, simply aping the cynical licentiousness of his elders, and thinking himself a mighty fine fellow in so doing. Life, movement, and gaiety do something to redeem the play. It may even be called remarkable that an Irish hobbledehoy, within the first few months of his stay in London, could produce so spirited an imitation of the current type of comedy. But the character of Roebuck admits of no defence. It is a sheer monstrosity, a boyish fanfaronade of vice. And here, indeed, Farquhar does descend to a grossness almost as vile as that of his contemporaries. Not quite as vile in my judgment—but that, I own, is a matter of opinion. On the other hand, however severely we may condemn this play, it is manifestly unjust to let its sins taint the whole of Farquhar's theatre, and treat as one of his general characteristics an excess into which he fell in his 'prentice work alone. In short, while I cannot admit that even *Love and a Bottle* bears out the charge of *exceptional* "coarseness of fibre," I hold it merely just to put aside this crude and boyish effort, and judge Farquhar by the plays, from *The Constant Couple* onwards, which display his talent and his character in some approach to maturity.

This sin of youth, then, being struck out of the record, we may inquire whether there are in Farquhar many, or any, of those passages of sheer nastiness at which the gorge rises in Wycherley, in Vanbrugh, and even in Congreve. Quotation being out of the question, one can only appeal to the experience of the unprejudiced reader. Morality, be it noted, is not the point at issue. So far as this particular argument is concerned, Farquhar may be as immoral as any of his fellows ; and I freely admit that in point of sensuality, of what was in those days called "lusciousness" of language, he was no whit behind them. But I cannot find that he ever showed the predilection for absolute loathsomeness, for fetid brutality of thought and expression, that was so strong in Wycherley and Vanbrugh. There is nothing in Farquhar to compare with the abominable ugliness of Gripe and Lady Flippant in Wycherley's *Love in a Wood;* no such intolerably nauseous speeches as Sir Simon Addleplot's in Act ii. sc. 1 of that play (beginning, "Though I can give a great guess"), or

Dapperwit's in Act iii. sc. 2 (beginning, " And then so neat "). Where in Farquhar shall we find anything so inhumanly vile as the Horner scenes in *The Country Wife*, or as a great part of *The Plain Dealer?* (Note especially a speech of Manly's in Act iv. sc. i, beginning, " But she was false to me before.") Wycherley, it may be said, belongs in reality to an earlier generation, and a touch of mediæval grossness clings to him. But what, then, of Vanbrugh? Is there anything in Farquhar so revolting as several passages in *The Provoked Wife*, not only in the character of Sir John Brute himself, but even in the conversation of Lady Brute and Belinda? Squire Sullen in *The Beaux' Stratagem* is no doubt cousin-german to Sir John Brute, but how much less repulsive! And when was Farquhar guilty of anything so unspeakable as the character of Coupler in *The Relapse?* Congreve is somewhat less brutal than the rest; but I can think of nothing in Farquhar so abominable as the passage in the first scene of *Love for Love*, beginning with Jeremy's speech, " Oh, sir, there's Trapland, the scrivener," &c. ; and others, scarcely more agreeable, might be cited. Amid all the lewdness that doubtless disfigures Farquhar's plays (especially *The Constant Couple* and its sequel) one is conscious, I think, of a sweeter, cleaner, healthier mind than can be claimed for Wycherley, Congreve, or Vanbrugh, to say nothing of Otway, or D'Urfey, or (alas !) Dryden. He never, like so many of his contemporaries, showed a love for the merely malodorous. His muse stands sadly in need of chastening, but not of disinfecting.

We come now to the second count of the indictment— that " his morality is no better than that of the most reckless of his contemporaries." Here a plain distinction strikes us of once. There is certainly one point of difference between Farquhar and the three contemporaries with whom he is usually bracketed : namely, that they do not, while he very distinctly does, rise from a lower to a higher moral plane. "Manly" Wycherley is as "beastly" in his last as in his first play. Congreve's cynicism is as inhuman in *The Way of the World* as in *The Old Bachelor*. If *The Confederacy* is a little less brutal than *The Relapse* and *The Provoked Wife*, it is only because it is translated from the French. It gives no proof of moral progress on Vanburgh's part. But

Farquhar, from play to play, becomes more decent and more humane. The criticism is summary indeed which lumps together *Love and a Bottle* and *The Beaux' Stratagem*, and speaks as though Farquhar's morality or immorality remained constant throughout his career. The fact is far otherwise ; and unless it can be proved that Farquhar started below the level of his fellows (which is scarcely possible) it follows that he must ultimately have risen above it.

The character which made Farquhar famous shows him at his lowest moral level. Sir Harry Wildair is undeniably a reprobate, a son of chaos, inadmissible in any moral order. But at the same time there is a grace, a humanity, a lightness of touch in his portraiture which distinguishes him for the better from the ferocious, cast-iron libertines of Wycherley and Congreve. The type is not an invention of Farquhar's. It is sketched in Etherege's Sir Frederick Frollick, and other precedents could be quoted. But Farquhar breathed into it a new and enduring vitality. He gave it a touch of bravery, a touch of race, above all, a touch of humour, which still appeals to us. We feel that Sir Harry's faults arise from thoughtlessness, not from wickedness in the grain. Here is a character which does indeed lend some colour to Lamb's defence of Restoration Comedy. In a non-moral fairyland, Sir Harry would be an agreeable sprite ; whereas no abrogation of moral law could render Wycherley's or Congreve's heroes other than detestable. It may be said that Farquhar, in this case, does more harm than his contemporaries, by making vice attractive. That would be true if comedy produced its effect solely or chiefly by inciting to direct imitation of particular characters. But its main effect proceeds rather from the subtle influence of its general atmosphere ; and the atmosphere in which Sir Harry Wildair moves is one of harum-scarum levity rather than of deliberate turpitude. Wycherley and Congreve were no doubt as desirous as Farquhar was to render their heroes attractive, and thought that they had done so. The difference of effect shows that in Farquhar's case we have to deal with a better and saner nature, one that had taken on the taint of the time, but was not fundamentally corrupt.

And Sir Harry, I repeat, shows Farquhar at his worst.

Even in the two plays in which he figures, we have another character of a much higher type—a type for which we may search Wycherley and Congreve in vain. Colonel Standard is a man with some approach to the instincts of a gentleman as we now conceive them. He is a bluff, honest soldier, not a saint, but still less a blackguard. The character is not very vividly drawn, and the incredible romance of his relation to Lady Lurewell impairs his claim to psychological consistency. But the question here at issue is not Farquhar's artistry, but the tone of his mind ; and Standard, I think, gives clear evidence of an innate decency of feeling (to rank it no higher) denied to the other playwrights of the time. In *The Twin-Rivals*, again, Hermes Wouldbe and Trueman are both good fellows enough, wholly different from the Congreve-Vanbrugh type of hero. The callousness with which Wouldbe receives the news of his father's death has been censured, with apparent reason. But it is to be observed, first, that the dramatic situation made it very difficult for him to give way to feeling ; second, that when he has time to reflect, he chides himself for his lack of "filial duty" ; third, that the people of that day took mortality more, and family affection less, as a matter of course than we do. In Farquhar's next play, *The Recruiting Officer*, the conduct of Justice Balance and Silvia, on learning of the death of his son and her brother, seems incredibly unfeeling. To say that it belonged to the manners of the day is not, of course, to justify it ; but another age may be as critical of our sensibility as we of the insensibility of the early eighteenth century. After all, there is nothing to show that the relation of Silvia to her brother had been at all intimate or tender. Perhaps they had seen very little of each other; perhaps they had been wholly unsympathetic. Mr Bernard Shaw's favourite thesis that near relatives always tend to hate each other, is flagrantly false ; but the opposite belief, that they always and necessarily love each other dearly, is a superstition of modern sentimentality. The fact that Farquhar does not interrupt the course of his comedies with scenes of lamentation cannot fairly be taken as a proof that he was deficient in natural feeling.

The ethical standards of *The Recruiting Officer* and of *The Beaux' Stratagem* cannot, certainly, be called high ; but there is in both a general tone of humanity which is far above the level of the age, and even above that of Farquhar's early plays, down to and including *Sir Harry Wildair.* Captain Plume, though a loose-living soldier, belongs rather to the company of Fielding's Tom Jones than to that of Wycherley's Horner or Manly, Congreve's Bellmour or Vainlove, Vanbrugh's Loveless or Worthy. As for Aimwell and Archer, adventurers though they be, they are neither brutal nor wholly unscrupulous. Aimwell, indeed, voluntarily foregoes the fruits of his intrigue, and confesses his personation, in the moment of its success—a trait of conscience inconceivable in the typical hero of the period. But it is not in definite and positive acts that the moral advance is chiefly to be noted. It is in the substitution of wholesome fresh air for the black, bitter, cruel atmosphere that weighs on us in the works of the three other playwrights. I shall try to show later that there are traces in *The Beaux' Stratagem* of an actual interest in moral problems, wholly different from the downright contempt for the very idea of morality which pervades the Restoration Comedy as a whole. In the meantime, it is sufficient to say that in all his plays, from *The Constant Couple* onwards, and especially in the last three, Farquhar gives a general preponderance to kindness over cruelty [1] and good over evil, which reverses the order of things prevailing in his contemporaries. Where shall we look in them for a sentiment like the following (*The Twin-Rivals,* Act ii. sc. I) :—

Constance. Are you sure he's well-bred ?
Aurelia. I tell you he's good-natured, and I take good manners to be nothing but a natural desire to be easy and agreeable to whatever conversation we fall into ; and a porter with this is mannerly in his way, and a duke without it has but the breeding of a dancing-master.

Such an utterance points forward to the nineteenth century rather than backward to the seventeenth. In the third act of the same play, the scene between Hermes Wouldbe

---

[1] It may be said that *The Recruiting Officer* treats heartlessly of the cruelties perpetrated under the Enlistment Acts. But denunciation of these abuses was scarcely to be expected from an officer actually employed in the work of recruitment ; and, on the other hand, though the comedy is gay and irresponsible in tone, it is no eulogy, but rather a satire, on the methods employed.

and Fairbank is conceived in a spirit of rectitude and kindliness quite unknown to Farquhar's compeers and rivals.

That Farquhar's nature was humane seems to me beyond question ; but he also moved with a general current setting towards humanity. To say that he was "reformed" by Jeremy Collier would be inexact, for the famous *Short View of the Immorality and Profaneness of the English Stage* appeared many months before Farquhar made his first essay as a dramatist. Collier's attack was nearly two years old when Farquhar scored his greatest success with the *The Constant Couple*, on which "the parson" had certainly no influence whatever. Nevertheless, there can be little doubt that Farquhar felt and welcomed the reaction in favour of decency, if not of speech, at any rate of feeling. One would like to think that he headed the reaction, but here the dates are unaccommodating. That distinction belongs to Steele. *The Funeral*, produced towards the end of 1701 (it is misdated in Genest), marked a long step on a path which Farquhar did not clearly begin to follow until a year later in *The Twin-Rivals*. Had he been minded to relapse into the old rut, the failure of that play would have afforded him an excuse. But he was not weary in better-doing, and may fairly share with Steele the credit of having set earnestly about the ventilation of English comedy.

We come now to the question of dialogue, which we shall find shading off into another and larger question. It may be admitted at once that Farquhar's dialogue has not the dry, hard polish—the "sparkle," as Professor Ward justly calls it—of Congreve, or of Vanbrugh at his best. He is not, like Congreve, a virtuoso in style. There is perhaps no part in his plays so well written, in the literary sense, as that of Lord Foppington in Vanbrugh's *Relapse*. He was not, in fact, specifically a literary man. His verse is uniformly execrable, and his non-dramatic prose has far more ease than distinction. But we must note that if, in his dialogue, he did not achieve the glitter of Congreve, it is partly, at least, because he did not aim at it. Farquhar had plenty of wit ; but he did not make wit the beginning and end of his endeavour. It would be a curious task for German industry (and by no means the idlest it has ever undertaken) to tell us how many times the word "wit" occurs in the comedies of Congreve and Farquhar respectively. I would lay a heavy wager that the proportion would prove to be at least twenty to one. Congreve's characters, both the wise men (such as they be) and the fools, are always thinking and talking about their wit. Wit and intrigue are the sole objects of their existence. "Leave business to idlers and wisdom to fools," cries Bellmour, on the first page of Congreve's first comedy; "wit be my faculty, and pleasure my occupation." No doubt it would be unjust to call this continual strain after similitude, paradox, and repartee a mere convention of the playhouse. There are social circles to-day in which the same self-conscious striving after brilliancy makes life an irritation and a toil. The great development of "polite" intercourse which followed the Restoration begot a new Euphuism which, being unrestrained by decency or good nature, was an easily-acquired and highly infectious fashion. It is quite probable that the Dapperwit, the Sparkish, the Novel of Wycherley, the Brisk and Tattle and Petulant and Witwoud of Congreve, had their originals in real life, and were not even very grossly caricatured. But the world to which they belonged —the fast or "smart" world, as we should nowadays call it —was a very small and superficial one. As the modern dramatist speaks of "our little parish of St James's," so Congreve might have called the whole province of his genius "our little parish of Covent Garden." In his plays especially, but also in those of Wycherley and Vanbrugh, we have a constant sense of frequenting a small coterie of exceedingly disagreeable people. Their talk is essentially coterie-talk, keyed up to the pitch of a particular and narrow set. It is Farquhar's great merit to have released comedy from this circle of malign enchantment. Even in *The Constant Couple* and *Sir Harry Wildair* his characters have not quite the coterie stamp. We feel, at any rate, that they are studied from an outside point of view, by one who does not mistake the conventions of the coterie for laws of nature. In *The Twin-Rivals* the coterie tone is scarcely heard at all. With the return to a recognition (rather too formal to be artistic) of the difference between right and wrong, we have something like a return to nature in the tone of conversation. In the excellent little scene (Act i. sc. 1) between Benjamin Wouldbe and the innkeeper Balderdash, there is nothing that can be called wit, but a great deal of humour ; while Mrs Mandrake is a realistic life-study of extraordinary power. Finally, in *The Recruiting Officer* and *The Beaux' Stratagem*, Farquhar broke away altogether from the purlieus of Covent Garden, and took comedy out into the highways and the byways. When Congreve strayed into the country, it was only to present to us that amazing "house party" of *The Double Dealer*—Lord and Lady Touchwood, Lord and Lady Froth, Sir Paul and Lady Plyant, Mellefont, Maskwell, Careless and Brisk—in a word, the coterie at its narrowest. When Vanbrugh went down to the shires, it was only to show Tom Fashion stealing away the daughter of Sir Tunbelly Clumsey. But Farquhar introduced us to the life of the inn, the market-place, and the manor house. He showed us the squire, the justice, the innkeeper, the highwayman, the recruiting sergeant, the charitable lady, the country belle, the chambermaid, and half a score of excellent rustic types. He introduced the picaresque element into English comedy, along with a note of sincere and original observation. To have made the good folk of Shrewsbury and Lichfield express themselves with the modish, stereotyped wit of the London chocolate-house and boudoir would have been the height of absurdity. Farquhar reduced wit within something like the limits of nature, subordinating it to humour, and giving it, at the same time, an accent, all his own, of unforced, buoyant gaiety. And he had for his reward the line : " What pert, low dialogue has Farquhar writ ! "

That Farquhar widened the range of comedy is obvious and generally admitted. But critics have, so far as I know, overlooked a subtler distinction between his work and that of his contemporaries, which seems to me real and important. If he was not specifically a literary man in the sense in which they were, he was specifically a dramatist in a sense in which they were not. That is to say, he was a dramatist and nothing else, whereas in Wycherley, Congreve and Vanbrugh the dramatist was as yet imperfectly differentiated from the social essayist. How often in their

plays does the action stand still while the characters ex-
patiate in reflection, generalisation, description and criticism
of other characters ; in short, in essays or leading articles
broken up into dialogue ! Comedy, as they conceived it,
meant *the introspection of the coterie.* The business of the
comic poet was to show the little circle, with which alone he
was conversant, in the act of observing, analysing, and dis-
cussing its own manners and customs, humours and foibles.
His characters were always intensely self-conscious, always
perfectly aware that they were playing parts, under the
critical eyes of their friends and acquaintances, upon the
coterie-stage of "the town." There is scarcely a comedy of
Wycherley, Congreve, or Vanbrugh from which long scenes
of sheer generalisation or episodic portraiture could not be
wholly excised, without leaving any sensible gap either in
the action of the play or in the characterisation necessary to
justify the action. As instances, let me mention in
Wycherley the scenes between Lady Fidget, Mrs Dainty
Fidget, and Mrs Squeamish (*Country Wife*, Act ii. sc. 1),
between Horner, Sparkish, and Dorilant (*Country Wife*,
Act iii. sc. 2), between Olivia, Eliza, Novel, and Plausible
(*Plain Dealer*, Act ii. sc. 1) ; in Congreve, the greater part
of the Petulant and Witwoud dialogue in *The Way of the
World;* and in Vanbrugh the scene between Lady Brute
and Belinda (*Provoked Wife*, Act iii. sc. 3), which opens
in this characteristic strain of reflection :—

Lady Brute. What hogs men turn, Belinda, when they grow
weary of women !
Belinda. And what owls they are whilst they are fond of 'em !

But whole scenes of this nature are, of course, compara-
tively rare. The essential point is that there is scarcely a
scene in any of these writers wherein the characters do not
pause, more or less frequently, to contemplate themselves or
each other from what may be called the essayist's point of
view, and to pass general remarks and theoretic judgments.
There is scarcely a scene in which one could not find the
text (and often a great part of the substance) of a *Tatler* or
Spectator essay. The dramatist, in fact, was not merely a
dramatist but a journalist as well. He suffered his
characters not only to reveal themselves in action, but to

explain and satirise themselves and each other, in un-dramatised or imperfectly dramatised disquisition. Even his valets and lady's-maids would not infrequently deliver themselves of neat little essays, wholly unnecessary to the progress of the plot.

When we come to Farquhar, we find the differentiation between the dramatist and the essayist rapidly completing itself. In *Love and a Bottle* it is still very imperfect, but from *The Constant Couple* onwards it is much more clearly marked than in any of the other three. His characters are not for ever feeling their own pulses, taking the social temperature, or noting the readings of the wit-barometer. It is impossible to prove a negative by quotation ; I can but state what I think is the fact and leave the reader to verify it. Farquhar's plots are as conventional as those of his contemporaries, his technical devices as crude ; but he confines his characters within the action, and keeps the action moving, better than they do. He is much less given to the elaborate portrayal of a Jonsonian "humour" for its own sake. We do not find in his comedies that characters are minutely described before they appear, and then do nothing throughout the rest of the play but, as it were, copy their own portrait. I remember but one exception to this rule : Captain Brazen, in *The Recruiting Officer*, who is heralded by his full-length portrait, drawn by Worthy and Balance. The few lines of introduction which precede Sir Harry Wildair's entrance are scarcely a case in point ; for Wildair is certainly a rounded character, not, like Dapperwit or Sparkish, or Tattle or Brisk, a mere incarnate "humour." This departure from the Jonsonian method is an additional evidence of the fact that the dramatist, properly so-called, was more highly developed in Farquhar than in his contemporaries.

Now history shows us that one of the chief literary phenomena of these years was precisely the differentiation of the journalist from the dramatist. Steele, who comes to the front as a dramatist two years later than Farquhar, and precedes him by a year in the movement towards a saner morality, presently abandons the stage (or nearly so) in order to devote himself to journalism. In other words, he distributes his essays and character-sketches in type through the coffee-houses and the boudoirs, instead of inviting the beaux, wits and ladies to come and listen to them in the theatre. Addison follows suit ; and as the essay gains ground, comedy declines. This means that specifically dramatic endowment was rare, and that, as soon as the non-dramatic element in Restoration Comedy was found readily separable from the dramatic framework, much of the talent which would otherwise have sought utterance in the theatre chose rather to express itself in a simple and natural than in a hybrid and highly artificial form. But Farquhar was the one man of the time who had dramatic talent highly developed and discursive talent scarcely at all. He had great fertility and facility ; his last and best play he wrote in six weeks, while in the grip of mortal illness. Had he lived to sixty instead of dying before thirty, we can scarcely doubt that he would have kept the drama more nearly abreast of the essay and its successor, the novel, than it has ever been from his day to our own. We might have had in him a Fielding of the theatre.

Even as it was, in his brief literary life of eight or nine years, cut short before he can be supposed to have reached full maturity, he contrived to do work which makes him, far more than any other of his group, an influential precursor of Fielding. In humour and humanity the two are distinctly congenial ; and, if we allow for difference of scale, Farquhar's power of character-drawing may quite well be measured with that of the " Great Harry." He had extraordinary ease in giving his personages individuality without caricature, or mechanical insistence or " humours." But what chiefly justifies us in regarding his too early death as one of the most notable of the many mischances that have befallen the English drama, is the steady growth we can perceive in him, not only of moral feeling, but of sober criticism of life. His first three comedies, as I have admitted, are entirely irresponsible ; but in the last act of the last of them we come upon a passage which, in ironic form, strikes a note of sincere indignation. So, at least, I read the short scene in *Sir Harry Wildair* (Act v. sc. 4) between Sir Harry and Lord Bellamy. The almost savage scorn with which Sir Harry here spits in the face of " smart " society—of what I have called the coterie—is not in his normal character. It reminds one of a tirade by one of the debauchee moralists of the younger Dumas. Farquhar is here uttering the bitterness of his own spirit ; and from this time onward he is no longer irresponsible, not even in the semi-Elizabethan *Inconstant* which he borrowed from Fletcher. Especially noteworthy is the growth of his sympathy with the finer aspects of womanhood. Leanthe in *Love and a Bottle* is a romantic impossibility, Lucinda a very vulgar personage. Angelica in *The Constant Couple* is a lay-figure, and in *Sir Harry Wildair* a convention ; while Lady Lurewell is, in *The Constant Couple*, a melodramatic man-hater, not unlike Dumas's *Étrangère*, and has become, in *Sir Harry Wildair*, a vapourish, corrupt fine-lady. But in the later plays the heroines are always natural, agreeable women, with as much refinement as the atmosphere of the age would permit. I have already quoted an admirable saying of Aurelia's in *The Twin-Rivals*. Silvia, in *The Recruiting Officer*, in spite of the absurdity of her disguise and the coarseness of some of the episodes that spring from it, seems to me to have more than a touch of the free, generous, self-reliant womanhood of Shakespeare's heroines in the past and Mr Meredith's in the future. Dorinda, in *The Beaux' Stratagem*, is a pleasant figure, and even Mrs Sullen is not the ordinary female rake of Restoration Comedy. Professor Ward writes of this play : "Some of the incidents are dubious, including one at the close—a separation by mutual consent, which throws a glaring light on the view taken by the author and his age on the sanctity of the marriage tie." I venture to suggest that what is here set down to Farquhar's discredit is, in fact, a remarkable proof of the increasing earnestness of his outlook upon life. We have in this comedy (especially in the scenes between Mrs Sullen and Dorinda at the end of Act iii., and between Squire Sullen and Sir Charles Freeman at the beginning of Act v.) a serious and very damaging criticism of the conventional view that there can be no immorality in marriage save breach of the marriage vow. These scenes are, in fact, a plea for what Farquhar regarded, rightly or wrongly, as a more rational law of divorce. We may or may not think the plea a sound one ; but it is certain that a serious discussion of the ethics of divorce was a homage to the idea of marriage which Wycherley, Congreve, or Vanbrugh would never have dreamt of paying. To them marriage meant nothing but a legal convention governing the transmission of property from (reputed) father to son. For the rest, it merely added a relish to libertinism. Where marriage constitutes no bond, divorce can have no function. When Farquhar seriously (and wittily) set himself to show that a certain type of marriage was loathsome and immoral, he broke once for all with the irresponsible licentiousness of his school. He admitted a moral standard, and subjected social convention, not to mere cynical persiflage, but to the criticism of reason. Having reached this point at twenty-nine, how far might he not have advanced if another twenty years had been vouchsafed him?

WILLIAM ARCHER.

THE

CONSTANT COUPLE

OR A

TRIP TO THE JUBILEE

A

COMEDY

Acted at the Theatre Royal in *Drury - Lane*,
By His Majesty's Servants.

The *Second Edition*, with a New Scene added
to the part of *Wildair*.

By Mr *GEORGE FARQUHAR*

Sive favore tuli, sive hanc ego carmine famam
Jure tibi grates, candide lector, ago.

OVID, Trist. lib. 4, Eleg. 10.

LONDON ;

Printed for *Ralph Smith* at the Bible under the *Piazza* of the *Royal Exchange, Cornhil*, and *Bennet Banbury* at the Blue Anchor in the *New Exchange*, in the *Strand*. 1700.

As to the date of this comedy (1699) and as to its relation to *The Adventures of Covent Garden*, see Introduction p. 7, Genest is probably right in saying that a hint for Lady Lurewell's character, and for the two Clinchers, was borrowed from D'Urfey's *Madam Fickle, or the Witty False One* (1676). It is possible, too, that in Lady Lurewell, Farquhar had in mind Mrs Manley, afterwards authoress of the *New Atlantis*. Her father was Sir Roger Manley, while Lady Lurewell's father is called Sir Oliver Manly; and the irregularity of Mrs Manley's marriage seems to have begotten in her a somewhat Lurewell-like frame of mind. The last performance of the play chronicled by Genest took place at the Haymarket in 1820, when Mrs Mardyn appeared as Sir Harry Wildair. This part was frequently—one might almost say generally—acted by women. It was one of Mrs Woffington's chief successes, and even Mrs Jordan played it repeatedly.

SIR ROGER MOSTYN, BART., OF MOSTYN HALL
IN FLINTSHIRE

SIR,

IS no small reflection on pieces of this nature, that panegyric is so much improved, and that dedication is grown more an art than poetry; that authors, to make their patrons more than men, make themselves less ; and that persons of honour are forced to decline patronising wit, because their modesty cannot bear the gross strokes of adulation.

But give me leave to say, Sir, that I am too young an author to have learned the art of flattery; and, I hope, the same modesty which recommended this play to the world, will also reconcile my addresses to you, of whom I can say nothing but what your merits may warrant, and all that have the honour of your acquaintance will be proud to vindicate.

The greatest panegyric upon you, Sir, is the unprejudiced and bare truth of your character, the fire of youth, with the sedateness of a senator, and the modern gaiety of a fine English gentleman, with the noble solidity of the Ancient Briton.

This is the character, Sir, which all men, but yourself, are proud to publish of you, and which more celebrated pens than mine should transmit to posterity.

The play has had some noble appearances to honour its representation ; and to complete the success, I have presumed to prefix so noble a name to usher it into the world. A stately frontispiece is the beauty of a building. But here I must transverse Ovid :

Materia superabit Opus.

I am,

Honourable Sir,

Your most devoted, and

Humble servant,

GEO. FARQUHAR.

PREFACE TO THE READER

 N affected modesty is very often the greatest vanity, and authors are sometimes prouder of their blushes than of the praises that occasioned them. I shan't therefore, like a foolish virgin, fly to be pursued, and deny what I chiefly wish for. I am very willing to acknowledge the beauties of this play, especially those of the third night, which not to be proud of were the height of impudence. Who is ashamed to value himself upon such favours, under-values those who conferred them.

As I freely submit to the criticisms of the judicious, so I cannot call this an ill play, since the Town has allowed it such success. When they have pardoned my faults, 'twere very ill manners to condemn their indulgence. Some may think (my acquaintance in town being too slender to make a party for the play) that the success must be derived from the pure merits of the cause. I am of another opinion : I have not been long enough in town to raise enemies against me ; and the English are still kind to strangers. I am below the envy of great wits, and above the malice of little ones. I have not displeased the ladies, nor offended the clergy ; both which are now pleased to say, that a comedy may be diverting without smut and profaneness.

Next to these advantages, the beauties of action gave the greatest life to the play, of which the town is so sensible, that all will join with me in commendation of the actors, and allow (without detracting from the merits of others) that the Theatre Royal affords an excellent and complete set of comedians. Mr Wilks's performance has set him so far above competition in the part of Wildair, that none can pretend to envy the praise due to his merit. That

35

he made the part, will appear from hence, that whenever the stage has the misfortune to lose him, Sir Harry Wildair may go to the Jubilee.

A great many quarrel at *the Trip to the Jubilee* for a misnomer : I must tell them, that perhaps there are greater trips in the play ; and when I find that more exact plays have had better success, I'll talk with the critics about decorums, &c. However, if I ever commit another fault of this nature, I'll endeavour to make it more excusable.

PROLOGUE

BY A FRIEND

OETS will think nothing so checks their fury
As wits, cits, beaux, and women, for their jury.
Our spark's half dead to think what medley's come,
With blended judgments to pronounce his doom.
'Tis all false fear; for in a mingled pit,
Why, what your grave don thinks but dully writ,
His neighbour i' th' great wig may take for wit.
Some authors court the few, the wise, if any;
Our youth's content, if he can reach the many,
Who go with much like ends to church and play,
Not to observe what priests or poets say;
No, no, your thoughts, like theirs, lie quite another way.
The ladies safe may smile: for here's no slander,
No smut, no lewd-tongued beau, no *double-entendre*.
'Tis true, he has a spark just come from France,
But then so far from beau—why, he talks sense!
Like coin oft carried out, but—seldom brought from thence.
There's yet a gang to whom our spark submits,
Your elbow-shaking fool, that lives by's wits,
That's only witty though, just as he lives, by fits.
Who, lion-like, through bailiffs scours away,
Hunts, in the face, a dinner all the day,
At night, with empty bowels, grumbles o'er the play.
And now the modish prentice he implores,
Who, with his master's cash, stolen out of doors,

37

Employs it on a brace of—honourable whores;
While their good bulky mother pleased sits by,
Bawd regent of the bubble gallery.
Next to our mounted friends we humbly move,
Who all your side-box tricks are much above,
And never fail to pay us—with your love. [1]
Ah, friends! Poor Dorset-Garden house [2] is gone;
Our merry meetings there are all undone:
Quite lost to us, sure for some strange misdeeds,
That strong dog Samson's pull'd it o'er our heads,
Snaps rope like thread; but when his fortune's told him,
He'll hear perhaps of rope will one day hold him:
At least I hope that our good-natured town
Will find a way to pull his prizes down.
    Well, that's [3] all! Now, gentlemen, for the play.
On second thoughts, I've but two words to say;
Such as it is for your delight design'd,
Hear it, read, try, judge, and speak as you find.

[1] The meaning of this triplet is far from clear. The "mounted friends" were doubtless spectators in the gallery, and the "side-box tricks" referred to were probably the tricks of the beaux to avoid payment. Note Archer's allusion in *The Beaux' Stratagem*, Act IV. sc. 2, "or be obliged to sneak into the side-box, and between both houses steal two acts of a play." Shadwell, in *The Humours of the Army*, has a similar passage, showing that when the Boxkeeper went round between the acts to collect the charges (after the old Restoration custom), the beau tried to dodge him by shifting about from box to box. But, according to this interpretation, it would seem to have been the denizens of the side-boxes, and not the "mounted friends" who payed "with their love."

[2] The Duke's Theatre in Dorset Gardens, Fleet Street, was opened, according to Downes, on November 9th 1671. It was a large and handsome house, where a good deal was attempted in the way of spectacle, but throughout its career it was more patronised by the City than by the Court. On the accession of James II. its name was changed to the Queen's. After 1697, theatrical performances at the Queen's were only occasional; and in 1699 it was let to one William Joy, calling himself Samson, a Kentish "strong man," alluded to below. For a short time in October, 1706, the Drury Lane Company acted at Dorset Gardens (*see* note, p. 12). An advertisement in *The Daily Courant* for June 1st, 1709, announces that "The Play House at Dorset Stairs is now pulling down," and that excellent firewood is to be had cheap.

[3] Query "that is"?

A NEW PROLOGUE

*In answer to my very good friend, Mr Oldmixon [1]; who,
having two plays damn'd at the Old House, had a mind to
curry favour, to have a third damn'd at the New.*

IS hard the author of this play in view,
Should be condemn'd, purely for pleas-
    ing you :
Charged with a crime, which you, his
    judges, own
Was only this, that he has pleased the
    town.
He touch'd no poet's verse, nor doctor's bills ;

[1] John Oldmixon had had two unsuccessful plays produced at
Drury Lane : *Amintas*, 1698, and *The Grove, or Love's Paradise*,
in 1700. For the latter, Farquhar wrote an epilogue, so that he
was then, no doubt, the author's friend ; but this prologue shows
that they had quarrelled. Now, *The Post Boy* of July 9-11, 1700,
contains the following paragraph : " In consideration of the great
success of a Play called *The Constant Couple, or a Trip to the
Jubelee* (*sic*), and in answer to a Scandulous (*sic*) Prologue spoken
against it at the New House : at the Theatre Royal in Drury Lane
on Saturday, the 13th of July, the said Play will be presented for
the benefit of the Author, it being the last time of the Company's
acting this summer." (Genest, Vol. II., p. 166, quotes an MS.
note, evidently based upon this paragraph). It would appear, then,
that *The Grove* was produced early in 1700 ; that subsequently to
its production, and in order to " curry favour " with the rival
company at Lincoln's Inn Fields, and secure the acceptance of a
play, Oldmixon wrote for them a prologue attacking *The Constant
Couple ;* and that this was Farquhar's retort, no doubt spoken on
his third, if not fourth, benefit night, the last of the season, July
13. As a matter of fact, Oldmixon's next play was produced at
L.I.F., though not until 1703.

No foe to B——re,[1] yet a friend to Wills.
No reputation stabb'd by sour debate ;
Nor had a hand in bankrupt Brisco's[2] fate :
And, as an ease to's tender conscience, vows,
He's none of those that broke the t'other house :
In perfect pity to their wretched cheer,
Because his play was bad—he brought it here.
The dreadful sin of murder cries aloud ;
And sure these poets ne'er can hope for good,
Who dipp'd their barbarous pens in that poor house's
    blood.
'Twas malice all : no malice like to theirs,
To write good plays, purpose to starve the players.
To starve by's wit, is still the poet's due,
But here are men whose wit is match'd by few ;
Their wit both starves themselves and others too.
Our plays are farce, because our house is cramm'd ;
Their plays all good ; for what?—because they're
    damn'd.
Because we pleasure you, you call us tools ;
And 'cause you please yourselves they call you fools.
By their good-nature, they are wits, true blue ;
And men of breeding, by their respects to you.
To engage the fair, all other means being lost,
They fright the boxes with old Shakspeare's ghost[3] ;
The ladies of such spectres should take heed ;
For 'twas the devil did raise that ghost indeed.

[1] Ewald says : "An allusion, I think, to Sir Richard Blackmore, doctor and poet" ; but the point of the allusion seems to be lost beyond recovery.

[2] Probably the bookseller referred to by Luttrell under May 12, 1698 :—"The Justices of Middlesex did not only present the play houses, but also Mr Congreve, for writing the *Double Dealer ;* Durfey, for *Don Quixote ;* and Tonson and Brisco, booksellers, for printing them ; and that women frequenting the play houses in masks tended much to debauchery and immorality." (Collier's *Short View* had been published in the previous March.)

[3] An allusion to Gildon's maltreatment of *Measure for Measure,* produced at Lincoln's Inn Fields, with an epilogue by Oldmixon, spoken by Verbruggen, in the character of Shakspeare's Ghost.

Their case is hard that such despair can show ;
They've disobliged all powers above, they know ;
And now must have recourse to powers below.
Let Shakspeare then lie still, ghosts do no good ;
The fair are better pleased with flesh and blood.
What is't to them, to mind the ancients' taste ?
But the poor folks are mad, and I'm in haste.

　　　　　　　　　　　　　　　　[*Runs off.*

DRAMATIS PERSONÆ

MEN

Sir Harry Wildair	An airy gentleman, affecting humorous gaiety and freedom in his behaviour.	Mr Wilks.
Standard	A disbanded Colonel, brave and generous.	Mr Powell.
Vizard	Outwardly pious, otherwise a great debauchee, and villainous.	Mr Mills.
Smuggler, an old Merchant.		Mr Johnson.
Clincher	A pert London 'Prentice turned Beau, and affecting travel.	Mr Pinkethman.
Clincher Jun.	His Brother, educated in the Country.	Mr Bullock.
Dicky, his Man.		Mr Norris.
Tom¹ Errand, a Porter.		Mr Haines.

WOMEN

Lurewell	A Lady of a jilting temper, proceeding from a resentment of her wrongs from Men.	Mrs Verbruggen.
Lady Darling	An old Lady, Mother to Angelica.	Mrs Powell.
Angelica, a Woman of Honour		Mrs Rogers.
Parly, Maid to Lurewell.		Mrs Moor.

Constable, Mob, Porter's Wife, Servants, &c.

SCENE—London.

¹ *See* note, p. 80.

ACT I

SCENE I.—*The Park.*

Enter VIZARD *with a letter*, Servant *following.*

VIZ. Angelica send it back un-opened! say you?

Serv. As you see, sir.

Viz. The pride of these virtuous women is more insufferable than the immodesty of prostitutes!—After all my encouragement, to slight me thus!

Serv. She said, sir, that imagining your morals sincere, she gave you access to her conversation; but that your late behaviour in her company has convinced her that your love and religion are both hypocrisy, and that she believes your letter like yourself, fair on the outside, foul within; so sent it back unopened.

Viz. May obstinacy guard her beauty till wrinkles bury it! Then may desire prevail to make her curse that untimely pride her disappointed age repents!—I'll be revenged the very first opportunity.—Saw you the old Lady Darling, her mother?

Serv. Yes, sir, and she was pleased to say much in your commendation.

Viz. That's my cue. — An esteem grafted in old

age is hardly rooted out, years stiffen their opinions
with their bodies, and old zeal is only to be cozened
by young hypocrisy.—Run to the Lady Lurewell's,
and know of her maid whether her ladyship will be at
home this evening. — [*Exit* Servant.]   Her beauty
is sufficient cure for Angelica's scorn.

> [*Pulls out a book, reads, and walks about.*

Enter Alderman SMUGGLER.

Smug. Ay, there's a pattern for the young men o'
th' times!—At his meditation so early; some book
of pious ejaculations, I'm sure.

Viz. [*Aside.*] This Hobbes is an excellent fellow!
—[*Aloud.*] O uncle Smuggler! To find you in this
end o' th' town is a miracle.

Smug. I have seen a miracle this morning indeed,
cousin Vizard.

Viz. What is it, pray, sir?

Smug. A man at his devotion so near the Court.—
I'm very glad, boy, that you keep your sanctity untainted
in this infectious place; the very air of this park is
heathenish, and every man's breath I meet scents of
atheism.

Viz. Surely, sir, some great concern must bring you
to this unsanctified end of the town.

Smug. A very unsanctified concern truly, cousin.

Viz. What is't?

Smug. A lawsuit, boy.—Shall I tell you?—My ship
the Swan is newly arrived from St Sebastian's, laden
with Portugal wines: now the impudent rogue of a tide-
waiter has the face to affirm, 'tis French wines in Spanish
casks, and has indicted me upon the statute.[1]—O conscience! conscience! these tide-waiters and surveyors
plague us more with their French wines, than the war
did with French privateers.

---

[1] This method of passing off French goods under cover of another
nationality was one of the most frequently practised among the
many forms of smuggling.

Enter Colonel STANDARD.

Ay, there's another plague of the nation—a red coat and feather.[1]

Viz. Colonel Standard, I'm your humble servant.

Stand. Maybe not, sir.

Viz. Why so !

Stand. Because—I'm disbanded.

Viz. How ? broke !

Stand. This very morning, in Hyde Park, my brave regiment, a thousand men that looked like lions yesterday, were scattered, and looked as poor and simple as the herd of deer that grazed beside 'em.

Smug. [*Singing,*] Tal, al, deral !—I'll have a bonfire this night as high as the Monument.

Stand. A bonfire ! thou dry, withered, ill nature ! had not these brave fellows' swords defended you, your house had been a bonfire ere this about your ears.—Did we not venture our lives, sir ?

Smug. And did not we pay you for your lives, sir ?—Venture your lives ! I'm sure we ventured our money, and that's life and soul to me.—Sir, we'll maintain you no longer.

Stand. Then your wives shall, old Actæon. There are five-and-thirty strapping officers gone this morning to live upon free quarter in the city.

Smug. O Lord ! O Lord ! I shall have a son within these nine months born with a leading staff in his hand.—Sir, you are—

Stand. What, sir ?

Smug. Sir, I say that you are—

Stand. What, sir ?

Smug. Disbanded, sir, that's all.—I see my lawyer yonder. [*Exit.*

[2] The struggle between King William and the Parliament of 1698 over the disbandment, or sweeping reduction, of the army, was the burning topic of 1698-99. The Dutch Guards had, as a matter of fact, been dismissed, and the British forces reduced to a minimum.

Viz. Sir, I'm very sorry for your misfortune.

Stand. Why so ? I don't come to borrow money of you ; if you're my friend, meet me this evening at the Rummer[1] ; I'll pay my way, drink a health to my king, prosperity to my country ; and away for Hungary to-morrow morning.

Viz. What ! you won't leave us ?

Stand. What ! a soldier stay here ! to look like an old pair of colours in Westminster Hall, ragged and rusty ! no, no.—I met yesterday a broken lieutenant, he was ashamed to own that he wanted a dinner, but begged eighteenpence of me to buy a new sheath for his sword.

Viz. Oh, but you have good friends, Colonel !

Stand. Oh, very good friends ! my father's a lord, and my elder brother a beau.

Viz. But your country may perhaps want your sword again.

Stand. Nay, for that matter, let but a single drum beat up for volunteers between Ludgate and Charing Cross, and I shall undoubtedly hear it at the walls of Buda.

Viz. Come, come, Colonel, there are ways of making your fortune at home. Make your addresses to the fair ; you're a man of honour and courage.

Stand. Ay, my courage is like to do me wondrous service with the fair. This pretty cross cut over my eye will attract a duchess. I warrant 'twill be a mighty grace to my ogling.—Had I used the stratagem of a certain brother colonel of mine, I might succeed.

Viz. What was it, pray ?

Stand. Why, to save his pretty face for the women,

[1] The "Rummer" was a tavern on the site of the present "Ship" restaurant, 45 Charing Cross, which is its direct descendant. It stood two doors from the more famous Locket's or Lockitt's, the site of which is now occupied by Drummond's Bank. The Rummer was at this time (until 1702) kept by Samuel Prior, an uncle of the poet, who here, according to Macaulay, "passed his boyhood in drawing corks." *See* Hogarth's *Night,* and Macmichael's *Charing Cross,* p. 47.

he always turned his back upon the enemy. He was a
man of honour—for the ladies.

Viz. Come, come, the loves of Mars and Venus will
never fail; you must get a mistress.

Stand. Prithee, no more on't. You have awakened
a thought, from which, and the kingdom, I would have
stolen away at once.—To be plain, I have a mistress.

Viz. And she's cruel?

Stand. No.

Viz. Her parents prevent your happiness?

Stand. Nor that.

Viz. Then she has no fortune?

Stand. A large one; beauty to tempt all mankind,
and virtue to beat off their assaults. O Vizard! such a
creature!—Heyday! who the devil have we here?

Viz. The joy of the playhouse, and life of the Park;

Enter Sir HARRY WILDAIR, *crosses the stage singing,*
with Footmen *after him.*

Sir Harry Wildair newly come from Paris.

Stand. Sir Harry Wildair! Did not he make a campaign in Flanders some three or four years ago?

Viz. The same.

Stand. Why, he behaved himself very bravely.

Viz. Why not? dost think bravery and gaiety are inconsistent? He's a gentleman of most happy circumstances, born to a plentiful estate, has had a genteel and
easy education, free from the rigidness of teachers and
pedantry of schools. His florid constitution being never
ruffled by misfortune, nor stinted in its pleasures, has
rendered him entertaining to others, and easy to himself:—turning all passion into gaiety of humour, by
which he chooses rather to rejoice his friends than be
hated by any; as you shall see.

Re-enter WILDAIR, Footman *attending.*

Sir Har. Ha! Vizard!

Viz. Sir Harry!

Sir Har. Who thought to find you out of the rubric so long? I thought thy hypocrisy had been wedded to a pulpit-cushion long ago.—Sir, if I mistake not your face, your name is Standard.

Stand. Sir Harry, I'm your humble servant.

Sir Har. Come, gentlemen, the news! the news o' th' town! for I'm just arrived.

Viz. Why, in the City end o' th' town we're playing the knave, to get estates.

Stand. And in the Court end, playing the fool in spending 'em.

Sir Har. Just so in Paris; I'm glad we're grown so modish.

Viz. We are all so reformed, that gallantry is taken for vice.

Stand. And hypocrisy for religion.

Sir Har. *A la mode de Paris*, again.

Viz. Not one whore between Ludgate and Aldgate.

Stand. But ten times more cuckolds than ever.

Viz. Nothing like an oath in the city.

Stand. That's a mistake; for my major swore a hundred and fifty last night to a merchant's wife in her bedchamber.

Sir Har. Psha! this is trifling; tell me news, gentlemen. What lord has lately broke his fortune at the Groom-porter's [1]? or his heart at Newmarket, for the loss of a race? What wife has been lately suing in Doctors'

---

[1] The Groom-porter was a Court official whose quarters in St James's Palace were, by an ancient custom, a legalised resort for high play. Gambling at Court was encouraged between Christmas and Epiphany, the authorised period for play in remoter times. See Evelyn, 6th January 1662 and 8th January 1668. Pepys on January 1, 1668, went to see the gaming at the Groom-porter's, and was mortified to find there many dirty apprentices and other idle people. *Flying Post*, January 10-13, 1699.—"Friday last being Twelf-day the King, according to custom, plaid at the Groom-porter's; where we hear Esqre Frampton was the greatest gainer." The Groom-porter's privileges were abolished at the accession of George III.

Commons for alimony? or what daughter run away with her father's valet? What beau gave the noblest ball at the Bath, or had the finest coach in the ring? I want news, gentlemen.

Stand. Faith, sir, these are no news at all.

Viz. But pray, Sir Harry, tell us some news of your travels.

Sir Har. With all my heart. You must know, then, I went over to Amsterdam in a Dutch ship ; I there had a Dutch whore for five stivers : I went from thence to Landen, [1] where I was heartily drubbed in the battle with the butt-end of a Swiss musket. I thence went to Paris, where I had half a dozen intrigues, bought half a dozen new suits, fought a couple of duels, and here I am again *in statu quo*.

Viz. But we heard that you designed to make the tour of Italy ; what brought you back so soon?

Sir Har. That which brought you into the world, and may perhaps carry you out of it : a woman.

Stand. What! quit the pleasures of travel for a woman !

Sir Har. Ay, Colonel, for such a woman ! I had rather see her *ruelle* [2] than the palace of Lewis le Grand. There's more glory in her smile than in the Jubilee at Rome; and I would rather kiss her hand than the Pope's toe.

Viz. You, Colonel, have been very lavish in the beauty and virtue of your mistress ; and Sir Harry here has been no less eloquent in the praise of his. Now will I lay you both ten guineas a-piece, that neither of them is so pretty, so witty, or so virtuous, as mine.

Stand. 'Tis done !

Sir Har. I'll double the stakes.—But, gentlemen,

---

[1] In the Battle of Landen (1693), William III. was defeated by the Duke of Luxemburg. "It was in this battle," Ewald notes, "that Corporal Trim was wounded."

[2] The space in a bed-chamber between the bedside and the wall.

now I think on't, how shall we be resolved? for I know
not where my mistress may be found; she left Paris
about a month before me, and I had an account—

Stand. How, sir! left Paris about a month before
you!

Sir Har. Ay, but I know not where, and perhaps
mayn't find her this fortnight.

Stand. Her name, pray, Sir Harry?

Viz. Ay, ay, her name; perhaps we know her.

Sir Har. Her name! Ay,—she has the softest,
whitest hand that ever was made of flesh and blood, her
lips so balmy sweet!

Stand. But her name, sir!

Sir Har. Then her neck and breast!—" Her breasts
do so heave, so heave "—   [*Singing.*

Viz. But her name, sir, her quality!

Sir Har. Then her shape, Colonel!

Stand. But her name I want, sir!

Sir Har. Then her eyes, Vizard!

Stand. Psha, Sir Harry, her name or nothing!

Sir Har. Then, if you must have it, she's called the
Lady——But then her foot, gentlemen! she dances to
a miracle.—Vizard, you have certainly lost your wager.

Viz. Why, you have lost your senses; we shall never
discover the picture unless you subscribe the name.

Sir Har. Then her name is Lurewell.

Stand. [*Aside.*] 'Sdeath, my mistress!

Viz. [*Aside.*] My mistress, by Jupiter!

Sir Har. Do you know her, gentlemen?

Stand. I have seen her, sir.

Sir Har. Canst tell where she lodges? Tell me,
dear colonel.

Stand. Your humble servant, sir.   [*Exit.*

Sir Har. Nay, hold, Colonel, I'll follow you, and
will know.   [*Runs out.*

Viz. The **Lady** Lurewell his mistress!—He loves her,
but she loves me.—But he's a baronet, and I plain

Vizard; he has a coach-and-six, and I walk a-foot; I was bred in London, and he in Paris.—That very circumstance has murdered me.—Then, some stratagem must be laid to divert his pretensions.

Re-enter WILDAIR.

Sir Har. Prithee, Dick, what makes the colonel so out of humour?

Viz. Because he's out of pay, I suppose.

Sir Har. 'Slife, that's true! I was beginning to mistrust some rivalship in the case.

Viz. And suppose there were; you know the colonel can fight, Sir Harry.

Sir Har. Fight! psha! but he can't dance, ha! We contend for a woman, Vizard! 'Slife, man, if ladies were to be gained by sword and pistol only, what the devil should all the beaux do?

Viz. [*Aside.*] I'll try him farther.—[*Aloud.*] But would not you, Sir Harry, fight for this woman you so much admire?

Sir Har. Fight?—Let me consider. I love her, that's true;—but then I love honest Sir Harry Wildair better. The Lady Lurewell is divinely charming—right—but, then, a thrust i' th' guts, or a Middlesex jury, is as ugly as the devil.

Viz. Ay, Sir Harry, 'twere a dangerous cast for a beau baronet to be tried by a parcel of greasy, grumbling, bartering boobies, who would hang you purely because you're a gentleman.

Sir Har. Ay, but on the t'other hand, I have money enough to bribe the rogues with: so, upon mature deliberation, I would fight for her.—But no more of her. Prithee, Vizard, can't you recommend a friend to a pretty mistress by the by, till I can find my own? You have store, I'm sure; you cunning poaching dogs make surer game than we that hunt open and fair. Prithee now, good Vizard!

Viz. Let me consider a little.—[*Aside.*] Now love and revenge inspire my politics.

[*Pauses, whilst* WILDAIR *walks singing.*

Sir Har. Psha ! thou'rt as long studying for a new mistress as a drawer is piercing a new pipe.

Viz. I design a new pipe for you, and wholesome wine ; you'll therefore bear a little expectation.

Sir Har. Ha ! sayest thou, dear Vizard ?

Viz. A girl of sixteen, Sir Harry.

Sir Har. Now sixteen thousand blessings light on thee !

Viz. Pretty and witty.

Sir Har. Ay, ay, but her name, Vizard ?

Viz. Her name ! yes,—she has the softest, whitest hand that ever was made of flesh and blood, her lips so balmy sweet !

Sir Har. Well, well, but where shall I find her, man ?

Viz. Find her !—-but, then, her foot, Sir Harry !—she dances to a miracle.

Sir Har. Prithee, don't distract me.

Viz. Well, then, you must know that this lady is the curiosity and ambition of the town ; her name's Angelica. She that passes for her mother is a private bawd, and called the Lady Darling ; she goes for a baronet's lady (no disparagement to your honour, Sir Harry), I assure you.

Sir Har. Psha, hang my honour ! But what street, what house ?

Viz. Not so fast, Sir Harry ; you must have my passport for your admittance, and you'll find my recommendation, in a line or two, will procure you very civil entertainment ; I suppose twenty or thirty pieces handsomely placed will gain the point ; I'll ensure her sound.

Sir Har. Thou dearest friend to a man in necessity !— [*To* Footman.] Here, sirrah, order my coach about to St James's ; I'll walk across the Park.

[*Exit* Footman.

Enter CLINCHER Senior

Clinch. Sen. Here, sirrah, order my coach about to
St James's, I'll walk across the Park too.[1]—Mr Vizard,
your most devoted.—Sir, [*To* WILDAIR] I admire the
mode of your shoulder-knot ; methinks it hangs very
emphatically, and carries an air of travel in it ; your
sword-knot too is most ornamentally modish, and bears
a foreign mien. Gentlemen, my brother is just arrived
in town, so that, being upon the wing to kiss his hands,
I hope you'll pardon this abrupt departure of, gentlemen,
your most devoted and most faithful humble servant.

[*Exit.*

Sir Har. Prithee, dost know him ?

Viz. Know him ! why, 'tis Clincher, who was
apprentice to my uncle Smuggler, the merchant in the
city.

Sir Har. What makes him so gay ?

Viz. Why, he's in mourning for his father ; the kind
old man, in Hertfordshire t'other day, broke his neck a
fox-hunting ; the son, upon the news, has broke his
indentures, whipped from behind the counter into the
side-box, forswears merchandise, where he must live
by cheating, and usurps gentility, where he may die by
raking. He keeps his coach and liveries, brace of
geldings, leash of mistresses, talks of nothing but wines,
intrigues, plays, fashions, and going to the Jubilee.[2]

Sir Har. Ha, ha, ha ! how many pounds of pulvil[3]
must the fellow use in sweetening himself from the
smell of hops and tobacco ? Faugh !—I' my conscience

---

[1] Speaking to a (doubtless imaginary) servant behind the scenes.

[2] From Luttrell's *Brief Relation of State Affairs*, September 23,
1699, " The Earl of Exeter is goeing to the jubilee at Rome " ;
and October 7, 1699, " The Earl of Exeter and other persons of
quality goeing to the jubilee at Rome are stopt by order of His
Majestie."

[3] " Pulvil," meant literally a small cushion or sachet filled with
scented powder (Lat. *pulvinulus*) : but the term came to be extended from the bag to its contents.

methought, like Olivia's lover, he stunk of Thames Street.[1] But now for Angelica—that's her name?— We'll to the Princess's chocolate-house,[2] where you shall write my passport. Allons.[3]   [*Exeunt.*

SCENE II.—*Lady Lurewell's Lodgings.*

Lady LUREWELL *and* her Maid PARLY.

Lady Lure. Parly, my pocket-book!—Let me see— Madrid, Venice, Paris, London.—Ay, London! They may talk what they will of the hot countries, but I find love most fruitful under this climate.—In a month's space have I gained—let me see—*imprimis*, Colonel Standard.

Par. And how will your ladyship manage him?

Lady Lure. As all soldiers should be managed: he shall serve me till I gain my ends, then I disband him.

Par. But he loves you, madam.

Lady Lure. Therefore I scorn him. I hate all that don't love me, and slight all that do. Would his whole deluding sex admire me, thus would I slight them all! My virgin and unwary innocence was wronged by faithless man, but now glance eyes, plot brain, dissemble face, lie tongue, and be a second Eve to tempt, seduce and damn the treacherous kind. Let me survey my captives.—The Colonel leads the van; next Mr Vizard, he courts me, out of the *Practice of Piety*,[4] therefore is a hypocrite; then Clincher, he adores me with orangery,[5]

---

[1] "Foh! I hate a lover that smells like Thames Street."— Wycherley, *The Plain Dealer*, ii. 1.
[2] Near the New Exchange in the Strand.—EWALD.
[3] In early editions "*Aloons*."
[4] No doubt this refers to *Of the Daily Practice of Piety; also Devotions and Praiers in Time of Captivity*, London, 1660.
[5] An expensive brand of snuff. See *Love and a Bottle*, ii. 2.

and is consequently a fool; then my old merchant Alderman Smuggler, he's a compound of both; out of which medley of lovers, if I don't make good diversion —what d'ye think, Parly?

Par. I think, madam, I'm like to be very virtuous in your service, if you teach me all those tricks that you use to your lovers.

Lady Lure. You're a fool, child; observe this, that though a woman swear, forswear, lie, dissemble, back-bite, be proud, vain, malicious, anything, if she secures the main chance, she's still virtuous; that's a maxim.

Par. I can't be persuaded though, madam, but that you really loved Sir Harry Wildair in Paris.

Lady Lure. Of all the lovers I ever had, he was my greatest plague, for I could never make him uneasy; I left him involved in a duel upon my account; I long to know whether the fop be killed or not.

Enter STANDARD.

O Lord! no sooner talk of killing, but the soldier is conjured up. You're upon hard duty, Colonel, to serve your king, your country, and a mistress too.

Stand. The latter, I must confess, is the hardest; for in war, madam, we can be relieved in our duty: but in love who would take our post is our enemy; emulation in glory is transporting, but rivals here intolerable.

Lady Lure. Those that bear away the prize in the field, should boast the same success in the bedchamber; and I think, considering the weakness of our sex, we should make those our companions who can be our champions.

Stand. I once, madam, hoped the honour of defending you from all injuries through a title to your lovely person; but now my love must attend my fortune. This commission, madam, was my passport to the fair; adding a nobleness to my passion, it stamped a value on my love; 'twas once the life of honour, but now its hearse, and with it must my love be buried.

Par. What ! disbanded, colonel ?

Stand. Yes, Mrs Parly.

Par. [*Aside.*] Faugh, the nauseous fellow ! he stinks of poverty already.

Lady Lure. [*Aside.*] His misfortune troubles me, 'cause it may prevent my designs.

Stand. I'll choose, madam, rather to destroy my passion by absence abroad, than have it starved at home.

Lady Lure. I'm sorry, sir, you have so mean an opinion of my affection, as to imagine it founded upon your fortune.   And to convince you of your mistake, here I vow by all that's sacred, I own the same affection now as before.   Let it suffice, my fortune is considerable.

Stand. No, madam, no; I'll never be a charge to her I love.   The man that sells himself for gold is the worst of prostitutes.

Lady Lure. [*Aside.*] Now were he any other creature but a man, I could love him.

Stand. This only last request I make, that no title recommend a fool, office introduce a knave, nor a coat a coward, to my place in your affections ; so farewell my country ! and adieu my love !   [*Exit.*

Lady Lure. Now the devil take thee for being so honourable ! — Here, Parly, call him back. — [*Exit* PARLY] I shall lose half my diversion else.

Re-enter PARLY *with* STANDARD.

Now for a trial of skill.—Sir, I hope you'll pardon my curiosity ; when do you take your journey ?

Stand. To-morrow morning, early, madam.

Lady Lure. So suddenly !   Which way are you designed to travel ?

Stand. That I can't yet resolve on.

Lady Lure. Pray sir, tell me, pray sir, I entreat you. Why are you so obstinate?

Stand. Why are you so curious, madam?

Lady Lure. Because—

Stand. What?

Lady Lure. Because, I—I—

Stand. Because what, madam? Pray tell me.

Lady Lure. Because I design—to follow you.

[*Crying.*

Stand. Follow me! by all that's great! I ne'er was proud before, but love from such a creature might swell the vanity of the proudest prince. Follow me! By Heavens, thou shalt not. What! expose thee to the hazards of a camp!—Rather I'll stay and here bear the contempt of fools, and worst of fortune.

Lady Lure. You need not, shall not; my estate for both is sufficient.

Stand. Thy estate! no, I'll turn a knave and purchase one myself; I'll cringe to that proud man I undermine, and fawn on him that I would bite to death; I'll tip my tongue with flattery, and smooth my face with smiles; I'll turn pimp, informer, office-broker, nay coward, to be great; and sacrifice it all to thee, my generous fair.

Lady Lure. And I'll dissemble, lie, swear, jilt, anything but I'll reward thy love, and recompense thy noble passion.

Stand. Sir Harry, ha, ha, ha! poor Sir Harry, ha, ha, ha! Rather kiss her hand than the Pope's toe, ha, ha, ha!

Lady Lure. What Sir Harry? Colonel, what Sir Harry?

Stand. Sir Harry Wildair, madam—

Lady Lure. What! is he come over?

Stand. Ay, and he told me—but I don't believe a syllable on't.

Lady Lure. What did he tell you?

Stand. Only called you his mistress, and pretending

to be extravagant in your commendation, would vainly insinuate the praise of his own judgment and good fortune in a choice—

Lady Lure. How easily is the vanity of fops tickled by our sex!

Stand. Why, your sex is the vanity of fops.

Lady Lure. O' my conscience, I believe so. This gentleman, because he danced well, I pitched on for a partner at a ball in Paris, and ever since he has so persecuted me with letters, songs, dances, serenading, flattery, foppery and noise, that I was forced to fly the kingdom.—And I warrant you he made you jealous?

Stand. Faith, madam, I was a little uneasy.

Lady Lure. You shall have a plentiful revenge. I'll send him back all his foolish letters, songs, and verses, and you yourself shall carry 'em; 'twill afford you opportunity of triumphing, and free me from his farther impertinence; for of all men he's my aversion.—I'll run and fetch them instantly.

Stand. Dear madam, a rare project!—[*Exit* Lady Lurewell.] How I shall bait him like Actæon, with his own dogs!—Well, Mrs Parly, 'tis ordered by Act of Parliament, that you receive no more pieces, Mrs Parly.—

Par. 'Tis provided by the same act, that you send no more messages by me, good Colonel; you must not pretend to send any more letters, unless you can pay the postage.

Stand. Come, come, don't be mercenary; take example by your lady, be honourable.

Par. A lack a day, sir! it shows as ridiculous and haughty for us to imitate our betters in their honour as in their finery; leave honour to nobility that can support it; we poor folks, Colonel, have no pretence to't; and truly, I think, sir, that your honour should be cashiered with your leading-staff.

Stand. [*Aside.*] 'Tis one of the greatest curses of poverty to be the jest of chambermaids!

Re-enter Lady LUREWELL.

Lady Lure. Here's the packet, Colonel; the whole magazine of love's artillery.   [*Gives him the packet*

Stand. Which since I have gained I will turn upon the enemy. Madam, I'll bring you the news of my victory this evening.—Poor Sir Harry, ha, ha, ha!

[*Exit.*

Lady Lure. To the right about! as you were!—march, Colonel! ha, ha, ha!

Vain man, who boasts of studied parts and wiles,
Nature in us your deepest art beguiles,
Stamping deep cunning in our frowns and smiles.
You toil for art, your intellects you trace;
Woman, without a thought, bears policy in her face.

ACT II

SCENE I.—*Clincher Junior's Lodgings.*

Enter CLINCHER Junior, *opening a letter,* DICKY *following.*

LINCHER *Jun.* [Reads.]
    Dear Brother,
    *I will see you presently. I have sent
    this lad to wait on you ; he can
    instruct you in the fashions of the
    town. I am your affectionate
    brother,* CLINCHER.

Very well, and what's your name, sir?

Dicky. My name is Dicky, sir.

Clinch. Jun. Dicky !

Dicky. Ay, Dicky, sir.

Clinch. Jun. Very well, a pretty name! And what can you do, Mr Dicky?

Dicky. Why, sir, I can powder a wig, and pick up a whore.

Clinch. Jun. O Lord! O Lord!—a whore! Why, are there many whores in this town?

Dicky. Ha, ha, ha! many whores? there's a question indeed! Why, sir, there are above five hundred surgeons in town. Hark'ee, sir, do you see that woman there in the velvet scarf, and red knots?

Clinch. Jun. Ay, sir ; what then?

60

Dicky. Why, she shall be at your service in three minutes, as I'm a pimp.

Clinch. Jun. O Jupiter Ammon! why, she's a gentlewoman.

Dicky. A gentlewoman! why, so are all the whores in town, sir.

Enter CLINCHER Senior.

Clinch. Sen. Brother, you're welcome to London.

Clinch. Jun. I thought, brother, you owed so much to the memory of my father as to wear mourning for his death.

Clinch. Sen. Why, so I do, fool: I wear this because I have the estate, and you wear that because you have not the estate: you have cause to mourn indeed, brother. Well, brother, I'm glad to see you, fare you well! [*Going.*

Clinch. Jun. Stay, stay, brother! Where are you going?

Clinch. Sen. How natural 'tis for a country booby to ask impertinent questions!—Hark'ee, sir, is not my father dead?

Clinch. Jun. Ay, ay, to my sorrow.

Clinch. Sen. No matter for that, he's dead. And am not I a young powdered extravagant English heir?

Clinch. Jun. Very right, sir.

Clinch. Sen. Why, then, sir, you may be sure that I am going to the Jubilee, sir.

Clinch. Jun. Jubilee! what's that?

Clinch. Sen. Jubilee! why, the Jubilee is—faith, I don't know what it is.

Dicky. Why, the Jubilee is the same thing with our Lord Mayor's day in the City; there will be pageants, and squibs, and raree-shows, and all that, sir.

Clinch. Jun. And must you go so soon, brother?

Clinch. Sen. Yes, sir, for I must stay a month in Amsterdam, to study poetry.

Clinch. Jun. Then I suppose, brother, you travel through Muscovy to learn fashions, don't you, brother?

Clinch. Sen. Brother!—Prithee, Robin, don't call me brother; "Sir" will do every jot as well.

Clinch. Jun. O Jupiter Ammon! why so?

Clinch. Sen. Because people will imagine that you have a spite at me.—But have you seen your cousin Angelica yet, and her mother the Lady Darling?

Clinch. Jun. No, my dancing-master has not been with me yet. How shall I salute them, brother?

Clinch. Sen. Psha! that's easy; 'tis only two scrapes, a kiss, and your humble servant; I'll tell you more when I come from the Jubilee. Come along.

[*Exeunt.*

SCENE II.—*Lady Darling's House.*

Enter WILDAIR, *with a letter.*

Sir Har. *Like light and heat incorporate we lay,*
　　　　We bless'd the night, and cursed the coming
　　　　　　day.

Well, if this paper-kite flies sure, I'm secure of my game.—Humph! the prettiest bordel I have seen; a very stately genteel one—[Footmen *cross the stage.*] Heyday! equipage too! Now for a bawd by the courtesy, and a whore with a coat of arms.—'Sdeath, I'm afraid I've mistaken the house!

Enter Lady DARLING.

No, this must be the bawd by her bulk.

Lady Dar. Your business, pray, sir?

Sir Har. Pleasure, madam.

Lady Dar. Then, sir, you have no business here.

Sir Har. This letter madam, will inform you farther;

Mr. Vizard sent it, with his humble service to your ladyship.

Lady Dar. How does my cousin, sir?

Sir Har. [*Aside.*] Ay, her cousin too:—that's right procuress again.

Lady Dar. [Reads.] *Madam—earnest inclination to serve—Sir Harry—madam—court my cousin—gentleman —fortune—your ladyship's most humble servant,*—VIZARD. Sir, your fortune and quality are sufficient to recommend you anywhere; but what goes farther with me, is the recommendation of so sober and pious a young gentleman as my cousin Vizard.

Sir Har. [*Aside.*] A right sanctified bawd, o' my word!

Lady Dar. Sir Harry, your conversation with Mr Vizard argues you a gentleman, free from the loose and vicious carriage of the town; I'll therefore call my daughter. [*Exit.*

Sir Har. Now go thy way for an illustrious bawd of Babylon!—She dresses up a sin so religiously, that the devil would hardly know it of his making.

Re-enter Lady DARLING *with* ANGELICA.

Lady Dar. [*Aside to* ANGELICA.] Pray, daughter, use him civilly; such matches won't offer every day. [*Exit.*

Sir Har. [*Aside.*] O all ye powers of love! an angel! 'Sdeath, what money have I got in my pocket? I can't offer her less than twenty guineas—and, by Jupiter, she's worth a hundred!

Angel. [*Aside.*] 'Tis he! the very same? and his person as agreeable as his character of good-humour.— Pray Heaven his silence proceed from respect.

Sir Har. [*Aside.*] How innocent she looks! How would that modesty adorn virtue, when it makes even vice look so charming!—By Heaven, there's such a commanding innocence in her looks that I dare not ask the question.

Angel. [*Aside.*] Now all the charms of real love and feigned indifference assist me to engage his heart, for mine is lost already.

Sir Har. Madam—I, I—[*Aside.*] Zoons! I cannot speak to her.—But she's a whore, and I will.—[*Aloud.*] Madam, in short I, I—[*Aside.*] O hypocrisy, hypocrisy! what a charming sin art thou!

Angel. [*Aside.*] He is caught; now to secure my conquest.—[*Aloud.*] I thought, sir, you had business to impart?

Sir Har. [*Aside.*] Business to impart! how nicely she words it!—[*Aloud.*] Yes, madam; don't you—don't you love singing birds, madam?

Angel. [*Aside.*] That's an odd question for a lover.—[*Aloud.*] Yes, sir.

Sir Har. Why, then, madam, here is a nest of the prettiest goldfinches that ever chirped in a cage; twenty young ones, I assure you, madam.

Angel. Twenty young ones! what then, sir?

Sir Har. Why, then, madam, there are twenty young ones.—'Slife, I think twenty is pretty fair.

Angel. [*Aside.*] He's mad, sure!—[*Aloud.*] Sir Harry, when you have learned more wit and manners you shall be welcome here again.   [*Exit.*

Sir Har. Wit and manners! Egad, now I conceive there is a great deal of wit and manners in twenty guineas.—I'm sure 'tis all the wit and manners I have about me at present. What shall I do?

Enter CLINCHER Junior *and* DICKY.

What the devil's here? Another cousin, I warrant ye! —Hark'ee, sir, can you lend me ten or a dozen guineas instantly? I'll pay you fifteen for them in three hours, upon my honour.

Clinch. Jun. [*Aside to* DICKY.] These London sparks are plaguy impudent! This fellow, by his wig and assurance, can be no less than a courtier.

Dicky. He's rather a courtier by his borrowing.

Clinch. Jun. Faith, sir, I han't above five guineas about me.

Sir Har. What business have you here then, sir? For to my knowledge twenty won't be sufficient.

Clinch. Jun. Sufficient! for what, sir?

Sir Har. What, sir! why, for that, sir; what the devil should it be, sir! I know your business notwithstanding all your gravity, sir.

Clinch. Jun. My business! why, my cousin lives here.

Sir Har. I know your cousin does live here, and Vizard's cousin, and—my cousin, and everybody's cousin. —Hark'ee, sir, I shall return immediately, and if you offer to touch her till I come back, I shall cut your throat, rascal!   [*Exit.*

Clinch. Jun. Why, the man's mad, sure!

Dicky. Mad, sir! ay. Why, he's a beau!

Clinch. Jun. A beau! what's that? Are all madmen beaux?

Dicky. No, sir; but most beaux are madmen.—But now for your cousin. Remember your three scrapes, a kiss, and your humble servant.

                    [*Exeunt, as into the house.*

SCENE III.—*The Street.*

Enter WILDAIR, STANDARD *following.*

Stand. Sir Harry! Sir Harry!

Sir Har. I'm in haste, Colonel; besides, if you're in no better humour than when I parted with you in the Park this morning, your company won't be very agreeable.

Stand. You're a happy man, Sir Harry, who are never

out of humour.   Can nothing move your gall, Sir
Harry?

Sir Har. Nothing but impossibilities, which are the
same as nothing.

Stand. What impossibilities?

Sir Har. The resurrection of my father to disinherit
me, or an Act of Parliament against wenching.   A man
of eight thousand pounds per annum to be vexed!—
No, no; anger and spleen are companions for younger
brothers.

Stand. Suppose one called you son of a whore behind
your back?

Sir Har. Why, then would I call him rascal behind
his back, and so we're even.

Stand. But suppose you had lost a mistress?

Sir Har. Why, then would I get another.

Stand. But suppose you were discarded by the woman
you love, that would surely trouble you?

Sir Har. You're mistaken, Colonel; my love is neither
romantically honourable, nor meanly mercenary.   'Tis
only a pitch of gratitude: while she loves me, I love
her; when she desists, the obligation's void.

Stand. But to be mistaken in your opinion, sir; if the
Lady Lurewell (only suppose it) had discarded you—I
say, only suppose it—and had sent your discharge by
me!

Sir Har. Psha! that's another impossibility.

Stand. Are you sure of that?

Sir Har. Why, 'twere a solecism in nature!—we're
finger and thumb, sir.   She dances with me, sings with
me, plays with me, swears with me, lies with me!

Stand. How, sir?

Sir Har. I mean in an honourable way; that is, she
lies for me.—In short, we are as like one another as a
couple of guineas!

Stand. Now that I have raised you to the highest
pinnacle of vanity, will I give you so mortifying a fall

as shall dash your hopes to pieces !—I pray your honour
to peruse these papers.   [*Gives him the packet.*

Sir Har. What is't ? The muster-roll of your regiment, Colonel?

Stand. No, no, 'tis a list of your forces in your last
love campaign ; and for your comfort, all disbanded !

Sir Har. Prithee, good metaphorical Colonel, what
d'ye mean ?

Stand. Read, sir, read ! these are the Sibyl's leaves
that will unfold your destiny.

Sir Har. So it be not a false deed to cheat me of my
estate, what care I !—[*Opening the packet.*] Humph !
my hand !—*To the Lady Lurewell !—To the Lady Lurewell !—To the Lady Lurewell !*—What devil hast thou
been tampering with to conjure up these spirits ?

Stand. A certain familiar of your acquaintance,
sir.

Sir Har. [Reading.] *Madam, my passion—so natural
—your beauty contending—force of charms—mankind—
eternal admirer,* WILDAIR !—I never was ashamed of my
name before !

Stand. What, Sir Harry Wildair out of humour ! ha,
ha; ha !—Poor Sir Harry ! more glory in her smile than
in the Jubilee at Rome, ha, ha, ha !—But then her foot,
Sir Harry ! she dances to a miracle, ha, ha ha !—Fy,
Sir Harry ! a man of your parts write letters not worth
a keeping !—What say'st thou, my dear knight-errant ?
ha, ha, ha !—You may go seek adventures now
indeed !

Sir Har. [*Sings.*] "No, no, let her wander," &c.

Stand. You are jilted to some tune, sir ! blown up
with false music, that's all !

Sir Har. Now, why should I be angry that a woman
is a woman ? Since inconstancy and falsehood are
grounded in their natures, how can they help it ?

Stand. Then they must be grounded in your nature
for you and she are finger and thumb, sir !

Sir Har. Here's a copy of verses, too ; I must turn poet in the devil's name !—[*Aside.*]   Stay !—'sdeath, what's here? This is her hand.—Oh, the charming characters !—[Reading.]   *My dear Wildair,*—That's I ;—*this huff bluff colonel*—that's he,—*is the rarest fool in nature,*—the devil he is !—*and as such have I used him ;* —with all my heart, faith !—*I had no better way of letting you know that I lodge in Pall Mall, near the Holy Lamb.*—[*Aloud.*]   Colonel, I'm you're most humble servant.

Stand. Hold, sir ! you shan't go yet ; I han't delivered half my message.

Sir Har. Upon my faith, but you have, Colonel !

Stand. Well, well, own your spleen ; out with it : I know you're like to burst.

Sir Har. I am so, by Gad, ha, ha, ha !

Stand. Ay, with all my heart, ha, ha !—[*Laugh and point at one another.*]   Well, well, that's all forced, Sir Harry.

Sir Har. I was never better pleased in all my life, by Jupiter !

Stand. Well, Sir Harry, 'tis prudence to hide your concern when there's no help for't.—But to be serious now, the lady has sent you back all your papers there. I was so just as not to look upon 'em.

Sir Har. I'm glad on't, sir ; for there were some things that I would not have you see.

Stand. All this she has done for my sake, and I desire you would decline any farther pretensions for your own sake. So, honest, good-natured Sir Harry, I'm your humble servant.   [*Exit.*

Sir Har. Ha, ha, ha ! poor Colonel !—Oh, the delight of an ingenious mistress ! what a life and briskness it adds to an amour ! like the loves of mighty Jove, still suing in different shapes. A legerdemain mistress, who, *Presto ! pass !* and she's vanished, then *Hey !* in an instant in your arms again.   [*Going.*

Enter VIZARD.

Viz. Well met, Sir Harry ; what news from the island of Love?

Sir Har. Faith, we made but a broken voyage by your card ; but now I am bound for another port : I told you the colonel was my rival.

Viz. [*Aside.*] The colonel! cursed misfortune! another!

Sir Har. But the civillest in the world : he brought me word where my mistress lodges. The story's too long to tell you now, for I must fly.

Viz. What! have you given over all thoughts of Angelica?

Sir Har. No, no, I'll think of her some other time. But now for the Lady Lurewell ; wit and beauty calls.

That mistress ne'er can pall her lover's joys,
Whose wit can whet whene'er her beauty cloys.
Her little amorous frauds all truths excel,
And make us happy, being deceived so well. [*Exit.*

Viz. The colonel, my rival too! how shall I manage? There is but one way : him and the knight will I set a-tilting, where one cuts t'other's throat, and the survivor's hanged. So there will be two rivals pretty decently disposed of. Since honour may oblige them to play the fool, why should not necessity engage me to play the knave? [*Exit.*

SCENE IV.—*Lady Lurewell's Lodgings.*

LUREWELL *and* PARLY.

Lady Lure. Has my servant brought me the money from my merchant?

Par. No, madam, he met Alderman Smuggler at

Charing Cross, who has promised to wait on you himself immediately.

Lady Lure. 'Tis odd that this old rogue should
pretend to love me, and at the same time cheat me of
my money.

Par. 'Tis well, madam, if he don't cheat you of your
estate; for you say the writings are in his hands.

Lady Lure. But what satisfaction can I get of him?—

Enter Alderman SMUGGLER.

Mr Alderman, your servant. Have you brought me any
money, sir?

Smug. Faith, madam, trading is very dead; what
with paying the taxes, raising the customs, losses at sea
abroad, and maintaining our wives at home, the bank
is reduced very low.

Lady Lure. Come, come, sir, these evasions won't
serve your turn; I must have money, sir;—I hope you
don't design to cheat me.

Smug. Cheat you, madam! have a care what you
say: I'm an alderman, madam. Cheat you, madam!
I have been an honest citizen these five-and-thirty
years!

Lady Lure. An honest citizen! bear witness, Parly!
I shall trap him in more lies presently.—Come, sir,
though I'm a woman I can take a course.

Smug. What course, madam? You'll go to law,
will ye? I can maintain a suit of law, be it right or
wrong, these forty years. I'm sure of that, thanks to the
honest practice of the court.

Lady Lure. Sir, I'll blast your reputation, and so ruin
your credit.

Smug. Blast my reputation! he, he, he!—Why, I'm
a religious man, madam! I have been very instrumental
in the reformation of manners. Ruin my credit! ah,
poor woman. There is but one way, madam,—you
have a sweet leering eye!

Lady Lure. You instrumental in reformation ! How?

Smug. I whipped all the whores, cut and long tail,[1] out of the parish.—Ah ! that leering eye !—Then I voted for pulling down the playhouse.—Ah, that ogle ! that ogle !—Then my own pious example.—Ah, that lip ! that lip !

Lady Lure. [*Aside to* PARLY.] Here's a religious rogue for you now ! As I hope to be saved, I have a good mind to beat the old monster.

Smug. Madam, I have brought you about a hundred and fifty guineas (a great deal of money as times go), and—

Lady Lure. Come, give it me.

Smug. Ah, that hand ! that hand ! that pretty, soft, white——I have brought it, you see ; but the condition of the obligation is such, that whereas that leering eye, that pouting lip, that pretty soft hand, that—you understand me ; you understand, I'm sure you do, you little rogue—

Lady Lure. [*Aside to* PARLY.] Here's a villain now, so covetous, that he won't wench upon his own cost, but would bribe me with my own money ! I will be revenged.—[*Aloud.*] Upon my word, Mr Alderman, you make me blush ; what d'ye mean, pray?

Smug. See here, madam.—[*Puts a piece of money in his mouth.*] Buss and guinea, buss and guinea, buss and guinea !

Lady Lure. Well, Mr Alderman, you have such pretty yellow teeth and green gums, that I will—ha, ha, ha, ha !

Smug. Will you indeed? he, he, he ! my little cocket ; and when? and where? and how?

Lady Lure. 'Twill be a difficult point, sir, to secure both our honours : you must therefore be disguised, Mr Alderman.

---

[1] Of all sorts and conditions. The phrase originally referred to a stable of horses or kennel of dogs. *Cf.* Slender in *The Merry Wives of Windsor*, iii. 4.

Smug. Psha! no matter, I am an old fornicator, I'm not half so religious as I seem to be. You little rogue; why, I am disguised as I am; our sanctity is all outside, all hypocrisy.

Lady Lure. No man is seen to come into this house after nightfall,; you must therefore sneak in when 'tis dark, in woman's clothes.

Smug. Egad so! cod so!—I have a suit a purpose, my little cocket! I love to be disguised; ecod, I make a very handsome woman, ecod, I do!

Enter Footman, *whispers* Lady LUREWELL, *and exit.*

Lady Lure. Oh! Mr Alderman, shall I beg you to walk into the next room? here are some strangers coming up.

Smug. Buss and guinea first; ah, my little cocket!

[*Exit.*

Enter WILDAIR, Footman *attending.*

Sir Har. *My life, my soul, my all that heaven can give!*

Lady Lure. *Death's life with thee, without thee death to live.*

Welcome, my dear Sir Harry, I see you got my directions.

Sir Har. Directions! in the most charming manner, thou dear Machiavel of intrigue!

Lady Lure. Still brisk and airy, I find, Sir Harry.

Sir Har. The sight of you, madam, exalts my air, and makes joy lighten in my face.

Lady Lure. I have a thousand questions to ask you, Sir Harry. How d'ye like France?

Sir Har. *Ah! est le plus beau pays du monde.*

Lady Lure. Then what made you leave it so soon?

Sir Har. *Madame vous voyez que je vous suis partout.*

Lady Lure. *O monsieur, je vous suis fort obligée.*— But where's the Court now?

Sir Har. At Marli, madam.

Lady Lure. And where my Count Le Valier?

Sir Har. His body's in the church of Nôtre Dame; I don't know where his soul is.

Lady Lure. What disease did he die of?

Sir Har. A duel, madam; I was his doctor.

Lady Lure. How d'ye mean?

Sir Har. As most doctors do, I killed him!

Lady Lure. En cavalier, my dear knight-errant? Well, and how? And how? What intrigues, what gallantries are carrying on in the *beau-monde?*

Sir Har. I should ask you that question, madam, since your ladyship makes the *beau-monde* wherever you come.

Lady Lure. Ah, Sir Harry! I've been almost ruined, pestered to death here, by the incessant attacks of a mighty colonel; he has besieged me as close as our army did Namur.[1]

Sir Har. I hope your ladyship did not surrender though?

Lady Lure. No, no, but was forced to capitulate;[2] but since you are come to raise the siege, we'll dance, and sing, and laugh.

Sir Har. And love and kiss.—*Montrez-moi vôtre chambre.*

Lady Lure. Attende, attende, un peu.—I remember, Sir Harry, you promised me in Paris never to ask that impertinent question again.

Sir Har. Psha, madam! that was above two months ago; besides, madam, treaties made in France are never kept.

Lady Lure. Would you marry me, Sir Harry?

<hr/>

[1] The siege of Namur lasted from July 2 to August 26, and ended in the surrender of Marshal Boufflers to William III. and his allies. "For the first time, men said, since France had Marshals, a Marshal of France was to deliver up a fortress to a victorious enemy."—MACAULAY.

[2] An obsolete sense of "capitulate" = "to treat, bargain, parley." It was so used, however, by the Duke of Wellington (1815), and by Southey (1816).—(*N.E.D.*)

Sir Har. Oh !—*Le mariage est un grand mal*—but I will marry you.

Lady Lure. Your word, sir, is not to be relied on : if a gentleman will forfeit his honour in dealings of business, we may reasonably suspect his fidelity in an amour.

Sir Har. My honour in dealings of business ! Why, madam, I never had any business in all my life.

Lady Lure. Yes, Sir Harry, I have heard a very odd story, and am sorry that a gentleman of your figure should undergo the scandal.

Sir Har. Out with it, madam.

Lady Lure. Why, the merchant, sir, that transmitted your bills of exchange to you in France, complains of some indirect and dishonourable dealings.

Sir Har. Who, old Smuggler !

Lady Lure. Ay, ay, you know him, I find.

Sir Har. I have no less than reason, I think ; why, the rogue has cheated me of above five hundred pound within these three years.

Lady Lure. 'Tis your business then to acquit yourself publicly ; for he spreads the scandal everywhere.

Sir Har. Acquit myself publicly !—[*To* Footman.] Here, sirrah, my coach ; I'll drive instantly into the City, and cane the old villain round the Royal Exchange ; he shall run the gauntlet through a thousand brushed beavers and formal cravats.

Lady Lure. Why, he is in the house now, sir.

Sir Har. What, in this house ?

Lady Lure. Ay, in the next room.

Sir Har. Then, sirrah, lend me your cudgel.

Lady Lure. Sir Harry, you won't raise a disturbance in my house.

Sir Har. Disturbance, madam ! no, no, I'll beat him with the temper of a philosopher.—Here, Mrs Parly, show me the gentleman.

[*Exit with* PARLY *and* Footman.

Lady Lure. Now shall I get the old monster well beaten, and Sir Harry pestered next term with blood-sheds, batteries, costs and damages, solicitors and attorneys; and if they don't tease him out of his good humour, I'll never plot again. [*Exit.*

SCENE V.—*Changes to another Room in the same House.*

Alderman SMUGGLER *discovered alone.*

Smug. Oh, this damned tide-waiter! A ship and cargo worth five thousand pound! why, 'tis richly worth five hundred perjuries.

Enter WILDAIR.

Sir Har. Dear Mr Alderman, I'm your most devoted and humble servant.

Smug. My best friend, Sir Harry! You're welcome to England.

Sir Har. I'll assure you, sir, there's not a man in the king's dominions I'm gladder to meet.

Smug. O Lord, sir, you travellers have the most obliging ways with you!

Sir Har. There is a business, Mr Alderman, fallen out, which you may oblige me infinitely by—I am very sorry that I am forced to be troublesome; but necessity, Mr Alderman——

Smug. Ay, sir, as you say, necessity—but upon my word, sir, I am very short of money, at present, but—

Sir Har. That's not the matter, sir, I'm above an obligation that way; but the business is, I am reduced to an indispensable necessity of being obliged to you for a beating. Here, take this cudgel.

Smug. A beating, Sir Harry! ha, ha, ha! I beat a knight-baronet! an alderman turn cudgel-player! ha, ha, ha!

Sir Har. Upon my word, sir, you must beat me, or I cudgel you; take your choice.

Smug. Psha, psha, you jest!

Sir Har. Nay, 'tis as sure as fate: so, Alderman, I hope you'll pardon my curiosity.   [*Strikes him.*

Smug. Curiosity! deuce take your curiosity, sir! what d'ye mean?

Sir Har. Nothing at all: I'm but in jest, sir.

Smug. Oh, I can take anything in jest; but a man might imagine by the smartness of the stroke that you were in downright earnest.

Sir Har. Not in the least, sir;—[*Strikes him*] not in the least, indeed, sir!

Smug. Pray, good sir, no more of your jests: for they are the bluntest jests that I ever knew.

Sir Har. [*Strikes.*] I heartily beg your pardon, with all my heart, sir.

Smug. Pardon, sir! well, sir, that is satisfaction enough from a gentleman; but seriously now, if you pass any more of your jests upon me, I shall grow angry.

Sir Har. I humbly beg your permission to break one or two more.   [*Striking him.*

Smug. O Lord, sir, you'll break my bones! Are you mad, sir? Murder! felony! manslaughter!

[WILDAIR *knocks him down.*

Sir Har. Sir, I beg you ten thousand pardons! but I am absolutely compelled to't, upon my honour, sir; nothing can be more averse to my inclinations than to jest with my honest, dear, loving, obliging friend, the alderman.

[*Striking him all this while.* SMUGGLER *tumbles over and over, and shakes out his pocket-book on the floor.*

Enter Lady LUREWELL.

Lady Lure. [*Aside.*] The old rogue's pocket-book;
this may be of use—[*Takes it up.*] O Lord, Sir Harry's
murdering the poor old man !

Smug. O dear, madam, I was beaten in jest, till I am
murdered in good earnest.

Lady Lure. Well, well, I'll bring you off.—[*To* Sir
HARRY.] *Seigneur, frappez, frappez !*

Smug. Oh, for charity's sake, madam, rescue a poor
citizen !

Lady Lure. Oh, you barbarous man ! hold, hold !—
Frappez plus rudement, frappez !—I wonder you are not
ashamed !—[*Holding* Sir HARRY.] A poor reverend
honest elder !—[*Helps* SMUGGLER *up.*] It makes me
weep to see him in this condition, poor man !—Now
the devil take you, Sir Harry—for not beating him
harder !—[*To* SMUGGLER.] Well, my dear, you shall
come at night, and I'll make you amends !

[*Here* Sir HARRY *takes snush.*

Smug. Madam, I will have amends before I leave the
place.—Sir, how durst you use me thus ?

Sir Har. Sir !

Smug. Sir, I say that I will have satisfaction !

Sir Har. With all my heart !

[*Throws snush into his eyes.*

Smug. Oh, murder ! blindness ! fire !—Oh, madam !
madam ! get me some water ! water ! fire ! fire ! water !

[*Exit with* Lady LUREWELL.

Sir Har. How pleasant is resenting an injury without
passion ! 'tis the beauty of revenge !

Let statesmen plot, and under business groan,
And settling public quiet lose their own ;
Let soldiers drudge and fight for pay or fame,
For when they're shot, I think 'tis much the same.
Let scholars vex their brains with mood and tense,
And mad with strength of reason, fools commence,

Losing their wits in searching after sense;
Their *summum bonum* they must toil to gain,
And seeking pleasure, spend their life in pain.
I make the most of life, no hour misspend,
Pleasure's the means, and pleasure is my end.
No spleen, no trouble, shall my time destroy;
Life's but a span, I'll every inch enjoy.   [*Exit.*

ACT III

SCENE I.—*The Street.*

Enter STANDARD *and* VIZARD.

TAND. I bring him word where she lodged! I, the civillest rival in the world!—'tis impossible!

Viz. I shall urge it no farther, sir. I only thought, sir, that my character in the world might add authority to my words, without so many repetitions.

Stand. Pardon me, dear Vizard; our belief struggles hard, before it can be brought to yield to the disadvantage of what we love: 'tis so great an abuse to our judgment, that it makes the faults of our choice our own failing.—But what said Sir Harry?

Viz. He pitied the poor credulous colonel; laughed heartily; flew away with all the raptures of a bridegroom, repeating these lines :—

> *A mistress ne'er can pall her lover's joys,*
> *Whose wit can whet whene'er her beauty cloys.*

Stand. A mistress ne'er can pall!—by all my wrongs, he whores her! and I'm made their property. Vengeance!—Vizard, you must carry a note for me to Sir Harry.

Viz. What! a challenge! I hope you don't design to fight?

Stand. What! wear the livery of my King, and pocket an affront!—'Twere an abuse to his Sacred Majesty! A soldier's sword, Vizard, should start of itself to redress its master's wrong!

Viz. However, sir, I think it not proper for me to carry any such message between friends.

Stand. I have ne'er a servant here; what shall I do?

Viz. There's Tom Errand, the porter, that plies at the Blue Posts,[1] and who knows Sir Harry and his haunts very well; you may send a note by him.

Stand. [*Calls.*] Here! you, friend.

Viz. I have now some business, and must take my leave; I would advise you, nevertheless, against this affair.

Stand. No whispering now, nor telling of friends to prevent us. He that disappoints a man of an honourable revenge, may love him foolishly like a wife, but never value him as a friend.

Viz. [*Aside.*] Nay, the devil take him that parts you, say I!   [*Exit.*

Enter TOM ERRAND,[2] *running.*

Err. Did your honour call a porter?

Stand. Is your name Tom Errand?

Err. People call me so, an't like your worship.

---

[1] The "Blue Posts" was a frequent designation for a tavern. Farquhar may have had in mind the "Blue Posts" in Spring Gardens, a noted Jacobite resort. It was quite near the "Rummer" before mentioned, p. 46.

[2] All modern editors make this character "Tim" Errand, no doubt because his wife, in Act iv. Sc. 1, refers to him as "Timothy;" but in the early editions he is consistently called "Tom," and never once "Tim." His second speech in this scene seems to show that he was called "out of his name." Possibly he was an actual character whom the audience would recognise. In Churchill's *Rosciad*, Yates, when playing the part of a gentleman, is said to "look like Tom Errand dress'd in Clincher's cloaths."

Stand. D'ye know Sir Harry Wildair?

Err. Ay, very well, sir; he's one of my masters; many a round half-crown have I had of his worship; he's newly come home from France, sir.

Stand. Go to the next coffee-house, and wait for me.—[*Exit* ERRAND.] O woman! woman!
How blest is man when favour'd by your smiles!
And how accursed when all those smiles are found
But wanton baits to soothe us to destruction!
Thus our chief joys with base allays are curst,
And our best things, when once corrupted, worst.

[*Exit.*

SCENE II.—*The same.*[1]

Enter WILDAIR, *and* CLINCHER Senior *following.*

Clinch. Sen. Sir, sir, sir! having some business of importance to communicate to you, I would beg your attention to a trifling affair that I would impart to you.

Sir Har. What is your trifling business of importance, pray, sweet sir?

Clinch. Sen. Pray, sir, are the roads deep between this and Paris?

Sir Har. Why that question, sir?

Clinch. Sen. Because I design to go to the Jubilee, sir; I understand that you are a traveller, sir; there is an air of travel in the tie of your cravat, sir, there is indeed, sir.—I suppose, sir, you bought this lace in Flanders?

Sir Har. No, sir; this lace was made in Norway.

---

[1] For convenience of quotation, we follow Leigh Hunt and other modern editors in making this a new scene; but it is not so marked in early editions, and there is no reason for so considering it.

Clinch. Sen. Norway, sir !

Sir Har. Yes, sir, of the shavings of deal boards.

Clinch. Sen. That's very strange now, faith !—Lace made of the shavings of deal boards ! Egad, sir, you travellers see very strange things abroad !—very incredible things abroad, indeed ! Well, I'll have a cravat of that very same lace before I come home.

Sir Har. But, sir, what preparations have you made for your journey ?

Clinch. Sen. A case of pocket-pistols for the bravoes—and a swimming-girdle.

Sir Har. Why these, sir ?

Clinch. Sen. O Lord ! sir, I'll tell you. Suppose us in Rome now ; away goes me, I, to some ball—for I'll be a mighty beau ! Then, as I said, I go to some ball, or some bear-baiting—'tis all one, you know ; then comes a fine Italian bona roba,[1] and plucks me by the sleeve, *Siegniour Angle ! Seigniour Angle !*—she's a very fine lady, observe that !—*Seigniour Angle !* says she ; *Seigniora !* says I, and trips after her to the corner of a street—suppose it Russel Street here, or any other street ; then, you know, I must invite her to the tavern —I can do no less. There, up comes her bravo ; the Italian grows saucy, and I give him an English douse of the face—I can box, sir, box tightly ; I was a 'prentice, sir.—But then, sir, he whips out his stiletto, and I whips out my bull-dog—slaps him through, trips down stairs, turns the corner of Russel Street again, and whips me into the ambassador's train, and there I'm safe as a beau behind the scenes !

Sir Har. Was your pistol charged, sir ?

Clinch. Sen. Only a brace of bullets, that's all, sir. —I design to shoot seven Italians a week, sir.

Sir Har. Sir, you won't have provocation.

Clinch. Sen. Provocation, sir !—Zauns, sir ! I'll kill any man for treading upon my corn !—and there will be

[1] A courtesan.

a devilish throng of people there.—They say that all the princes in Italy will be there.

Sir Har. And all the fops and fiddlers in Europe.— But the use of your swimming-girdle, pray, sir?

Clinch. Sen. O Lord, sir! that's easy. Suppose the ship cast away;—now, whilst other foolish people are busy at their prayers, I whips on my swimming-girdle, claps a month's provision into my pockets, and sails me away like an egg in a duck's belly.—And harkee, sir; I have a new project in my head. Where d'ye think my swimming-girdle shall carry me upon this occasion?— 'tis a new project.

Sir Har. Where, sir?

Clinch. Sen. To Civita Vecchia, faith and troth! and so save the charges of my passage. Well, sir, you must pardon me now, I'm going to see my mistress.

[*Exit.*

Sir. Har. This fellow's an accomplished ass before he goes abroad.—Well! this Angelica has got into my heart, and I can't get her out of my head. I must pay her t'other visit. [*Exit.*

SCENE III.—*Lady Darling's House.*

ANGELICA *sola.*

Angel. Unhappy state of woman! whose chief virtue is but ceremony, and our much boasted modesty but a slavish restraint. The strict confinement on our words makes our thoughts ramble more; and what preserves our outward fame, destroys our inward quiet.—'Tis hard that love should be denied the privilege of hatred; that scandal and detraction should be so much indulged, yet sacred love and truth debarred our conversation.

Enter LADY DARLING, CLINCHER Junior, *and* DICKY.

Lady Dar. This is my daughter, cousin.

Dicky. [*Aside to him.*] Now, sir, remember your three scrapes.

Clinch. Jun. [*Saluting* ANGELICA.] One, two, three— [*Kisses her*] your humble servant.—Was not that right, Dicky?

Dicky. Ay, faith, sir; but why don't you speak to her?

Clinch. Jun. I beg your pardon, Dicky, I know my distance. Would you have me speak to a lady at the first sight?

Dicky. Ay, sir, by all means; the first aim is the surest.

Clinch. Jun. Now for a good jest to make her laugh heartily.—By Jupiter Ammon, I'll go give her a kiss.

[*Goes towards her.*

Enter WILDAIR, *interposing.*

Sir Har. 'Tis all to no purpose, I told you so before; your pitiful five guineas will never do.—You may march, sir, for as far as five hundred pounds will go, I'll outbid you.

Clinch. Jun. What the devil! the madman's here again.

Lady Dar. Bless me, cousin! what d'ye mean? Affront a gentleman of his quality in my house!

Clinch. Jun. Quality! why, madam, I don't know what you mean by your madmen, and your beaux, and your quality.—They're all alike, I believe.

Lady Dar. Pray, sir, walk with me into the next room.

[*Exit, leading* CLINCHER Junior, DICKY *following.*

Angel. Sir, if your conversation be no more agreeable than 'twas the last time, I would advise you to make it as short as you can.

Sir Har. The offences of my last visit, madam, bore their punishment in the commission; and have made me as uneasy till I receive pardon as your ladyship can be till I sue for it.

Angel. Sir Harry, I did not well understand the offence, and must therefore proportion it to the greatness of your apology; if you would therefore have me think it light, take no great pains in an excuse.

Sir Har. How sweet must be the lips that guard that tongue!—Then, madam, no more of past offences, let us prepare for joys to come; let this seal 'my pardon.— [*Kisses her hand.*] And this—[*Kisses again*] initiate me to farther happiness.

Angel. Hold, sir,—one question, Sir Harry, and pray answer plainly : d'ye love me?

Sir Har. Love you! does fire ascend? do hypocrites dissemble? usurers love gold, or great men flattery? Doubt these, then question that I love.

Angel. This shows your gallantry, sir, but not your love.

Sir Har. View your own charms, madam, then judge my passion. Your beauty ravishes my eye, your voice my ear, and your touch has thrilled my melting soul.

Angel. If your words be real, 'tis in your power to raise an equal flame in me.

Sir Har. Nay, then—I seize—

Angel. Hold, sir! 'tis also possible to make me detest and scorn you worse than the most profligate of your deceiving sex.

Sir Har. [*Aside.*] Ha! a very odd turn this.—[*Aloud.*] I hope, madam, you only affect anger, because you know your frowns are becoming.

Angel. Sir Harry, you being the best judge of your own designs, can best understand whether my anger should be real or dissembled. Think what strict modesty should bear, then judge of my resentments.

Sir Har. Strict modesty should bear! Why, faith,

madam, I believe the strictest modesty may bear
fifty guineas, and I don't believe 'twill bear one farthing
more.

Angel. What d'ye mean, sir?

Sir Har. Nay, madam, what do you mean? If you
go to that, I think now fifty guineas is a very fine offer
for your strict modesty, as you call it.

Angel. 'Tis more charitable, Sir Harry, to charge the
impertinence of a man of your figure on his defect in
understanding, than on his want of manners.—I'm afraid
you're mad, sir.

Sir Har. Why, madam, you're enough to make any
man mad. 'Sdeath, are you not a—

Angel. What, sir?

Sir Har. Why, a lady of—strict modesty, if you will
have it so.

Angel. I shall never hereafter trust common report,
which represented you, sir, a man of honour, wit, and
breeding; for I find you very deficient in them all.

[Exit.

Sir Har. [*solus.*] Now I find that the strict pretences
which the ladies of pleasure make to strict modesty, is
the reason why those of quality are ashamed to wear it.

Enter VIZARD.

Viz. Ah, Sir Harry! have I caught you? Well, and
what success?

Sir Har. Success! 'Tis a shame for you young
fellows in town here to let the wenches grow so saucy:
I offered her fifty guineas, and she was in her airs presently. I could have had two countesses in Paris for
half the money, and *Je vous remercie* into the bargain.

Viz. Gone in her airs, say you? and did not you
follow her?

Sir Har. Whither should I follow her?

Viz. Into her bedchamber, man: she went on
purpose. You a man of gallantry, and not understand

that a lady's best pleased when she puts on her airs, as
you call it !

Sir Har. She talked to me of strict modesty, and stuff.

Viz. Certainly most women magnify their modesty,
for the same reason that cowards boast their courage,
because they have least on't. Come, come, Sir Harry,
when you make your next assault, encourage your spirits
with brisk burgundy ; if you succeed, 'tis well ; if not,
you have a fair excuse for your rudeness. I'll go in, and
make your peace for what's past.—Oh, I had almost
forgot—Colonel Standard wants to speak with you about
some business.

Sir Har. I'll wait upon him presently; d'ye know
where he may be found ?

Viz. In the Piazza of Covent Garden, about an hour
hence, I promised to see him, and there you may meet
him.—[*Aside.*] To have your throat cut.—[*Aloud.*] I'll
go in and intercede for you.

Sir Har. But no foul play with the lady, Vizard !
[*Exit.*

Viz. No fair play, I can assure you. [*Exit.*

———————

SCENE IV.—*The Street before Lady
Lurewell's Lodgings.*[1]

CLINCHER Senior *and* Lady LUREWELL *coquetting in the
balcony. Enter below* Colonel STANDARD.

Stand How weak is reason in disputes of love ![2]
That daring reason which so oft pretends

———

[1] This and the following scene are taken from *The Adventures of
Covent Garden* (1699). *See* Introduction, p. 7. Mr W. J.
Lawrence writes : "Scenes like this are peculiar to the period, and
occur frequently in the comedies of Mrs Behn. The balcony used
was a permanent one, situated over the proscenium entrance-door."

[2] The whole speech printed as prose in early editions.

To question works of high omnipotence,
Yet poorly truckles to our weakest passions,
And yields implicit faith to foolish love,
Paying blind zeal to faithless woman's eyes.
I've heard her falsehood with such pressing proofs,
That I no longer should distrust it.
Yet still my love would baffle demonstration,
And make impossibilities seem probable.   [*Looks up.*
Ha! that fool too! what! stoop so low as that animal!
—'Tis true, women once fallen, like cowards in de-
spair, will stick at nothing; there's no medium in their
actions. They must be bright as angels, or black as
fiends. But now for my revenge; I'll kick her cully
before her face, call her a whore, curse the whole sex,
and so leave her.   [*Goes in.*

SCENE V.—*The Scene changes to a Dining Room.*

Enter Lady LUREWELL *with* CLINCHER Senior.

Lady Lure. O Lord, sir, 'tis my husband! What will
become of you?

Clinch. Sen. Eh! your husband! oh, I shall be
murdered! what shall I do? where shall I run! I'll
creep into an oven; I'll climb up the chimney; I'll
fly! I'll swim!—I wish to the Lord I were at the
Jubilee now!

Lady Lure. Can't you think of anything, sir?

Enter TOM ERRAND.

What do you want, sir?

Err. Madam, I am looking for Sir Harry Wildair; I
saw him come in here this morning, and did imagine he
might be here still.

Lady Lure. A lucky hit!—Here, friend, change clothes with this gentleman, quickly; strip!

Clinch Sen. Ay, ay, quickly, strip! I'll give you half-a-crown. Come, here : so. [*They change clothes.*

Lady Lure. [*To* CLINCHER.] Now slip you down stairs, and wait at the door till my husband be gone. —[*Exit* CLINCHER.] And get you in there till I call you. [*Puts* ERRAND *into the next room.*

Enter STANDARD.

Oh, sir! are you come? I wonder, sir, how you have the confidence to approach me after so base a trick!

Stand. Oh, madam, all your artifices won't prevail.

Lady Lure. Nay, sir, your artifices won't avail. I thought, sir, that I gave you caution enough against troubling me with Sir Harry Wildair's company when I sent his letters back by you; yet you, forsooth, must tell him where I lodged, and expose me again to his impertinent courtship.

Stand. I expose you to his courtship!

Lady Lure. I'll lay my life you'll deny it now. Come, come, sir; a pitiful lie is as scandalous to a red coat as an oath to a black. Did not Sir Harry himself tell me that he found out by you where I lodged?

Stand. You're all lies! First, your heart is false, your eyes are double; one look belies another; and then your tongue does contradict them all. Madam, I see a little devil just now hammering out a lie in your pericranium.

Lady Lure. [*Aside.*] As I hope for mercy, he's in the right on't.—[*Aloud.*] Hold, sir, you have got the playhouse cant upon your tongue, and think that wit may privilege your railing; but I must tell you, sir, that what is satire upon the stage is ill manners here.

Stand. What is feigned upon the stage, is here in reality real falsehood. Yes, yes, madam; I exposed you to the courtship of your fool Clincher too : I

hope your female wiles will impose that upon me
also—

Lady Lure. Clincher! nay, now you're stark mad. I
know no such person.

Stand. Oh, woman in perfection! not know him!
'Slife, madam, can my eyes, my piercing jealous eyes,
be so deluded?   Nay, madam, my nose could not
mistake him ; for I smelt the fop by his pulvilio from
the balcony down to the street.

Lady Lure. The balcony! ha, ha, ha! the balcony!
I'll be hanged but he has mistaken Sir Harry Wildair's
footman, with a new French livery, for a beau.

Stand. 'Sdeath, madam, what is there in me that
looks like a cully?   Did I not see him?

Lady Lure. No, no, you could not see him ; you're
dreaming, Colonel.   Will you believe your eyes, now
that I have rubbed them open?—Here, you friend!
                                                    [*Calls.*

Re-enter ERRAND *in* CLINCHER'S *clothes.*

Stand. This is illusion all; my eyes conspire against
themselves! 'tis legerdemain!

Lady Lure. Legerdemain! Is that all your acknowledgment for your rude behaviour? Oh, what a curse
is it to love as I do! But don't presume too far, sir,
on my affection ; for such ungenerous usage will soon
return my tired heart.—[*To* ERRAND.] Begone, sir, to
your impertinent master, and tell him I shall never be
at leisure to receive any of his troublesome visits.—
Send to me to know when I should be at home!—Begone, sir!—I am sure he has made me an unfortunate
woman.   [*Weeps.—Exit* ERRAND.

Stand. Nay, then there is no certainty in Nature;
and truth is only falsehood well disguised.

Lady Lure. Sir, had not I owned my fond foolish
passion, I should not have been subject to such unjust
suspicions : but 'tis an ungrateful return.   [*Weeping.*

Stand. [*Aside.*] Now, where are all my firm resolves?
I will believe her just. My passion raised my jealousy;
then why mayn't love be blind in finding faults as in
excusing them?—[*Aloud.*] I hope, madam, you'll
pardon me, since jealousy, that magnified my suspicion,
is as much the effect of love as my easiness in being
satisfied.

Lady Lure Easiness in being satisfied! You men
have got an insolent way of extorting pardon by per-
sisting in your faults. No, no, sir, cherish your suspicions, and feed upon your jealousy : 'tis fit meat for
your squeamish stomach.

With me all women should this rule pursue :
Who thinks us false, should never find us true.
[*Exit in a rage.*

Re-enter CLINCHER Senior.

Clinch. Sen. [*Aside.*] Well, intriguing is the prettiest,
pleasantest thing for a man of my parts! How shall we
laugh at the husband when he is gone!—How sillily he
looks! He's in labour of horns already :—to make a
colonel a cuckold! 'Twill be rare news for the
aldermen.

Stand. All this Sir Harry has occasioned; but he's
brave, and will afford me just revenge.—Oh, this is
the porter I sent the challenge by.—Well, sir, have you
found him?

Clinch. Sen. [*Aside.*] What the devil does he mean
now?

Stand. Have you given Sir Harry the note, fellow?

Clinch. Sen. The note!—what note?

Stand. The letter, blockhead! which I sent by you
to Sir Harry Wildair. Have you seen him?

Clinch. Sen. [*Aside.*] O Lord! what shall I say
now?—[*Aloud.*] Seen him?—yes, sir—no, sir.—I have,
sir—I have not, sir.

Stand. The fellow's mad! Answer me directly, sirrah, or I'll break your head!

Clinch. Sen. I know Sir Harry very well, sir; but as, to the note, sir, I can't remember a word on't: truth is, I have a very bad memory.

Stand. Oh, sir, I'll quicken your memory!

[Strikes him.

Clinch. Sen. Zauns, sir, hold! I did give him the note.

Stand. And what answer?

Clinch. Sen. I mean, sir, I did not give him the note.

Stand. What! d'ye banter, rascal?

[Strikes him again.

Clinch. Sen. Hold, sir! hold!—He did send an answer.

Stand. What was't, villain?

Clinch. Sen. Why, truly, sir, I have forgot it: I told you that I had a very treacherous memory.

Stand. I'll engage you shall remember me this month, rascal!   [*Beats him off and exit.*

Re-enter Lady LUREWELL with PARLY.

Lady Lure. Fort bon! fort bon! fort bon![1]—this is better than I expected; but fortune still helps the industrious.

Re-enter CLINCHER Senior.

Clinch. Sen. Ah, the devil take all intriguing, say I! and him who first invented canes! That cursed colonel has got such a knack of beating his men, that he has left the mark of a collar of bandoleers about my shoulders.

Lady Lure. Oh, my poor gentleman! and was it beaten?

Clinch. Sen. Yes, I have been beaten: but where's my clothes? my clothes?

---

[1] Early editions: "*Fortboon, fortboon, fortboon!*"

Lady Lure. What! you won't leave me so soon, my dear, will ye?

Clinch. Sen. Will ye!—If ever I peep into a colonel's tent again, may I be forced to run the gauntlet!—But my clothes, madam.

Lady Lure. I sent the porter downstairs with them, did not you meet him?

Clinch. Sen. Meet him! no, not I.

Par. No? He went out of the back door, and is run clear away, I'm afraid.

Clinch. Sen. Gone, say you? and with my clothes? my fine Jubilee clothes!—Oh, the rogue! the thief!—I'll have him hanged for murder. But how shall I get home in this pickle?

Par. I'm afraid, sir, the colonel will be back presently; for he dines at home.

Clinch. Sen. Oh, then I must sneak off!—was ever man so managed! to have his coat well thrashed, and lose his coat too? [*Exit.*

Lady Lure. Thus the noble poet spoke truth :—

*Nothing suits worse with vice than want of sense :
Fools are still wicked at their own expense.*

Par. Methinks, madam, the injuries you have suffered by men must be very great to raise such heavy resentments against the whole sex.

Lady Lure. The greatest injury that woman could sustain : they robbed me of that jewel which, preserved, exalts our sex almost to angels; but destroyed, debases us below the worst of brutes—mankind.

Par. But I think, madam, your anger should be only confined to the author of your wrongs.

Lady Lure. The author!—Alas! I know him not; which makes my wrongs the greater.

Par. Not know him! 'tis odd, madam, that a man should rob you of that same jewel you mentioned, and you not know him!

Lady Lure. Leave trifling!—'tis a subject that always sours my temper. But since, by thy faithful service, I have some reason to confide in your secrecy, hear the strange relation. Some twelve years ago I lived at my father's house in Oxfordshire, blest with innocence, the ornamental but weak guard of blooming beauty. I was then just fifteen, an age oft fatal to the female sex:—our youth is tempting, our innocence credulous, romances moving, love powerful, and men are—villains! Then it happened, that three young gentlemen, from the university, coming into the country, and being benighted, and strangers, called at my father's: he was very glad of their company, and offered them the entertainment of his house.

Par. Which they accepted, no doubt.—Oh! these strolling collegians are never abroad but upon some mischief!

Lady Lure. They had some private frolic or design in their heads, as appeared by their not naming one another; which my father perceiving, out of civility, made no inquiry into their affairs. Two of them had a heavy, pedantic, university air, a sort of disagreeable scholastic boorishness in their behaviour; but the third!—

Par. Ay, the third, madam!—the third of all things, they say, is very critical.

Lady Lure. He was—but, in short, nature cut him out for my undoing!—He seemed to be about eighteen.

Par. A fit match for your fifteen as could be.

Lady Lure. He had a genteel sweetness in his face, a graceful comeliness in his person, and his tongue was fit to soothe soft innocence to ruin. His very looks were witty, and his expressive eyes spoke softer, prettier things, than words could frame.

Par. There will be mischief by-and-bye; I never heard a woman talk so much of eyes but there were tears presently after.

Lady Lure. His discourse was directed to my father, but his looks to me. After supper, I went to my chamber, and read Cassandra; then went to bed, and dreamt of him all night; rose in the morning, and made verses: so fell desperately in love. My father was so well pleased with his conversation, that he begged their company next day; they consented; and next night, Parly—

Par. Ay, next night, madam,—next night (I'm afraid) was a night indeed.

Lady Lure. He bribed my maid, with his gold, out of her honesty; and me, with his rhetoric, out of my honour. She admitted him to my chamber, and there he vowed, and swore, and wept, and sighed — and conquered. [*Weeps.*

Par. Alack-a-day, poor fifteen! [*Weeps.*

Lady Lure. He swore that he would come down from Oxford in a fortnight, and marry me.

Par. [*Aside.*] The old bait! the old bait!—I was cheated just so myself.—[*Aloud.*] But had not you the wit to know his name all this while?

Lady Lure. Alas! what wit had innocence like mine? He told me, that he was under an obligation to his companions of concealing himself then, but that he would write to me in two days, and let me know his name and quality. After all the binding oaths of constancy, joining hands, exchanging hearts, I gave him a ring with this motto, *Love and Honour.* Then we parted; but I never saw the dear deceiver more.

Par. No, nor never will, I warrant you.

Lady Lure. I need not tell my griefs, which my father's death made a fair pretence for; he left me sole heiress and executrix to three thousand pounds a year. At last, my love for this single dissembler turned to a hatred of the whole sex; and, resolving to divert my melancholy, and make my large fortune subservient to my pleasure and revenge I went to travel, where, in most Courts of Europe, I have done some execution. Here I will play my last scene; then retire to my country house, live solitary, and die a penitent.

Par. But don't you still love this dear dissembler?

Lady Lure. Most certainly: 'tis love of him that keeps my anger warm, representing the baseness of mankind full in view, and makes my resentments work.——We shall have that old impotent lecher Smuggler here to-night; I have a plot to swinge him, and his precise nephew Vizard.

Par. I think, madam, you manage everybody that comes in your way.

Lady Lure. No, Parly; those men whose pretensions I found just and honourable, I fairly dismissed, by letting them know my firm resolutions never to marry. But those villains that would attempt my honour, I've seldom failed to manage.

Par. What d'ye think of the colonel, madam? I suppose his designs are honourable.

Lady Lure. That man's a riddle; there's something of honour in his temper that pleases: I'm sure he loves me too, because he's soon jealous, and soon satisfied. But he's a man still. When I once tried his pulse about marriage, his blood ran as low as a coward's. He swore, indeed, that he loved me, but could not marry me forsooth, because he was engaged elsewhere. So poor a pretence made me disdain his passion, which otherwise might have been uneasy to me. But hang him, I have teased him enough. Besides, Parly, I begin to be tired of my revenge.—But this " buss and guinea " I must maul once more: I'll hansel his woman's clothes for him! Go, get me pen and ink; I must write to Vizard too. [*Exit* PARLY.

Fortune this once assist me as before,
Two such machines can never work in vain,
As thy propitious wheel, and my projecting brain.
[*Exit.*

ACT IV

SCENE I.—*Covent Garden.*

WILDAIR *and* STANDARD *meeting.*

TAND. I thought, Sir Harry, to have met you ere this in a more convenient place; but since my wrongs were without ceremony, my revenge shall be so too. Draw, sir!

Sir Har. Draw, sir? What shall I draw?

Stand. Come, come, sir, I like your facetious humour well enough; it shows courage and unconcern. I know you brave; and therefore use you thus. Draw your sword.

Sir Har. Nay, to oblige you, I will draw; but the devil take me if I fight!—Perhaps, Colonel, this is the prettiest blade you have seen.

Stand. I doubt not but the arm is good; and therefore think both worthy my resentment. Come, sir.

Sir Har. But prithee, Colonel, dost think that I am such a madman as to send my soul to the devil and my body to the worms upon every fool's errand?

Stand. I hope you're no coward, sir.

Sir Har. Coward, sir! I have eight thousand pounds a year, sir.

Stand. You fought in Flanders to my knowledge.

97

Sir Har. Ay, for the same reason that I wore a red coat, because 'twas fashionable.

Stand. Sir, you fought a French count in Paris.

Sir Har. True, sir; he was a beau like myself. Now you're a soldier, Colonel, and fighting's your trade; and I think it downright madness to contend with any man in his profession.

Stand. Come, sir, no more dallying: I shall take very unseemly methods if you don't show yourself a gentleman

Sir Har. A gentleman! why there again now? A gentleman! I tell you once more, Colonel, that I am a baronet, and have eight thousand pounds a year. I can dance, sing, ride, fence, understand the languages. Now, I can't conceive how running you through the body should contribute one jot more to my gentility. But pray, Colonel, I had forgot to ask you: what's the quarrel?

Stand. A woman, sir.

Sir Har. Then I put up my sword.—Take her.

Stand. Sir, my honour's concerned.

Sir Har. Nay, if your honour be concerned with a woman, get it out of her hands as soon as you can. An honourable lover is the greatest slave in nature; some will say, the greatest fool. Come, come, Colonel, this is something about the Lady Lurewell, I warrant; I can give you satisfaction in that affair.

Stand. Do so then immediately.

Sir Har. Put up your sword first; you know I dare fight: but I had much rather make you a friend than an enemy. I can assure you, this lady will prove too hard for one of your temper. You have too much honour, too much in conscience, to be a favourite with the ladies.

Stand. I am assured, sir, she never gave you any encouragement

Sir Har. A man can never hear reason with a sword

in his hand. Sheathe your weapon; and then if I don't satisfy you, sheathe it in my body.

Stand. Give me but demonstration of her granting you any favour, and 'tis enough.

Sir Har. Will you take my word?

Stand. Pardon me, sir, I cannot.

Sir Har. Will you believe your own eyes?

Stand. 'Tis ten to one whether I shall or no; they have deceived me already.

Sir Har. That's hard.—But some means I shall devise for your satisfaction. We must fly this place, else that cluster of mob will overwhelm us. [*Exeunt.*

Enter Mob, TOM ERRAND'S *wife hurrying in* CLINCHER Senior *in* ERRAND'S *clothes.*

Wife. Oh, the villain! the rogue! he has murdered my husband: ah, my poor Timothy! [*Crying.*

Clinch. Sen. Dem your Timothy!—Your husband has murdered me, woman; for he has carried away my fine Jubilee clothes.

Wife. Ay, you cut-throat, have you not got his clothes upon your back there?—Neighbours, don't you know poor Timothy's coat and apron?

Mob. Ay, ay, 'tis the same.

1 *Mob.* What shall we do with him, neighbours?

2 *Mob.* We'll pull him in pieces.

1 *Mob.* No, no; then we may be hanged for murder: but we'll drown him.

Clinch. Sen. Ah, good people, pray don't drown me; for I never learned to swim in all my life.—Ah, this plaguy intriguing!

Mob. Away with him! away with him to the Thames!

Clinch. Sen. Oh, if I had but my swimming-girdle now!

Enter Constable.

Const. Hold, neighbours! I command the peace.

Wife. Oh, Mr Constable, here's a rogue that has murdered my husband, and robbed him of his clothes.

Const. Murder and robbery! then he must be a gentleman.—Hands off there! he must not be abused.—Give an account of yourself: are you a gentleman?

Clinch. Sen. No, sir, I am a beau.

Const. Then you have killed nobody, I'm persuaded. How came you by these clothes, sir?

Clinch. Sen. You must know, sir, that walking along, sir, I don't know how, sir, I can't tell where, sir; and— so the porter and I changed clothes, sir.

Const. Very well.   The man speaks reason and like a gentleman.

Wife. But pray, Mr Constable, ask him how he changed clothes with him.

Const. Silence, woman! and don't disturb the court. —Well, sir, how did you change clothes?

Clinch. Sen. Why, sir, he pulled off my coat, and I drew off his; so I put on his coat, and he puts on mine.

Const. Why, neighbours, I don't find that he's guilty. Search him; and if he carries no arms about him, we'll let him go.

[*They search his pockets, and pull out his pistols.*

Clinch. Sen. O gemini! my Jubilee pistols!

Const. What, a case of pistols! then the case is plain. —Speak, what are you, sir? whence came you, and whither go you?

Clinch. Sen. Sir, I came from Russel Street, and am going to the Jubilee.

Wife. You shall go to the gallows, you rogue!

Const. Away with him! away with him to Newgate, straight!

Clinch. Sen. I shall go to the Jubilee now, indeed.

[*Exeunt.*

Re-enter WILDAIR *and* STANDARD.

Sir Har. In short, Colonel, 'tis all nonsense.   Fight

for a woman!—Hard by is the lady's house; if you please we'll wait on her together: you shall draw your sword, I'll draw my snuff-box: you shall produce your wounds received in war, I'll relate mine by Cupid's dart : you shall look big, I'll ogle : you shall swear, I'll sigh : you shall sa ! sa ! and I'll coupee :¹ and if she flies not to my arms like a hawk to its perch, my dancing-master deserves to be damned !

Stand. With the generality of women, I grant you, these arts may prevail.

Sir Har. Generality of women! why, there again you're out. They're all alike, sir; I never heard of any one that was particular, but one.

Stand. Who was she, pray ?

Sir Har. Penelope, I think, she's called ; and that's a poetical story too. When will you find a poet in our age make a woman so chaste ?

Stand. Well, Sir Harry, your facetious humour can disguise falsehood, and make calumny pass for satire. But you have promised me ocular demonstration that she favours you : make that good, and I shall then maintain faith and female to be as inconsistent as truth and falsehood.

Sir Har. Nay, by what you have told me, I am satisfied that she imposes on us all ; and Vizard, too, seems what I still suspected him ; but his honesty once mistrusted, spoils his knavery.—But will you be convinced, if our plot succeeds ?

Stand. I rely on your word and honour, Sir Harry ; which if I doubted, my distrust would cancel the obligation of their security.

Sir Har. Then meet me half-an-hour hence at the Rummer.² You must oblige me by taking a hearty glass with me toward the fitting me out for a certain project which this night I undertake.

¹ Terms in fencing and dancing respectively.
² See note, p. 46.

Stand. I guess by the preparation that woman's the design.

Sir Har. Yes, faith.—I am taken dangerously ill with two foolish maladies, modesty and love ; the first I'll cure with burgundy, and my love by a night's lodging with the damsel. A sure remedy. *Probatum est !*

Stand. I'll certainly meet you, sir.

[*Exeunt severally.*

SCENE II.—*The same.* [1]

Enter CLINCHER Junior *and* DICKY.

Clinch. Jun. Ah, Dicky, this London is a sad place ! a sad vicious place ! I wish that I were in the country again.—And this brother of mine! I'm sorry he's so great a rake : I had rather see him dead than see him thus.

Dicky. Ay, sir, he'll spend his whole estate at this same Jubilee. Who d'ye think lives at this same Jubilee?

Clinch. Jun. Who, pray?

Dicky. The Pope.

Clinch. Jun. The devil he does ! My brother go to the place where the Pope dwells ! he's bewitched sure.

Enter TOM ERRAND *in* CLINCHER Senior's *clothes.*

Dicky. Indeed I believe he is, for he's strangely altered.

Clinch. Jun. Altered ! why he looks like a Jesuit already.

Err. [*Aside.*] This lace will sell. What a blockhead was the fellow to trust me with his coat ! If I can get across the Garden, down to the water side, I'm pretty secure.

Clinch. Jun. Brother!—Alaw! O gemini! are you my brother?

Dicky. I seize you in the king's name, sir.

Err. [*Aside.*] O Lord! should this prove some parliament man now!

Clinch. Jun. Speak, you rogue, what are you?

Err. A poor porter, sir, and going of an errand.

Dicky. What errand? speak, you rogue.

Err. A fool's errand, I'm afraid.

Clinch. Jun. Who sent you?

Err. A beau, sir.

Dicky. No, no, the rogue has murdered your brother, and stripped him of his clothes.

Clinch. Jun. Murdered my brother! O crimini! O my poor Jubilee brother!—Stay, by Jupiter Ammon, I'm heir though!—Speak, sirrah, have you killed him? Confess that you have killed him, and I'll give you half-a-crown.

Err. Who, I, sir? Alack-a-day, sir, I never killed any man but a carrier's horse once.

Clinch. Jun. Then you shall certainly be hanged; but confess that you killed him, and we'll let you go.

Err. [*Aside.*] Telling the truth hangs a man, but confessing a lie can do no harm; besides, if the worst comes to the worst, I can but deny it again.—[*Aloud.*] Well, sir, since I must tell you, I did kill him.

Clinch. Jun. Here's your money, sir:—but are you sure you killed him dead?

Err. Sir, I'll swear it before any judge in England.

Dicky. But are you sure that he's dead in law?

Err. Dead in law! I can't tell whether he be dead in law: but he's dead as a door-nail; for I gave him seven knocks on the head with a hammer.

Dicky. Then you have the estate by the statute. Any man that's knocked o' th' head is dead in law.

Clinch. Jun. But are you sure he was *compos mentis* when he was killed ?

Err. I suppose he was, sir ; for he told me nothing to the contrary afterwards.

Clinch. Jun. Hey ! then I go to the Jubilee.—Strip, sir, strip ! by Jupiter Ammon, strip !

　　　　　　　[*Exchanges clothes with* TOM ERRAND.

Dicky. Ah ! don't swear, sir.

Clinch. Jun. Swear, sir ! Zoons, han't I got the estate, sir ?　Come, sir, now I'm in mourning for my brother.

Err. I hope you'll let me go now, sir—

Clinch. Jun. Yes, yes, sir ; but you much first do me the favour to swear positively before a magistrate that you killed him dead, that I may enter upon the estate without any trouble.　By Jupiter Ammon, all my religion's gone since I put on these fine clothes !—Hey ! call me a coach somebody.

Err Ay, master, let me go, and I'll call one immediately.

Clinch. Jun. No, no, Dicky, carry this spark before a justice, and when he has made oath, you may discharge him.—[*Exeunt* DICKY *and* ERRAND.]　And I'll go see Angelica.　Now that I'm an elder brother, I'll court, and swear, and rant, and rake, and go to the Jubilee with the best of them.　　　　　　　　　　　[*Exit.*

SCENE III.—*A Room in Lady Lurewell's House.*

Enter Lady LUREWELL *and* PARLY.

Lady Lure. Are you sure that Vizard had my letter?

Par. Yes, yes, madam ; one of your ladyship's footmen gave it to him in the Park, and he told the bearer, with all transports of joy, that he would be punctual to a minute.

Lady Lure. Thus most villains, sometime or other, are punctual to their ruin; and hypocrisy, by imposing on the world, at last deceives itself. Are all things prepared for his reception?

Par. Exactly to your ladyship's order; the alderman, too, is just come, dressed and cooked up for iniquity.

Lady Lure. Then he has got woman's clothes on?

Par. Yes, madam, and has passed upon the family for your nurse.

Lady Lure. Convey him into that closet, and put out the candles, and tell him I'll wait on him presently.— [*As* PARLY *goes to put out the candles, somebody knocks.*] This must be some clown without manners, or a gentleman above ceremony.—Who's there?

SONG.

Sir Har. [*Without.*] Thus Damon knock'd at
   Celia's door,
He sigh'd, and begg'd, and wept, and swore;
   The sign was so;   [*Knocks.*
   She answer'd, no,
   No, no, no.   [*Knocks thrice.*

Again he sigh'd, again he pray'd;—
"No, Damon, no, I am afraid;
Consider, Damon, I'm a maid,
   Consider; no,
   I am a maid.
   No, no, no."

At last his sighs and tears made way,
She rose, and softly turned the key;
"Come in," said she, "but do not stay.
   I may conclude
   You will be rude,
But, if you are, you may." [*Exit* PARLY.

Lady Lure. 'Tis too early for serenading, Sir Harry.

Sir Har. Wheresoever love is, there music is proper; there's an harmonious consent in their natures, and, when rightly joined, they make up the chorus of earthly happiness.

Lady Lure. But, Sir Harry, what tempest drives you here at this hour?

Sir Har. No tempest, madam, but as fair weather as ever enticed a citizen's wife to cuckold her husband in fresh air:—love, madam.

[*Taking her by the hand.*

Lady Lure. *As pure and white as angels' soft desires.—* Is't not so?

Sir Har. *Fierce as when ripe consenting beauty fires.*

Lady Lure. [*Aside.*] O villain! What privilege has man to our destruction, that thus they hunt our ruin? [Wildair *drops a ring, she takes it up.*] If this be a love-token, your mistress's favours hang very loose about you, sir.

Sir Har. I can't justly, madam, pay your trouble of taking it up by anything but desiring you to wear it.

Lady Lure. You gentlemen have the cunningest ways of playing the fool, and are so industrious in your profuseness! Speak seriously, am I beholden to chance or design for this ring?

Sir Har. To design, upon my honour, [*Aside.*] and I hope my design will succeed.

Lady Lure. [Singing.] *And what shall I give you for such a fine thing?*

Sir Har. [Singing]. *You'll give me another, you'll give me another fine thing.*

Lady Lure. Shall I be free with you, Sir Harry?

Sir Har. With all my heart, madam, so I may be free with you.

Lady Lure. Then, plainly, sir, I shall beg the favour

to see you some other time, for at this very minute I have two lovers in the house.

Sir Har. Then, to be as plain, I must be gone this minute, for I must see another mistress within these two hours.

Lady Lure. Frank and free.

Sir Har. As you with me.—Madam, your most humble servant. [*Exit.*

Lady Lure. Nothing can disturb his humour.—Now for my merchant and Vizard.

[*Exit, and takes the candles with her.*

Re-enter PARLEY, *leading in* SMUGGLER, *dressed in woman's clothes.*

Par. This way, Mr Alderman.

Smug. Well, Mrs Parly, I'm obliged to you for this trouble ; here are a couple of shillings for you. Times are hard, very hard indeed, but next time I'll steal a pair of silk stockings from my wife, and bring them to you.—What are you fumbling about my pockets for?

Par. Only settling the plaits of your gown. Here, sir, get into this closet, and my lady will wait on you presently.

[*Puts him into the closet, runs out, and returns with* VIZARD.

Viz. Where wouldst thou lead me, my dear auspicious little pilot?

Par. You're almost in port, sir; my lady's in the closet, and will come out to you immediately.

Viz. Let me thank thee as I ought. [*Kisses her.*

Par. [*Aside.*] Psha ! who has hired me best—a couple of shillings or a couple of kisses? [*Exit.*

Viz. Propitious darkness guides the lover's steps, and night that shadows outward sense, lights up our inward joy. Night ! the great awful ruler of mankind, which, like the Persian monarch, hides its royalty to raise

the veneration of the world. Under thy easy reign
dissemblers may speak truth; all slavish forms and
ceremonies laid aside, and generous villany may act
without constraint.

Smug. [*Peeping out of the closet.*] Bless me! what
voice is this?

Viz. Our hungry appetites, like the wild beasts of
prey, now scour abroad to gorge their craving maws;
the pleasure of hypocrisy, like a chained lion once broke
loose, wildly indulges its new freedom, ranging through
all unbounded joys.

Smug. [*Aside.*] My nephew's voice, and certainly
possessed with an evil spirit; he talks as profanely as
an actor possessed with a poet.

Viz. Ha! I hear a voice.—Madam—my life, my
happiness, where are you, madam?

Smug. [*Aside.*] Madam! He takes me for a woman
too; I'll try him.—[*Aloud.*] Where have you left your
sanctity, Mr Vizard?

Viz. Talk no more of that ungrateful subject—I left
it where it has only business, with daylight; 'tis needless
to wear a mask in the dark.

Smug. [*Aside.*] O the rogue, the rogue!—[*Aloud.*]
The world takes you for a very sober, virtuous gentleman.

Viz. Ay, madam, that adds security to all my
pleasures. With me a cully-squire [1] may squander his
estate, and ne'er be thought a spendthrift: with me
a holy elder may zealously be drunk, and toast his
tuneful nose in sack, to make it hold forth clearer:
but what is most my praise, the formal rigid she, that
rails at vice and men, with me secures her loosest
pleasures, and her strictest honour. She who with
scornful mien and virtuous pride disdains the name of
whore, with me can wanton, and laugh at the deluded
world.

---

[1] A "cully" meant a dupe or gull.

Smug. [*Aside.*] How have I been deceived!—[*Aloud.*] Then you are very great among the ladies?

Viz. Yes, madam: they know that, like a mole in the earth, I dig deep, but invisible; not like those fluttering noisy sinners, whose pleasure is the proclamation of their faults; those empty flashes who no sooner kindle, but they must blaze to alarm the world.—But come, madam, you delay our pleasures.

Smug. [*Aside.*] He surely takes me for the Lady Lurewell; she has made him an appointment too; but I'll be revenged of both.—[*Aloud.*] Well, sir, what are those you are so intimate with?

Viz. Come, come, madam, you know very well— those who stand so high, that the vulgar envy even their crimes, whose figure adds privilege to their sin, and makes it pass unquestioned; fair, high, pampered females, whose speaking eyes and piercing voice would arm the statue of a Stoic, and animate his cold marble with the soul of an Epicure; all ravishing, lovely, soft, and kind, like you!

Smug. [*Aside.*] I am very lovely and soft indeed! you shall find me much harder than you imagine, friend!— [*Aloud.*] Well, sir, but I suppose your dissimulation has some other motive besides pleasure?

Viz. Yes, madam, the honestest motive in the world —interest. You must know, madam, that I have an old uncle, Alderman Smuggler—you have seen him, I suppose?

Smug. Yes, yes, I have some small acquaintance with him.

Viz. 'Tis the most knavish, precise, covetous old rogue that ever died of a gout.

Smug. [*Aside.*] Ah! the young son of a whore!— [*Aloud.*] Well, sir, and what of him?

Viz. Hell hungers not more for wretched souls than he for ill-got pelf: and yet (what's wonderful) he that would stick at no profitable villainy himself, loves holi-

ness in another. He prays all Sunday for the sins of
the week past ; he spends all dinner-time in too tedious
graces ; and what he designs a blessing to the meat,
proves a curse to his family. He's the most—

Smug. Well, well, sir, I know him very well.

Viz. Then madam, he has a swinging estate, which
I design to purchase as a saint, and spend like a gentleman. He got it by cheating, and should lose it by deceit. By the pretence of my zeal and sobriety, I'll
cozen the old miser one of these days out of a settlement and deed of conveyance—

Smug. [*Aside.*] It shall be a deed to convey you to
the gallows, then, you young dog !

Viz. And no sooner he's dead, but I'll rattle over his
grave with a coach-and-six, to inform his covetous ghost
how genteelly I spend his money.

Smug. [*Aside.*] I'll prevent you, boy ; for I'll have my
money buried with me.

Viz. Bless me, madam ! here's a light coming this way ;
I must fly immediately ! When shall I see you, madam ?

Smug. Sooner than you expect, my dear !

Viz. Pardon me, dear madam, I would not be seen
for the world. I would sooner forfeit my life, nay, my
pleasure, than my reputation.   [*Exit.*

Smug. Reputation ! reputation ! that poor word suffers
a great deal. Well, thou art the most accomplished
hypocrite that ever made a grave plodding face over a
dish of coffee and a pipe of tobacco ! He owes me for
seven years' maintenance, and shall pay me by seven
years' imprisonment ; and when I die, I'll leave him to
the fee-simple of a rope and a shilling !—Who are these !
I begin to be afraid of some mischief. I wish that I
were safe within the city liberties.—I'll hide myself.
                              [*Stands close.*

Enter Butler *and* Footmen *with lights.*

But. I say, there are two spoons wanting, and I'll

search the whole house. Two spoons will be no small gap in my quarter's wages.

Foot. When did you miss them, James?

But. Miss them? why, I miss them now; in short, they must be among you; and if you don't return them, I'll go to the cunning-man [1] to-morrow morning; my spoons I want, and my spoons I will have.

Foot. Come, come, search about.—[*Search and discover* SMUGGLER.] Ah! who's this?

But. Hark'ee, good woman, what makes you hide yourself? what are you ashamed of?

Smug. Ashamed of!—O Lord, sir! I'm an honest old woman that never was ashamed of anything.

But. What are you? a midwife then? Speak, did not you see a couple of stray spoons in your travels?

Smug. Stray spoons?

But. Ay, ay, stray spoons; in short, you stole them, and I'll shake your old limbs to pieces if you don't deliver them presently.

Smug. [*Aside.*] Bless me, a reverend elder of seventy years old accused for petty larceny!—[*Aloud.*] Why, search me, good people, search me; and if you find any spoons about me, you shall burn me for a witch.

But. Ay, ay, we will search you, mistress.

[*They search and pull the spoons out of his pocket.*

Smug. Oh, the devil! the devil!

But. Where? where is he?—Lord bless us! she is a witch in good earnest, maybe!

Smug. Oh, it was some devil, some Covent Garden or St. James's devil that put them in my pocket!

But. Ay, ay, you shall be hanged for a thief, burned for a witch, and then carted for a bawd. Speak, what are you?

Re-enter Lady LUREWELL.

Smug. I'm the Lady Lurewell's nurse.

[1] Wizard, clairvoyant.

Lady Lure. What noise is this?

But. Here is an old succubus,[1] madam, that has stole two silver spoons, and says she's your nurse.

Lady Lure. My nurse! Oh the impudent old jade! I never saw the withered creature before.

Smug. [*Aside.*] Then I'm finely caught!—[*Aloud.*] O madam, madam! don't you know me? don't you remember buss and guinea?

Lady Lure. Was ever such impudence!—I know thee! why, thou'rt as brazen as a bawd in the side-box.—Take her before a justice, and then to Newgate. Away!

Smug. [*Aside to* Lady LUREWELL] Oh! consider, madam, that I'm an alderman.

Lady Lure. [*Aside to* SMUGGLER.] Consider, sir, that you're a compound of covetousness, hypocrisy, and knavery, and must be punished accordingly. You must be in petticoats, gouty monster, must ye! you must "buss and guinea" too! you must tempt a lady's honour, old satyr!—[*Aloud.*] Away with him!

[Butler *and* Footmen *hurry* SMUGGLER *off.*

Still may our sex thus frauds of men oppose,
Still may our arts delude these tempting foes:
May honour rule, and never fall betray'd,
But vice be caught in nets for virtue laid.

[1] The Butler means *succuba*, properly a female demon, but often applied to a witch.

ACT V

SCENE I.—*Lady Darling's House.*

Lady DARLING *and* ANGELICA.

ADY DAR. Daughter, since you have to deal with a man of so peculiar a temper, you must not think the general arts of love can secure him; you may therefore allow such a courtier some encouragement extraordinary, without reproach to your modesty.

Angel. I am sensible, madam, that a formal nicety makes our modesty sit awkward, and appears rather a chain to enslave than bracelet to adorn us: it should show, when unmolested, easy and innocent as a dove, but strong and vigorous as a falcon when assaulted.

Lady Dar. I'm afraid, daughter, you mistake Sir Harry's gaiety for dishonour.

Angel. Though modesty, madam, may wink, it must not sleep, when powerful enemies are abroad. I must confess, that of all men's, I would not see Sir Harry Wildair's faults; nay, I could wrest his most suspicious words a thousand ways to make them look like honour. —But, madam, in spite of love, I must hate him, and curse those practices which taint our nobility, and rob all virtuous women of the bravest men.

Lady Dar. You must certainly be mistaken, Angelica; for I'm satisfied Sir Harry's designs are only to court and marry you.

Angel. His pretence, perhaps, was such; but women now, like enemies, are attacked; whether by treachery or fairly conquered, the glory of triumph is the same. Pray, madam, by what means were you made acquainted with his designs?

Lady Dar. Means, child! Why, my cousin Vizard, who, I'm sure, is your sincere friend, sent him. He brought me this letter from my cousin.

[*Gives her the letter, which she opens.*

Angel. [*Aside*] Ha! Vizard! then I'm abused in earnest. Would Sir Harry, by his instigation, fix a base affront upon me? No, I can't suspect him of so un-genteel a crime. This letter shall trace the truth.— [*Aloud.*] My suspicions, madam, are much cleared; and I hope to satisfy your ladyship in my management when next I see Sir Harry.

Enter Footman.

Foot. Madam, here's a gentleman below calls himself Wildair.

Lady Dar. Conduct him up. — [*Exit* Footman.] Daughter, I won't doubt your discretion.   [*Exit.*

Enter WILDAIR.

Sir Har. Oh, the delights of love and burgundy!— Madam, I have toasted your ladyship fifteen bumpers successively, and swallowed Cupids like loaches,[1] to every glass.

Angel. And what then, sir?

Sir Har. Why then, madam, the wine has got into my head, and the Cupids into my heart; and unless by quenching quick my flame, you kindly ease the smart, I'm a lost man, madam.

[1] A small fresh-water fish, *cobitis barbatula.*

Angel. Drunkenness, Sir Harry, is the worst pretence a gentleman can make for rudeness: for the excuse is as scandalous as the fault.—Therefore, pray consider who you are so free with, sir; a woman of condition, that can call half-a-dozen footmen upon occasion.

Sir Har. Nay, madam, if you have a mind to toss me in a blanket, half-a-dozen chambermaids would do better service. — Come, come, madam, though the wine makes me lisp, yet has it taught me to speak plainer. By all the dust of my ancient progenitors, I must this night quarter my coat-of-arms with yours.

Angel. Nay then—Who waits there?   [*Calls.*

Enter Footmen.

Take hold of that madman, and bind him.

Sir Har. Nay, then burgundy's the word, and slaughter will ensue. Hold!—do you know, scoundrels, that I have been drinking victorious burgundy? [*Draws.*

Foot. We know you're drunk, sir.

Sir Har. Then, how have you the impudence, rascals, to assault a gentleman with a couple of flasks of courage in his head?

Foot. Sir, we must do as our young mistress commands us.

Sir Har. Nay, then have among ye, dogs!

    [*Throws money among them; they scramble, and take it up. He, pelting them out, shuts the door, and returns.*

Rascals! Poltroons!—I have charmed the dragon, and now the fruit's my own.

Angel. Oh, the mercenary wretches! this was a plot to betray me.

Sir Har. I have put the whole army to flight: and now take the general prisoner.   [*Laying hold of her.*

Angel. I conjure you, sir, by the sacred name of honour, by your dead father's name, and the fair reputation of your mother's chastity, that you offer not the

least offence!—Already you have wronged me past
redress.

Sir Har. Thou art the most unaccountable creature!

Angel. What madness, Sir Harry, what wild dream of
loose desire could prompt you to attempt this baseness?
View me well. The brightness of my mind, methinks,
should lighten outwards, and let you see your mistake in
my behaviour. I think it shines with so much innocence
in my face,

That it should dazzle all your vicious thoughts.[1]

Think not I am defenceless 'cause alone.

Your very self is guard against yourself:

I'm sure, there's something generous in your soul;

My words shall search it out,

And eyes shall fire it for my own defence.

Sir Har. [*Mimicking.*][2] Tall ti dum, ti dum, tall ti
didi, didum.—A million to one now but this girl is just
come flush from reading the *Rival Queens.*[3]—Egad, I'll
at her in her own cant.—*O my Statira! O my angry
dear! Turn thy eyes on me,* — behold thy beau in
buskins.

Angel. Behold me, sir; view me with a sober thought,
free from those fumes of wine that throw a mist before
your sight, and you shall find that every glance from
my reproaching eyes is arm'd with sharp resentment,
and with a virtuous pride that looks dishonour dead.

Sir Har. [*Aside.*] This is the first whore in heroics
that I have met with.—[*Aloud.*] Look ye, madam, as to
that slender particular of your virtue, we sha'n't quarrel
about it; you may be as virtuous as any woman in
England, if you please; you may say your prayers all
the time.—But pray, madam, be pleased to consider
what is this same virtue that you make such a mighty

---

[1] These lines printed as prose in early editions.

[2] The "new scene added to the part of Wildair" in Q. 2, begins
at this point. The original scene, as it stood in Q. 1, will be
found in the Appendix, p. 135.

[3] *The Rival Queens, or Alexander the Great,* by Nat. Lee.

noise about? Can your virtue bespeak you a front row in the boxes? No; for the players can't live upon virtue. Can your virtue keep you a coach and six? No, no, your virtuous women walk a-foot. Can your virtue hire you a pew in a church? Why, the very sexton will tell you, no. Can your virtue stake for you at picquet? No. Then what business has a woman with virtue? Come, come, madam, I offered you fifty guineas: there's a hundred.—The devil! Virtuous still! Why, 'tis a hundred, five score, a hundred guineas.

Angel. O indignation!
Were I a man, you durst not use me thus; [1]
But the mean, poor abuse you throw on me,
Reflects upon yourself!
Our sex still strikes an awe upon the brave,
And only cowards dare affront a woman.

Sir Har. Affront! 'Sdeath, madam! a hundred guineas will set you up at basset,[2] a hundred guineas will furnish out your lodgings with china; a hundred guineas will give you an air of quality; a hundred guineas will buy you a rich escritoir for your billets-doux, or a fine Common-Prayer-book for your virtue. A hundred guineas will buy a hundred fine things, and fine things are for fine ladies; and fine ladies are for fine gentlemen; and fine gentlemen are—egad, this burgundy makes a man speak like an angel.—Come, come, madam, take it and put it to what use you please.

Angel. I'll use it as I would the base unworthy giver —thus.

[*Throws down the purse and stamps upon it.*

Sir Har. I have no mind to meddle in State affairs; but these women will make me a parliament man 'spite of my teeth, on purpose to bring in a bill against their

[1] Printed as prose in early editions.
[2] Basset (sometimes accented on last syllable), "an obsolete game at cards, resembling Faro" (*N.E.D.*).

extortion. She tramples underfoot that deity which all the world adores.—Oh, the blooming pride of beautiful eighteen! Psha, I'll talk to her no longer; I'll make my markets with the old gentlewoman; she knows business better.—[*Goes to the door, and calls.*] Here, you friend, pray desire the old lady to walk in.—Hark'ee, by Gad, madam, I'll tell your mother.

Re-enter Lady DARLING.

Lady Dar. Well, Sir Harry, and how d'ye like my daughter, pray?

Sir Har. Like her, madam!—Hark'ee, will you take it?—Why, faith, madam, take the money, I say, or egad, all's out.

Angel. All shall out. Sir, you're a scandal to the name of gentleman.

Sir Har. With all my heart, madam.—In short, madam, your daughter has used me somewhat too familiarly, though I have treated her like a woman of quality.

Lady Dar. How, sir?

Sir Har. Why, madam I have offered her a hundred guineas.

Lady Dar. A hundred guineas! upon what score?

Sir Har. Upon what score! Lord! Lord! how these old women love to hear bawdy! Why, faith, madam, I have ne'er a *double-entendre* ready at present, but I'll sing you a song.   [*Sings.*

Behold the goldfinches, tall al de rall,
And a man of my inches, tall al de rall;
You shall take 'em, believe me, tall al de rall,
If you will give me your—tall al de rall.

A modish minuet, madam, that's all.

Lady Dar. Sir, I don't understand you.

Sir Har. [*Aside.*] Ay, she will have it in plain terms.
—[*Aloud.*] Then, madam, in downright English, I offered your daughter a hundred guineas to—

Angel. Hold, sir, stop your abusive tongue! too loose for modest ears to bear. Madam, I did before suspect that his designs were base, now they're too plain; this knight, this mighty man of wit and humours, is made a tool to a knave : Vizard has sent him of a bully's errand, to affront a woman; but I scorn the abuse, and him that offered it.

Lady Dar. How, sir, come to affront us! D'ye know who we are, sir?

Sir Har. Know who ye are? Why your daughter there is Mr Vizard's cousin, I suppose :—and for you, madam,—[*Aside.*] now to call her procuress *à la mode France,*—[Aloud.] *J'estime votre occupation——*

Lady Dar. Pray, sir, speak English.

Sir Har. [*Aside.*] Then to define her office, *à la mode Londres!*—[*Aloud.*] I suppose your ladyship to be one of those civil, obliging, discreet old gentlewomen, who keep their visiting days for the entertainment of their presenting friends, whom they treat with imperial tea, a private room, and a pack of cards. Now I suppose you do understand me.

Lady Dar. This is beyond sufferance! But say, thou abusive man, what injury have you e'er received from me or mine thus to engage you in this scandalous aspersion?

Angel. Yes, sir, what cause, what motives, could induce you thus to debase yourself below your rank?

Sir Har. Heyday! Now, dear Roxana, and you my fair Statira,[1] be not so very heroic in your styles; Vizard's letter may resolve you, and answer all the impertinent questions you have made me.

Both Women. We appeal to that.

Sir Har. And I'll stand to't; he read it to me, and the contents were pretty plain, I thought.

Angel. Here, sir, peruse it, and see how much we are injured, and you deceived.

[1] The rival queens in Lee's tragedy (see note p. 116).

Sir Har. [*Opening the letter.*] But hold, madam—[*To* Lady DARLING] before I read, I'll make some condition. Mr Vizard says here, that I won't scruple 30 or 40 pieces. Now, madam, if you have clapped in another cipher to the account, and made it three or four hundred, by Gad, I will not stand to't.

Angel. Now can't I tell whether disdain or anger be the most just resentment for this injury.

Lady Dar. The letter, sir, shall answer you.

Sir Har. Well then!—[Reads.] *Out of my earnest inclination to serve your ladyship, and my cousin Angelica* —Ay, ay, the very words, I can say it by heart—*I have sent Sir Harry Wildair—to court my cousin.*—What the devil's this?—*Sent Sir Harry Wildair to court my cousin!*—He read to me quite a different thing.—*He's a gentleman of great parts and fortune*—He's a son of a whore, and a rascal!—*And would make your daughter very happy* [Whistles] *in a husband.*—Oh, poor Sir Harry! what have thy angry stars designed?

[*Looks foolish, and hums a song.*

Angel. Now, sir, I hope you need no instigation to redress our wrongs, since even the injury points the way.

Lady Dar. Think, sir, that our blood for many generations has run in the purest channel of unsullied honour.

Sir Har. Ay, madam.   [*Bows to her.*

Angel. Consider what a tender blossom is female reputation, which the least air of foul detraction blasts.

Sir Har. Yes, madam.   [*Bows to* ANGELICA.

Lady Dar. Call then to mind your rude and scandalous behaviour.

Sir Har. Right, madam.   [*Bows again.*

Angel. Remember the base price you offered me.

[*Exit.*

Sir Har. Very true, madam.—Was ever man so catechised?

Lady Dar. Then think that Vizard, villain Vizard, caused all this, yet lives. That's all, farewell! [*Going.*

Sir Har. Stay, madam, one word. Is there no other way to redress your wrongs, but by fighting?

Lady Dar. Only one, sir, which if you can think of, you may do ; you know the business I entertained you for.

Sir Har. I understand you, madam.—[*Exit* Lady DARLING.] Here am I brought to a very pretty dilemma : I must commit murder or commit matrimony! Which is best, now? a licence from Doctors' Commons, or a sentence from the Old Bailey? If I kill my man, the law hangs me; if I marry my woman, I shall hang myself.—But, damn it! cowards dare fight; I'll marry! That's the most daring action of the two. So, my dear cousin Angelica, have at you.

[*Exit.*

SCENE II.—*Newgate.*

CLINCHER Senior *solus.*

Clinch. Sen. How severe and melancholy are Newgate reflections! Last week my father died; yesterday I turned beau ; to-day I am laid by the heels, and to-morrow shall be hung by the neck.—I was agreeing with a bookseller about printing an account of my journey through France to Italy; but now, the history of my travels through Holborn to Tyburn—*The last and dying speech of Beau Clincher, that was going to the Jubilee.—Come, a halfpenny apiece !*—A sad sound, a sad sound, faith! 'Tis one way to have a man's death make a great noise in the world.

Enter SMUGGLER *and* Jailer.

Smug. Well, friend, I have told you who I am : so

send these letters into Thames Street, as directed ; they
are to gentlemen that will bail me.—[*Exit* Jailer.]   Eh !
this Newgate is a very populous place : here's robbery
and repentance in every corner.—Well, friend, what are
you ? a cut-throat or a bum-bailiff ?

Clinch. Sen. What are you, mistress ? a bawd or a
witch ?   Hark'ee, if you are a witch, d'ye see, I'll give
you a hundred pounds to mount me on a broom-staff
and whip me away to the Jubilee

Smug. The Jubilee !   Oh, you young rakehell, what
brought you here ?

Clinch. Sen. Ah, you old rogue, what brought you
here, if you go to that.

Smug. I knew, sir, what your powdering, your prink-
ing, your dancing, and your frisking, would come to.

Clinch. Sen. And I knew what your cozening, your
extortion, and your smuggling would come to.

Smug. Ay, sir, you must break your indentures, and
run to the devil in a full-bottom wig, must you ?

Clinch. Sen. Ay, sir, and you must put off your gravity,
and run to the devil in petticoats ?   You design to
swing in masquerade, master, d'ye ?

Smug. Ay, you must go to the plays, too, sirrah !
Lord ! Lord ! what business has a 'prentice at a playhouse, unless it be to hear his master made a cuckold,
and his mistress a whore ! 'Tis ten to one now, but some
malicious poet has my character upon the stage within
this month.   'Tis a hard matter now that an honest sober
man can't sin in private for this plaguy stage.   I gave an
honest gentleman five guineas myself towards writing a
book against it : and it has done no good, we see.

Clinch. Sen. Well, well, master, take courage ; our
comfort is, we have lived together, and shall die
together : only with this difference, that I have lived
like a fool, and shall die like a knave ; and you have
lived like a knave and shall die like a fool.

Smug. No, sirrah ! I have sent a messenger for my

clothes, and shall get out immediately, and shall be upon your jury by-and-by.—Go to prayers, you rogue! go to prayers!   [*Exit.*

Clinch. Sen. Prayers! 'tis a hard taking when a man must say grace to the gallows. Ah, this cursed intriguing! Had I swung handsomely in a silken garter now, I had died in my duty; but to hang in hemp, like the vulgar, 'tis very ungenteel.

Enter TOM ERRAND.

A reprieve! a reprieve! Thou dear, dear—damned rogue, where have you been? Thou art the most welcome—son of a whore! Where's my clothes?

Err. Sir, I see where mine are: come, sir, strip, sir, strip!

Clinch. Sen. What, sir! will you abuse a gentleman?

Err. A gentleman! ha, ha, ha! D'ye know where you are, sir? We're all gentlemen here. I stand up for liberty and property. Newgate's a commonwealth. No courtier has business among us. Come, sir!

Clinch. Sen. Well, but stay, stay till I send for my own clothes: I shall get out presently.

Err. No, no, sir! I'll ha' you into the dungeon, and uncase you.

Clinch. Sen. Sir, you can't master me; for I'm twenty thousand strong.   [*Exeunt struggling.*

SCENE III.—*Lady Darling's House.*

Enter WILDAIR *with letters,* Footmen *following.*

Sir Har. Here, fly all around, and bear these as directed;—you to Westminster, you to St. James's, and you into the City. Tell all my friends a bridegroom's joy invites their presence. Look all of ye like bridegrooms also: all appear with hospitable looks, and bear a welcome in your faces. Tell 'em I'm married. If any ask to whom, make no reply, but tell 'em that I'm married, that joy shall crown the day, and love the night. Begone! fly! [*Exeunt* Footmen.

Enter STANDARD.

A thousand welcomes, friend! My pleasure's now complete, since I can share it with my friend. Brisk joy shall bound from me to you; then back again; and like the sun grow warmer by reflection!

Stand. You're always pleasant, Sir Harry; but this transcends yourself! Whence proceeds it?

Sir Har. Canst thou not guess, my friend? Whence flows all earthly joy? What is the life of man and soul of pleasure?—woman! What fires the heart with transport, and the soul with raptures?—lovely woman! What is the master-stroke and smile of the creation, but charming, virtuous woman? When nature, in the general composition, first brought woman forth, like a flushed poet ravished with his fancy, with ecstasy she blessed the fair production![1]—Methinks, my friend, you relish not my joy; what is the cause?

Stand. Canst thou not guess? What is the bane of man and scourge of life, but woman? What is the heathenish idol man sets up, and is damned for worshipping?—treacherous woman. What are those, whose eyes, like basilisks, shine beautiful for sure destruction, whose smiles are dangerous as the grin of fiends, but false, deluding woman? Woman! whose composition inverts humanity: their body's heavenly, but their souls are clay!

Sir Har. Come, come, Colonel, this is too much. I

[1] Early editions: "like a flush'd Poet, ravish'd with his Fancy, with Extasie: The blest, the fair Production." Emended in later 18th century editions: "with ecstasy it blessed the fair production" The emendation adopted in the text is apparently Leigh Hunt's.

know your wrongs received from Lurewell may excuse your resentments against her : but 'tis unpardonable to charge the failings of a single woman upon the whole sex. I have found one, whose virtues—

Stand. So have I, Sir Harry ; I have found one, whose pride's above yielding to a prince. And if lying, dissembling, perjury, and falsehood, be no breaches in woman's honour, she's as innocent as infancy.

Sir Har. Well, Colonel, I find your opinion grows stronger by opposition : I shall now therefore waive the argument, and only beg you for this day to make a show of complaisance at least.—Here comes my charming bride.

Enter Lady DARLING *and* ANGELICA.

Stand. [*Saluting* ANGELICA.] I wish you, madam, all the joys of love and fortune.

Enter CLINCHER Junior.

Clinch. Jun. Gentlemen and ladies, I'm just upon the spur, and have only a minute to take my leave.

Sir Har. Whither are you bound, sir?

Clinch. Jun. Bound, sir ! I'm going to the Jubilee, sir.

Lady Dar. Bless me, cousin ! how came you by these clothes ?

Clinch. Jun. Clothes ! ha, ha, ha ! the rarest jest ! ha, ha, ha ! I shall burst, by Jupiter Ammon, I shall burst !

Lady Dar. What's the matter, cousin ?

Clinch. Jun. The matter ! ha, ha, ha ! Why, an honest porter—ha, ha, ha !—has knocked out my brother's brains, ha, ha, ha !

Sir Har. A very good jest, i' faith ! ha, ha, ha !

Clinch. Jun. Ay, sir, but the best jest of all is, he knocked out his brains with a hammer, and so he is as dead as a door-nail, ha, ha, ha !

Lady Dar. And do you laugh, wretch ?

Clinch. Jun. Laugh ! ha, ha, ha !—Let me see e'er a

younger brother in England that won't laugh at such a
jest.

Angel. You appeared a very sober pious gentleman
some hours ago.

Clinch. Jun. Psha! I was a fool then; but now,
madam, I'm a wit: I can rake now. As for your part,
madam, you might have had me once: but now, madam,
if you should chance fall to eating chalk, or gnawing the
sheets, 'tis none of my fault. Now, madam, I have got
an estate, and I must go to the Jubilee.

Enter CLINCHER Senior *in a blanket.*

Clinch. Sen. Must you so, rogue? must ye?—You
will go to the Jubilee, will you?

Clinch. Jun. A ghost! a ghost!—Send for the dean
and chapter presently.

Clinch. Sen. A ghost! no, no, sirrah; I'm an elder
brother, rogue!

Clinch. Jun. I don't care a farthing for that; I'm
sure you're dead in law.

Clinch. Sen. Why so, sirrah? why so?

Clinch. Jun. Because, sir, I can get a fellow to swear
he knocked out your brains.

Sir Har. An odd way of swearing a man out of his
life!

Clinch. Jun. Smell him, gentlemen; he has a deadly
scent about him!

Clinch. Sen. Truly, the apprehensions of death may
have made me savour a little! [*Aside.*] O Lord! the
colonel!—The apprehension of him may make me
savour worse, I'm afraid.

Clinch. Jun. In short, sir, were you ghost, or brother,
or devil, I will go to the Jubilee, by Jupiter Ammon!

Stand. Go to the Jubilee! go to the bear-garden!
The travel of such fools as you doubly injures our
country; you expose our native follies, which ridicules
us among strangers; and return fraught only with their

vices, which you vend here for fashionable gallantry. A travelling fool is as dangerous as a home-bred villain. Get ye to your native plough and cart; converse with animals like yourselves—sheep and oxen; men are creatures you don't understand.

Sir. Har. Let 'em alone, Colonel, their folly will be now diverting.—Come, gentlemen, we'll dispute this point some other time; I hear some fiddles tuning, let's hear how they can entertain us.—Be pleased to sit.

[*Here singing and dancing; after which a* Footman *enters and whispers* WILDAIR.

Sir Har. [*To* Lady DARLING.] Madam, shall I beg you to entertain the company in the next room for a moment?

Lady Dar. With all my heart.—Come, gentlemen.

[*Exeunt Omnes but* WILDAIR.

Sir Har. A lady to inquire for me! Who can this be?

Enter Lady LUREWELL.

Oh, madam, this favour is beyond my expectation, to come uninvited to dance at my wedding!—What d'ye gaze at, madam?

Lady Lure. A monster!—If thou art married, thou'rt the most perjured wretch that e'er avouched deceit!

Sir Har. Heyday! why, madam, I'm sure I never swore to marry you! I made, indeed, a slight promise, upon condition of your granting me a small favour; but you would not consent, you know.

Lady Lure. [*Aside.*] How he upbraids me with my shame!—[*Aloud.*] Can you deny your binding vows. When this appears a witness 'gainst your falsehood?[1]

[*Showing a ring.*

Methinks the motto of this sacred pledge
Should flash confusion in your guilty face!
Read!
Read here the binding words of *Love and Honour;*

[1] This speech printed as prose in early editions.

Words not unknown to your perfidious eyes,
Though utter strangers to your treacherous heart!

Sir Har The woman's stark staring mad, that's
certain!

Lady Lure. Was it maliciously designed to let me find
my misery when past redress? to let me know you, only
to know you false? Had not cursed chance showed
me the surprising motto, I had been happy. The first
knowledge I had of you was fatal to me, and this second
worse.

Sir Har. What the devil's all this! Madam, I'm not
at leisure for raillery at present; I have weighty affairs
upon my hands; the business of pleasure, madam—
Any other time—   [*Going.*

Lady Lure. Stay, I conjure you, stay!

Sir Har. Faith, I can't! my bride expects me.—But
hark'ee, when the honeymoon is over, about a month or
two hence, I may do you a small favour.   [*Exit.*

Lady Lure. Grant me some wild expressions, Heavens,
or I shall burst! Woman's weakness, man's falsehood,
my own shame, and love's disdain, at once swell up my
breast!—Words, words, or I shall burst!   [*Going.*

Re-enter STANDARD.

Stand. Stay, madam, you need not shun my sight;
for if you are perfect woman, you have confidence to
outface a crime, and bear the charge of guilt without a
blush.

Lady Lure. The charge of guilt!—What, making a
fool of you? I've done't, and glory in the act! the
height of female justice were to make you all hang or
drown! Dissembling to the prejudice of men is virtue;
and every look, or sign, or smile, or tear that can
deceive is meritorious.

Stand. Very pretty principles truly! If there be truth
in woman, 'tis now in thee.—Come, madam, you know
that you re discovered, and being sensible you can't

escape, you would now turn to bay.—That ring, madam, proclaims you guilty.

Lady Lure. O monster! villain! perfidious villain! has he told you?

Stand. I'll tell it you, and loudly too.

Lady Lure. Oh, name it not!—Yes, speak it out, 'tis so just a punishment for putting faith in man, that I will bear it all; and let credulous maids, that trust their honour to the tongues of men, thus hear their shame proclaimed.—Speak now what his busy scandal, and your improving malice, both dare utter.

Stand. Your falsehood can't be reached by malice nor by satire; your actions are the justest libel on your fame. Your words, your looks, your tears, I did believe in spite of common fame: nay, 'gainst my own eyes I still maintained your truth. I imagined Wildair's boasting of your favours to be the pure result of his own vanity. At last he urged your taking presents of him; as a convincing proof of which you yesterday from him received that ring:—which ring, that I might be sure he gave it, I lent him for that purpose. [1]

Lady Lure. Ha! you lent him for that purpose?

Stand. Yes, yes, madam, I lent him for that purpose —no denying it.—I know it well, for I have worn it long, and desire you now, madam, to restore it to the just owner.

Lady Lure. The just owner! Think, sir, think but of what importance 'tis to own it. If you have love and honour in your soul, 'tis then most justly yours; if not, you are a robber, and have stolen it basely.

Stand. Ha! your words, like meeting flints, have struck a light to show me something strange.—But tell me instantly, is not your real name Manly?

Lady Lure. Answer me first: did not you receive this ring about twelve years ago?

[1] This plot had apparently been concocted between Wildair and Standard during their absence from the stage in Act iv. Sc. 1— an odd example of Farquhar's technique.

Stand. I did.

Lady Lure. And were not you about that time entertained two nights at the house of Sir Oliver Manly in
Oxfordshire?

Stand. I was! I was!—[*Runs to her, and embraces
her.*] The blest remembrance fires my soul with transport! I know the rest—you are the charming she, and
I the happy man.

Lady Lure. How has blind Fortune stumbled on the
right!—But where have you wandered since?—'Twas
cruel to forsake me.

Stand. The particulars of my fortune were too tedious
now; but to discharge myself from the stain of dishonour, I must tell you, that immediately upon my return to the university, my elder brother and I quarrelled.
My father, to prevent farther mischief, posts me away
to travel: I writ to you from London, but fear the letter
came not to your hands.

Lady Lure. I never had the least account of you, by
letter or otherwise.

Stand. Three years I lived abroad, and at my return,
found you were gone out of the kingdom; though none
could tell me whither. Missing you thus, I went to
Flanders, served my king till the peace [1] commenced;
then fortunately going on board at Amsterdam, one ship
transported us both to England. At the first sight I
loved, though ignorant of the hidden cause.—You may
remember, madam, that talking once of marriage, I told
you I was engaged; to your dear self I meant.

Lady Lure. Then men are still most generous and
brave—and to reward your truth, an estate of three
thousand pounds a year waits your acceptance; and
if I can satisfy you in my past conduct, and the reasons
that engaged me to deceive all men, I shall expect
the honourable performance of your promise, and that
you would stay with me in England.

---

[1] The peace of Ryswick, 1697.

Stand. Stay!—not fame nor glory e'er shall part us more. My honour can be nowhere more concerned than here.

Re-enter WILDAIR, ANGELICA, *both* CLINCHERS.

O Sir Harry, Fortune has acted miracles! The story's strange and tedious, but all amounts to this: that woman's mind is charming as her person, and I am made a convert too to beauty.

Sir Har. I wanted only this to make my pleasure perfect.

Enter SMUGGLER.

Smug. So, gentlemen and ladies, is my gracious nephew Vizard among ye?

Sir Har. Sir, he dares not show his face among such honourable company, for your gracious nephew is—

Smug. What, sir? Have a care what you say—

Sir Har. A villain, sir.

Smug. With all my heart:—I'll pardon you the beating me for that very word. And pray, Sir Harry, when you see him next, tell him this news from me, that I have disinherited him, that I will leave him as poor as a disbanded quartermaster. And this is the positive and stiff resolution of threescore and ten; an age that sticks as obstinately to its purpose, as to the old fashion of its cloak.

Sir Har. [*To* ANGELICA.] You see, madam, how industriously Fortune has punished his offence to you.

Angel. I can scarcely, sir, reckon it an offence, considering the happy consequence of it.

Smug. O, Sir Harry, he is as hypocritical—

Lady Lure. As yourself, Mr Alderman: how fares my good old nurse, pray, sir?

Smug. O madam, I shall be even with you before I part with your writings and money, that I have in my hands!

Stand. A word with you, Mr Alderman: do you know this pocket-book?

Smug. [*Aside.*] O Lord, it contains an account of all my secret practices in trading!—[*Aloud.*] How came you by it, sir?

Stand. Sir Harry here dusted it out of your pocket, at this lady's house yesterday. It contains an account of some secret practices in your merchandizing; among the rest, the counterpart of an agreement with a correspondent at Bordeaux, about transporting French wine in Spanish casks.—First return this lady all her writings, then I shall consider whether I shall lay your proceedings before the parliament or not; whose justice will never suffer your smuggling to go unpunished.

Smug. Oh, my poor ship and cargo!

Clinch. Sen. Hark'ee, master, you had as good come along with me to the Jubilee now.

Angel. Come, Mr Alderman, for once let a woman advise. Would you be thought an honest man, banish covetousness, that worst gout of age; avarice is a poor pilfering quality of the soul, and will as certainly cheat, as a thief would steal.—Would you be thought a reformer of the times, be less severe in your censures, less rigid in your precepts, and more strict in your example.

Sir Har. Right, madam; virtue flows freer from imitation than compulsion; of which, Colonel, your conversion and mine are just examples.

In vain are musty morals taught in schools,
By rigid teachers, and as rigid rules,
Where virtue with a frowning aspect stands,
And frights the pupil from its rough commands.
But woman,—
Charming woman, can true converts make;
We love the precepts for the teacher's sake.
Virtue in them appears so bright, so gay,
We hear with transport, and with pride obey.

FINIS.

EPILOGUE,

OW all depart, each his respective
    way,
To spend an evening's chat upon
    the play;
Some to Hippolito's; one home-
    ward goes,
And one with loving she retires to
    th' Rose.[1]
The amorous pair, in all things frank and free,
Perhaps may save the play—in Number Three.
The tearing spark, if Phillis aught gainsays,
Breaks th' drawer's head, kicks her, and murders Bays.
To coffee some retreat to save their pockets,
Others, more generous, damn the play at Locket's;[2]
But there, I hope, the author's fears are vain,
Malice ne'er spoke in generous champagne.
That poet merits an ignoble death,
Who fears to fall over a brave Monteth.[3]
The privilege of wine we only ask,
You'll taste again before you damn the flask.

[1] The Rose Tavern in Russell Street, adjoining Drury Lane
Theatre.   For numerous allusions to it, from Pepys to Gibbon,
see Wheatley & Cunningham : *London Past and Present*, iii., 170.
See also *The Recruiting Officer*, p. 344.
[2] A well-known ordinary. See note, p. 46.
[3] A large punch-bowl, usually of silver, with a movable rim,
called after its inventor :—
      " New things produce new words, and thus Monteith
      Has by one vessel sav'd his name from death."
Quoted in Ashton's *Social Life in the Reign of Queen Anne*, i., 183.

Our author fears not you; but those he may,
Who in cold blood murder a man in tea :
Those men of spleen who, fond the world should know it,
Sit down, and for their twopence damn a poet.
Their criticism's good, that we can say for't,
They understand a play—too well to pay for't.
From box to stage, from stage to box they run,
First steal the play, then damn it when they've done.[1]
But now, to know what fate may us betide,
Among our friends, in Cornhill and Cheapside :
But those, I think, have but one rule for plays ;
They'll say they're good, if so the world [2] says.
If it should please them, and their spouses know it,
They straight inquire what kind of man's the poet.
But from side-box we dread a fearful doom,
All the good-natured beaux are gone to Rome.
The ladies' censure I'd almost forgot,
Then for a line or two t' engage their vote :
But that way's old, below our author's aim,
No less than his whole play is compliment to them.
For their sakes then the play can't miss succeeding,
Though critics may want wit, they have good breeding.
They won't, I'm sure, forfeit the ladies' graces,
By showing their ill-nature to their faces,
Our business with good manners may be done,
Flatter us here, and damn us when you're gone.

[1] See Note 1, p. 38.
[2] Farquhar apparently pronounced this word " wurruld.

APPENDIX

ORIGINAL FORM OF "THE CONSTANT COUPLE," ACT V.
SCENE I

HE misunderstanding between Sir Harry Wildair and Angelica was evidently found so delectable by the original audiences that Farquhar was induced to develop and elaborate it in a new scene. I here reproduce the original scene, as it appeared in the first quarto, which no previous editor seems to have examined.[1] It is, in truth, comparatively tame and comparatively decent ; yet surely worth recovering, if only for Sir Harry's delightful phrase about "the chastest, purest passion, with a large and fair estate." The two versions diverge after Angelica's speech (p. 116), concluding, " My words shall search it out, And eyes shall fire it for my own defence." From that point the remainder of the scene in the first edition runs as follows :—

Sir Har. Ha ! Her voice bears a commanding accent ! Every syllable is pointed.—By Heavens, I love her :—I feel her piercing words turn the wild current of my blood and thrill through all my veins.

Angel. View me well : consider me with a sober thought, free from those fumes of wine that cast a mist before your sight ; and you shall find that every glance from my reproaching eye is armed with sharp resentment and with repelling rays that look dishonour dead.

[1] Dr. Schmid (*op. cit.* on p. 3) offers one or two mistaken conjectures as to which was the added scene.

Sir Har. I cannot view you, madam : for when you speak all the faculties of my charmed soul crowd to my attentive ears ; desert my eyes, which gaze insensibly.—Whatever charm inspires your looks, whether of innocence or vice, 'tis lovely past expression.

Angel. If my beauty has power to rouse a flame, be sure it is a virtuous one ; if otherwise, 'tis owing to the foulness of your own thought, which, throwing this mean affront upon my honour, has alarm'd my soul, and fires it with a brave disdain.

Sir Har. Where can the difference lie 'twixt such hypocrisy and truth ? Madam, whate'er my unruly passion did at first suggest, I must now own you've turn'd my love to veneration, and my unmannerly demands to a most humble prayer.—Your surprising conduct has quench'd the gross material flame ; but raised a subtil piercing fire, which flies like lambent lightning through my blood [and] disdaining common fuel, preys upon the nobler part, my soul.

Angel. [*aside.*] Grant, Heavens, his words be true ! [*Aloud.*] Then, as you hope that passion should be happy, tell me without reserve what motives have engaged you thus to affront my virtue?

Sir Har. [*aside.*] Affront her virtue ! Ah, something I fear.—[*Aloud.*] Your question, madam, is a riddle and cannot be resolved ; but the most proper answer the old gentlewoman can make, who passes for your mother.

Angel. Passes for my mother ! O indignation ! Were I a man, you durst not use me thus ! But the mean, poor abuse you cast on me reflects upon yourself. Our sex still strikes an awe upon the brave, and only cowards dare affront a woman.

Sir Har. Then, madam, I have a fair claim to courage ; for, by all hopes of happiness, I ne'er was aw'd so much, nor ever felt the power of fear before. But, since I can't dissolve this knot, I'll cut it at a stroke. Vizard (who I fear is a villain) told me you were a prostitute ; that he had known you, and sent a letter, intimating my designs, to the old gentlewoman, who, I supposed, had licensed my proceedings by leaving us so oft in private.

Angel. That Vizard is a villain, damn'd beyond the

curses of an injured woman, is most true ; but that his letter signified any dishonourable proceedings, is as false.

Sir Har. I appeal to that for pardon or condemnation. He read it to me, and the contents were as I have declared, only with this addition, that I would scruple no price for the enjoyment of my pleasure.

Angel. No price ! What have I suffered? To be made a prostitute for sale ! 'Tis an unequalled curse upon our sex that woman's virtue should so much depend on lying fame and scandalous tongues of men. Read that : then judge how far I'm injur'd and you deceived.

Sir Har. [*reads.*]

Out of my earnest inclination to serve your Ladyship and my Cousin Angelica, I have sent Sir Harry Wildair to court my cousin.—[The villain read me a clean different thing]. *He's a gentleman of great parts and fortune.*—[Damn his compliment !] *and would make your daughter very happy in a husband.*—[O Lord, O Lord, what have I been doing !] *I hope your Ladyship will entertain him as becomes his birth and fortune, and the friend of, madam,*

Your Ladyship's most devoted
and humble Servant,
VIZARD.

Angel. Now, sir, I hope you need no instigation to redress my wrongs, since honour points the way.

Sir Har. Redress your wrongs ! Instruct me, madam ; for all your injuries tenfold recoil'd on me. I have abus'd innocence, murdered honour, stabb'd it in the nicest part : a fair lady's fame. Instruct me, madam, for my reason's fled, and hides its guilty face, as conscious of its master's shame.

Angel. Think, sir, that my blood, for many generations has run in the purest channel of unsully'd honour. Consider what a tender flower is woman's reputation, which the least air of foul detraction blasts. Call then to mind your rude and scandalous behaviour : remember the base price you offered : then think that Vizard, villain Vizard, caused all this, yet lives. That's all.—Farewell !   [*Going.*

Sir Har. Stay, madam ! He's too base an offering for such purity : but justice has inspired me with a nobler

thought. I throw a purer victim at your feet, my honourable love and fortune. If chastest, purest passion, with a
large and fair estate, can make amends, they're yours this
moment. The matrimonial tie shall bind us friends this
hour. Nay, madam, no reply unless you smile. Let but a
pleasing look forerun my sentence : then raise me up to
joy.

Angel. Rise, sir. [*Smiling*] I'm pleased to find my senti-
ments of you, which were always generous, so generously
answered. And since I have met a man above the common
level of your sex, I think myself disengaged from the
formality of mine, and shall therefore venture to inform you
that with joy I receive your honourable love.

Sir Har. Beauty without art! Virtue without pride!
And love without ceremony! The day breaks glorious to
my o'erclouded thought, and darts its smiling beams into
my soul. My love is heightened by a glad devotion ; and
virtue rarifies the bliss to feast the purer mind.

Angel. You must promise me, Sir Harry, to have a care
of burgundy henceforth.

Sir Har. Fear not, sweet innocence : your presence, like
a guardian angel, shall fright away all vice.

> In your sweet eyes and words there is a charm
> To settle madness, or a fiend disarm
> Of all his spite, his torments and his cares :
> And make him change his curses into prayers.

[*Exeunt.*

THE

TWIN - RIVALS

A

COMEDY

Acted at the

THEATRE ROYAL

By Her Majesty's Servants

Written by Mr FARQUHAR

Sic vos non vobis

LONDON

Printed for *Bernard Lintott* at the Post-House in the *Middle-Temple-Gate* in *Fleetstreet.* MDCCIII.

As to the date of this comedy (1702) *see* Introduction, p. 9. Genest chronicles ten revivals of it. At Lincoln's Inn Fields in 1725 Wilks still played the Elder Wouldbe, and Mrs Oldfield was the Aurelia. In this revival the name of Mrs Mandrake was altered to Mrs Midnight; but the part was still played by a man (Miller). In 1736, at Drury Lane, Mills played the Elder Wouldbe and Mrs Clive Aurelia. At Covent Garden in 1755 Aurelia was played by Peg Woffington. At Drury Lane in 1758 "Mrs Midnight" was played by a woman, Mrs Macklin; and thenceforward this was always the case. The last performance in London appears to have taken place at Covent Garden, 21st October 1778; but the comedy was revived at Bath in 1812, when, it is interesting to note, its plain-speaking shocked the audience. When "Mrs Midnight" in the fifth act said, "Only a poor gentlewoman in labour," the hissing was so violent as to stop the play.

THE DEDICATION

TO

HENRY BRET, ESQ.[1]

THE Commons of England have a right of petitioning ; and since by your place in the Senate you are obliged to hear and redress the subject, I presume upon the privilege of the people to give you the following trouble.

As prologues introduce plays on the stage, so dedications usher them into the great Theatre of the World ; and as we choose some stanch actor to address the audience, so we pitch upon some gentleman of undisputed ingenuity to recommend us to the reader. Books, like metals, require to be stamped with some valuable effigies before they become popular and current.

To escape the critics, I resolved to take sanctuary with one of the best ; one who differs from the fraternity in this, that his good-nature is ever predominant, can discover an author's smallest fault, and pardon the greatest.

Your generous approbation, Sir, has done this play service, but has injured the author ; for it has made him insufferably vain, and he thinks himself authorised to stand up for the merit of his performance, when so great a master of wit has declared in its favour.

The Muses are the most coquettish of their sex, fond of being admired, and always putting on their best airs to the

---

[1] Henry Brett, known after 1705 as Colonel Brett, married in 1700 the divorced Countess of Macclesfield (alleged to have been the mother of Richard Savage). Brett was a member of Addison's coterie, and had at one time a share in the Drury Lane Patent. Died 1724. See Cibber's *Apology*, chap. xi.

finest gentleman : but alas, Sir ! their addresses are stale, and their fine things but repetition ; for there is nothing new in wit, but what is found in your own conversation.

Could I write by the help of study, as you talk without it, I would venture to say something in the usual strain of dedication ; but as you have too much wit to suffer it, and I too little to undertake it, I hope the world will excuse my deficiency, and you will pardon the presumption of,

Sir,

Your most obliged, and most humble servant,

GEORGE FARQUHAR.

December 23, 1702.[1]

---

[1] This date does not appear in all copies of Q 1.

THE PREFACE

THE success and countenance that debauchery has met with in plays, was the most severe and reasonable charge against their authors in Mr Collier's *Short View*;[1] and indeed this gentleman had done the drama considerable service, had he arraigned the stage only to punish its misdemeanours, and not to take away its life; but there is an advantage to be made sometimes of the advice of an enemy, and the only way to disappoint his designs, is to improve upon his invective, and to make the stage flourish, by virtue of that satire by which he thought to suppress it.

I have therefore in this piece endeavoured to show, that an English comedy may answer the strictness of poetical justice; but indeed the greater share of the English audience, I mean that part which is no farther read than in plays of their own language, have imbibed other principles, and stand up as vigorously for the old poetic licence, as they do for the liberty of the subject. They take all innovations for grievances; and, let a project be never so well laid for their advantage, yet the undertaker is very likely to suffer by't. A play without a beau, cully, cuckold, or coquette, is as poor an entertainment to some palates, as their Sunday's dinner would be without beef and pudding. And this I take to be one reason that the galleries were so thin during the run of this play. I thought indeed to have soothed the splenetic zeal of the city, by making a gentleman a knave, and punishing their great grievance—a whoremaster; but a certain

---

[1] Jeremy Collier's *Short View of the Immorality and Profaneness of the English Stage*, published in 1698. See Introduction, pp. 5 and 22.

143

virtuoso of that fraternity has told me since, that the citizens
were never more disappointed in any entertainment : " For,"
said he, " however pious we may appear to be at home, yet
we never go to that end of the town but with an intention to
be lewd."

There was an odium cast upon this play, before it
appeared, by some persons who thought it their interest to
have it suppressed. The ladies were frighted from seeing
it by formidable stories of a midwife, and were told, no
doubt, that they must expect no less than a labour upon the
stage ; but I hope the examining into that aspersion will be
enough to wipe it off, since the character of the midwife is
only so far touched as is necessary for carrying on the plot,
she being principally deciphered in her procuring capacity ;
and I dare not affront the ladies so far as to imagine they
could be offended at the exposing of a bawd.

Some critics complain, that the design is defective for
want of Clelia's appearance in the scene ; but I had rather
they should find this fault, than I forfeit my regard to the
fair, by showing a lady of figure under a misfortune ; for
which reason I made her only nominal, and chose to expose,
the person that injured her ; and if the ladies don't agree
that I have done her justice in the end, I'm very sorry
for't.

Some people are apt to say, that the character of Richmore points at a particular person ; though I must confess
I see nothing but what is very general in his character,
except his marrying his own mistress ; which, by the way,
he never did, for he was no sooner off the stage but he
changed his mind, and the poor lady is still *in statu quo.*
But upon the whole matter, 'tis application only makes the
ass ; and characters in plays are like Long Lane[1] clothes,
not hung out for the use of any particular people, but to be
bought by only [those] that they happen to fit.

The most material objection against this play is the importance of the subject, which necessarily leads into senti-
ments too grave for diversion, and supposes vices too great
for comedy to punish. 'Tis said, I must own, that the

---

[1] Long Lane leads from Smithfield to the junction of Aldersgate
Street and Barbican. It was inhabited by pawnbrokers and
second hand clothes dealers. See Congreve, *The Way of the World,*
Act iii. Sc. 1.

business of comedy is chiefly to ridicule folly ; and that the punishment of vice falls rather into the province of tragedy ; but if there be a middle sort of wickedness, too high for the sock, and too low for the buskin, is there any reason that it should go unpunished ? What are more obnoxious to human society, than the villainies exposed in this play, the frauds, plots, and contrivances upon the fortunes of men, and the virtue of women ? But the persons are too mean for the heroic ; then what must we do with them ? Way, they must of necessity drop into comedy ; for it is unreasonable to imagine that the lawgivers in poetry would tie themselves up from executing that justice which is the foundation of their constitution ; or to say, that exposing vice is the business of the drama, and yet make rules to screen it from persecution.

Some have asked the question, why the Elder Wouldbe, in the fourth act, should counterfeit madness in his confinement ? Don't mistake, there was no such thing in his head ; and the judicious could easily perceive, that it was only a start of humour put on to divert his melancholy ; and when gaiety is strained to cover misfortune, it may very naturally be overdone, and rise to a semblance of madness, sufficient to impose on the constable, and perhaps on some of the audience ; who, taking everything at sight, impute that as a fault, which I am bold to stand up for, as one of the most masterly strokes of the whole piece.

This I think sufficient to obviate what objections I have heard made ; but there was no great occasion for making this defence, having had the opinion of some of the greatest persons in England, both for quality and parts, that the play has merit enough to hide more faults than have been found ; and I think their approbation sufficient to excuse some pride that may be incident to the author upon this performance.

I must own myself obliged to Mr Longueville¹ for some

---

¹ In the Index Volume of the *Dictionary of National Biography* (though, oddly enough, not in the body of the work), this Mr Longueville is identified as William Longueville (1639-1721), the friend of Samuel Butler and of the Norths, of whom Roger North wrote : "His discourse was fluent, witty, literate, copious and instructive." The identification is probably right ; but if so, we must suppose Farquhar to use "foreign" assistance, a few lines

lines in the part of Teague, and something of the Lawyer ;
but above all, for his hint of the twins, upon which I
formed my plot. But having paid him all due satisfaction
and acknowledgment, I must do myself the justice to believe,
that few of our modern writers have been less beholden to
foreign assistance in their plays, than I have been in the
following scenes.

further down, in the unusual sense of "outside" assistance. The
expression suggests, at first sight, that "Longueville" was a French
playwright ; but there seems to have been none of that name.

PROLOGUE,

BY MR MOTTEUX [1]

AND SPOKEN BY MR WILKS

An Alarm sounded.

ITH drums and trumpets, in this
    warring age,
A martial prologue should alarm
    the stage.
New plays, ere acted, a full
    audience near,
Seem towns invested, when
    siege they fear.
Prologues are like a forlorn hope, sent out
Before the play, to skirmish and to scout:
Our dreadful foes, the critics, when they spy,
They cock, they charge, they fire, then—back they fly.
The siege is laid, there gallant chiefs abound,
Here foes intrench'd, there glittering troops around,
And the loud batteries roar from yonder rising ground.
In the first act brisk sallies (miss or hit),
With volleys of small shot, or snip-snap wit,
Attack, and gall the trenches of the pit.
The next: the fire continues, but at length
Grows less, and slackens like a bridegroom's strength.
The third: feints, mines, and countermines abound,
Your critic engineers safe underground,
Blow up our works, and all our art confound.

---

[1] Peter Anthony Motteux (1660-1718) collaborated with Farquhar
in a farce called *The Stage Coach.* *See* Introduction, p. 10.

The fourth brings on most action, and 'tis sharp,
Fresh foes crowd on, at your remissness carp,
And desperate, though unskill'd, insult our counterscarp.
Then comes the last ; the general storm is near,
The poet-governor now quakes for fear ;
Runs wildly up and down, forgets to huff,
And would give all h'as plunder'd—to get off.
So, Don and Monsieur, bluff before the siege,
Were quickly tamed at Venloo, and at Liège : [1]
'Twas *Viva Spagnia ! Vive France !* before ;
Now, *Quartier ! Monsieur ! Quartier ! Ah, Señor !*
But what your resolution can withstand?
You master all, and awe the sea and land.
In war your valour makes the strong submit ;
Your judgment humbles all attempts in wit.
What play, what fort, what beauty can endure
All fierce assaults, and always be secure !
Then grant 'em generous terms who dare to write,
Since now that seems as desperate as to fight :
If we must yield, yet ere the day be fixt,
Let us hold out the third, and, if we may, the sixth. [2]

[1] Venloo was taken by Marlborough, 23rd September 1702, and Liège on the 29th of the following month.
[2] The author's nights

THE TWIN-RIVALS

A COMEDY

DRAMATIS PERSONÆ

MEN

ELDER WOULDBE [Hermes].	Mr WILKS.
YOUNG WOULDBE [Benjamin].	Mr CIBBER.
RICHMORE.	Mr HUSBAND.
TRUEMAN.	Mr MILLS.
SUBTLEMAN.	Mr PINKETHMAN.
BALDERDASH and ALDERMAN.	Mr JOHNSON.
CLEARACCOUNT, a Steward.	Mr FAIRBANK.
FAIRBANK, a Goldsmith.	Mr MINNS.
TEAGUE.	Mr BOWEN.

WOMEN

CONSTANCE.	Mrs ROGERS.
AURELIA.	Mrs HOOK.
MANDRAKE.	Mr BULLOCK.
STEWARD'S WIFE.	Mrs MOOR.

Constable, Watch, etc.

SCENE—LONDON.

ACT I

SCENE I.—[Benjamin Wouldbe's] *Lodgings.*

The Curtain drawn up, discovers Young Wouldbe
a-dressing and his Valet *buckling his shoes.*

EN. WOULD. Here is such a plague
every morning, with buckling shoes,
gartering, combing and powdering!
—Psha! cease thy impertinence, I'll
dress no more to-day.—[*Exit* Jack.]
Were I an honest brute, that rises
from his litter, shakes himself, and so
is dressed, I could bear it.

Enter Richmore.

Rich. No farther yet, Wouldbe? 'tis almost one.

Ben. Would. Then blame the clockmakers, they made
it so; the sun has neither fore nor afternoon. Prithee,
what have we to do with time? Can't we let it alone as
nature made it? Can't a man eat when he's hungry, go
to bed when he's sleepy, rise when he wakes, dress
when he pleases, without the confinement of hours to
enslave him?

Rich. Pardon me, sir, I understand your stoicism—
you have lost your money last night.

Ben. Would. No, no, Fortune took care of me there—
I had none to lose.

Rich. 'Tis that gives you the spleen.

Ben. Would. Yes, I have got the spleen; and something else.—Hark'ee—   [*Whispers.*

Rich. How!

Ben. Would. Positively. The lady's kind reception was the most severe usage I ever met with. Sha'n't I break her windows, Richmore?

Rich. A mighty revenge truly! Let me tell you, friend, that breaking the windows of such houses are no more than writing over a vintner's door as they do in Holland, *Vin te koop.* 'Tis no more than a bush to a tavern, a decoy to trade, and to draw in customers; but upon the whole matter, I think, a gentleman should put up an affront got in such little company; for the pleasure, the pain, and the resentment, are all alike scandalous.

Ben. Would. Have you forgot, Richmore, how I found you one morning with the *Flying Post*[1] in your hand, hunting for physical advertisements?

Rich. That was in the days of dad, my friend, in the days of dirty linen, pit-masks, hedge-taverns, and beef-steaks; but now I fly at nobler game; the Ring, the Court, Pawlet's,[2] and the Park: I despise all women that I apprehend any danger from, less than the having my throat cut: and should scruple to converse even with a lady of fortune, unless her virtue were loud enough to give me pride in exposing it.—Here's a letter I received this morning; you may read it.

[*Gives a letter.*

Ben. Would. [Reads.] *If there be solemnity in pro-testation, justice in heaven, or fidelity on earth, I may still*

---

[1] A newspaper started on May 11, 1695 (immediately after the lapse of the Licensing Act), by one George Ridpath, a Scotch "stickit minister."

[2] Under the date June 30, 1702, Isaac Reed (*Notitia Dramatica* in B.M. Manuscript Room) records "a concert at Pawlett's Great Dancing-Room, near Dowgate. Singing by Mr Hughes. Tickets, 1s. 6d."

depend on the faith of my Richmore. Though I may con-
ceal my love, I no longer can hide the effects on't from the
world.   Be careful of my honour, remember your vows,
and fly to the relief of the disconsolate   CLELIA.

The fair, the courted, blooming Clelia!

Rich. The credulous, troublesome, foolish Clelia.
Did you ever read such a fulsome harangue? *Lard,*
sir, I am near my time and want your assistance! Does
the silly creature imagine that any man would come
near her in those circumstances, unless it were Doctor
Chamberlain?[1]   You may keep the letter.

Ben. Would. But why would you trust it with me?
You know I can't keep a secret that has any scandal
in't.

Rich. For that reason I communicate: I know thou
art a perfect gazette, and will spread the news all over
the town: for you must understand that I am now
besieging another; and I would have the fame of my
conquests upon the wing, that the town may surrender
the sooner.

Ben. Would. But if the report of your cruelty goes
along with that of your valour, you'll find no garrison
of any strength will open their gates to you.

Rich. No, no, women are cowards, and terror prevails
upon them more than clemency: my best pretence to
my success with the fair is my using 'em ill.   'Tis turning their own guns upon 'em, and I have always found
it the most successful battery to assail one reputation by
sacrificing another.

Ben. Would. I could love thee for thy mischief did I
not envy thee for thy success in't.

Rich. You never attempt a woman of figure.

Ben. Would. How can I? this confounded hump of
mine is such a burden at my back, that it presses me

[1] Hugh Chamberlain (or Chamberlen) was a noted *accoucheur.*
—EWALD.

down here in the dirt and diseases of Covent Garden, the low suburbs of pleasure. Curst fortune! I am a younger brother, and yet cruelly deprived of my birthright of a handsome person; seven thousand a year in a direct line would have straightened my back to some purpose. But I look, in my present circumstances, like a branch of another kind, grafted only upon the stock which makes me grow so crooked.

Rich. Come, come, 'tis no misfortune, your father is so as well as you.

Ben. Would. Then why should not I be a lord as well as he? Had I the same title to the deformity I could bear it.

Rich. But how does my lord bear the absence of your twin-brother?

Ben. Would. My twin-brother! Ay, 'twas his crowding me that spoiled my shape, and his coming half an hour before me that ruined my fortune. My father expelled me his house some two years ago, because I would have persuaded him that my twin-brother was a bastard. He gave me my portion, which was about fifteen hundred pound, and I have spent two thousand of it already. As for my brother, he don't care a farthing for me.

Rich. Why so, pray?

Ben. Would. A very odd reason—because I hate him.

Rich. How should he know that?

Ben. Would. Because he thinks it reasonable it should be so.

Rich. But did your actions ever express any malice to him?

Ben. Would. Yes: I would fain have kept him company; but being aware of my kindness, he went abroad. He has travelled these five years, and, I am told, is a grave sober fellow, and in danger of living a great while. All my hope is, that when he gets into his honour and estate, the nobility will soon kill him by

drinking him up to his dignity. But come, Frank, I
have but two eyesores in the world, a brother before me
and a hump behind me, and thou art still laying 'em in
my way. Let us assume an argument of less severity—
canst thou lend me a brace of hundred pounds?

Rich. What would you do with 'em?

Ben. Would. Do with 'em! there's a question indeed!
Do you think I would eat 'em?

Rich. Yes, o' my troth, would you, and drink 'em together. Look'ee, Mr Wouldbe, whilst you kept well
with your father, I could have ventured to have lent you
five guineas: but as the case stands, I can assure you, I
have lately paid off my sister's fortune, and—

Ben. Would. Sir, this put-off looks like an affront;
and you know I don't use to take such things.

Rich. Sir, your demand is rather an affront, when you
know I don't use to give such things.

Ben. Would. Sir, I'll pawn my honour.

Rich. That's mortgaged already for more than it is
worth; you had better pawn your sword there, 'twill
bring you forty shillings.

Ben. Would. 'Sdeath, sir.—

[*Takes his sword off the table.*

Rich. Hold, Mr Wouldbe! suppose I put an end to
your misfortunes all at once?

Ben. Would. How, sir?

Rich. Why, go to a magistrate, and swear you would
have robbed me of two hundred pounds. Look'ee, sir,
you have been often told, that your extravagance would
some time or other be the ruin of you; and it will go a
great way in your indictment, to have turned the pad
upon your friend.

Ben. Would. This usage is the height of ingratitude
from you, in whose company I have spent my fortune.

Rich. I'm therefore a witness, that it was very ill
spent. Why would you keep company, be at equal expenses with me, that have fifty times your estate?

What was gallantry in me, was prodigality in you;
mine was my health, because I could pay for't; yours a
disease, because you could not.

Ben. Would. And is this all I must expect from our
friendship?

Rich. Friendship! sir, there can be no such thing
without an equality.

Ben. Would. That is, there can be no such thing
when there is occasion for't.

Rich. Right, sir; our friendship was over a bottle
only; and whilst you can pay your club of friendship
I'm that way your humble servant; but when once you
come borrowing, I'm this way—your humble servant.
                                                    [*Exit.*

Ben. Would. Rich, big, proud, arrogant villain! I
have been twice his second, thrice sick of the same love,
and thrice cured by the same physic, and now he drops
me for a trifle. That an honest fellow in his cups
should be such a rogue when he's sober! The narrow-
hearted rascal has been drinking coffee this morning.
Well, thou dear, solitary half-crown, adieu!—Here, Jack!

Re-enter JACK.

Take this; pay for a bottle of wine, and bid Balderdash
bring it himself.—[*Exit* JACK.] How melancholy are
my poor breeches; not one chink!—Thou art a
villanous hand, for thou hast picked my pocket.—This
vintner now has all the marks of an honest fellow:
a broad face, a copious look, a strutting belly, and a jolly
mien. I have brought him above three pound a night.
for these two years successively. The rogue has money
I'm sure, if he will but lend it.

Enter BALDERDASH *with a bottle and glass[es]*,[1]
JACK *attending.*

Oh, Mr Balderdash, good morrow.

---

[1] *See* note on a similar passage in *The Beaux' Stratagem*, Act I.,
Sc. 1.

Bald. Noble Mr Wouldbe, I'm your most humble servant. I have brought you a whetting-glass, the best old hock in Europe; I know 'tis your drink in a morning.

Ben. Would. I'll pledge you, Mr Balderdash.

Bald. Your health, sir.   [*Drinks.*

Ben. Would. Pray, Mr Balderdash, tell me one thing —but first sit down : now tell me plainly what you think of me?

Bald. Think of you, sir! I think that you are the honestest, noblest gentleman, that ever drank a glass of wine; and the best customer that ever came into my house.

Ben. Would. And you really think as you speak?

Bald. May this wine be my poison, sir, if I don't speak from the bottom of my heart!

Ben. Would. And how much money do you think I have spent in your house?

Bald. Why truly, sir, by a moderate computation, I do believe that I have handled of your money the best part of five hundred pounds within these two years.

Ben. Would. Very well! And do you think that you lie under any obligation for the trade I have promoted to your advantage?

Bald. Yes, sir ; and if I can serve you in any respect, pray command me to the utmost of my ability.

Ben. Would. Well! thanks to my stars, there is still some honesty in wine.—Mr Balderdash, I embrace you and your kindness : I am at present a little low in cash, and must beg you to lend me a hundred pieces.

Bald. Why, truly, Mr Wouldbe, I was afraid it would come to this. I have had it in my head several times to caution you upon your expenses : but you were so very genteel in my house, and your liberality became you so very well, that 1 was unwilling to say anything that might check your disposition ; but truly, sir, I can forbear no longer to tell you, that you have been a little too extravagant.

Ben. Would. But since you reaped the benefit of my extravagance, you will, I hope, consider my necessity.

Bald. Consider your necessity! I do with all my heart, and must tell you, moreover, that I will be no longer accessory to it: I desire you, sir, to frequent my house no more.

Ben. Would. How, sir!

Bald. I say, sir, that I have an honour for my good lord your father, and will not suffer his son to run into any unconvenience. Sir, I shall order my drawers not to serve you with a drop of wine. Would you have me connive at a gentleman's destruction?

Ben. Would. But methinks, sir, that a person of your nice conscience should have cautioned me before.

Bald. Alas! sir, it was none of my business. Would you have me be saucy to a gentleman that was my best customer? Lackaday, sir, had you money to hold it out still, I had been hanged rather than be rude to you. But truly, sir, when a man is ruined, 'tis but the duty of a Christian to tell him of it.

Ben. Would. Will you lend me the money, sir?

Bald. Will you pay me this bill, sir?

Ben. Would. Lend me the hundred pound, and I will pay the bill.

Bald. Pay me the bill, and I will not lend the hundred pound, sir. But pray consider with yourself now, sir, would not you think me an arrant coxcomb, to trust a person with money that has always been so extravagant under my eye? whose profuseness I have seen, I have felt, I have handled? Have not I known you, sir, throw away ten pound of a night upon a covey of pit-partridges, and a setting-dog? Sir, you have made my house an ill house: my very chairs will bear you no longer. In short, sir, I desire you to frequent the Crown no more, sir.

Ben. Would. Thou sophisticated tun of iniquity, have
I fattened your carcass, and swelled your bags with my
vital blood?   Have I made you my companion to be
thus saucy to me?   But now I will keep you at your
due distance.   [*Kicks him.*
    Jack. Welcome, sir!
    Ben. Would. Well said, Jack.   [*Kicks him again.*
    Jack. Very welcome, sir! I hope we shall have your
company another time.   Welcome, sir!
                        [BALDERDASH *is kicked off.*
    Ben. Would. Pray wait on him downstairs, and give
him a welcome at the door too.—[*Exit* JACK.]   This is
the punishment of hell; the very devil that tempted me
to the sin, now upbraids me with the crime.—I have
villanously murdered my fortune; and now its ghost,
in the lank shape of Poverty, haunts me: is there no
charm to conjure down the fiend?

                    Re-enter JACK.

    Jack. O sir, here's sad news!
    Ben. Would. Then keep it to thyself, I have enough
of that already.
    Jack. Sir, you will hear it too soon.
    Ben. Would. What! is Broad [1] below?
    Jack. No, no, sir; better twenty such as he were
hanged.   Sir, your father's dead.
    Ben. Would. My father!—Good night, my lord!—
Has he left me anything?
    Jack. I heard nothing of that, sir.
    Ben. Would. Then I believe you heard all there was
of it.—Let me see.—My father dead! and my elder
brother abroad!—If necessity be the mother of inven-

---

[1] Doubtless a reference to Jacob Broad, a celebrated bailiff. *See
The Comical and Tragical History of the Lives and Adventures of the
most noted Bayliffs in and about London and Westminster . . . and
particularly the Life of Jacob Broad of Merry Memory,* by Captain
Alexander Smith, 1723.

tion, she was never more pregnant than with me.—
[*Pauses.*] Here, sirrah, run to Mrs Mandrake, and bid
her come hither presently. — [*Exit* JACK.] That
woman was my mother's midwife when I was born, and
has been my bawd these ten years. I have had her
endeavours to corrupt my brother's mistress; and now
her assistance will be necessary to cheat him of his
estate; for she's famous for understanding the right
side of a woman, and the wrong side of the law. [*Exit.*

SCENE II.—*Scene changes to* [*a Room in* Mrs]
MANDRAKE'S *House.*

Mrs MANDRAKE *discovered.*

Mrs Man. [*Calls.*]   Who is there?

Enter Maid.

Maid. Madam !

Mrs Man. Has any message been left for me to-day?

Maid. Yes, madam : here has been one from my lady
Stillborn, that desired you not to be out of the way, for
she expected to cry out every minute.

Mrs Man. How ! every minute !—Let me see.—
[*Takes out a pocket-book.*] Stillborn—ay—she reckons
with her husband from the first of April ; and with Sir
James, from the first of March.—Ay, she's always a
month before her time.—[*Knocking at the door.*] Go
see who's at the door.

Maid. Yes, madam.   [*Exit.*

Mrs Man. Well, certainly there is not a woman in
the world so willing to oblige mankind as myself ! and
really I have been so ever since the age of twelve, as I
can remember. I have delivered as many women of
great bellies, and helped as many to 'em, as any person

in England ; but my watching and cares have broken
me quite, I am not the same woman I was forty years
ago.

Enter RICHMORE.

Oh, Mr Richmore ! you're a sad man, a barbarous man,
so you are ! What will become of poor Clelia, Mr
Richmore ? The poor creature is so big with her misfortunes, that they are not to be borne.   [*Weeps.*

Rich. You, Mrs Mandrake, are the fittest person in
the world to ease her of 'em.

Mrs Man. And won't you marry her, Mr Richmore ?

Rich. My conscience won't allow it ; for I have sworn
since to marry another.

Mrs Man. And will you break your vows to Clelia ?

Rich. Why not, when she has broke hers to me ?

Mrs Man. How's that, sir ?

Rich. Why, she swore a hundred times never to grant
me the favour ; and yet you know she broke her word.

Mrs Man. But she loved, Mr Richmore, and that
was the reason she forgot her oath.

Rich. And I love Mr Richmore, and that is the
reason I forgot mine. Why should she be angry that I
follow her own example, by doing the very same thing
from the very same motive ?

Mrs Man. Well, well ! Take my word, you'll never
thrive. I wonder how you can have the face to come
near me, that am the witness of your horrid oaths and
imprecations ! Are not you afraid that the guilty
chamber above-stairs should fall down upon your head ?
Yes, yes, I was accessory, I was so ; but if ever you
involve my honour in such a villainy the second time—
Ah, poor Clelia ! I loved her as I did my own daughter
—You seducing man !   [*Weeps.*

Rich. Heigh-ho, my Aurelia !

Mrs Man. Heigh-ho, she's very pretty !

Rich. Dost thou know her, my dear Mandrake ?

Mrs Man. Heigh-ho, she's very pretty! Ah, you're a sad man! Poor Clelia was handsome, but indeed, breeding, puking, and longing, has broken her much. 'Tis a hard case, Mr Richmore, for a young lady to see a thousand things, and long for a thousand things, and yet not dare to own that she longs for one. She had liked to have miscarried t'other day for the pith of a loin of veal.—Ah, you barbarous man!—

Rich. But, my Aurelia! confirm me that you know her, and I'll adore thee.

Mrs Man. You would fling five hundred guineas at my head, that you knew as much of her as I do. Why, sir, I brought her into the world; I have had her sprawling in my lap. Ah! she was as plump as a puffin, sir.

Rich. I think she has no great portion to value herself upon; her reputation only will keep up the market. We must first make that cheap, by crying it down, and then she'll part with it at an easy rate.

Mrs Man. But won't you provide for poor Clelia?

Rich. Provide! why, ha'n't I taught her a trade? Let her set up when she will, I'll engage her customers enough, because I can answer for the goodness of the ware.

Mrs Man. Nay, but you ought to set her up with credit, and take a shop; that is, get her a husband. Have you no pretty gentleman your relation now, that wants a young virtuous lady with a handsome fortune? No young Templar that has spent his estate in the study of the law, and starves by the practice? No spruce officer that wants a handsome wife to make court for him among the major-generals? Have you none of these, sir?

Rich. Pho, pho, madam! you have tired me upon that subject. Do you think a lady that gave me so much trouble before possession shall ever give me any after it? No, no; had she been more obliging to me

when I was in her power, I should be more civil to
her now she's in mine: my assiduity beforehand was an
overprice; had she made a merit of the matter, she
should have yielded sooner.

Mrs Man. Nay, nay, sir; though you have no regard
to her honour, yet you shall protect mine. How d'ye
think I have secured my reputation so long among the
people of best figure, but by keeping all mouths stopped?
Sir, I'll have no clamours at me. Heavens help me, I
have clamours enough at my door early and late in my
t'other capacity! In short, sir, a husband for Clelia, or
I banish you my presence for ever.

Rich. [*Aside.*] Thou art a necessary devil, and I can't
want thee.

Mrs Man. Look'ee, sir, 'tis your own advantage; 'tis
only making over your estate into the hands of a
trustee; and though you don't absolutely command the
premises, yet you may exact enough out of 'em for
necessaries, when you will.

Rich. Patience a little, madam! I have a young
nephew that is captain of horse: he mortgaged
the last morsel of his estate to me, to make up his
equipage for the last campaign. Perhaps you know
him; he's a brisk fellow, much about Court, Captain
Trueman.

Mrs Man. Trueman! ads my life, he's one of my
babies! I can tell you the very minute he was born
—precisely at three o'clock next St George's day
Trueman will be two-and-twenty; a stripling, the
prettiest, good-natured child, and your nephew! He
must be the man; and shall be the man; I have a
kindness for him.

Rich. But we must have a care; the fellow wants
neither sense nor courage.

Mrs Man. Phu, phu! never fear her part, she sha'n't
want instructions; and then for her lying-in a little
abruptly, 'tis my business to reconcile matters there, a

fright or a fall excuses that. Lard, sir! I do these
things every day.

Rich. 'Tis pity then to put you out of your road; and
Clelia shall have a husband.

Mrs Man. Spoke like a man of honour! and now I'll
serve you again. This Aurelia, you say—

Rich. Oh, she distracts me! Her beauty, family, and
virtue, make her a noble pleasure.

Mrs Man. And you have a mind for that reason to
get her a husband?

Rich. Yes, faith; I have another young relation at
Cambridge is just going into orders; and I think such
a fine woman, with fifteen hundred pound, is a better
presentation than any living in my gift; and why should
he like the cure the worse that an incumbent was there
before?

Mrs Man. Thou art a pretty fellow! At the same
moment you would persuade me that you love a
woman to madness, are you contriving how to part
with her.

Rich. If I loved her not to madness I should not
run into these contradictions. Here, my dear mother,
Aurelia's the word.   [*Offers her money.*

Mrs Man. Pardon me, sir!—[*Refusing the money.*]
Did you ever know me mercenary? No, no, sir; virtue
is its own reward.

Rich. Nay, but, madam, I owe you for the teeth-
powder you sent me.

Mrs Man. Oh, that's another matter, sir!—[*Takes the
money.*] I hope you liked it, sir?

Rich. Extremely, madam. — [*Aside.*] But it was
somewhat dear of twenty guineas.

Enter Footman.

Foot. Madam, here is Mr Wouldbe's footman below
with a message from his master.

Mrs Man. I come to him presently.—[*Exit* Footman.] Do you know that Wouldbe loves Aurelia's cousin and companion, Mrs Constance, with the great fortune, and that I solicit for him?

Rich. Why, she's engaged to his elder brother! Besides, young Wouldbe has no money to prosecute an affair of such consequence. You can have no hopes of success there, I'm sure.

Mrs Man. Truly, I have no great hopes; but an industrious body, you know, would do anything rather than be idle. The aunt is very near, her time, and I have access to the family when I please.

Rich. Now I think on't: prithee, get the letter from Wouldbe that I gave him just now. It would be proper to our designs upon Trueman that it should not be exposed.

Mrs Man. And you showed Clelia's letter to Wouldbe?

Rich. Yes.

Mrs Man. Eh, you barbarous man! Who the devil would. oblige you? What pleasure can you take in exposing the poor creature? Dear little child, 'tis pity, indeed it is!

Rich. Madam, the messenger waits below: so I'll take my leave. [*Exit.*

Mrs Man. Ah, you're a sad man! [*Exit.*

ACT II

SCENE I.—*The Park.*

CONSTANCE *and* AURELIA.

UR. Prithee, cousin Constance, be cheerful; let the dead lord sleep in peace, and look up to the living. Take pen, ink, and paper, and write immediately to your lover, that he is now a baron of England, and that you long to be a baroness.

Con. Nay, Aurelia, there is some regard due to the memory of the father, for the respect I bear the son; besides, I don't know how, I could wish my young lord were at home in this juncture. This brother of his—some mischief will happen—I had a very ugly dream last night. In short, I am eaten up with the spleen, my dear.

Aur. Come, come, walk about and divert it; the air will do you good; think of other people's affairs a little. When did you see Clelia?

Con. I'm glad you mentioned her; don't you observe her gaiety to be much more forced than formerly? Her humour don't sit so easy upon her.

Aur. No, nor her stays neither, I assure you.

Con. Did you observe how she devoured the pomegranates yesterday?

Aur. She talks of visiting a relation in Leicester-shire.

Con. She fainted away in the country dance t'other night.

Aur. Richmore shunned her in the Walk last week.

Con. And his footman laughed.

Aur. She takes laudanum to make her sleep a' nights.

Con. Ah, poor Clelia! What will she do, cousin?

Aur. Do! Why, nothing till the nine months be up.

Con. That's cruel, Aurelia. How can you make merry with her misfortunes? I am positive she was no easy conquest; some singular villainy has been practised upon her.

Aur. Yes, yes, the fellow would be practising upon me too, I thank him.

Con. Have a care, cousin; he has a promising person.

Aur. Nay, for that matter, his promising person may as soon be broke as his promising vows. Nature indeed has made him a giant, and he wars with heaven like the giants of old.

Con. Then why will you admit his visits?

Aur. I never did: but all the servants are more his than our own; he has a golden key to every door in the house. Besides, he makes my uncle believe that his intentions are honourable; and, indeed, he has said nothing yet to disprove it. But, cousin, do you see who comes yonder, sliding along the Mall?

Con. Captain Trueman, I protest! The campaign has improved him; he makes a very clean, well furnished figure.

Aur. Youthful, easy, and good-natured. I could wish he would know us.

Con. Are you sure he's well-bred?

Aur. I tell you he's good-natured, and I take good manners to be nothing but a natural desire to be easy

and agreeable to whatever conversation we fall into ;
and a porter with this is mannerly in his way, and a
duke, without it, has but the breeding of a dancing-master.

Con. I like him for his affection to my young lord.

Aur. And I like him for his affection to my young
person.

Con. How, how, cousin ? You never told me that.

Aur. How should I ? He never told it to me ; but I
have discovered it by a great many signs and tokens,
that are better security for his heart than ten thousand
vows and promises.

Con. He's Richmore's nephew.

Aur. Ah, would he were his heir too ! He's a pretty
fellow. But, then, he's a soldier ; and must share his
time with his mistress, Honour, in Flanders. No, no, I'm
resolved against a man that disappears all the summer,
like a woodcock.

*As these last words are spoken, TRUEMAN enters
behind them, as passing over the stage.*

True. That's for me, whoever spoke it.—[*The* Ladies
turn about.] Aurelia ! [*surprised*]

Con. What, Captain, you're afraid of everything but
the enemy.

True. I have reason, ladies, to be most apprehensive
where there is most danger. The enemy is satisfied
with a leg or an arm, but here I'm in hazard of losing
my heart.

Aur. None in the world, sir. Nobody here designs
to attack it.

True. But suppose it be assaulted and taken already,
madam ?

Aur. Then we'll return it without ransom.

True. But suppose, madam, the prisoner choose to
stay where it is ?

Aur. That were to turn deserter, and you know,
Captain, what such deserve.

True. The punishment it undergoes this moment—shot to death.

Con. Nay, then, 'tis time for me to put in.—Pray sir, have you heard the news of my lord Wouldbe's death?

True. [*To* CONSTANCE.] People mind not the death of others, madam, that are expiring themselves —[*To* AURELIA.] Do you consider, madam, the penalty of wounding a man in the Park?

Aur. Heyday! Why, Captain, d'ye intend to make a Vigo[1] business of it, and break the boom at once? Sir, if you only rally, pray let my cousin have her share; or, if you would be particular, pray be more respectful; not so much upon the declaration, I beseech you, sir.

True. I have been, fair creature, a perfect coward in my passion; I have had hard strugglings with my fear before I durst engage, and now perhaps behave but too desperately.

Aur. Sir, I am very sorry you have said so much; for I must punish you for't, though it be contrary to my inclination.—Come, cousin, will you walk?

Con. Servant, sir!   [*Exeunt* Ladies.

True. Charming creature!—*I must punish you for't, though it be contrary to my inclination.*—Hope and despair in a breath. But I'll think the best.   [*Exit.*

SCENE II.—BENJAMIN WOULDBE'S *Lodgings.*

BENJAMIN WOULDBE *and* Mrs MANDRAKE, *meeting.*

Ben. Would. Thou life and soul of secret dealings, welcome!

---

[1] In October 1702, a fleet under Admiral Rooke and the Duke of Ormonde broke the boom which protected the Spanish treasure-fleet in Vigo Bay, and destroyed the enemy's ships, securing booty to the amount of about £1,000,000.

Mrs Man. My dear child, bless thee!—Who would have imagined that I brought this great rogue into the world? He makes me an old woman, I protest.—But, adso, my child, I forgot; I'm sorry for the loss of your father, sorry at my heart, poor man!—[*Weeps.*] Mr Wouldbe, have you a drop of brandy in your closet? I an't very well to-day.

Ben. Would. That you sha'n't want; but please to sit, my dear mother.—[*Calls to* Servant.] Here, Jack, the brandy bottle.—Now, madam, I have occasion to use you in dressing up a handsome cheat for me.

Mrs Man. I defy any chambermaid in England to do it better. I have dressed up a hundred and fifty cheats in my time.

Enter JACK *with the brandy bottle.*

Here, boy, this glass is too big; carry it away, I'll take a sup out of the bottle.   [*Exit* JACK.

Ben. Would. Right, madam. And my business being very urgent—in three words, 'tis this—

Mrs Man. Hold, sir, till I take advice of my counsel.—[*Drinks.*] There is nothing more comfortable to a poor creature, and fitter to revive wasting spirits, than a little plain brandy. I an't for your hot spirits, your rosa solis, your ratafias, your orange-waters, and the like: a moderate glass of cool Nantes is the thing.

Ben. Would. But to our business, madam.—My father is dead, and I have a mind to inherit his estate.

Mrs Man. You put the case very well.

Ben. Would. One of two things I must choose—either to be a lord or a beggar.

Mrs Man. Be a lord to choose:—though I have known some that have chosen both.

Ben. Would. I have a brother that I love very well; but, since one of us must want, I had rather he should starve than I.

Mrs Man. Upon my conscience, dear heart, you're in the right on't.

Ben. Would. Now your advice upon these heads.

Mrs Man. They be matters of weight, and I must consider.—[*Drinks.*] Is there a will in the case?

Ben. Would. There is; which excludes me from every foot of the estate.

Mrs Man. That's bad.—Where's your brother?

Ben. Would. He's now in Germany, in his way to England, and is expected very soon.

Mrs Man. How soon?

Ben. Would. In a month or less.

Mrs Man. O ho! a month is a great while! our business must be done in an hour or two. We must—[*Drinks*] suppose your brother to be dead; nay, he shall be actually dead—and, my lord, my humble service t'ye!

Ben. Would. O madam, I'm your ladyship's most devoted! Make your words good, and I'll—

Mrs Man. Say no more, sir; you shall have it, you have it.

Ben. Would. Ay, but how, dear Mrs Mandrake?

Mrs Man. Mrs Mandrake! Is that all? Why not mother, aunt, grandmother? Sir, I have done more for you this moment than all the relations you have in the world.

Ben. Would. Let me hear it.

Mrs Man. By the strength of this potent inspiration, I have made you a peer of England, with seven thousand pound a year.—My lord, I wish you joy.
[*Drinks.*

Ben. Would. The woman's mad, I believe!

Mrs Man. Quick, quick, my lord! Counterfeit a letter presently from Germany, that your brother is killed in a duel; let it be directed to your father, and fall into the hands of the steward when you are by.—What sort of fellow is the steward?

Ben. Would. Why, a timorous, half-honest man, that a little persuasion will make a whole knave. He wants courage to be thoroughly just or entirely a villain; but good backing will make him either.

Mrs Man. And he sha'n't want that! I tell you the letter must come into his hands when you are by; upon this you take immediate possession, and so you have the best part of the law on your side.

Ben. Would. But suppose my brother comes in the meantime?

Mrs Man. This must be done this very moment. Let him come while you're in possession, I'll warrant we'll find a way to keep him out.

Ben. Would. But how, my dear contriver?

Mrs Man. By your father's will, man, your father's will:—that is, one that your father might have made and which we will make for him. I'll send you a nephew of my own, a lawyer, that shall do the business. Go, get into possession, possession, I say; let us have but the estate to back the suit, and you'll find the law too strong for justice, I warrant you.

Ben. Would. My oracle! How shall we revel in delight when this great prediction is accomplished!— But one thing yet remains: my brother's mistress, the charming Constance—let her be mine.

Mrs Man. Pho! pho! she's yours o' course; she's contracted to you; for she's engaged to marry no man but my lord Wouldbe's son and heir; now, you being the person, she's recoverable by law.

Ben. Would. Marry her! No, no, she's contracted to him; 'twere injustice to rob a brother of his wife— an easier favour will satisfy me.

Mrs Man. Why, truly, as you say, that favour is so easy that I wonder they make such a bustle about it. But get you gone and mind your affairs, I must about mine.—Oh—I had forgot—where's that foolish letter you had this morning from Richmore?

Ben. Would. I have posted it up in the chocolate-house.

Mrs Man. Yaw!—[*Shrieks.*] I shall fall into fits; hold me—

Ben. Would. No, no, I did but jest; here it is. But be assured, madam, I wanted only time to have exposed it.

Mrs Man. Ah, you barbarous man! why so?

Ben. Would. Because, when knaves of our sex, and fools of yours meet, they make the best jest in the world.

Mrs Man. Sir, the world has a better share in the jest when we are the knaves and you the fools. But look'ee, sir, if ever you open your mouth about this trick, I'll discover all your tricks; therefore, silence and safety on both sides.

Ben. Would. Madam, you need not doubt my silence at present; because my own affairs will employ me sufficiently; so there's your letter.—[*Gives the letter.*] And now to write my own.

Mrs Man. Adieu, my lord!—[*Exit* WOULDBE.] Let me see.—[*Opens the letter and reads.*] *If there be solemnity in protestations*—that's foolish, very foolish! Why should she expect solemnity in protestations?— Um, um, um.—*I may still depend on the faith of my Richmore.*—Ah, poor Clelia!—Um, um, um.—*I can no longer hide the effects on't from the world.*—The effects on't! How modestly is that expressed! Well, 'tis a pretty letter, and I'll keep it.

[*Puts the letter in her pocket and exit.*

SCENE III.—Lord WOULDBE's *House.*

Enter Steward [CLEARACCOUNT] *and his wife.*

Mrs Clear. You are to blame, you are much to blame, husband, in being so scrupulous.

Clear. 'Tis true; this foolish conscience of mine has been the greatest bar to my fortune.

Mrs Clear. And will ever be so. Tell me but one that thrives, and I'll show you a hundred that starve by it. Do you think 'tis fourscore pound a year makes my lord Gouty's steward's wife live at the rate of four hundred? Upon my word, my dear, I'm as good a gentlewoman as she, and I expect to be maintained accordingly. 'Tis conscience I warrant that buys her the point-heads and diamond necklace? Was it conscience that bought her the fine house in Jermyn Street? Is it conscience that enables the steward to buy when the lord is forced to sell?

Clear. But what would you have me do?

Mrs Clear. Do! Now's your time: that small morsel of an estate your lord bought lately, a thing not worth mentioning; take it towards your daughter Molly's portion. What's two hundred a year? 'Twill never be missed.

Clear. 'Tis but a small matter, I must confess; and as a reward for my past faithful service, I think it but reasonable I should cheat a little now.

Mrs Clear. Reasonable! all the reason that can be; if the ungrateful world won't reward an honest man, why let an honest man reward himself. There's five hundred pounds you received but two days ago: lay them aside. You may easily sink it in the charge of the funeral. Do my dear now, kiss me, and do it.

Clear. Well, you have such a winning way with you! But, my dear, I'm so much afraid of my young lord's coming home; he's a cunning close man, they say, and will examine my accounts very narrowly.

Mrs Clear. Ay, my dear: would you had the younger brother to deal with! You might manage him as you pleased. I see him coming. Let us weep, let us weep. [*They pull out their handkerchiefs, and seem to mourn.*

Enter BENJAMIN WOULDBE.

Clear. Ah, sir! we have all lost a father, a friend, and a supporter.

Ben. Would. Ay, Mr Steward, we must submit to fate, as he has done. And it is no small addition to my grief, honest Mr Clearaccount, that it is not in my power to supply my father's place to you and yours. Your sincerity and justice to the dead merits the greatest regard from those that survive him. Had I but my brother's ability, or he my inclinations, I'll assure you, Mrs Clearaccount, you should not have such cause to mourn.

Mrs Clear. Ah, good, noble sir!

Clear. Your brother, sir, I hear, is a very severe man.

Ben. Would. He is what the world calls a prudent man, Mr Steward. I have often heard him very severe upon men of your business; and has declared, that for form's sake indeed he would keep a steward, but that he would inspect into all his accounts himself.

Mrs Clear. Ay, Mr Wouldbe, you have more sense than to do these things; you have more honour than to trouble your head with your own affairs. Would to Heavens we were to serve you!

Ben. Would. Would I could serve you, madam— without injustice to my brother.

Enter Footman.

Foot. A letter for my lord Wouldbe.

Clear. It comes too late, alas! for his perusal. Let me see it.   [*Opens and reads.*
Frankfort, Octob. 10, *new style.*
Frankfort! where's Frankfort, sir?

Ben. Would. In Germany. This letter must be from my brother; I suppose he's a-coming home.

Clear. 'Tis none of his hand.   Let me see.

[*Reads.*

My Lord,

  I am troubled at this unhappy occasion of sending to your lordship; your brave son, and my dear friend, was yesterday unfortunately killed in a duel by a German Count—

I shall love a German Count as long as I live.—My lord, my lord, now I may call you so, since your elder brother's—dead.

Ben. Would., Mrs Clear. How?

Clear. Read there.

[*Gives the letter,* WOULDBE *peruses it.*

Ben. Would. Oh, my fate! a father and a brother in one day! Heavens! 'tis too much.—Where is the fatal messenger?

Foot. A gentleman, sir, who said he came post on purpose. He was afraid the contents of the letter would unqualify my lord for company; so he would take another time to wait on him.   [*Exit.*

Ben. Would. Nay, then, 'tis true; and there is truth in dreams.   Last night I dreamed—

Mrs. Clear. Nay, my lord, I dreamed too; I dreamed I saw your brother dressed in a long minister's gown (Lord bless us!), with a book in his hand, walking before a dead body to the grave.

Ben. Would. Well, Mr Clearaccount, get mourning ready.

Clear. Will your lordship have the old coach covered, or a new one made?

Ben. Would. A new one. The old coach, with the grey horses, I give to Mrs Clearaccount here; 'tis not fit she should walk the streets.

Mrs Clear. [*Aside.*] Heavens bless the German count, I say!—[*Aloud.*] But, my lord—

Ben. Would. No reply, madam, you shall have it:

and receive it but as the earnest of my favours.—
Mr Clearaccount, I double your salary, and all the
servants' wages, to moderate their grief for our great
losses. Pray, sir, take order about these affairs.

Clear. I shall, my lord.

[*Exit with* Mrs CLEARACCOUNT.

Ben. Would. So! I have got possession of the castle,
and if I had but a little law to fortify me now, I believe
we might hold it out a great while. Oh! here comes
my attorney.

Enter SUBTLEMAN.

Mr Subtleman, your servant.

Sub. My lord, I wish you joy; my aunt Mandrake
has sent me to receive your commands.

Ben. Would. Has she told you anything of the affair?

Sub. Not a word, my lord.

Ben. Would. Why then—come nearer—can you make
a man right heir to an estate during the life of an elder
brother?

Sub. I thought you had been the eldest.

Ben. Would. That we are not yet agreed upon; for
you must know, there is an impertinent fellow that takes
a fancy to dispute the seniority with me; for, look'ee,
sir, my mother has unluckily sowed discord in the
family, by bringing forth twins. My brother, 'tis true,
was first-born; but, I believe from the bottom of my
heart, I was the first-begotten.

Sub. I understand—you are come to an estate and
dignity, that by justice indeed is your own, but by law
it falls to your brother.

Ben. Would. I had rather, Mr Subtleman, it were
his by justice and mine by law; for I would have the
strongest title, if possible.

Sub. I am very sorry there should happen any breach
between brethren : so I think it would be but a Christian
and charitable act to take away all farther disputes, by

making you true heir to the estate by the last will of your father. Look'ee, I'll divide stakes; you shall yield the eldership and honour to him, and he shall quit his estate to you.

Ben. Would. Why, as you say, I don't much care if I do grant him the eldest, half an hour is but a trifle. But how shall we do about this will? Who shall we get to prove it?

Sub. Never trouble yourself for that : I expect a cargo of witnesses and usquebaugh by the first fair wind.

Ben. Would. But we can't stay for them ; it must be done immediately.

Sub. Well, well; we'll find somebody, I warrant you, to make oath of his last words.

Ben. Would. That's impossible ; for my father died of an apoplexy, and did not speak at all.

Sub. That's nothing, sir : he's not the first dead man that I have made to speak.

Ben. Would. You're a great master of speech, I don't question, sir; and I can assure you there will be ten guineas for every word you extort from him in my favour.

Sub. O sir, that's enough to make your great-grand-father speak.

Ben. Would. Come then, I'll carry you to my steward ; he shall give you the names of the manors, and the true titles and denominations of the estate, and then you shall go to work.   [*Exeunt.*

SCENE IV.—*The Park.*

Richmore *and* Trueman, *meeting.*

Rich. O brave cuz ! you're very happy with the fair, I find. Pray which of those two ladies you encountered just now has your adoration ?

True. She that commands by forbidding it : and since I had courage to declare to herself, I dare now own it to the world : Aurelia, sir, is my angel.

Rich. Ha!—[*A long pause.*] Sir, I find you're of everybody's religion ; but methinks you make a bold flight at first. Do you think your captain's pay will stake against so high a gamester ?

True. What do you mean ?

Rich. Mean ! bless me, sir, mean !—You're a man of mighty honour, we all know.—But I'll tell you a secret —the thing is public already.

True. I should be proud that all mankind were acquainted with it ; I should despise the passion that could make me either ashamed or afraid to own it.

Rich. Ha, ha, ha ! prithee, dear Captain, no more of these rodomontados ; you may as soon put a standing-army upon us. I'll tell you another secret—five hundred pound is the least penny.

True. Nay, to my knowledge, she has fifteen hundred.

Rich. Nay, to my knowledge, she took five.

True. Took five ! how ? where ?

Rich. In her lap, in her lap, Captain ! Where should it be ?

True. I'm amazed !

Rich. So am I ; that she could be so unreasonable.— Fifteen hundred pound ! 'sdeath ! had she that price from you ?

True. 'Sdeath ! I meant her portion.

Rich. Why, what have you to do with her portion ?

True. I loved her up to marriage, by this light.

Rich. Marriage ! ha, ha, ha ! I love the gipsy for her cunning. A young, easy, amorous, credulous fellow of two-and-twenty, was just the game she wanted ; I find she presently singled you out from the herd.

True. You distract me !

Rich. A soldier too, that must follow the wars abroad, and leave her to engagements at home.

True. Death and furies! I'll be revenged!

Rich. Why, what can you do? You'll challenge her, will you?

True. Her reputation was spotless when I went over.

Rich. So was the reputation of Mareschal Boufflers [1]; but d'ye think, that while you were beating the French abroad, that we were idle at home? No, no, we have had our sieges, our capitulations, and surrendries, and all that. We have cut ourselves out good winter-quarters as well as you.

True. And are you billeted there?

Rich. Look'ee, Trueman, you ought to be very trusty to a secret, that has saved you from destruction. In plain terms, I have buried five hundred pounds in that little spot, and I should think it very hard if you took it over my head.

True. Not by a lease for life, I can assure you; but I shall—

Rich. What! you han't five hundred pounds to give? Look'ee, since you can make no sport, spoil none. In a year or two, she dwindles to a perfect basset-bank; everybody may play at it that pleases, and then you may put in for a piece or two.

True. Dear sir, I could worship you for this.

Rich. Not for this, nephew; for I did not intend it; but I came to seek you upon another affair. Were not you in the presence last night?

True. I was.

Rich. Did not you talk to Clelia, my lady Taper's niece?

True. A fine woman.

Rich. Well, I met her upon the stairs, and handing her to her coach, she asked me if you were not my nephew; and said two or three warm things, that persuade me she likes you. Her relations have interest at Court, and she has money in her pocket.

¹ See note, p. 73.

True. But—this devil Aurelia still sticks with me.

Rich. What then! the way to love in one place with success, is to marry in another with convenience. Clelia has four thousand pound; this applied to your reigning ambition, whether love or advancement, will go a great way: and for her virtue and conduct, be assured that nobody can give a better account of it than myself.

True. I am willing to believe, from this late accident, that you consult my honour and interest in what you propose, and therefore I am satisfied to be governed.

Rich. I see the very lady in the walk. We'll about it.

True. I wait on you.   [*Exeunt.*

SCENE V.—Lord WOULDBE'S *House.*

BENJAMIN WOULDBE, SUBTLEMAN, *and* CLEARACCOUNT.

Ben. Would. Well, Mr Subtleman, you are sure the will is firm and good in law?

Sub. I warrant you, my lord: and for the last words to prove it, here they are.—Look'ee, Mr Clearaccount— *Yes*—that is an answer to the question that was put to him (you know) by those about him when he was a-dying—yes, or no, he must have said; so we have chosen yes— *Yes, I have made my will, as it may be found in the custody of Mr Clearaccount my steward; and I desire it may stand as my last will and testament.*—Did you ever hear a dying man's words more to the purpose? An apoplexy! I tell you, my lord had intervals to the last.

Clear. Ay, but how shall these words be proved?

Sub. My lord shall speak 'em now.

Ben. Would. Shall he, faith?

Sub. Ay, now—if the corpse ben't buried. Look'ee, sir, these words must be put into his mouth, and drawn

out again before us all; and if they won't be his last
words then—I'll be perjured.

Ben. Would. What! violate the dead! It must not
be, Mr Subtleman.

Sub. With all my heart, sir! But I think you had
better violate the dead of a tooth or so, than violate the
living of seven thousand pound a year.

Ben Would. But is there no other way?

Sub. No, sir. Why, d'ye think Mr Clearaccount here
will hazard soul and body to swear they are his last
words, unless they be made his last words? For my
part, sir, I'll swear to nothing but what I see with my
eyes come out of a man's mouth.

Ben Would. But it looks so unnatural.

Sub. What! to open a man's mouth, and put in a bit
of paper?—This is all.

Ben. Would. But the body is cold, and his teeth
can't be got asunder.

Sub. But what occasion has your father for teeth now?
I tell you what—I knew a gentleman, three days buried,
taken out of his grave, and his dead hand set to his last
will, (unless somebody made him sign another afterwards,) and I know the estate to be held by that tenure
to this day; and a firm tenure it is; for a dead hand
holds fastest; and let me tell you, dead teeth will fasten
as hard.

Ben. Would. Well, well, use your pleasure; you
understand the law best.—[*Exeunt* SUBTLEMAN *and*
CLEARACCOUNT.] What a mighty confusion is brought
into families by sudden death! Men should do well to
settle their affairs in time. Had my father done this
before he was taken ill, what a trouble had he saved us!
But he was taken suddenly, poor man!

Re-enter SUBTLEMAN.

Sub. Your father still bears you the old grudge, 1

find. It was with much struggling he consented; I never knew a man so loath to speak in my life.

Ben. Would. He was always a man of few words.

Sub. Now I may safely bear witness myself, as the scrivener there present: I love to do things with a clear conscience. [*Subscribes.*

Ben. Would. But the law requires three witnesses.

Sub. Oh! I shall pick up a couple more, that perhaps may take my word for't. But is not Mr Clearaccount in your interest?

Ben. Would. I hope so.

Sub. Then he shall be one; a witness in the family goes a great way; besides, these foreign evidences are risen confoundedly since the wars. I hope, if mine escape the privateers, to make a hundred pound an ear of every head of 'em. But the steward is an honest man, and shall save you the charges. [*Exit.*

Ben. Would. The pride of birth, the heats of appetite, and fears of want, are strong temptations to injustice.— But why injustice?—The world has broke all civilities with me, and left me in the eldest state of nature, wild, where force or cunning first created right. I cannot say I ever knew a father; 'tis true, I was begotten in his lifetime, but I was posthumous born, and lived not till he died. My hours indeed I numbered, but ne'er enjoyed 'em till this moment.—My brother! what is brother? we are all so; and the first two were enemies. He stands before me in the road of life to rob me of my pleasures. My senses, formed by nature for delight, are all alarmed. My sight, my hearing, taste and touch, call loudly on me for their objects, and they shall be satisfied. [*Exit.*

ACT III

SCENE I.—[Lord Wouldbe's *House.*]

A Levee. Benjamin Wouldbe *dressing, and several*
Gentlemen *whispering him by turns.*

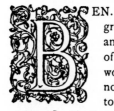EN. WOULD. [*Aside.*] Surely, the greatest ornament of quality is a clean and a numerous levee! Such a crowd of attendance for the cheap reward of words and promises, distinguishes the nobility from those that pay wages to their servants. — [*A* Gentleman *whispers.*] Sir, I shall speak to the Commissioners, and use all my interest, I can assure you, sir.—[*Another whispers.*] Sir, I shall meet some of your board this evening: let me see you to-morrow.—[*A third whispers.*] Sir, I'll consider of it.—[*Aside.*] That fellow's breath stinks of tobacco.—O Mr Comic, your servant!

Com. My lord, I wish you joy; I have something to show your lordship.

Ben. Would. What is it, pray, sir?

Com. I have an elegy upon the dead lord, and a panegyric upon the living one.—*In utrumque paratus,* my lord.

Ben. Would. Ha! ha! very pretty, Mr Comic. But pray, Mr Comic, why don't you write plays? It would give one an opportunity of serving you.

Com. My lord, I have writ one.

Ben. Would. Was it ever acted?

Com. No, my lord; but it has been a-rehearsing these three years and a half.[1]

Ben. Would. A long time. There must be a great deal of business in it surely.

Com. No, my lord, none at all. I have another play just finished, but that I want a plot for't.

Ben. Would. A plot! you should read the Italian and Spanish plays, Mr Comic. I like your verses here mightily.—Here, Mr Clearaccount!

Com. [*Aside.*] Now for five guineas at least.

Ben. Would. Here, give Mr Comic, give him—give him the Spanish play that lies in the closet window.— [*To a* Gentleman.] Captain, can I do you any service?

Fourth Gent. Pray, my lord, use your interest with the general for that vacant commission: I hope, my lord, the blood I have already lost may entitle me to spill the remainder in my country's cause.

Ben. Would. All the reason in the world.—Captain, you may depend upon me for all the service I can.

Fifth Gent. I hope your lordship won't forget to speak to the general about that vacant commission. Although I have never made a campaign, yet, my lord, my interest in the country can raise me men, which I think should prefer me to that gentleman, whose bloody disposition frightens the poor people from listing.

Ben. Would. All the reason in the world, sir; you may depend upon me for all the service in my power.— Captain, I'll do your business for you.—Sir, I'll speak to the general; I shall see him at the House—

Enter a Citizen.

Oh, Mr Alderman, your servant!—Gentlemen all, I beg your pardon!—[*Exeunt* Levee.] Mr Alderman, have you any service to command me?

[1] This may perhaps be a hit at Oldmixon. See note, p. 39.

Ald. Your lordship's humble servant!—I have a favour to beg. You must know, I have a graceless son, a fellow that drinks and swears eternally, keeps a whore in every corner of the town : in short, he's fit for no kind of thing but a soldier. I am so tired of him that I intend to throw him into the army, let the fellow be ruined, if he will.

Ben. Would. I commend your paternal care, sir! Can I do you any service in this affair?

Ald. Yes, my lord: there is a vacant company in Colonel Whatd'yecalum's regiment, and if your lordship would but speak to the general—

Ben. Would. Has your son ever served?

Ald. Served! Yes, my lord: he's an ensign in the trainbands.

Ben. Would. Has he ever signalised his courage?

Ald. Often, often, my lord ; but one day particularly, you must know, his captain was so busy shipping off a cargo of cheeses, that he left my son to command in his place—would you believe it, my lord? he charged up Cheapside, in the front of the buff-coats, with such bravery and courage, that I could not forbear wishing, in the loyalty of my heart, for ten thousand such officers upon the Rhine. Ah! my lord, we must employ such fellows as him, or we shall never humble the French king.—Now, my lord, if you could find a convenient time to hint these things to the general—

Ben. Would. All the reason in the world, Mr Alderman—I'll do you all the service I can.

Ald. You may tell him he's a man of courage, fit for the service; and then he loves hardship—he sleeps every other night in the round-house.

Ben. Would. I'll do you all the service I can.

Ald. Then, my lord, he salutes with his pike so very handsomely, it went to his mistress's heart, t'other day. —Then he beats a drum like an angel.

Ben. Would. Sir, I'll do you all the service I can—
   [*Not taking the least notice of the* Alderman *all this
   while, but dressing himself in the glass.*

Ald. But, my lord, the hurry of your lordship's affairs
may put my business out of your head; therefore, my
lord, I'll presume to leave you some memorandum.

Ben. Would. I'll do you all the service I can.
                                     [*Not minding him.*

Ald. Pray, my lord,—[*Pulling him by the sleeve*] give
me leave for a memorandum; my glove, I suppose, will
do.   Here, my lord, pray remember me—
             [*Lays his glove upon the table, and exit.*

Ben. Would. I'll do you all the service I can.—What,
is he gone? 'Tis the most rude familiar fellow!—Faugh,
what a greasy gauntlet is here!—[*A purse drops out of
the glove.*] Oh! no, no; the glove is a clean well-made
glove, and the owner of it—the most respectful person
I have seen this morning; he knows what distance—
[*Chinking the purse*] is due to a man of quality.—But
what must I do for this?—[*To his* Valet.] Frisure, do
you remember what the alderman said to me?

Fris. No, my lord, I thought your lordship had.

Ben. Would. This blockhead thinks a man of quality
can mind what people say—when they do something,
'tis another case.—Here, call him back.—[*Exit* FRISURE.]
He talked something of the general, and his son, and
trainbands, I know not what stuff.

           Re-enter FRISURE *with* Alderman.

Oh, Mr Alderman, I have put your memorandum in
my pocket.

Ald. Oh, my lord, you do me too much honour!

Ben. Would. But, Mr Alderman, the business you
were talking of—it shall be done, but if you gave a short
note of it to my secretary, it would not be amiss.—But
Mr Alderman, han't you the fellow to this glove? it fits
me mighty well—[*Putting on the glove.*] It looks so

like a challenge to give a man an odd glove—and I would have nothing that looks like enmity between you and I, Mr Alderman.

Ald. Truly, my lord, I intended the other glove for a memorandum to the colonel, but since your lordship has a mind to't—   [*Gives the glove.*

Ben. Would. Here, Frisure, lead this gentleman to my secretary, and bid him take a note of his business.

Ald. But, my lord, *don't* do me all the service you can now.

Ben. Would. Well, I *won't* do you all the service I can.[1]—[*Exeunt* FRISURE *and* Alderman.] These citizens have a strange capacity of soliciting sometimes.

Re-enter CLEARACCOUNT.

Clear. My lord, here are your tailor, your vintner, your bookseller, and half-a-dozen more with their bills at the door, and they desire their money.

Ben. Would. Tell 'em, Mr Clearaccount, that when I was a private gentleman, I had nothing else to do but to run in debt, and now that I have got into a higher rank, I'm so very busy I can't pay it. As for that clamorous rogue of a tailor, speak him fair till he has made up my liveries: then, about a year and a half hence, be at leisure to put him off for a year and a half longer.

Clear. My lord, there's a gentleman below calls himself Mr Basset; he says your lordship owes him fifty guineas that he won of you at cards.

Ben. Would. Look'ee, sir, the gentleman's money is a debt of honour, and must be paid immediately.

Clear. Your father thought otherwise, my lòrd. He always took care to have the poor tradesmen satisfied,

---

[1] The *don't* and *won't* are italicised in Q. 1 and early editions. The allusion is, of course, to the stereotyped phrase used by Benjamin Wouldbe above, which implied no intention of doing anything whatever.

whose only subsistence lay in the use of their money, and was used to say, that nothing was honourable but what was honest.

Ben. Would. My father might say what he pleased, he was a nobleman of very singular humours : but in my notion there are not two things in nature more different than honour and honesty. Now your honesty is a little mechanic quality, well enough among citizens, people that do nothing but pitiful mean actions according to law ; but your honour flies a much higher pitch, and will do anything that's free and spontaneous, but scorns to level itself to what is only just.

Clear. But I think it a little hard to have these poor people starve for want of their money, and yet pay this sharping rascal fifty guineas.

Ben. Would. Sharping rascal ! what a barbarism that is ! Why, he wears as good wigs, as fine linen, and keeps as good company, as any at White's ; and between you and I, sir, this sharping rascal, as you are pleased to call him, shall make more interest among the nobility with his cards and counters, than a soldier shall with his sword and pistol. Pray let him have fifty guineas immediately.   [*Exeunt.*

SCENE II.—*The Street* [*before* Lord WOULDBE'S *House*].

ELDER [HERMES] WOULDBE, *writing in a pocket-book, in a riding-habit.*

Herm. Would. *Monday the* [14*th of December,*][1] 1702, *I arrived safe in London, and so concluding my travels—*
[*Puts up the book.*
Now welcome country, father, friends,
My brother too, if brothers can be friends :

[1] Date left blank in Q. 1.

But above all, my charming fair, my Constance.
Through all the mazes of my wandering steps,
Through all the various climes that I have run,
Her love has been the loadstone of my course,
Her eyes the stars that pointed me the way.
Had not her charms my heart entire possessed,
Who knows what Circe's artful voice and look
Might have ensnared my travelling youth,
And fixed me to enchantment?
Here comes my fellow-traveller.

Enter TEAGUE,[1] *with a portmantle.   He throws it down and sits on it.*

What makes you sit upon the portmantle, Teague?
you'll rumple the things.

Teague. Be me shoul, maishter, I did carry the portmantle till it tired me ; and now the portmantle shall
carry me till I tire him.

Herm. Would. And how d'ye like London, Teague,
after our travels?

Teague. Fet, dear joy, 'tis the bravest plaase I have
sheen in my peregrinations, exshepting my nown brave
shitty of Carick-Vergus.—Uf, uf, dere ish a very fragrant
shmell hereabouts.—Maishter, shall I run to that
paishtry-cook's for shix pennyworths of boiled beef?

Herm. Would. Though this fellow travelled the world
over, he would never lose his brogue nor his stomach.—
Why, you cormorant, so hungry and so early!

Teague. Early! Deel tauke me, maishter, 'tish a great
deal more than almost twelve a-clock.

Herm. Would. Thou art never happy unless thy guts
be stuffed up to thy eyes.

---

[1] "Teague" was the general nickname for Irishmen, until sup-
planted by "Paddy" late in the eighteenth century.   It occurs so
early as 1632 in Shirley's *Hyde Park*.   The famous "Teague" of
Sir Robert Howard's *Committee* (acted in 1663) was already in
possession of the stage when Farquhar wrote.   On "Teague" and
his "brogue" see a very interesting letter by Mr Albert Matthews
in the *Nation* (N. Y.), July 21, 1904.

Teague. O maishter, dere ish a dam way of distance, and the deel a bit between.

Enter BENJAMIN WOULDBE *in a chair, with four or five* Footmen *before him, and passes over the stage.*

Herm. Would. Heyday, who comes here? with one, two, three, four, five footmen! Some young fellow just tasting the sweet vanity of fortune.—Run, Teague, inquire who that is.

Teague. Yes, maishter.—[*Runs to one of the* Footmen.] Sir, will you give my humble shervish to your maishter, and tell him to send me word fat naam ish upon him.

Foot. You would know fat naam ish upon him?

Teague. Yesh, fet would I.

Foot. Why, what are you, sir?

Teague. Be me shoul, I am a shentleman bred and born, and dere ish my maishter.

Foot. Then your master would know it?

Teague. Arrah, you fool, ish it not the saam ting?

Foot. Then tell your master 'tis the young lord Wouldbe, just come to his estate by the death of his father and elder brother.   [*Exit.*

Herm. Would. What do I hear?

Teague. You hear that you are dead, maishter; fere vil you please to be buried?

Herm. Would. But art thou sure it was my brother?

Teague. Be me shoul, it was him nown self; I know'd him fery well, after his man told me.

Herm. Would. The business requires that I be convinced with my own eyes; I'll follow him, and know the bottom on't. Stay here till I return.

Teague. Dear maishter, have a care upon yourshelf: now they know you are dead, by my shoul, they may kill you.

Herm. Would. Don't fear; none of his servants know me, and I'll take care to keep my face from his sight. It concerns me to conceal myself, till I know the

engines of this contrivance.—Be sure you stay till I come
to you; and let nobody know whom you belong to.

[*Exit.*

Teague. Oh, oh, hon, poor Teague is left all alone!

[*Sits on the portmantle.*

Enter SUBTLEMAN *and* CLEARACCOUNT.

Sub. And you won't swear to the will?

Clear. My conscience tells me I dare not do't with
safety.

Sub. But if we make it lawful, what should you fear?
We now think nothing against conscience, till the cause
be thrown out of court.

Clear. In you, sir, 'tis no sin; because 'tis the
principle of your profession: but in me, sir, 'tis downright perjury indeed. You can't want witnesses enough,
since money won't be wanting. And you must lose no
time; for I heard just now that the true lord Wouldbe
was seen in town, or his ghost.

Sub. It was his ghost, to be sure; for a nobleman
without an estate is but the shadow of a lord. Well,
take no care; leave me to myself; I'm near the Friars,[1]
and ten to one shall pick up an evidence.

Clear. Speed you well, sir!   [*Exit.*

Sub. There's a fellow that has hunger and the
gallows pictured in his face, and looks like my countryman.—How now, honest friend, what have you got
under you there?

Teague. Noting, dear joy.

Sub. Nothing? Is it not a portmantle?

Teague. That is noting to you.

Sub. The fellow's a wit.

Teague. Fet am I; my grandfader was an Irish poet.
He did write a great book of verses concerning the vars
between St Patrick and the wolf-dogs.

Sub. Then thou art poor, I'm afraid?

[1] Whitefriars or Alsatia.

Teague. Be me shoul, my fole ¹ generation ish so.   I have noting but thish poor portmantle, and dat itshelf is not my own.

Sub. Why, who does it belong to ?

Teague. To my maishter, dear joy.

Sub. Then you have a master ?

Teague. Fet have I, but he's dead.

Sub. Right !—And how do you intend to live ?

Teague. By eating, dear joy, fen I can get it, and by sleeping fen I can get none : 'tish the fashion of Ireland.

Sub. What was your master's name, pray ?

Teague. [*Aside.*] I will tell a lee now ; but it shall be a true one.—[*Aloud.*] Macfadin, dear joy, was his naam. He vent over vith King Jamish into France.—[*Aside.*] He was my master once.   Deere ish de true lee noo.

Sub. What employment had he ?

Teague. *Je ne sçay pas.*

Sub. What, can you speak French ?

Teague. *Oui, monsieur.* — I did travel France, and Spain, and Italy.   Dear joy, I did kish the Pope's toe, and dat will excuse me all the sins of my life ; and fen I am dead, St Patrick will excuse the rest.

Sub. [*Aside.*] A rare fellow for my purpose !—[*Aloud.*] Thou look'st like an honest fellow ; and if you'll go with me to the next tavern, I'll give thee a dinner, and a glass of wine.

Teague. Be me shoul, 'tis dat I wanted, dear joy, come along, I will follow you.

[*Runs out before* SUBTLEMAN *with the portmantle on his back.*

Re-enter HERMES WOULDBE.

Herm. Would. My father dead ! my birthright lost ; How have my drowsy stars slept o'er my fortune ?—Ha ! [*Looking about*] my servant gone !   The simple, poor,

---

¹ So in Q. 1, evidently meaning " whole."   *Cf.* below " fen " for " when."   Later editions read " sole "—quite meaninglessly.

ungrateful wretch has left me. I took him up from
poverty and want; and now he leaves me just as I found
him. My clothes and money too!—But why should I
repine? Let man but view the dangers he has passed,
and few will fear what hazards are to come. That
Providence that has secured my life from robbers,
shipwreck, and from sickness, is still the same; still
kind whilst I am just.[1]—My death, I find, is firmly
believed; but how it gained so universal credit I fain
would learn.—Who comes here?—honest Mr Fairbank!
my father's goldsmith, a man of substance and integrity.
The alteration of five years' absence, with the report of
my death, may shade me from his knowledge, till I
inquire some news.

Enter FAIRBANK.

Sir, your humble servant!

Fair. Sir, I don't know you.   [*Shunning him.*

Herm. Would. I intend you no harm, sir; but seeing
you come from my lord Wouldbe's house, I would ask
you a question or two.—Pray what distemper did my
lord die of?

Fair. I am told it was an apoplexy.

Herm. Would. And pray, sir, what does the world
say? Is his death lamented?

Fair. Lamented! my eyes that question should
resolve. Friend, thou knewest him not: else thy own
heart had answered thee.

Herm. Would. [*Aside.*] His grief, methinks, chides
my defect of filial duty.—[*Aloud.*] But, I hope, sir, his
loss is partly recompensed in the merits of his successor.

Fair. It might have been; but his eldest son, heir to
his virtue and his honour, was lately and unfortunately
killed in Germany.

Herm. Would. How unfortunately, sir?

[1] Down to this point the speech is evidently intended to be in
blank verse, as Farquhar understood it.

Fair. Unfortunately for him and us. I do remember him. He was the mildest, humblest, sweetest youth—

Herm. Would. [*Aside.*] Happy indeed had been my part in life if I had left this human stage whilst this so spotless and so fair applause had crowned my going off. —[*Aloud.*] Well, sir.

Fair. But those that saw him in his travels, told such wonders of his improvement, that the report recalled his father's years ; and with the joy to hear his Hermes praised, he oft would break the chains of gout and age, and leaping up with strength of greenest youth, cry, *My Hermes is myself : methinks I live my sprightly days again, and I am young in him.*

Herm. Would. [*Aside.*] Spite of all modesty, a man must own a pleasure in the hearing of his praise.

Fair. You're thoughtful, sir—had you any relation to the family we talk of ?

Herm. Would. None, sir, beyond my private concern in the public loss. But pray, sir, what character does the present lord bear ?

Fair. Your pardon, sir. As for the dead, their memories are left unguarded, and tongues may touch them freely : but for the living, they have provided for the safety of their names by a strong inclosure of the law. There is a thing called *scandalum magnatum*, sir.

Herm. Would. I commend your caution, sir ; but be assured I intend not to entrap you. I am a poor gentleman ; and having heard much of the charity of the old Lord Wouldbe, I had a mind to apply to his son : and therefore enquired his character.

Fair. Alas ! sir, things are changed. That house was once what poverty might go a pilgrimage to seek, and have its pains rewarded. The noble lord, the truly noble lord, held his estate, his honour, and his house, as if they were only lent upon the interest of doing good to others. He kept a porter, not to exclude, but serve the poor. No creditor was seen to guard his going out, or watch his coming in : no craving eyes, but looks of smiling gratitude.—But now, that family, which, like a garden fairly kept, invited every stranger to its fruit and shade, is now run o'er with weeds. Nothing but wine and revelling within, a crowd of noisy creditors without, a train of servants insolently proud. Would you believe it, sir, as I offered to go in just now, the rude porter pushed me back with his staff. I am at this present (thanks to Providence and my industry) worth twenty thousand pounds. I pay the fifth part of this to maintain the liberty of the nation ; and yet this slave, the impudent Swiss slave, offered to strike me !

Herm. Would. 'Twas hard, sir, very hard : and if they used a man of your substance so roughly, how will they manage me, that am not worth a groat ?

Fair. I would not willingly defraud your hopes of what may happen. If you can drink and swear, perhaps—

Herm. Would. I shall not pay that price for his lordship's bounty, would it extend to half he's worth. Sir, I give you thanks for your caution, and shall steer another course.

Fair. Sir, you look like an honest, modest gentleman. Come home with me ; I am as able to give you a dinner as my lord ; and you shall be very welcome to eat at my table every day, till you are better provided.

Herm. Would. [*Aside.*] Good man !—[*Aloud.*] Sir, I must beg you to excuse me to-day : but I shall find a time to accept of your favours, or at least to thank you for 'em.

Fair. Sir, you shall be very welcome whenever you please.   [*Exit.*

Herm. Would. Gramercy, citizen ! Surely, if Justice were an herald, she would give this tradesman a nobler coat of arms than my brother.—But 1 delay : I long to vindicate the honour of my station, and to displace this bold usurper.—But one concern methinks is nearer still : my Constance ! Should she, upon the rumour of my

death, have fixed her heart elsewhere,—then I were dead
indeed. But if she still proves true,—brother, sit fast—
I'll shake your strength, all obstacles remove,
Sustain'd by justice, and inspired by love.

[*Exit.*

SCENE III.—*An Apartment.*

CONSTANCE, AURELIA.

Con. For Heaven's sake, cousin, cease your impertinent consolation! It but makes me angry, and raises
two passions in me instead of one. You see I commit
no extravagance, my grief is silent enough : my tears
make no noise to disturb anybody. I desire no companion in my sorrows : leave me to myself and you comfort me.

Aur. But, cousin, have you no regard to your
reputation ?—This immoderate concern for a young
fellow—what will the world say ? You lament him like
a husband.

Con. No, you mistake : I have no rule nor method for
my grief; no pomp of black and darkened rooms ; no
formal month for visits on my bed. I am content with
the slight mourning of a broken heart ; and all my form
is tears. [*Weeps.*

Enter Mrs MANDRAKE.

Mrs Man. Madam Aurelia, madam, don't disturb her.
Everything must have its vent. 'Tis a hard case to be
crossed in one's first love. But you should consider,
madam, [*To* CONSTANCE] that we are all born to die ;
some young, some old.

Con. Better we all died young, than be plagued with
age as I am. I find other folks' years are as troublesome to us as our own.

Mrs Man. You have reason, you have cause to
mourn : he was the handsomest man, and the sweetest
babe, that I know. Though I must confess too, that
Ben had much the finer complexion when he was
born. But then Hermes—O yes, Hermes had the
shape, that he had ! But of all the infants that I ever
beheld with my eyes, I think Ben had the finest ear !
—waxwork, perfect waxwork ! And then he did so
sputter at the breast ! His nurse was a hale, well-
complexioned, sprightly jade as ever I saw ; but her
milk was a little too stale, though, at the same time,
'twas as blue and clear as a cambric.

Aur. Do you intend all this, madam, for a consolation to my cousin ?

Mrs Man. No, no, madam, that's to come.—I tell
you, fair lady, you have only lost the man ; the estate
and title are still your own ; and this very moment I
would salute you Lady Wouldbe, if you pleased.

Con. Dear madam, your proposal is very tempting ;
let me but consider till to-morrow, and I'll give you an
answer.

Mrs Man. I knew it, I knew it ! I said, when you
were born, you would be a lady; I knew it ! To-
morrow, you say ?—My lord shall know it immediately.   [*Exit.*

Aur. What d'ye intend to do, cousin ?

Con. To go into the country this moment, to be
free from the impertinence of condolence, the persecution of that monster of a man, and that devil of a
woman. O Aurelia, I long to be alone ! I am become
so fond of grief, that I would fly where I might enjoy it
all, and have no interruption in my darling sorrow.

Enter HERMES WOULDBE *unperceived.*

Herm. Would. In tears ! perhaps for me ! I'll try.
        [*Drops a miniature, and goes back to
                the entrance, and listens.*

Aur. If there be aught in grief delightful, don't grudge me a share.

Con. No, my dear Aurelia, I'll engross it all. I loved him so, methinks I should be jealous if any mourned his death besides myself. What's here!—[*Takes up the miniature.*] Ha! see, cousin—the very face and features of the man! Sure, some officious angel has brought me this for a companion in my solitude! Now I'm fitted out for sorrow! With this I'll sigh, with this converse, gaze on his image till I grow blind with weeping!

Aur. I'm amazed! how came it here?

Con. Whether by miracle or human chance, 'tis all alike; I have it here: nor shall it ever separate from my breast. It is the only thing could give me joy, because it will increase my grief.

Herm. Would. [*Coming forward.*] Most glorious woman! now I am fond of life.

Aur. Ha! what's this!—Your business, pray, sir?

Herm. Would. With this lady.—[*Goes to* CONSTANCE, *takes her hand, and kneels.*] Here let me worship that perfection whose virtue might attract the listening angels, and make 'em smile to see such purity, so like themselves in human shape!

Con. Hermes!

Herm. Would. Your living Hermes, who shall die yours too!

Con. [*Aside.*] Now passion, powerful passion, would bear me like a whirlwind to his arms!—But my sex has bounds.—[*Aloud.*] 'Tis wondrous, sir!

Herm. Would. Most wondrous are the works of fate for man; and most closely laid is the serpentine line that guides him into happiness! That hidden power which did permit those arts to cheat me of my birthright, had this surprise of happiness in store, well knowing that grief is the best preparative for joy.

Con. I never found the true sweets of love till this

romantic turn.—Dead, and alive!—my stars are poetical! For Heaven's sake, sir, unriddle your fortune!

Herm. Would. That my dear brother must do ; for he made the enigma.

Aur. Methinks I stand here like a fool all this while! Would I had somebody or other to say a fine thing or two to me!

Herm. Would. Madam, I beg ten thousand pardons! I have my excuse in my hand.

Aur. My lord, I wish you joy!

Herm. Would. Pray, madam, don't trouble me with a title till I am better equipped for it. My peerage would look a little shabby in these robes.

Con. You have a good excuse, my lord : you can wear better when you please.

Herm. Would. I have a better excuse, madam : these are the best I have.

Con. How, my lord?

Herm. Would. Very true, madam ; I am at present, I believe, the poorest peer in England. Heark'ee, Aurelia, prithee lend me a piece or two.

Aur. Ha, ha, ha! poor peer indeed! he wants a guinea.

Con. I'm glad on't, with all my heart!

Herm. Would. Why so, madam?

Con. Because I can furnish you with five thousand.

Herm. Would. Generous woman!

Enter TRUEMAN.

Ha, my friend too!

True. I'm glad to find you here, my lord. Here's a current report about town that you were killed. I was afraid it might reach this family ; so I came to disprove the story by your letter to me by the last post.

Aur. [*Aside.*] I'm glad he's come ; now it will be my turn, cousin.

True. Now, my lord, I wish you joy; and I expect the same from you.

Herm. Would. With all my heart; but upon what score?

True. The old score—marriage.

Herm. Would. To whom?

True. To a neighbour lady here.

[*Looking at* AURELIA.

Aur. [*Aside.*] Impudence!—[*Aloud.*] The lady mayn't be so near as you imagine, sir.

True. The lady mayn't be so near as you imagine, madam.

Aur. Don't mistake me, sir; I did not care if the lady were in Mexico.

True. Nor I neither, madam.

Aur. You're very short, sir!

True. The shortest pleasures are the sweetest, you know.

Aur. Sir, you appear very different to me from what you were lately.

True. Madam, you appear very indifferent to me, to what you were lately.

Aur. Strange!

[*This while* CONSTANCE *and* WOULDBE *entertain one another in dumb-show.*

True. Miraculous!

Aur. I could never have believed it.

True. Nor I, as I hope to be saved!

Aur. Ill manners!

True. Worse.

Aur. How have I deserved it, sir?

True. How have I deserved it, madam?

Aur. What?

True. You.

Aur. Riddles!

True. Women!—My lord, you'll hear of me at White's.—Farewell!   [*Runs off.*

Herm. Would. What, Trueman gone?

Aur. Yes.   [*Walks about in disorder.*

Con. Bless me! what's the matter, cousin?

Aur. Nothing.

Con. Why are you uneasy?

Aur. Nothing.

Con. What ails you then?

Aur. Nothing.—I don't love the fellow!—yet, to be affronted—I can't bear it!

[*Bursts out a-crying, and runs off.*

Con. Your friend, my lord, has affronted Aurelia.

Herm. Would. Impossible! his regard to me were sufficient security for his good behaviour here, though it were in his nature to be rude elsewhere. She has certainly used him ill

Con. Too well rather.

Herm. Would. Too well? Have a care, madam! That, with some men, is the greatest provocation to a slight.

Con. Don't mistake, my lord; her usage never went further than mine to you; and I should take it very ill to be abused for it.

Herm. Would. I'll follow him, and know the cause of it.

Con. No, my lord, we'll follow her, and know it. Besides, your own affairs with your brother require you at present.   [*Exeunt.*

ACT IV

SCENE I.—Lord Wouldbe's *House.*

Benjamin Wouldbe *and* Subtleman.

EN. WOULD. Returned! who saw him? who spoke with him?—He can't be returned.

Sub. My lord, he's below at the gate parleying with the porter, who has private orders from me to admit nobody till you send him word, that we may have the more time to settle our affairs.

Ben. Would. 'Tis a hard case, Mr Subtleman, that a man can't enjoy his right without all this trouble.

Sub. Ay, my lord, you see the benefit of law now, what an advantage it is to the public for securing of property! Had you not the law o' your side, who knows what devices might be practised to defraud you of your right!—But I have secured all.—The will is in true form ; and you have two witnesses already to swear to the last words of your father.

Ben. Would. Then you have got another?

Sub. Yes, yes, a right one; and I shall pick up another time enough before the term : and I have planted three or four constables in the next room to take care of your brother if he should be boisterous.

Ben. Would. Then you think we are secure?

Sub. Ay, ay; let him come now when he pleases. I'll go down, and give orders for his admittance.

[*Exit.*

Ben. Would. Unkind brother! to disturb me thus, just in the swing and stretch of my full fortune! Where is the tie of blood and nature when brothers will do this? Had he but staid till Constance had been mine, his presence or his absence had been then indifferent.

Enter Mrs MANDRAKE.

Mrs Man. Well, my lord,—[*Pants as out of breath*] you'll ne'er be satisfied till you have broken my poor heart. I have had such ado yonder about you with Madam Constance!—But she's your own.

Ben. Would. How! my own! Ah, my dear help-mate, I'm afraid we are routed in that quarter: my brother's come home.

Mrs Man. Your brother come home! then I'll go travel. [*Going.*

Ben. Would. Hold, hold, madam, we are all secure; we have provided for his reception; your nephew Subtleman has stopped up all passages to the estate.

Mrs Man. Ay, Subtleman is a pretty, thriving, ingenious boy. Little do you think who is the father of him! I'll tell you:—Mr Moabite, the rich Jew in Lombard Street.

Ben. Would. Moabite the Jew!

Mrs Man. You shall hear, my lord. One evening, as I was very grave in my own house, reading the— *Weekly Preparation*—ay, it was the *Weekly Preparation*, I do remember particularly well—what hears me I—but pat, pat, pat, very softly at the door. Come in, cries I; and presently enters Mr Moabite, followed by a snug chair, the windows close drawn, and in it a fine young virgin just upon the point of being delivered. We were all in a great hurly-burly for a

while, to be sure; but our production was a fine boy.
I had fifty guineas for my trouble, the lady was wrapped
up very warm, placed in her chair, and reconveyed to
the place she came from. Who she was, or what she
was, I could never learn, though my maid said that the
chair went through the Park—but the child was left
with me. The father would have made a Jew on't
presently, but I swore, if he committed such a barbarity
on the infant, that I would discover all. So I had him
brought up a good Christian, and bound 'prentice to an
attorney.

Ben Would. Very well!

Mrs Man. Ah, my lord! there's many a pretty fellow
in London that knows as little of their true father and
mother as he does. I have had several such jobs in my
time;—there was one Scotch nobleman that brought me
four in half a year.

Ben. Would. Four! and how were they all provided
for?

Mrs Man. Very handsomely indeed; they were two
sons and two daughters; the eldest son rides in the first
troop of guards, and the t'other is a very pretty fellow,
and his father's valet-de-chambre.

Ben. Would. And what is become of the daughters,
pray?

Mrs Man. Why, one of 'em is a manteau-maker, and
the youngest has got into the playhouse.—Ay, ay, my
lord, let Subtleman alone, I'll warrant he'll manage your
brother.—Ads my life, here's somebody coming! I would
not be seen.

Ben. Would. 'Tis my brother, and he'll meet you upon
the stairs; 'adso, get into this closet till he be gone.

[*Shuts her into the closet.*

Re-enter SUBTLEMAN *with* HERMES WOULDBE.

My brother! dearest brother, welcome!

[*Runs and embraces him.*

Herm. Would. I can't dissemble, sir, else I would return your false embrace.

Ben. Would. False embrace! still suspicious of me! I thought that five years' absence might have cooled the unmanly heats of our childish days. That I am overjoyed at your return, let this testify: this moment I resign all right and title to your honour, and salute you, lord.

Herm. Would. I want not your permission to enjoy my right; here I am lord and master without your resignation: and the first use I make of my authority is to discard that rude, bull-faced fellow at the door.—Where's my steward?

Enter CLEARACCOUNT.

Mr Clearaccount, let that pampered sentinel below this minute be discharged.—Brother, I wonder you could feed such a swarm of lazy, idle drones about you, and leave the poor industrious bees, that fed you from their hives, to starve for want.—Steward, look to't; if I have not discharges for every farthing of my father's debts upon my toilet to-morrow morning, you shall follow the tipstaff, I can assure you.

Ben. Would. Hold, hold, my lord, you usurp too large a power, methinks, o'er my family.

Herm. Would. Your family!

Ben. Would. Yes, my family: you have no title to lord it here.—Mr Clearaccount, you know your master.

Herm. Would. How! a combination against me!— Brother, take heed how you deal with one that, cautious of your falsehood, comes prepared to meet your arts, and can retort your cunning to your infamy. Your black, unnatural designs against my life, before I went abroad, my charity can pardon: but my prudence must remember to guard me from your malice for the future.

Ben. Would. Our father's weak and fond surmise! which he upon his death-bed owned: and to recompense me for that injurious, unnatural suspicion, he left me sole heir to his estate.   Now, my lord, my house and servants are—at your service.

Herm. Would. Villainy beyond example! Have I not letters from my father, of scarce a fortnight's date, where he repeats his fears for my return, lest it should again expose me to your hatred?

Sub. Well, well, these are no proofs, no proofs, my lord; they won't pass in court against positive evidence. Here is your father's will, *signatum et sigillatum*, besides his last words to confirm it, to which I can take my positive oath in any court of Westminster.

Herm. Would. What are you, sir?

Sub. Of Clifford's Inn, my lord; I belong to the law.

Herm. Would. Thou art the worm and maggot of the law, bred in the bruised and rotten parts, and now art nourished on the same corruption that produced thee. The English law, as planted first, was like the English oak, shooting its spreading arms around, to shelter all that dwelt beneath its shade: but now whole swarms of caterpillars, like you, hang in such clusters upon every branch, that the once thriving tree now sheds infectious vermin on our heads.

Ben. Would. My lord, I have some company above; if your lordship will drink a glass of wine, we shall be proud of the honour; if not, I shall attend you at any court of judicature, whenever you please to summon me.   [*Going.*

Herm. Would. Hold, sir!—[*Aside.*] Perhaps my father's dying weakness was imposed on, and he has left him heir; if so, his will shall freely be obeyed.—[*Aloud.*] Brother, you say you have a will?

Sub. Here it is.   [*Showing a parchment.*

Herm. Would. Let me see it.

Sub. There's no precedent for that, my lord.

Herm. Would. Upon my honour, I'll restore it.

Ben. Would. Upon my honour, but you sh'an't.

[*Takes it from* SUBTLEMAN *and puts it in his pocket.*

Herm. Would. This over-caution, brother, is suspicious.

Ben. Would. Seven thousand pound a year is worth looking after.

Herm. Would. Therefore you can't take it ill, that I am a little inquisitive about it.—Have you witnesses to prove my father's dying words?

Ben. Would. A couple, in the house.

Herm. Would. Who are they?

Sub. Witnesses, my lord! 'Tis unwarrantable to inquire into the merits of the cause out of court. My client shall answer no more questions.

Herm. Would. Perhaps, sir, upon a satisfactory account of his title, I intend to leave your client to the quiet enjoyment of his right, without troubling any court with the business; I therefore desire to know what kind of persons are these witnesses.

Sub. [*Aside.*] Oho, he's a-coming about!—[*Aloud.*] I told your lordship already that I am one; another is in the house, one of my lord's footmen.

Herm. Would. Where is this footman?

Ben. Would. Forthcoming.

Herm. Would. Produce him.

Sub. That I shall presently.—[*Aside to* BENJAMIN WOULDBE.] The day's our own, sir—[*To* HERMES WOULDBE.] But you shall engage first to ask him no cross questions.

Herm. Would. I am not skilled in such.—[*Exit.* SUBTLEMAN.] But pray, brother, did my father quite forget me? left me nothing!

Ben. Would. Truly, my lord, nothing. He spoke but little; left no legacies.

Herm. Would. 'Tis strange! he was extremely just, and loved me too;—but perhaps—

Re-enter SUBTLEMAN *with* TEAGUE.

Sub. My lord, here's another evidence.
Herm. Would. Teague!
Ben. Would. My brother's servant!
　　　　　[*They all four stare upon one another.*
Sub. His servant!
Teague. Maishter! see here, maishter, I did get all dish—[*Chinks money*] for being an evidensh, dear joy! and be me shoul, I will give the half of it to you, if you will give me your permission to maake swear against you.
Herm. Would. My wonder is divided between the villainy of the fact, and the amazement of the discovery! Teague! my very servant! sure I dream.
Teague. Fet, dere ish no dreaming in the cashe; I'm sure the croon pieceish are awake, for I have been taaking with dem dish half hour.
Ben. Would. [*Aside to* SUBTLEMAN.] Ignorant, unlucky man, thou hast ruined me! why had not I a sight of him before?
Sub. I thought the fellow had been too ignorant to be a knave.
Teague. Be me shoul, you lee, dear joy. I can be a knave as well as you, fen I think it conveniency.
Herm. Would. Now, brother!—Speechless!—Your oracle too silenced!—Is all your boasted fortune sunk to the guilty blushing for a crime?—But I scorn to insult: let disappointment be your punishment.—But for your lawyer there—Teague, lay hold of him.
Sub. Let none dare to attach me without a legal warrant.
Teague. Attach! no, dear joy, I cannot attach you—but I can catch you by the troat, after the fashion of Ireland.　　　[*Takes* SUBTLEMAN *by the throat.*
Sub. An assault! an assault!
Teague. No, no, 'tish nothing but choking, nothing but choking.

Herm. Would. Hold him fast, Teague.—[*To* BEN-JAMIN WOULDBE.] Now, sir, because I was your brother, you would have betrayed me; and because I am your brother I forgive it.—Dispose yourself as you think fit—I'll order Mr Clearaccount to give you a thousand pounds. Go take it, and pay me by your absence.

Ben. Would. I scorn your beggarly benevolence! Had my designs succeeded, I would not have allowed you the weight of a wafer, and therefore will accept none.—As for that lawyer, he deserves to be pilloried, not for his cunning in deceiving you, but for his ignorance in betraying me. The villain has defrauded me of seven thousand pounds a year. Farewell—

[*Going.*

Re-enter Mrs MANDRAKE *out of the closet, runs to* BENJAMIN WOULDBE *and kneels.*

Mrs Man. My lord! my dear Lord Wouldbe, I beg you ten thousand pardons!

Ben. Would. What offence hast thou done to me?

Mrs Man. An offence the most injurious. I have hitherto concealed a secret in my breast, to the offence of justice, and the defrauding your lordship of your true right and title. You, Benjamin Wouldbe, with the crooked back, are the eldest-born, and true heir to the estate and dignity.

All. How!

Teague. Arah, how?

Mrs Man. None, my lord, can tell better than I, who brought you both into the world. My deceased lord, upon the sight of your deformity, engaged me by a considerable reward, to say you were the last born, that the beautiful twin, likely to be the greater ornament to the family, might succeed him in his honour. This secret my conscience has long struggled with. Upon the news that you were left heir to the estate, I thought justice was satisfied, and I was resolved to keep it a secret still; but by strange chance overhearing what passed just now, my poor conscience was racked, and I was forced to declare the truth.

Ben. Would. By all my forward hopes, I could have sworn it! I found the spirit of eldership in my blood; my pulses beat, and swelled for seniority.—Mr Hermes Wouldbe,—I'm your most humble servant. [*Foppishly.*

Herm. Would. Hermes is my name, my Christian name; of which I am prouder than of all titles that honour gives, or flattery bestows. But thou, vain bubble, puffed up with the empty breath of that more empty woman; to let thee see how I despise thy pride, I'll call thee lord, dress thee up in titles like a King at Arms; you shall be blazoned round, like any church in Holland; thy pageantry shall exceed the lord mayor's; and yet this Hermes, plain Hermes, shall despise thee.

Sub. Well, well, this is nothing to the purpose.— Mistress, will you make an affidavit of what you have said, before a Master in Chancery?

Mrs Man. That I can, though I were to die the next minute after it.

Teague. Den, dear joy, you would be dam the next minute after dat.

Herm. Would. All this is trifling: I must purge my house of this nest of villany at once.—Here, Teague! —[*Whispers* TEAGUE.] Go, make haste!

Teague. Dat I can.

  [*As he runs out,* BENJAMIN WOULDBE *stops him.*

Ben. Would. Where are you going, sir?

Teague. Only for a pot of ale, dear joy, for you and my maishter, to drink friends.

Ben. Would. You lie, sirrah!   [*Pushes him back.*

Teague. Fet, I do so.

Herm. Would. What! violence to my servant! Nay, then, I'll force him a passage.   [*Draws.*

Sub. An assault! an assault upon the body of a peer!
—Within there!

Enter three or four Constables, *one of them with a
black patch on his eye. They disarm* HERMES
WOULDBE, *and secure* TEAGUE.

Herm. Would. This plot was laid for my reception.—
Unhand me, constable!

Ben. Would. Have a care, Mr Constable, the man is
mad; he's possessed with an odd frenzy, that he's my
brother, and my elder too: so, because I would not
very willingly resign my house and estate, he attempted
to murder me.

Sub. Gentlemen, take care of that fellow: he made
an assault upon my body, *vi et armis.*

Teague. Arah, fat is dat *wy at armish?*

Sub. No matter, sirrah; I shall have you hanged.

Teague. Hanged! dat is nothing, dear joy:—we are
used to't.

Herm. Would. Unhand me, villains! or by all—

Teague. Have a caar, dear maishter, don't swear; we
shall be had in the Croon-Offish.—You know dere ish
sharpers about us.

                    [*Looking about on them that hold him.*
Ben. Would. Mr Constable, you know your directions; away with 'em!

Herm. Would. Hold!—

Constab. No, no; force him away.

            [*They all hurry off except* BENJAMIN WOULDBE
                and Mrs MANDRAKE.

Ben. Would. Now, my dear prophetess, my sibyl, by
all my dear desires and ambitions, I do believe you have
spoken the truth!—I am the elder.

Mrs Man. No, no, sir, the devil a word on't is true.
I would not wrong my consience neither; for, faith and
troth, as I am an honest woman, you were born above
three-quarters of an hour after him;—but I don't much

care if I do swear that you are the eldest.—What a blessing it was that I was in the closet at that pinch! Had I
not come out that moment, you would have sneaked off;
your brother had been in possession, and then we had
lost all. But now you are established: possession gets
you money, that gets you law, and law, you know—
Down on your knees, sirrah, and ask me blessing.

Ben. Would. No, my dear mother, I'll give thee a blessing, a rent-charge of five hundred pound a year, upon
what part of the estate you will, during your life.

Mrs Man. Thank you, my lord: that five hundred a
year will afford me a leisurely life, and a handsome re-
tirement in the country, where I mean to repent me of
my sins, and die a good Christian: for, Heaven knows,
I am old, and ought to bethink me of another life.—
Have you none of the cordial left that we had in the
morning?

Ben. Would. Yes, yes, we'll go to the fountain-head.

[*Exeunt.*

SCENE II.—*The Street.*

Enter TEAGUE.

Teague. Deel tauke me but dish ish a most shweet
business indeed! Maishters play the fool, and shervants
must shuffer for it. I am prishoner in the constable's
house, be me shoul, and shent abrode to fetch some
bail for my maishter; but foo shall bail poor Teague
agra?

Enter CONSTANCE.

Oh dere ish my maishter's old love. Indeed, I fear
dish bishness will spoil his fortune.

Con. Who's here? Teague!   [*He turns from her.*

Teague. [*Aside.*] Deel tauke her, I did tought she could not know me again.—[CONSTANCE *goes about to look him in the face. He turns from her.*] Dish ish not shivil, be me shoul, to know a shentleman fither he will or no.

Con. Why this, Teague? what's the matter? are you ashamed of me, or yourself, Teague?

Teague. Of bote, be my shoul.

Con. How does your master, sir?

Teague. Very well, dear joy, and in prishon.

Con. In prison! how? where?

Teague. Why, in the little Bashtile yonder, at the end of the street.

Con. Show me the way immediately.

Teague. Fet, I can show you the hoose yonder : shee yonder ; be me shoul, I she his faace yonder, peeping troo the iron glash window!

Con. I'll see him, though a dungeon were his confine-ment.   [*Runs out.*

Teague. Ah! auld kindnesh, be me shoul, cannot be forgotten. Now, if my maishter had but grash enough to get her wit child, her word would go for two ; and she would bail him and I bote.   [*Exit.*

SCENE III.—*A Room miserably furnished* [*in a Spunging-House*].

HERMES WOULDBE *sitting and writing.*

Herm. Would. The Tower confines the great,
        The spunging-house the poor ;.
Thus there are degrees of state
        That ev'n the wretched must endure.

Virgil, though cherish'd in courts,
        Relates but a splenetic tale :

> Cervantes revels and sports,
>   Although he writ in a jail.

Then hang reflections!—[*Starts up.*] I'll go write a comedy.—Ho, within there! Tell the Lieutenant of the Tower that I would speak with him.

Enter Constable.

Constab. Ay, ay, the man is mad. Lieutenant o' th' Tower! ha, ha, ha!—Would you could make your words good, master.

Herm. Would. Why, am not I a prisoner there? I know it by the stately apartments. What is that, pray, that hangs streaming down upon the wall yonder?

Cnstab. Yonder! 'tis cobweb, sir.

Herm. Would. 'Tis false, sir! 'tis as fine tapestry as any in Europe.

Constab. The devil it is!

Herm. Would. Then your damask bed, here; the flowers are so bold, I took 'em for embroidery. And then the headwork! *Point de Venise*, I protest.

Constab. As good Kidderminster as any in England, I must confess; and though the sheets be a little soiled, yet I can assure you, sir, that many an honest gentleman has lain in them.

Herm. Would. Pray, sir, what did those two Indian pieces cost, that are fixed up in the corner of the room?

Constab. Indian pieces! What the devil, sir, they are my old jack boots, my militia boots!

Herm. Would. I took 'em for two china jars, upon my word! But heark'ee, friend, art thou content that these things should be as they are?

Constab. Content! ay, sir.

Herm. Would. Why then should I complain?

Servant. [*Without.*] Mr Constable, here's a woman will force her way upon us: we can't stop her.

Constab. Knock her down then, knock her down; let no woman come up, the man's mad enough already.

Enter CONSTANCE.

Con. Who dares oppose me?
　　　　　[*Throws him a handful of money.*
Constab. Not I truly, madam.
　　　　　[*Gathers up the money.*
Herm. Would. My Constance! my guardian angel, here! Then naught can hurt me.

Constab. Heark'ee, sir, you may suppose the bed to be a damask bed for half an hour if you please—

Con. No, no, sir, your prisoner must along with me.

Constab. Ay? Faith, the woman's madder than the man.

Enter TRUEMAN *and* TEAGUE.

Herm. Would. Ha! Trueman too! I'm proud to think that many a prince has not so many true friends in his palace, as I have here in prison.—Two such—

Teague. Tree, be me shoul.

True. My lord, just as I heard of your confinement, I was going to make myself a prisoner. Behold the fetters! I had just bought the wedding ring.

Con. I hope they are golden fetters, Captain.

True. They weigh four thousand pound, madam, besides the purse, which is worth a million.—My lord, this very evening was I to be married; but the news of your misfortune has stopped me: I would not gather roses in a wet hour.

Herm. Would. Come, the weather shall be clear; the thoughts of your good fortune will make me easy, more than my own can do, if purchased by your disappointment.

True. Do you think, my lord, that I can go to the bed of pleasure whilst you lie in a hovel?—Here, where is this constable? How dare you do this, insolent rascal?

Constab. Insolent rascal! do you know who you speak to, sir?

True. Yes, sirrah, don't I call you by your proper name? How dare you confine a peer of the realm?

Constab. Peer of the realm! you may give good words though, I hope.

Herm. Would. Ay, ay, Mr Constable is in the right, he did but his duty; I suppose he had twenty guineas for his pains.

Constab. No, I had but ten.

Herm. Would. Heark'ee, Trueman, this fellow must be soothed, he'll be of use to us. I must employ you too in this affair with my brother.

True. Say no more, my lord, I'll cut his throat—'tis but flying the kingdom.

Herm. Would. No, no, 'twill be more revenge to worst him at his own weapons. Could I but force him out of his garrison, that I might get into possession, his claim would vanish immediately.—Does my brother know you?

True. Very little, if at all.

Herm. Would. Heark'ee.   [*Whispers.*

True. It shall be done.—Look'ee, constable, you're drawn into a wrong cause, and it may prove your destruction if you don't change sides immediately. We desire no favour, but the use of your coat, wig, and staff, for half an hour.

Constab. Why truly, sir, I understand now, by this gentlewoman that I know to be our neighbour, that he is a lord, and I heartily beg his worship's pardon, and if I can do your honour any service, your grace may command me.

Herm Would. I'll reward you.—But we must have the black patch for the eye too.

Teague. I can give your lordship wan; here fet, 'tis a

plaishter for a shore finger, and I have worn it but twice.

Con. But pray, Captain, what was your quarrel at Aurelia to-day?

True. With your permission, madam, we'll mind my lord's business at present; when that's done, we'll mind the lady's.—My lord, I shall make an excellent constable; I never had the honour of a civil employment before. We'll equip ourselves in another place.—Here, you Prince of Darkness, have you ne'er a better room in your house? These iron grates frighten the lady.

Constab. I have a handsome, neat parlour below, sir.

True. Come along then, you must conduct us.— [*Aside.*] We don't intend to be out of your sight, that you mayn't be out of ours.   [*Exeunt.*

SCENE IV.—*An Apartment.*

Enter AURELIA *in a passion*, RICHMORE *following.*

Aur. Follow me not! Age and deformity, with quiet, were preferable to this vexatious persecution. For Heaven's sake, Mr Richmore, what have I ever shown to vindicate this presumption of yours.

Rich. You show it now, madam; your face, your wit, your shape, are all temptations to undergo even the rigour of your disdain, for the bewitching pleasure of your company.

Aur. Then be assured, sir, you shall reap no other benefit by my company; and if you think it a pleasure to be constantly slighted, ridiculed, and affronted, you shall have admittance to such entertainment whenever you will.

Rich. I take you at your word, madam; I am armed with submission against all the attacks of your severity, and your ladyship shall find that my resignation can bear much longer than your rigour can inflict.

Aur. That is, in plain terms, your sufficiency will presume much longer than my honour can resist. Sir, you might have spared the unmannerly declaration to my face, having already taken care to let me know your opinion of my virtue, by your impudent settlement, proposed by Mrs Mandrake.

Rich. By those fair eyes, I'll double the proposal! This soft, this white, this powerful hand—[*Takes her hand*] shall write its own conditions.

Aur. Then it shall write this—[*Strikes him*] and if you like the terms, you shall have more another time.
                                                    [*Exit.*

Rich. Death and madness! a blow!—Twenty thousand pound sterling for one night's revenge upon her dear, proud, disdainful person!—Am I rich as many a sovereign prince, wallow in wealth, yet can't command my pleasure?—Woman!—If there be power in gold, I yet shall triumph o'er thy pride.

                Enter Mrs MANDRAKE.

Mrs Man. O' my troth, and so you shall, if I can help it.

Rich. Madam, madam, here, here, here's money, gold, silver! take, take, all, all, my rings too! All shall be yours, make me but happy in this presumptuous beauty; I'll make thee rich as avarice can crave; if not, I'll murder thee, and myself too.

Mrs Man. Your bounty is too large, too large indeed, sir.

Rich. Too large! no, 'tis beggary without her. Lordships, manors, acres, rents, tithes and trees, all, all shall fly for my dear sweet revenge!

Mrs Man. Say no more, this night I'll put you in a way.

Rich. This night !

Mrs Man. The lady's aunt is very near her time—she goes abroad this evening a-visiting; in the meantime I send to your mistress, that her aunt has fallen in labour at my house: she comes in a hurry, and then—

Rich. Shall I be there to meet her !

Mrs Man. Perhaps.

Rich. In a private room ?

Mrs Man. Mum.

Rich. No creature to disturb us ?

Mrs Man. Mum, I say ; but you must give me your word not to ravish her ; nay, I can tell you she won't be ravished.

Rich. Ravish !—Let me see, I'm worth five thousand pound a year, twenty thousand guineas in my pocket, and may not I force a toy that's scarce worth fifteen hundred pound ?   I'll do't.

> Her beauty sets my heart on fire ; beside
> The injurious blow has set on fire my pride ;
> The bare fruition were not worth my pain,
> The joy will be to humble her disdain ;
> Beyond enjoyment will the transport last
> In triumph when the ecstasy is past.   [*Exeunt.*

ACT V

SCENE I.—Lord WOULDBE's *House.*

BENJAMIN WOULDBE, *alone.*

 EN. WOULD. Show me that proud stoic that can bear success and champagne! Philosophy can support us in hard fortune, but who can have patience in prosperity? The learned may talk what they will of human bodies, but I am sure there is not one atom in mine but what is truly epicurean. My brother is secured, I guarded with my friends, my lewd and honest midnight friends—Holla, who waits there?

Enter Footman.

Foot. My lord?

Ben. Would. A fresh battalion of bottles to reinforce the cistern. Are the ladies come?

Foot. Half an hour ago, my lord; they're below in the bathing-chamber.

Ben. Would. Where did you light on 'em?

Foot. One in the passage at the old playhouse, my lord—I found another, very melancholy, paring her nails by Rosamond's Pond,[1]—and a couple I got at the Chequer ale-house in Holborn; the two last came to town yesterday in a west-country waggon.

Ben. Would. Very well, order Baconface to hasten supper; and—d'ye hear?—and bid the Swiss admit no stranger without acquainting me. —[*Exit* Footman.] Now, Fortune, I defy thee; this night's my own at least.

Re-enter Footman.

Foot. My lord, here's the constable below with the black eye, and he wants to speak with your lordship in all haste.

Ben. Would. Ha! the constable!—Should Fortune jilt me now?—Bid him come up.—[*Exit* Footman.]   I fear some cursed chance to thwart me.

Enter TRUEMAN, *in the* Constable's *clothes.*

True. Ah! my lord, here is sad news—your brother is—

Ben. Would. Got away, made his escape, I warrant you.

True. Worse, worse, my lord.

Ben. Would. Worse, worse!   What can be worse?

True. I dare not speak it.

Ben. Would. Death and hell, fellow, don't distract me!

True. He's dead.

Ben. Would. Dead!

True. Positively.

Ben. Would. *Coup de grace, ciel gramercy!*

True. [*Aside.*] Villain, I understand you.

---

[1] A sheet of water in the south-west corner of St James's Park, "long consecrated to disastrous love and elegiac poetry" (Warburton).   It was filled up in 1770.   For numerous allusions to it, in Southerne, Cibber, Congreve, Swift, Pope, etc., see Wheatley & Cunningham's *London Past and Present*, Vol. III., p. 168.

Ben. Would. But, how, how, Mr Constable? Speak it aloud, kill me with the relation.

True. I don't know how; the poor gentleman was very melancholy upon his confinement, and so he desired me to send for a gentlewoman that lives hard by here : mayhap your worship may know her.

Ben. Would. At the gilt balcony in the square?

True. The very same, a smart woman truly. I went for her myself, but she was otherwise engaged ; not she truly! she would not come. Would you believe it, my lord, at hearing of this the poor man was like to drop down dead.

Ben. Would. Then he was but likely to drop dead?

True. Would it were no more! Then I left him, and coming about two hours after, I found him hanged in his sword-belt.

Ben. Would. Hanged!

True. Dangling.

Ben. Would. Le coup d'éclat! done like the noblest Roman of 'em all!—But are you sure he's past all recovery? Did you send for no surgeon to bleed him?

True. No, my lord, I forgot that—but I'll send immediately.

Ben. Would. No, no, Mr Constable, 'tis too late now, too late.—And the lady would not come, you say?

True, Not a step would she stir.

Ben. Would. Inhuman, barbarous—dear, delicious woman, thou now art mine!—Where is the body, Mr Constable? I must see it.

True. By all means, my lord ; it lies in my parlour There's a power of company come in, and among the rest one—one—one Trueman, I think they call him ; a devilish hot fellow, he had like to have pulled the house down about our ears, and swears—— I told him he should pay for his swearing ; he gave me a slap in the face, said he was in the army, and had a commission for't.

Ben. Would. Captain Trueman ! a blustering kind of rakehelly officer.

True. Ay, my lord, one of those scoundrels that we pay wages to for being knocked o' th' head for us.

Ben. Would. Ay, ay, one of those fools that have only brains to be knocked out.

True. [*Aside.*] Son of a whore !—[*Aloud.*] He's a plaguy impudent fellow, my lord ; he swore that you were the greatest villain upon the earth.

Ben. Would. Ay, ay ; but he durst not say that to my face, Mr Constable.

True. No, no, hang him, he said it behind your back, to be sure.   And he swore, moreover,—have a care, my lord,—he swore that he would cut your throat whenever he met you.

Ben. Would. Will you swear that you heard him say so?

True. Heard him ! ay, as plainly as you hear me : he spoke the very words that I speak to your lordship.

Ben. Would. Well, well, I'll manage him.—But now I think on't, I won't go see the body; it will but increase my grief.   Mr Constable, do you send for the coroner : they must find him *non compos*.   He was mad before, you know.   Here—something for your trouble.   [*Gives money.*

True. Thank your honour.- -But pray, my lord, have a care of that Trueman ; he swears that he'll cut your throat, and he will do't it, my lord, he will do't.

Ben. Would. Never fear, never fear.

True. But he swore it, my lord, and he will certainly do't.   Pray have a care.   [*Exit.*

Ben. Would. Well, well,—so,—the devil's in't if I ben't the eldest now.   What a pack of civil relations have I had here !   My father takes a fit of the apoplexy, makes a face, and goes off one way ; my brother takes a fit of the spleen, makes a face, and goes off t'other way. —Well, I must own he has found the way to mollify me, and I do love him now with all my heart. Since he was so very civil to justle into the world before me, I think he did very civilly to justle out of it before me.— But now my joys!—Without there—hollo!—Take off the inquisition of the gate; the heir may now enter unsuspected.

The wolf is dead, the shepherds may go play:
Ease follows care; so rolls the world away.

'Tis a question whether adversity or prosperity makes the most poets.

Re-enter Footman.

Foot. My lord, a footman brought this letter, and waits for an answer.

Ben. Would. Nothing from the Elysian fields, I hope. —[*Opening the letter.*] What do I see, *CONSTANCE!* Spells and magic in every letter of the name!—Now for the sweet contents.

My Lord,
I'm pleased to hear of your happy change of fortune, and shall be glad to see your lordship this evening to wish you joy.

CONSTANCE.

Now the devil's in this Mandrake! she told me this afternoon that the wind was chopping about; and has it got into the warm corner already?—Here, my coach-and-six to the door: I'll visit my sultana in state. As for the seraglio below stairs, you, my bashaws, may possess 'em.

[*Exit,* Footman *following.*]

SCENE II.—*The Street* [*before* Mrs MANDRAKE'S *House*].

Enter TEAGUE *with a lantern*, TRUEMAN *in the* Constable's *habit, following.*

True. Blockhead, thou hast led us out of the way ; we have certainly passed the constable's house.

Teague. Be me shoul, dear joy, I am never out of my ways; for poor Teague has been a vanderer ever since he was borned.

True. Hold up the lantern —What sign is that? the St Alban's tavern ! [1]—Why, you blundering fool, you have led me directly to St. James's Square, when you should have gone towards Soho.—[*Shrieking within.*] Hark ! what noise is that over the way? A woman's cry !

Teague. Fet is it; shome daumsel in distress I believe, that has no mind to be relieved.

True. I'll use the privilege of my office to know what the matter is.

Teague. Hold, hold, maishter Captain, be me fet, dat ish not the way home.

Aur. [*Within.*] Help! help! murder! help!

True. Ha! here must be mischief.—Within there, open the door in the king's name, or I'll force it open. —Here, Teague, break down the door.

[TEAGUE *takes the staff, thumps at the door.*

Teague. Deel tauke him, I have knock so long as I am able. Arah, maishter, get a great long ladder to get in the window of the firsht room, and sho open the door, and let in yourshelf.

---

[1] This tavern, in St Alban's Street, Pall Mall, survived throughout the eighteenth century, and was "celebrated for political and fashionable dinners and meetings." Here, in 1812, the Roxburghe Club was founded, after the sale of the Duke of Roxburghe's library.

Aur. [*Within.*] Help! help! help!

True. Knock harder; let's raise the mob.

Teague. O maishter, I have tink just now of a brave invention to maake dem come out; and be St Patrick, dat very bushiness did maake my nown self and my fader run like de devil out of my nown hoose in my nown country :—be me shoul, set the hoose a-fire.

Enter Mob.

Mob. What's the matter, Master Constable?

True. Gentlemen, I command your assistance in the king's name to break into the house : there is murder cried within.

Mob. Ay, ay, break open the door.

Mrs Man. [*From the balcony.*] What noise is that below?

Teague. Arah, vat noise ish dat above?

Mrs Man. Only a poor gentlewoman in labour; 'twill be over presently.—Here, Mr Constable; there's something for you to drink.

[*Throws down a purse,* TEAGUE *takes it up.*

Teague. Come, maishter, we have no more to shay, be me shoul.—[*Going.*] Arah, if you vill play de constable right now, fet you vill come away.

True. No, no; there must be villainy by this bribe.— Who lives in this house?

Mob. A midwife, a midwife ; 'tis none of our business : let us be gone.

Aur. [*At the window.*] Gentlemen, dear gentlemen, help :—A rape! a rape! villainy?

True. Ha! that voice I know.—Give me the staff; I'll make a breach, I warrant you.

[*Breaks open the door and all go in.*

SCENE III.—*The Inside of the House.*

Enter TRUEMAN *and* Mob.

True. Gentlemen, search all about the house; let not a soul escape.

[*Enter* AURELIA, *running, with her hair about her ears, and out of breath.*

Aur. Dear Mr Constable—had you—staid but a moment longer—I had been ruined.

True. [*Aside.*] Aurelia! [*Aloud.*] Are you safe, madam?

Aur. Yes, yes; I am safe—I think—but with enough ado: he's a devilish strong fellow.

True. Where is the villain that attempted it?

Aur. Psha!—never mind the villain;—look out the woman of the house, the devil, the monster, that decoyed me hither.

Enter TEAGUE, *haling in* Mrs MANDRAKE *by the hair.*

Teague. Be me shoul, I have taaken my shaare of the plunder. Let me shee fat I have gotten.—[*Takes her to the light.*] Ububboo a witch! a witch! the very saame witch dat would swaar my maishter was the youngest.

True. [*Aside.*] How! Mandrake! this was the luckiest disguise—[*Aloud.*] Come, my dear Proserpine, I'll take care of you.

Mrs Man. Pray, sir, let me speak with you.

True. No, no; I'll talk with you before a magistrate. —A cart, Bridewell,—you understand me?—Teague, let her be your prisoner: I'll wait on this lady.

Aur. Mr Constable, I'll reward you.

Teague. It ish convenient noo by the law of armsh, that I search my prishoner, for fear she may have some pocket-pishtols.—Dere is a joak for you!

[*Searches her pockets.*

Mrs Man. Ah! don't use an old woman so barbar-ously.

Teague. Dear joy, den fy vere you an old woman? Dat is your falt, not mine, joy!—Uboo, here ish nothing but scribble-scrabble papers, I tink.

[*Pulls out a handful of letters.*

True. Let me see 'em ; they may be of use.—[*Looks over the letters.*] For Mr Richmore—Ay, does he traffic here-abouts ?

Aur. That is the villain that would have abused me.

True. [*Aside.*] Ha! then he has abused you! Villain indeed!—[*Aloud.*] Was his name Richmore, mistress? a lusty, handsome man ?

Aur. Ay, ay, the very same : a lusty, ugly fellow.

True. Let me see—[*Opening a letter.*] Whose scrawl is this?—[*Aside.*] Death and confusion to my sight! Clelia, my bride, his whore!—I've passed a precipice unseen, which to look back upon, shivers me with terror —This night, this very moment, had not my friend been in confinement, had not I worn this dress, had not Aurelia been in danger, had not Teague found this letter, had the least minutest circumstance been omitted, what a monster had I been!—[*Aloud.*] Mistress, is this same Richmore in the house still, think'ee?

Aur. 'Tis very probable he may.

True. Very well.—Teague, take these ladies over to the tavern, and stay there till I come to you.—[*To* AURELIA.] Madam, fear no injury ; your friends are near you.

Aur. [*Aside.*] What does he mean ?

Teague. Come, dear joy, I vill give you a pot of wine out of your own briberies here.

[*Hales out* Mrs MANDRAKE, AURELIA *and* Mob *following.*

Enter RICHMORE.

Rich. [*Aside.*] Since my money won't prevail on this

cross fellow, I'll try what my authority can do.—[*Aloud*].
What's the meaning of this riot, constable? I have the
commission of the peace, and can command you. Go
about your business, and leave your prisoners with me.

True. No, sir; the prisoners shall go about their business, and I'll be left with you.—Look'ee, master, we
don't use to make up these matters before company:
so you and I must be in private a little.—You say, sir,
that you are a justice of peace?

Rich. Yes, sir; I have my commission in my pocket.

True. I believe it.—Now, sir, one good turn deserves
another: and, if you will promise to do me a kindness,
why, you shall have as good as you bring.

Rich. What is it?

True. You must know, sir, there is a neighbour's
daughter that I had a woundy kindness for. She had
a very good repute all over the parish, and might
have married very handsomely, that I must say; but,
I don't know how, we came together after a very
kindly, natural manner, and I swore, that I must say,
I did swear confoundedly, that I would marry her;
but, I don't know how, I never cared for marrying of
her since.

Rich. How so?

True. Why, because I did my business without it;
that was the best way, I thought. The truth is, she
has some foolish reasons to say she's with child, and
threatens mainly to have me taken up with a warrant,
and brought before a justice of the peace. Now, sir, I
intend to come before you, and I hope your worship
will bring me off.

Rich. Look'ee, sir, if the woman prove with child,
and you swore to marry her, you must do't.

True. Ay, master; but I am for liberty and property.
I vote for parliament-men: I pay taxes, and truly
I don't think matrimony consistent with the liberty of
he subject.

Rich. But, in this case, sir, both law and justice will oblige you.

True. Why, if it be the law of the land—I found a letter here—I think it is for your worship.

Rich. Ay, sir; how came you by it?

True. By a very strange accident truly.—Clelia—she says here you swore to marry her. Eh?—Now, sir, I suppose that what is law for a petty-constable may be law for a justice of peace.

Rich. This is the oddest fellow—

True. Here was the t'other lady that cried out so —I warrant now, if I were brought before you for ravishing a woman—the gallows would ravish me for't.

Rich. But I did not ravish her.

True. [*Aside.*] That I'm glad to hear : I wanted to be sure of that.

Rich. [*Aside.*] I don't like this fellow.—[*Aloud.*] Come, sir, give me my letter, and go about your business ; I have no more to say to you.

True. But I have something to say to you.
[*Coming up to him.*

Rich. What?

True. Dog! [*Strikes him.*

Rich. Ha! struck by a peasant!—[*Draws.*] Slave, thy death is certain. [*Runs at* TRUEMAN.

True. O brave Don John,[1] rape and murder in one night! [*Disarms him.*

Rich. Rascal, return my sword, and acquit your prisoners, else will I prosecute thee to beggary. I'll give some pettifogger a thousand pound to starve thee and thy family according to law.

True. I'll lay you a thousand pound you won't.
[*Discovering himself.*

Rich. Ghosts and apparitions! Trueman!

True. Words are needless to upbraid you : my very

[1] An allusion to Shadwell's *Libertine* (produced 1676), in which Don Juan's name was Anglicized and became Don John.

looks are sufficient; and, if you have the least sense of shame, this sword would be less painful in your heart than my appearance is in your eye.

Rich. Truth, by Heavens!

True. Think on the contents of this,—[*Showing the letter*] think next on me; reflect upon your villainy to Aurelia; then view thyself.

Rich. Trueman, canst thou forgive me?

True. Forgive thee!—[*A long pause.*] Do one thing and I will.

Rich. Anything :—I'll beg thy pardon.

True. The blow excuses that.

Rich. I'll give thee half my estate.

True. Mercenary!

Rich. I'll make thee my sole heir.

True. I despise it.

Rich. What shall I do?

True. You shall—marry Clelia.

Rich. How! That's too hard.

True. Too hard! why was it then imposed on me? If you marry her yourself, I shall believe you intended me no injury; so your behaviour will be justified, my resentment appeased, and the lady's honour repaired.

Rich. 'Tis infamous.

True. No, by Heavens, 'tis justice! and what is just is honourable. If promises from man to man have force, why not from man to woman? Their very weakness is the charter of their power, and they should not be injured because they can't return it.

Rich. Return my sword.

True. In my hand 'tis the sword of justice, and I should not part with it.

Rich. Then sheathe it here; I'll die before I consent so basely.

True. Consider, sir, the sword is worn for a distinguishing mark of honour: promise me one, and receive t'other.

Rich. I'll promise nothing, till I have that in my power.

True. Take it.   [*Throws him his sword.*

Rich. I scorn to be compelled even to justice; and now, that I may resist, I yield. Trueman, I have injured thee, and Clelia I have severely wronged.

True. Wronged indeed, sir;—and, to aggravate the crime, the fair afflicted loves you. Marked you with what confusion she received me? She wept, the injured Innocence wept, and with a strange reluctance gave consent; her moving softness pierced my heart, though I mistook the cause.

Rich. Your youthful virtue warms my breast, and melts it into tenderness.

True. Indulge it, sir; justice is noble in any form. Think of the joys and raptures will possess her when she finds you instead of me! you, the dear dissembler, the man she loves, the man she gave for lost, to find him true, returned, and in her arms.

Rich. No new possession can give equal joy. It shall be done—the priest that waits for you shall tie the knot this moment; in the morning I'll expect you'll give me joy.   [*Exit.*

True. So—is not this better now than cutting of throats? I have got my revenge, and the lady will have hers without bloodshed.   [*Exit.*

SCENE IV.—*An Apartment.*

CONSTANCE *and* Footman.

Foot. He's just a-coming up, madam.   [*Exit.*

Con. My civility to this man will be as great a constraint upon me as rudeness would be to his brother:

but I must bear it a little, because our designs require it.

Enter BENJAMIN WOULDBE.

—[*Aside.*] His appearance shocks me.—[*Aloud.*] My
lord, I wish you joy.

Ben. Would. Madam, 'tis only in your power to give
it; and would you honour me with a title to be really
proud of, it should be that of your humblest servant.

Con. I never admitted anybody to the title of an
humble servant, that I did not intend should command
me. If your lordship will bear with the slavery, you
shall begin when you please, provided you take upon
you the authority when I have a mind.

Ben. Would. Our sex, madam, make much better
lovers than husbands; and I think it highly unreasonable that you should put yourself in my power, when
you can so absolutely keep me in yours.

Con. No, my lord, we never truly command till we
have given our promise to obey; and we are never in
more danger of being made slaves, than when we have
'em at our feet.

Ben. Would. True, madam, the greatest empires are
in most danger of falling; but it is better to be absolute
there, than to act by a prerogative that's confined.

Con. Well, well, my lord, I like the constitution we
live under; I'm for a limited power, or none at all.

Ben. Would. You have so much the heart of the
subject, madam, that you may rule as you please; but
you have weak pretences to a limited sway, where your
eyes have already played the tyrant. I think one
privilege of the people is to kiss their sovereign's hand.
[*Taking her hand.*

Con. Not till they have taken the oaths, my lord;
and he that refuses them in the form the law prescribes
is, I think, no better than a rebel.

Ben. Would. [*Kneeling.*] By shrines and altars! by

all that you think just, and I hold good! by this, [*Taking her hand*] the fairest, and the dearest vow—

[*Kisses her hand.*

Con. Fy, my lord!   [*Seemingly yielding.*

Ben. Would. Your eyes are mine, they bring me tidings from your heart that this night I shall be happy.

Con. Would not you despise a conquest so easily gained?

Ben. Would. Yours will be the conquest, and I shall despise all the world but you.

Con. But will you promise to make no attempts upon my honour?

Ben. Would. [*Aside.*] That's foolish. [*Aloud.*] Not angels sent on messages to earth shall visit with more innocence.

Con. [*Aside.*] Ay, ay, to be sure. [*Aloud.*] My lord I'll send one to conduct you.   [*Exit.*

Ben. Would. Ha, ha, ha! no attempts upon her honour! When I can find the place where it lies, I'll tell her more of my mind. Now do I feel ten thousand Cupids tickling me all over with the points of their arrows. Where's my deformity now? I have read somewhere these lines :—

> Though Nature cast me in a rugged mould,
> Since Fate has changed the bullion into gold,
> Cupid returns, breaks all his shafts of lead,
> And tips each arrow with a golden head.
> Feather'd with title, the gay lordly dart
> Flies proudly on, whilst every virgin's heart
> Swells with ambition to receive the smart.

Enter HERMES WOULDBE *behind him.*

Herm. Would. Thus to adorn dramatic story,
> Stage-hero struts in borrowed glory,
> Proud and august as ever man saw,
> And ends his empire in a stanza.

[*Slaps him on the shoulder.*

Ben. Would. Ha! my brother!

Herm. Would. No, perfidious man; all kindred and relation I disown! The poor attempts upon my fortune I could pardon, but thy base designs upon my love I never can forgive. My honour, birthright, riches, all I could more freely spare, than the least thought of thy prevailing here.

Ben. Would. How! my hopes deceived! Curst be the fair delusions of her sex! Whilst only man opposed my cunning, I stood secure; but soon as woman interposed, luck changed hands, and the devil was immediately on her side. Well, sir, much good may do you[1] with your mistress, and may you love, and live, and starve together.   [*Going.*

Herm. Would. Hold, sir! I was lately your prisoner, now you are mine; when the ejectment is executed, you shall be at liberty.

Ben. Would. Ejectment!

Herm. Would. Yes, sir; by this time, I hope, my friends have purged my father's house of that debauched and riotous swarm that you had hived together.

Ben. Would. Confusion! Sir, let me pass; I am the elder, and will be obeyed.   [*Draws.*

Herm. Would. Darest thou dispute the eldership so nobly?

Ben. Would. I dare, and will, to the last drop of my inveterate blood.   [*They fight.*

Enter TRUEMAN *and* TEAGUE.

True. [*Striking down their swords.*] Hold, hold, my lord! I have brought those shall soon decide the controversy.

Ben. Would. If I mistake not, that is the villain that decoyed me abroad.

[*Runs at* TRUEMAN, TEAGUE *catches his arm behind, and takes away his sword.*

' So in all editions: but surely a misprint for "you do."

Teague. Ay, be me shoul, thish ish the besht guard upon the rules of fighting, to catch a man behind his back.

True. My lord, a word. — [*Whispers* HERMES WOULDBE.] Now, gentlemen, please to hear this venerable lady.

[*Goes to the door and brings in* Mrs MANDRAKE.

Herm. Would.[1] Mandrake in custody!

Teague. In my custody, fet.

True. Now, madam, you know what punishment is destined for the injury offered to Aurelia, if you don't immediately confess the truth.

Mrs Man. Then I must own, (Heaven forgive me!)— [*Weeping.*] I must own, that Hermes, as he was still esteemed, so he is the first-born.

Teague. A very honesht woman, be me shoul!

Ben. Would. That confession is extorted by fear, and therefore of no force.

True. Ay, sir; but here is your letter to her, with the ink scarce dry, where you repeat your offer of five hundred pound a year to swear in your behalf.

Teague. Dat was Teague's finding out, and I believe St Patrick put it in my toughts to pick her pockets.

Enter CONSTANCE *and* AURELIA.

Con. I hope, Mr Wouldbe, you will make no attempts upon my person.

Ben. Would. Damn your person!

Herm. Would. But pray, madam, where have you been all this evening? [*To* AURELIA.

Aur. Very busy, I can assure you, sir. Here's an honest constable that I could find in my heart to marry, had the greasy rogue but one drop of genteel blood in his veins; what's become of him? [*Looking about.*

Con. Bless me, cousin, marry a constable!

[1] Q. 1 and later editions give this speech to "Elder Wouldbe," but it ought surely to be assigned to the younger, Benjamin.

Aur. Why truly, madam, if that constable had not come in a very critical minute, by this time I had been glad to marry anybody.

True. I take you at your word, madam; you shall marry him this moment; and if you don't say that I have genteel blood in my veins by to-morrow morning—

Aur. And was it you, sir?

True. Look'ee, madam, don't be ashamed; I found you a little in the *déshabillé*, that's the truth on't; but you made a brave defence.

Aur. I am obliged to you; and though you were a little whimsical to-day, this late adventure has taught me how dangerous it is to provoke a gentleman by ill usage; therefore, if my lord and this lady will show us a good example, I think we must follow our leaders, Captain.

True. As boldly as when honour calls.

Con. My lord, there was taken among your brother's jovial crew, his friend Subtleman, whom we have taken care to secure.

Herm. Would. For him the pillory.—For you, madam—   [*To* Mrs MANDRAKE.

Teague. Be me shoul, she shall be married to maishter Fuller.[1]

Herm. Would. For you, brother—

Ben. Would. Poverty and contempt—
    To which I yield as to a milder fate
    Than obligations from the man I hate.   [*Exit.*

Herm Would. Then take thy wish.—And now, I hope, all parties have received their due rewards and punishments?

---

[1] Ewald is no doubt right in suggesting that the reference is to William Fuller (1670-1717?), "impostor, cheat and false accuser," who had recently stood three times in the pillory, and was now in prison. His *Narrative. . . proving the pretended Prince of Wales to be a grand Cheat upon the Nation*, was an effort entirely in the spirit of Mrs Mandrake.

Teague. But what will you do for poor Teague, maishter?

Herm. Would. What shall I do for thee?—

Teague. Arah, maak me a justice of peash, dear joy.

Herm. Would. Justice of peace! thou art not qualified, man.

Teague. Yest,[1] fet am I—I can take the oats, and write my mark—I can be an honesht man myshelf, and keep a great rogue for my clark.

Herm. Would. Well, well, you shall be taken care of.—And now, Captain, we set out for happiness:—

Let none despair whate'er their fortunes be—
Fortune must yield, would men but act like me.
Choose a brave friend as partner of your breast,
Be active when your right is in contest;
Be true to love, and Fate will do the rest.

[Exeunt omnes.

[1] So in Q. 1 and other editions; but surely Farquhar wrote " yesh."

EPILOGUE

SPOKEN BY MRS HOOK.

UR poet open'd with a loud warlike blast,
But now weak woman is his safest cast
To bring him off with quarter at the
last:
Not that he's vain to think that I can
say,
Or he can write, fine things to help the play.
The various scenes have drain'd his strength and art;
And I, you know, had a hard struggling part:
But then he brought me off with life and limb;
Ah, would that I could do as much for him!—
Stay, let me think—your favours to excite,
I still must act the part I play'd to-night.
For whatsoe'er may be your sly pretence,
You like those best that make the best defence:
But this is needless—'tis in vain to crave it—
If you have damn'd the play, no power can save it.
Not all the wits of Athens and of Rome,
Not Shakspeare, Jonson, could revoke its doom:
Nay, what is more—if once your anger rouses,
Not all the courted beauties of both houses.
He would have ended here—but I thought meet,
To tell him there was left one safe retreat,
Protection sacred, at the ladies' feet.
To that he answer'd in submissive strain,
He paid all homage to this female reign,

And therefore turn'd his satire 'gainst the men.
From your great Queen [1] this sovereign right ye draw,
To keep the wits, as she the world, in awe :
To her bright sceptre, your bright eyes, they bow ;
Such awful splendour sits on every brow,
All scandal on the sex were treason now.
The play can tell with what poetic care
He labour'd to redress the injured fair,
And if you won't protect, the men will damn him there.
Then save the Muse, that flies to ye for aid ;
Perhaps my poor request may some persuade
Because it is the first I ever made.

[1] Queen Anne had ascended the throne, March 8, 1702. This epilogue was spoken on December 14.

THE

RECRUITING OFFICER

A

COMEDY

As it is Acted at the

THEATRE ROYAL

in

DRYRY - LANE,

By Her MAJESTY's Servants

Written by Mr FARQUHAR

𝕿𝔥𝔢 𝕾𝔢𝔠𝔬𝔫𝔡 𝕰𝔡𝔦𝔱𝔦𝔬𝔫 𝕮𝔬𝔯𝔯𝔢𝔠𝔱𝔢𝔡

——*Captique dolis, donisque coacti.*
Virg. Lib. II. Æneid.

LONDON
Printed for BERNARD LINTOTT at the *Cross Keys* next
Nando's Coffee-House near *Temple Bar.*
Price 1s. 6d.

As to the date of this comedy (1706), see Introduction, p. 12. It was very popular throughout the 18th century. Ryan succeeded Wilks in the part of Plume, and it was afterwards acted by Garrick (1742), Barry (1756), Palmer (1758), Smith (1763), Charles Kemble (1797), and other leading actors. Garrick, at the age of eleven, appeared in an amateur performance as Sergeant Kite—the first part he ever played. At Covent Garden on 21st November 1740, Peg Woffington made her first appearance in the part of Silvia, which was afterwards played by Mrs Pritchard, Mrs Crawford and Mrs Jordan, among many others. Woodward was celebrated as Brazen, and the part was also played by Macklin. Costar Pearmain was among the parts played by Garrick during his first season on the stage (Goodman's Fields, 1741-42). It was afterwards acted by Liston, Munden and Keeley. *The Recruiting Officer* was the first play ever seen in Australia. A party of convicts acted it at Sydney, on 4th June 1789, in a hut fitted up for the occasion (Collins's *History of New South Wales*).

TO ALL

FRIENDS

ROUND THE

WREKIN

My Lords and Gentlemen,

NSTEAD of the mercenary expecta-
tions that attend addresses of this
nature, I humbly beg, that this may
be received as an acknowledgment
of the favours you have already con-
ferred. I have transgressed the rules
of dedication in offering you anything
in that style, without first asking your
leave : but the entertainment I found in Shropshire commands me to be grateful, and that's all I intend.

'Twas my good fortune to be ordered some time ago into
the place which is made the scene of this comedy ; I was a
perfect stranger to everything in Salop, but its character of
loyalty, the number of its inhabitants, the alacrity of the
gentlemen in recruiting the army, with their generous and
hospitable reception of strangers.

This character I found so amply verified in every
particular, that you made recruiting, which is the greatest
fatigue upon earth to others, to be the greatest pleasure in
the world to me.

The kingdom cannot show better bodies of men, better
inclinations for the service, more generosity, more good
understanding, nor more politeness, than is to be found at
the foot of the Wrekin.

245

Some little turns of humour that I met with almost within the shade of that famous hill, gave the rise to this comedy ; and people were apprehensive that, by the example of some others, I would make the town merry at the expense of the country-gentlemen. But they forgot that I was to write a comedy, not a libel ; and that whilst I held to nature, no person of any character in your country could suffer by being exposed. I have drawn the justice and the clown in their *puris naturalibus :* the one an apprehensive, sturdy, brave blockhead ; and the other a worthy, honest, generous gentleman, hearty in his country's cause, and of as good an understanding as I could give him, which I must confess is far short of his own.

I humbly beg leave to interline a word or two of the adventures of *The Recruiting Officer* upon the stage. Mr Rich, who commands the company for which those recruits were raised, has desired me to acquit him before the world of a charge which he thinks lies heavy upon him, for acting this play on Mr Durfey's third night.

Be it known unto all men by these presents, that it was my act and deed, or rather Mr Durfey's ; for he *would* play his third night against the first of mine. He brought down a huge flight of frightful birds upon me, when (Heaven knows !) I had not a feathered fowl in my play, except one single *Kite ;* but I presently made *Plume* a bird, because of his name, and *Brazen* another, because of the feather in his hat ; and with these three I engaged his whole empire, which I think was as great a *Wonder* as any *in the Sun.*[1]

But to answer his complaints more gravely, the season was far advanced ; the officers that made the greatest figures in my play were all commanded to their posts abroad,[2] and waited only for a wind, which might possibly turn in less time than a day : and I know none of Mr Durfey's birds that had posts abroad but his *Woodcocks,* and their season is over ; so that he might put off a day with less prejudice than the Recruiting Officer could ; who has this farther to

[1] Durfey's opera, produced at the Haymarket, April 5, 1706, three days before Farquhar's play, bore the title of *Wonders in the Sun, or, the Kingdom of the Birds.*
[2] The battle of Ramillies was fought just six weeks after the first night of the play.

say for himself, that he was posted before the other spoke, and could not with credit recede from his station.

These and some other rubs this comedy met with before it appeared. But, on the other hand, it had powerful helps to set it forward : the Duke of Ormond encouraged the author, and the Earl of Orrery approved the play. My recruits were reviewed by my General and my Colonel, and could not fail to pass muster ; and still to add to my success, they were raised among my *Friends round the Wrekin.*

This health has the advantage over our other celebrated toasts, never to grow worse for the wearing : 'tis a lasting beauty, old without age, and common without scandal. That you may live long to set it cheerfully round, and to enjoy the abundant pleasures of your fair and plentiful country, is the hearty wish of,

My Lords and Gentlemen,

Your most obliged,

and most obedient Servant,

GEO. FARQUHAR.

PROLOGUE

N ancient times, when Helen's fatal charms
    charms
Roused the contending universe to
    arms,
The Grecian council happily deputes
The sly Ulysses forth—to raise
    recruits.
The artful captain found, without delay,
Where great Achilles, a deserter, lay.
Him Fate hath warn'd to shun the Trojan blows:
Him Greece required—against their Trojan foes.
All the recruiting arts were needful here
To raise this great, this tim'rous volunteer.
Ulysses well could talk: he stirs, he warms
The warlike youth.—He listens to the charms
Of plunder, fine laced coats, and glitt'ring arms.
Ulysses caught the young aspiring boy,
And listed him who wrought the fate of Troy.
Thus by recruiting was bold Hector slain:
Recruiting thus fair Helen did regain.
If for one Helen such prodigious things
Were acted, that they even listed kings;
If for one Helen's artful, vicious charms,
Half the transported world was found in arms;
What for so many Helens may we dare,

Whose minds, as well as faces, are so fair?
If by one Helen's eyes old Greece could find
Its Homer fired to write—even Homer blind ;
The Britons sure beyond compare may write,
That view so many Helens every night.

DRAMATIS PERSONÆ

MEN

Mr Balance,		⌐ Mr Keen.
Mr Scale,	three Justices,	⟨ Mr Phillips.
Mr Scruple,		⌐ Mr Kent.

Mr Worthy, a Gentleman of Shropshire, Mr Williams.

Captain Plume,	two Recruiting	⌐ Mr Wilks.
Captain Brazen,	Officers,	⌐ Mr Cibber.

Kite, Sergeant to Plume, . . . Mr Estcourt.

Bullock, a Country Clown, . . . Mr Bullock.

Costar Pearmain,	two Recruits,	⌐ Mr Norris.
Thomas Appletree,		⌐ Mr Fairbank.

[Pluck, a Butcher.]

[Thomas, a Smith.]

WOMEN

Melinda, a Lady of Fortune, . . Mrs Rogers.

Silvia, Daughter to Balance, . . Mrs Oldfield.
    in love with Plume.

Lucy, Melinda's Maid, . . . Mrs Sapsford.

Rose, a Country Wench, . . . Mrs Mountfort.

Constable, Recruits, Mob, Servants and Attendants
[&c., &c.]

SCENE—Shrewsbury.

ACT I

SCENE I.—*The Market-Place.*

Enter Drummer, *beating the* "*Grenadier's March,*" Serjeant KITE, COSTAR PEARMAIN, THOMAS APPLE-TREE, *and* Mob *following.*[1]

ITE. [*Making a speech.*] If any gentlemen soldiers, or others, have a mind to serve her Majesty, and pull down the French king: if any prentices have severe masters, any children have undutiful parents: if any servants have too little wages, or any husband too much wife: let them repair to the noble Serjeant Kite, at the sign of the Raven in this good town of Shrewsbury, and they shall receive present relief and entertainment.— Gentlemen, I don't beat my drums here to ensnare or inveigle any man; for you must know, gentlemen, that I am a man of honour. Besides, I don't beat up for common soldiers ; no, I list only grenadiers—grenadiers,

---

[1] The stage-direction in early editions is "Scene, the Market-Place—Drum beats the Granadeer March. Enter Serjeant Kite, followed by the Mob." Neither Pearmain nor Appletree is named, and the speeches here assigned to Pearmain are simply marked "Mob." The "Grenadier March," it may be mentioned, was not the "British Grenadiers," but a composition printed as early as 1686 in Playford's *Dancing Master*, and reproduced in 1690, 1703 and other editions.

gentlemen. Pray, gentlemen, observe this cap. This is the cap of honour, it dubs a man a gentleman in the drawing of a trigger; and he that has the good fortune to be born six foot high, was born to be a great man.— [*To* Costar Pearmain.] Sir, will you give me leave to try this cap upon your head?

Pear. Is there no harm in't? Won't the cap list me?

Kite. No, no, no more than I can.—Come, let me see how it becomes you?

Pear. Are you sure there be no conjuration in it? no gunpowder plot upon me?

Kite. No, no, friend; don't fear, man.

Pear. My mind misgives me plaguily.—Let me see it. —[*Going to put it on.*] It smells woundily of sweat and brimstone. Pray, serjeant, what writing is this upon the face of it?

Kite. The Crown, or the Bed of Honour.[1]

Pear. Pray now, what may be that same bed of honour?

Kite. Oh! a mighty large bed! bigger by half than the great bed of Ware—ten thousand people may lie in it together, and never feel one another.

Pear. My wife and I would do well to lie in't, for we don't care for feeling one another.—But do folk sleep sound in this same bed of honour?

Kite. Sound! Ay, so sound that they never wake.

Pear. Wauns! I wish again that my wife lay there.

Kite. Say you so? then, I find, brother—

Pear. Brother! hold there, friend; I am no kindred to you that I know of yet. Look'ee, serjeant, no coaxing, no wheedling, d'ye see: if I have a mind to list, why so; if not, why 'tis not so; therefore take your cap and

---

[1] The first badge of the Grenadier Guards was the Crown above the royal cipher (or monogram) reversed—the cipher, of course, varying with the reign. The Sergeant's speech seems as though it referred to some motto, but I cannot find that any such motto was ever used by the regiment. The cap would be the "tall, pointed cloth caps" of the period.

your brothership back again, for I an't disposed at this present writing.—No coaxing, no brothering me, faith!

Kite. I coax! I wheedle! I'm above it! Sir, I have served twenty campaigns. But, sir, you talk well, and I must own that you are a man every inch of you, a pretty young sprightly fellow. I love a fellow with a spirit; but I scorn to coax, 'tis base : though I must say, that never in my life have I seen a man better built [1]; how firm and strong he treads! he steps like a castle; but I scorn to wheedle any man.—Come, honest lad, will you take share of a pot?

Pear. Nay, for that matter, I'll spend my penny with the best he that wears a head, that is, begging your pardon, sir, and in a fair way.

Kite. Give me your hand then; and now, gentlemen, I have no more to say, but this—here's a purse of gold, and there is a tub of humming ale at my quarters! 'tis the queen's money, and the queen's drink.—She's a generous queen, and loves her subjects—I hope, gentlemen, you won't refuse the queen's health?

Mob. No, no, no!

Kite. Huzza then! huzza for the queen, and the honour of Shropshire!

Mob. Huzza!

Kite. Beat drum.

[*Exeunt*, Drummer *beating the "Grenadier's March."*

Enter PLUME *in a Riding Habit.*

Plume. By the Grenadier March, that should be my drum, and by that shout, it should beat with success.— Let me see—[*Looking on his watch.*]—four o'clock. At ten yesterday morning I left London.—A hundred and twenty miles in thirty hours is pretty smart riding, but nothing to the fatigue of recruiting.

---

[1] Q. 1. "better built man."

Re-enter KITE.

Kite. Welcome to Shrewsbury, noble Captain! From the banks of the Danube to the Severn side, noble Captain, you're welcome!

Plume. A very elegant reception indeed, Mr Kite! I find you are fairly entered into your recruiting strain. Pray, what success?

Kite. I have been here but a week, and I have recruited five.

Plume. Five! pray what are they?

Kite. I have listed the strong man of Kent,[1] the king of the gipsies, a Scotch pedlar, a scoundrel attorney, and a Welsh parson.

Plume. An attorney! wert thou mad? List a lawyer? Discharge him, discharge him this minute.

Kite. Why, sir?

Plume. Because I will have nobody in my company that can write; a fellow that can write, can draw petitions.—I say this minute discharge him.

Kite. And what shall I do with the parson?

Plume. Can he write?

Kite. Hum! He plays rarely upon the fiddle.

Plume. Keep him by all means.—But how stands the country affected? were the people pleased with the news of my coming to town?

Kite. Sir, the mob are so pleased with your honour, and the justices and better sort of people are so delighted with me, that we shall soon do our business.—But, sir, you have got a recruit here that you little think of.

Plume. Who?

Kite. One that you beat up for last time you were in the country: you remember your old friend Molly at the Castle?

Plume, She's not with child, I hope?

Kite. No, no, sir—she was brought to bed yesterday.

Plume. Kite, you must father the child.

<hr>

' See note 2, p. 38.

Kite. And so her friends will oblige me to marry the mother.

Plume. If they should, we'll take her with us; she can wash, you know, and make a bed upon occasion.

Kite. Ay, or unmake it upon occasion. But your honour knows that I am married already.

Plume. To how many?

Kite. I can't tell readily—I have set them down here upon the back of the muster-roll.—[*Draws it out.*] Let me see,—*Imprimis*, Mrs Sheely Snikereyes; she sells potatoes upon Ormond Key in Dublin—Peggy Guzzle, the brandy-woman, at the Horse-guard at Whitehall— Dolly Waggon, the carrier's daughter at Hull— Mademoiselle Van-Bottomflat at the Buss.—Then Jenny Oakam, the ship-carpenter's widow, at Portsmouth; but I don't reckon upon her, for she was married at the same time to two lieutenants of marines, and a man-of-war's boatswain.

Plume. A full company!—You have named five— come, make 'em half-a-dozen, Kite. Is the child a boy or a girl?

Kite. A chopping boy.

Plume. Then set the mother down in your list, and the boy in mine. Enter him a grenadier by the name of Francis Kite, absent upon furlough.[1] I'll allow you a man's pay for his subsistence; and now go comfort the wench in the straw.

Kite. I shall, sir.

Plume. But hold; have you made any use of your German doctor's habit since you arrived?

Kite. Yes, yes, sir, and my fame's all about the country for the most faithful[2] fortune-teller that ever told a lie.—I was obliged to let my landlord into the secret, for the convenience of keeping it so; but he's an

[1] Not an impossible incident in those days, or even later. See J. H. Burton, *The Reign of Queen Anne*, vol. i. p. 205.
[2] Q. 1. "famous."

honest fellow, and will be faithful[1] to any roguery that is trusted[2] to him. This device, sir, will get you men and me money, which, I think, is all we want at present. —But yonder comes your friend Mr Worthy.—Has your honour any farther commands?

Plume. None at present.—[*Exit* KITE.] 'Tis indeed the picture of Worthy, but the life's departed.

Enter WORTHY.

What! arms a-cross, Worthy! Methinks, you should hold 'em open when a friend's so near.—The man has got the vapours in his ears, I believe : I must expel this melancholy spirit.

Spleen, thou worst of fiends below,

Fly, I conjure thee by this magic blow.

[*Slaps* WORTHY *on the shoulder.*

Wor. Plume! my dear Captain, welcome. Safe and sound returned?

Plume. I 'scaped safe from Germany, and sound, I hope, from London ; you see I have lost neither leg, arm, nor nose. Then for my inside, 'tis neither troubled with sympathies nor antipathies ; and I have an excellent stomach for roast-beef.

Wor. Thou art a happy fellow ; once I was so.

Plume. What ails thee, man? No inundations nor earthquakes in Wales, I hope? Has your father rose from the dead, and reassumed his estate?

Wor. No.

Plume. Then you are married, surely ?

Wor. No.

Plume. Then you are mad, or turning Quaker?

Wor. Come, I must out with it.—Your once gay, roving friend is dwindled into an obsequious, thoughtful, romantic, constant coxcomb.

Plume. And, pray, what is all this for?

Wor. For a woman.

Q. I. "trusty."   [2] Q. I. "confided."

Plume. Shake hands, brother; if you go to that, behold me as obsequious, as thoughtful, and as constant a coxcomb as your worship.

Wor. For whom?

Plume. For a regiment. — But for a woman!— 'Sdeath! I have been constant to fifteen at a time, but never melancholy for one; and can the love of one bring you into this pickle? Pray, who is this miraculous Helen?

Wor. A Helen indeed, not to be won under a ten years' siege: as great a beauty, and as great a jilt.

Plume. A jilt! pho! Is she as great a whore?

Wor. No, no.

Plume. 'Tis ten thousand pities. But who is she? do I know her?

Wor. Very well.

Plume. Impossible!—I know no woman that will hold out a ten years' siege.

Wor. What think you of Melinda?

Plume. Melinda! Why, she began to capitulate [1] this time twelvemonth, and offered to surrender upon honourable terms; and I advised you to propose a settlement of five hundred pounds a year to her, before I went last abroad.

Wor. I did, and she hearkened to't, desiring only one week to consider: when, beyond her hopes, the town was relieved, and I forced to turn my siege into a blockade.

Plume. Explain, explain!

Wor. My lady Richly, her aunt in Flintshire, dies, and leaves her, at this critical time, twenty thousand pounds.

Plume. Oh! the devil! What a delicate woman was there spoiled! But, by the rules of war now, Worthy, blockade [2] was foolish. After such a convoy of provisions was entered the place, you could have no thought

[1] See note, p. 73.   [2] Q. 1. "your blockade."

of reducing it by famine; you should have redoubled your attacks, taken the town by storm, or have died upon the breach.

Wor. I did make one general assault, and pushed it with all my forces; but I was so vigorously repulsed, that, despairing of ever gaining her for a mistress, I have altered my conduct, given my addresses the obsequious and distant turn, and court her now for a wife.

Plume. So as you grew obsequious, she grew haughty; and because you approached her as a goddess, she used you like a dog?

Wor. Exactly.

Plume. 'Tis the way of 'em all. Come, Worthy, your obsequious and distant airs will never bring you together; you must not think to surmount her pride by your humility. Would you bring her to better thoughts of you, she must be reduced to a meaner opinion of herself. Let me see: the very first thing that I would do, should be to lie with her chamber-maid, and hire three or four wenches in the neighbourhood to report that I had got them with child. Suppose we lampooned all the pretty women in town, and left her out? Or what if we made a ball, and forgot to invite her, with one or two of the ugliest?

Wor. These would be mortifications, I must confess; but we live in such a precise, dull place, that we can have no balls, no lampoons, no——

Plume. What! no bastards! and so many recruiting officers in town! I thought 'twas a maxim among them to leave as many recruits in the country as they carried out.

Wor. Nobody doubts your good-will, noble captain, in serving your country with your best blood; witness our friend Molly at the Castle. There have been tears in town about that business, Captain.

Plume. I hope Silvia has not heard of 't?

Wor. O sir, have you thought of her? I began to fancy you had forgot poor Silvia.

Plume. Your affairs had put mine [1] quite out of my head. 'Tis true, Silvia and I had once agreed to go to bed together, could we have adjusted preliminaries; but she would have the wedding before consummation, and I was for consummation before the wedding; we could not agree. She was a pert, obstinate fool, and would lose her maidenhead her own way; so she may keep it for Plume.

Wor. But do you intend to marry upon no other conditions?

Plume. Your pardon, sir, I'll marry upon no condition at all. If I should, I am resolved never to bind myself to a woman for my whole life, till I know whether I shall like her company for half an hour. Suppose I married a woman that wanted a leg!—such a thing might be, unless I examined the goods beforehand. If people would but try one another's constitutions before they engaged, it would prevent all these elopements, divorces, and the devil knows what.

Wor. Nay, for that matter, the town did not stick to say, that——

Plume. I hate country towns for that reason. If your town has a dishonourable thought of Silvia it deserves to be burned to the ground. I love Silvia, I admire her frank, generous disposition. There's something in that girl more than woman. Her sex is but a foil to her—the ingratitude, dissimulation, envy, pride, avarice, and vanity of her sister females, do but set off their contraries in her. In short, were I once a general, I would marry her.

Wor. Faith, you have reason; for were you but a corporal she would marry you. But my Melinda coquettes it with every fellow she sees. I'll lay fifty pound she makes love to you.

Plume. I'll lay fifty pound that I return it, if she does. Look'ee, Worthy, I'll win her, and give her to you afterwards.

[1] Q. 1. "my own."

Wor. If you win her you shall wear her. Faith, I would not value [1] the conquest without the credit of the victory.

Re-enter KITE.

Kite. Captain, captain, a word in your ear.

Plume. You may speak out, here are none but friends.

Kite. You know, sir, that you sent me to comfort the good woman in the straw, Mrs Molly—my wife, Mr Worthy.

Wor. O ho! very well! I wish you joy, Mr Kite.

Kite. Your worship very well may, for I have got both a wife and a child in half-an-hour. But, as I was saying, you sent me to comfort Mrs Molly—my wife, I mean—but what d'ye think, sir? she was better comforted before I came.

Plume. As how?

Kite. Why, sir, a footman in a blue livery had brought her ten guineas to buy her baby-clothes.

Plume. Who, in the name of wonder, could send them?

Kite. Nay, sir, I must whisper that [*Whispers.*]—Mrs Silvia.

Plume. Silvia! generous creature!

Wor. Silvia! impossible!

Kite. Here be the guineas, sir; I took the gold as part of my wife's portion. Nay, farther, sir, she sent word the child should be taken all imaginable care of, and that she intended to stand godmother. The same footman, as I was coming to you with this news, called after me, and told me, that his lady would speak with me. I went, and, upon hearing that you were come to town, she gave me half-a-guinea for the news; and ordered me to tell you that Justice Balance, her father, who is just come out of the country, would be glad to see you.

Plume. There's a girl for you, Worthy! Is there

[1] Q. 1. "give a fig for."

anything of woman in this? No, 'tis noble, generous, manly friendship. Show me another woman that would lose an inch of her prerogative, that way, without tears, fits, and reproaches! The common jealousy of her sex, which is nothing but their avarice of pleasure, she despises; and can part with the lover, though she dies for the man.—Come, Worthy: where's the best wine? for there I'll quarter.

Wor. Horton has a fresh pipe of choice Barcelona, which I would not let him pierce before, because I reserved the maidenhead of it for your welcome to town.

Plume. Let's away then.—Mr Kite, wait on the lady with my humble service, and tell her I shall only refresh a little, and wait upon her.

Wor. Hold, Kite!—Have you seen the other recruiting-captain?

Kite. No, sir.

Plume. Another! who is he?

Wor. My rival in the first place, and the most unaccountable fellow—but I'll tell you more as we go.

[*Exeunt.*

SCENE II.—*Melinda's Apartment.*

MELINDA *and* SILVIA *meeting.*

Mel. Welcome to town, cousin Silvia—[*Salute*]. I envied you your retreat in the country; for Shrewsbury, methinks, and all your heads of shires, are the most irregular places for living. Here we have smoke, noise, scandal, affectation, and pretension; in short, everything to give the spleen—and nothing to divert it. Then the air is intolerable.

Silv. O madam! I have heard the town commended for its air.

Mel. But you don't consider, Silvia, how long I have lived in't! for I can assure you, that to a lady, the least nice in her constitution, no air can be good above half a year. Change of air I take to be the most agreeable of any variety in life.

Silv. As you say, cousin Melinda, there are several sorts of airs.

Mel. Psha! I talk only of the air we breathe, or more properly of that we taste. Have not you, Silvia, found a vast difference in the taste of airs?

Silv. Pray, cousin, are not vapours a sort of air? Taste air! you might as well tell me, I may feed upon air. But prithee, my dear Melinda, don't put on such an air to me. Your education and mine were just the same; and I remember the time when we never troubled our heads about air, but when the sharp air from the Welsh mountains made our fingers ache in a cold morning at the boarding-school.

Mel. Our education, cousin, was the same, but our temperaments had nothing alike; you have the constitution of a horse.

Silv. So far as to be troubled with neither spleen, colic, nor vapours. I need no salts for my stomach, no hartshorn for my head, nor wash for my complexion; I can gallop all the morning after the hunting-horn, and all the evening after a fiddle. In short, I can do everything with my father, but drink, and shoot flying; and I am sure, I can do everything my mother could, were I put to the trial.

Mel. You are in a fair way of being put to't; for I am told your captain is come to town.

Silv. Ay, Melinda, he is come; and I'll take care he sha'n't go without a companion.

Mel. You are certainly mad, cousin!

Silv. And there's a pleasure in being mad, which none but madmen know.[1]

[1] There is a pleasure, sure, in being mad,
Which none but madmen know.
—DRYDEN, *The Spanish Friar*, act ii. sc. I.

Mel. Thou poor romantic Quixote! Hast thou the vanity to imagine that a young sprightly officer, that rambles o'er half the globe in half a year, can confine his thoughts to the little daughter of a country justice, in an obscure part [1] of the world?

Silv. Psha! what care I for his thoughts? I should not like a man with confined thoughts, it shows a narrowness of soul. Constancy is but a dull sleepy quality at best, they will hardly admit it among the manly virtues; nor do I think it deserves a place with bravery, knowledge, policy, justice, and some other qualities that are proper to that noble sex. In short, Melinda, I think a petticoat a mighty simple thing, and I am heartily tired of my sex.

Mel. That is, you are tired of an appendix to our sex, that you can't so handsomely get rid of in petticoats, as if you were in breeches. O' my conscience, Silvia, hadst thou been a man, thou hadst been the greatest rake in Christendom.

Silv. I should have endeavoured to know the world, which a man can never do thoroughly without half a hundred friendships, and as many amours. But now I think on't, how stands your affair with Mr Worthy?

Mel. He's my aversion!

Silv. Vapours!

Mel. What do you say, madam?

Silv. I say, that you should not use that honest fellow so inhumanly. He's a gentleman of parts and fortune; and besides that, he's my Plume's friend, and by all that's sacred, if you don't use him better, I shall expect satisfaction.

Mel. Satisfaction! You begin to fancy yourself in breeches in good earnest. But to be plain with you, I like Worthy the worse for being so intimate with your captain, for I take him to be a loose, idle, unmannerly coxcomb.

[1] Q. I. "corner."

Silv. O madam! You never saw him, perhaps, since you were mistress of twenty-thousand pounds; you only knew him when you were capitulating with Worthy for a settlement, which perhaps might encourage him to be a little loose and unmannerly with you.

Mel. What do you mean, madam?

Silv. My meaning needs no interpretation, madam.

Mel. Better it had, madam; for methinks you are too plain.

Silv. If you mean the plainness of my person, I think your ladyship's as plain as me to the full.

Mel. Were I sure of that, I should be glad to take up with a rakehelly officer, as you do.

Silv. Again!—Look'ee, madam, you're in your own house.

Mel. And if you had kept in yours, I should have excused you.

Silv. Don't be troubled, madam, I sha'n't desire to have my visit returned.

Mel. The sooner, therefore, you make an end of this the better.

Silv. I am easily persuaded to follow my inclinations, so, madam, your humble servant.   [*Exit.*

Mel. Saucy thing!

Enter LUCY.

Lucy. What's the matter, madam!

Mel. Did you not see the proud nothing, how she swelled [1] upon the arrival of her fellow?

Lucy. Her fellow has not been long enough arrived to occasion any great swelling, madam; I don't believe she has seen him yet.

Mel. Nor sha'n't if I can help it.—Let me see—I have it!—Bring me pen and ink.—Hold, I'll go write in my closet.

[1] Q. I. "swells."

Lucy. An answer to this letter, I hope, madam.

                                        [*Presents a letter.*

Mel. Who sent it?

Lucy. Your captain, madam.

Mel. He's a fool, and I am tired of him. Send it back unopened.

Lucy. The messenger's gone, madam.

Mel. Then how should[1] I send an answer? Call him back immediately, while I go write.   [*Exeunt.*

---

[1] Q. 1. "shall."

ACT II

SCENE I.—*An Apartment in* Justice BALANCE'S
House.

Enter Justice BALANCE *and* PLUME.

AL. Look'ee, Captain, give us but blood for our money, and you sha'n't want men. I remember that, for some years of the last war, [1] we had no blood nor wounds, but in the officers' mouths; nothing for our millions but news-papers not worth a reading. Our armies did nothing but play at prison bars and hide-and-seek with the enemy; but now ye have brought us colours, and standards, and prisoners. Ad's my life, Captain, get us but another Marshal of France, [2] and I'll go myself for a soldier.

Plume. Pray, Mr Balance, how does your fair daughter?

Bal. Ah, Captain! what is my daughter to a Marshal of France? We're upon a nobler subject, I want to have a particular description of the battle of Hockstat.

Plume. The battle, sir, was a very pretty battle as one should desire to see, but we were all so intent upon

---

[1] The war which ended with the Peace of Ryswick in 1697 had been sluggish and unexciting.
[2] Marshal Tallard was taken prisoner at Blenheim (or Hochstadt,) August 13, 1704.

victory, that we never minded the battle. All that I
know of the matter is, our general commanded us to beat
the French, and we did so; and if he pleases but to say
the word, we'll do't again. But pray, sir, how does Mrs
Silvia?

Bal. Still upon Silvia! For shame, Captain! you are
engaged already, wedded to the war. Victory is your
mistress, and 'tis below a soldier to think of any other.

Plume. As a mistress, I confess, but as a friend, Mr
Balance.

Bal. Come, come, Captain, never mince the matter:
would not you debauch my daughter if you could?

Plume. How, sir! I hope she's not to be debauched.

Bal. Faith, but she is, sir; and any woman in
England of her age and complexion, by a man of your
youth and vigour. Look'ee, Captain, once I was
young, and once an officer as you are; and I can guess
at your thoughts now, by what mine were then; and I
remember very well, that I would have given one of my
legs to have deluded the daughter of an old plain
country gentleman, as like me as I was then like you.

Plume. But, sir, was that country gentleman your
friend and benefactor?

Bal. Not much of that.

Plume. There the comparison breaks: the favours,
sir, that——

Bal. Pho, I hate speeches! If I have done you any
service, Captain, 'twas to please myself, for I love thee;
and if I could part with my girl, you should have her as
soon as any young fellow I know. But I hope you have
more honour than to quit the service, and she more
prudence than to follow the camp; but she's at her own
disposal, she has fifteen hundred pound in her pocket;
and so—Silvia, Silvia!   [*Calls.*

Enter SILVIA.

Silv. There are some letters, sir, come by the post

from London ; I left them upon the table in your closet.

Bal. And here is a gentleman from Germany.—
[*Presents* PLUME *to her.*] Captain, you'll excuse me,
I'll go read my letters, and wait on you.   [*Exit.*

Silv. Sir, you are welcome to England.

Plume. You are indebted to me a welcome, madam,
since the hopes of receiving it from this fair hand was
the principal cause of my seeing England.

Silv. I have often heard that soldiers were sincere ;
shall I venture to believe public report ?

Plume. You may, when 'tis backed by private in-
surance : for I swear, madam, by the honour of my profession, that whatever dangers I went upon, it was with
the hope of making myself more worthy of your esteem ;
and, if ever I had thoughts of preserving my life, 'twas
for the pleasure of dying at your feet.

Silv. Well, well, you shall die at my feet, or where you
will ; but you know, sir, there is a certain will and testament to be made beforehand.

Plume. My will, madam, is made already, and there it
is [*Gives her a parchment.*] ; and if you please to open
that parchment, which was drawn the evening before the
battle of Blenheim, you will find whom I left my
heir.

Silv. [*Opens the will and reads.*]   *Mrs Silvia
Balance.*—Well, Captain, this is a handsome and a
substantial compliment ; but I can assure you, I am
much better pleased with the bare knowledge of your
intention, than I should have been in the possession of
your legacy.   But methinks, sir, you should have left
something to your little boy at the Castle

Plume. [*Aside.*] That's home !—[*Aloud.*]   My little
boy ! Lack-a-day, madam, that alone may convince
you 'twas none of mine.   Why the girl, madam, is my
serjeant's wife, and so the poor creature gave out that I
was father, in hopes that my friends might support her

in case of necessity—that was all, madam.—My boy! no, no, no.

Enter a Servant.

Ser. Madam, my master has received some ill news from London, and desires to speak with you immediately, and he begs the Captain's pardon, that he can't wait on him as he promised. [*Exit.*

Plume. Ill news! Heavens avert it! Nothing could touch me nearer than to see that generous worthy gentleman afflicted. I'll leave you to comfort him ; and be assured, that if my life and fortune can be any way serviceable to the father of my Silvia, he shall freely command both.

Silv. The necessity must be very pressing that would engage me to endanger either. [*Exeunt severally.*

SCENE II.—*Another Apartment.*

Enter BALANCE *and* SILVIA.

Silv. Whilst there is life there is hopes, sir ; perhaps my brother may recover.

Bal. We have but little reason to expect it ; Doctor Kilman acquaints me here, that before this comes to my hands, he fears I shall have no son. Poor Owen !— But the decree is just : I was pleased with the death of my father, because he left me an estate, and now I'm punished with the loss of an heir to inherit mine. I must now look upon you as the only hopes of my family ; and I expect that the augmentation of your fortune will give you fresh thoughts, and new prospects.

Silv. My desire of being punctual in my obedience, requires that you would be plain in your commands, sir.

Bal. The death of your brother makes you sole heiress to my estate, which you know is about twelve hundred pounds a year. This fortune gives you a fair claim to quality, and a title ; you must set a just value upon yourself, and, in plain terms, think no more of Captain Plume.

Silv. You have often commended the gentleman, sir.

Bal. And I do so still; he's a very pretty fellow. But though I liked him well enough for a bare son-in-law, I don't approve of him for an heir to my estate and family. Fifteen hundred pounds indeed I might trust in his hands, and it might do the young fellow a kindness; but od's my life! twelve hundred pounds a year would ruin him—quite turn his brain! A captain of foot worth twelve hundred pounds a year ! 'tis a prodigy in nature. Besides this, I have five or six thousand pounds in woods upon my estate ; oh, that would make him stark mad! For you must know that all captains have a mighty aversion to timber; they can't endure to see trees standing. Then I should have some rogue of a builder, by the help of his damned magic art, transform my noble oaks and elms into cornices, portals, sashes, birds, beasts, and devils, to adorn some maggotty, new-fashioned bauble upon the Thames ; and then you should have a dog of a gardener bring a *habeas corpus* for my *terra firma*, remove it to Chelsea or Twittenham, and clap it into grass-plats and gravel-walks.

Enter a Servant.

Ser. Sir, here's one below with a letter for your worship, but he will deliver it into no hands but your own.

Bal. Come, show me the messenger.

[*Exit with* Servant.

Silv. Make the dispute between love and duty, and

I am prince Prettyman[1] exactly. If my brother dies, ah poor brother! if he lives, ah poor sister! 'Tis bad both ways; I'll try it again. Follow my own inclinations, and break my father's heart; or obey his commands, and break my own? Worse and worse. Suppose I take it thus?—a moderate fortune, a pretty fellow, and a pad; or a fine estate, a coach-and-six, and an ass. That will never do neither.

Re-enter BALANCE *and* Servant.

Bal. [*To* Servant.] Put four horses into the coach. —[*Exit* Servant.] Ho, Silvia!

Silv. Sir.

Bal. How old were you when your mother died?

Silv. So young that I don't remember I ever had one; and you have been so careful, so indulgent to me since, that indeed I never wanted one.

Bal. Have I ever denied you anything you asked of me?

Silv. Never that I remember.

Bal. Then, Silvia, I must beg that, once in your life, you would grant me a favour.

Silv. Why should you question it, sir?

Bal. I don't; but I would rather counsel than command. I don't propose this with the authority of a parent, but as the advice of your friend: that you would take the coach this moment, and go into the country.

Silv. Does this advice, sir,[2] proceed from the contents of the letter you received just now?

Bal. No matter; I will be with you in three or four days, and then give you my reasons. But before you go, I expect you will make me one solemn promise.

[1] A slip on Silvia's part. It is Prince Volscius who, in *The Rehearsal* (act iii. sc. 5) is torn two ways between the claims of Love and Honour.

[2] Q. 1. Omits "sir."

Silv. Propose the thing, sir.

Bal. That you will never dispose of yourself to any man without my consent.

Silv. I promise.

Bal. Very well; and to be even with you, I promise that I will never dispose of you without your own consent. And so, Silvia, the coach is ready; farewell! —[*Leads her to the door, and returns.*] Now she's gone, I'll examine the contents of this letter a little nearer.   [*Reads.*

> *Sir,*
>
> *My intimacy with Mr Worthy has drawn a secret from him that he had from his friend Captain Plume; and my friendship and relation to your family oblige me to give you timely notice of it: the Captain has dishonourable designs upon my cousin Silvia. Evils of this nature are more easily prevented than amended; and that you would immediately send my cousin into the country, is the advice of, sir, your humble servant,*   MELINDA.

Why, the devil's in the young fellows of this age! they are ten times worse than they were in my time. Had he made my daughter a whore, and forswore it like a gentleman, I could have almost pardoned it; but to tell tales beforehand is monstrous. Hang it, I can fetch down a woodcock or a snipe, and why not a hat and feather? I have a case of good pistols, and have a good mind to try.

Enter WORTHY.

Worthy, your servant.

Wor. I'm sorry, sir, to be the messenger of ill news.

Bal. I apprehend it, sir: you have heard that my son Owen is past recovery.

Wor. My letters [1] say he's dead, sir.

Bal. He's happy, and I'm satisfied. The strokes of

---

[1] Q. 1. "advices."

Heaven I can bear; but injuries from men, Mr Worthy, are not so easily supported.

Wor. I hope, sir, you're under no apprehension of wrong from anybody?

Bal. You know I ought to be.

Wor. You wrong my honour, sir, in believing I could know anything to your prejudice without resenting it as much as you should.

Bal. This letter, sir, which I tear in pieces to conceal the person that sent it, informs me that Plume has a design upon Silvia, and that you are privy to't.

[*Tears the letter.*

Wor. Nay then, sir, I must do myself justice, and endeavour to find out the author.—[*Takes up a fragment of the letter.*] Sir, I know the hand, and if you refuse to discover the contents, Melinda shall tell me. [*Going.*

Bal. Hold, sir! The contents I have told you already, only with this circumstance, that her intimacy with Mr Worthy has drawn the secret from him.

Wor. Her intimacy with me!—Dear sir, let me pick up the pieces of this letter; 'twill give me such a power over[1] her pride, to have her own an intimacy under her hand.—[*Gathering up the letter.*] 'Twas the luckiest accident! The aspersion, sir, was nothing but malice, the effect of a little quarrel between her and Mrs Silvia.

Bal. Are you sure of that, sir?

Wor. Her maid gave me the history of part of the battle just now, as she overheard it. But I hope, sir, your daughter has suffered nothing upon the account?

Bal. No, no, poor girl; she's so afflicted with the news of her brother's death, that to avoid company she begged leave to be gone into the country.

Wor. And is she gone?

Bal. I could not refuse her, she was so pressing; the coach went from the door the minute before you came.

Wor. So pressing to be gone, sir! I find her fortune

[1] Q. 1. "such a hank upon."

will give her the same airs with Melinda and then
Plume and I may laugh at one another.

Bal. Like enough; women are as subject to pride as
we are, and why mayn't great women, as well as great
men, forget their old acquaintance? But come, where's
this young fellow? I love him so well, it would break
the heart of me to think him a rascal.—[*Aside.*] I'm
glad my daughter's gone fairly off, though.—[*Aloud.*]
Where does the captain quarter?

Wor. At Horton's; I am to meet him there two
hours hence, and we should be glad of your company.

Bal. Your pardon, dear Worthy; I must allow a day
or two to the death of my son; the decorum of mourning is what we owe the world, because they pay it to
us. Afterwards,[1] I'm yours over a bottle, or how you
will.

Wor. Sir, I'm your humble servant.
                    [*Exeunt severally.*

SCENE III.—*The Street.*

Enter KITE, *leading* COSTAR PEARMAIN *in one hand,
and* THOMAS APPLETREE *in the other, both drunk.*[2]

KITE *sings.*

Our prentice Tom may now refuse
To wipe his scoundrel master's shoes;

---

[1] Q. 1 and Q. 2. "because they pay it to us afterwards. I'm yours,"
etc. An obvious misprint, corrected in many eighteenth century
editions, but reproduced without remark by Leigh Hunt and Ewald.
[2] Early editions: "Enter Kite, with a Mob in each hand,
drunk." The speeches of the Rustics are assigned to "1st Mob"
and "2nd Mob" throughout. In the indications of their dialect we
follow Q. 1. A few changes introduced in Q. 2 are more probably
due to the printer than to the poet.

For now he's free to sing and play—
Over the hills and far away,
Over the hills, &c.   [*The* Mob *sing the Chorus.*[1]

We all shall lead more happy lives
By getting rid of brats and wives,
That scold and brawl both night and day—
Over the hills and far away.
Over the hills, &c.[2]

Hey, boys! thus we soldiers live; drink, sing, dance,
play! We live, as one should say—we live—'tis impossible to tell how we live. We are all princes. Why—
why, you are a king, you are an emperor, and I'm a
prince. Now, ain't we—

Apple. No, serjeant, I'll be no emperor.

Kite. No!

Apple. No, I'll be a justice of peace.

Kite. A justice of peace, man!

Apple. Ay, wauns will I; for since this Pressing Act,[3]
they are greater than any emperor under the sun.

Kite. Done! you are a justice of peace, and you are a
king, and I am a duke; and a rum duke, an't I?

Pear. Ay, but I'll be no king.

Kite. What then?

Pear. I'll be a queen.

Kite. A queen!

Pear. Ay, Queen of England; that's greater than any
king of 'em all

---

[1] This stage-direction of Q. 1 and Q. 2 means that the two Rustics
join Kite in singing the Chorus, which consists of the quatrain sung
by Plume as he enters, on p. 276.

[2] "On September 16, 1706, *The Recruiting Officer* was acted at
Bath—several persons of quality were present—the news of the
victory gained by the Duke of Savoy and Prince Eugene reached
Bath that day—Estcourt added to the song in the second act,—
      The noble Captain Prince Eugene
      Has beat the French, Orleans and Marsin,
      And march'd up and relieved Turin,
      Over the hills and far away." *Genest*, vol. ii. p. 340.

[3] See note, p. 336.

Kite. Bravely said, faith! Huzza for the Queen!—
[*Huzza.*] But heark'ee, you Mr Justice, and you Mr
Queen, did you ever see the Queen's picture?

Both. No, no, no.

Kite. I wonder at that; I have two of 'em, set in gold,
and as like her Majesty, God bless the mark!—See here,
they are set in gold.

> [*Takes two broad pieces out of his pocket, and
> gives one to each.*

Apple. The wonderful works of Nature!

> [*Looking at it.*

Pear. What's this written about? Here's a posy, I
believe,—*Ca-ro-lus.*—What's that, serjeant?

Kite. Oh, Carolus!—Why, Carolus is Latin for
Queen Anne,—that's all.

Pear. 'Tis a fine thing to be a scollard!—Serjeant,
will you part with this? I'll buy it on you, if it come
within the compass of a crown.

Kite. A crown! Never talk of buying; 'tis the same
thing among friends, you know; I'll present them to ye
both: you shall give me as good a thing. Put 'em up,
and remember your old friend, when I am over the
hills and far away! [*They sing and put up the money.*

Enter PLUME, *singing.*

Plume.   *Over the hills and o'er the main,*
      To Flanders, Portugal, or Spain:
      The queen commands, and we'll obey—
      Over the hills and far away.

Come on, my men of mirth, away with it, I'll make one
among ye.—Who are these hearty lads?

Kite. Off with your hats; 'ounds, off with your hats!
This is the captain, the captain.

Apple. We have seen captains afore now, mun.

Pear. Ay, and lieutenant-captains too; flesh, I'se keep
on my nab!

Apple. And I'se scarcely doff mine for any captain in England. My vether's a freeholder.

Plume. Who are these jolly lads, serjeant?

Kite. A couple of honest brave fellows, that are willing to serve the Queen: I have entertained 'em just now, as volunteers, under your honour's command.

Plume. And good entertainment they shall have. Volunteers are the men I want, those are the men fit to make soldiers, captains, generals!

Pear. Wauns, Tummas, what's this! Are you listed?

Apple. Flesh, not I: are you, Costar?·

Pear. Wauns, not I!

Kite. What, not listed! Ha, ha, ha! a very good jest, faith!

Pear. Come, Tummas, we'll go home.

Apple. Ay, ay, come.

Kite. Home! for shame, gentlemen, behave yourselves better before your captain! Dear Tummas, honest Costar—

Apple. No, no, we'll be gone.

Kite. Nay then, I command you to stay: I place you both sentinels in this place for two hours: to watch the motion of St Mary's clock, you; and you the motion of St Chad's. And he that dares stir from his post till he be relieved, shall have my sword in his guts the next minute.

Plume. What's the matter, serjeant? I'm afraid you are too rough with these gentlemen.

Kite. I'm too mild, sir: they disobey command, sir, and one of 'em should be shot for an example to the other.

Pear. Shot, Tummas!

Plume. Come, gentlemen, what's the matter?

Pear. We don't know; the noble serjeant is pleased to be in a passion, sir, but—

Kite. They disobey command; they deny their being listed.

Apple. Nay, sergeant, we don't downright deny it

neither; that we dare not do, for fear of being shot; but we humbly conceive in a civil way, and begging your worship's pardon, that we may go home.

Plume. That's easily known. Have either of you received any of the Queen's money?

Pear. Not a brass farthing, sir.

Kite. Sir, they have each of 'em received three-and-twenty shillings and sixpence, and 'tis now in their pockets.

Pear. Wauns, if I have a penny in my pocket but a bent sixpence, I'll be content to be listed, and shot into the bargain!

Apple. And I.   Look ye here, sir.

Pear. Ay, here's my stock too: nothing but the Queen's picture, that the serjeant gave me just now.

Kite. See there, a broad-piece! three-and-twenty shillings and sixpence; the t'other has the fellow on't.

Plume. The case is plain, gentlemen; the goods are found upon you.   Those pieces of gold are worth three-and-twenty and sixpence each.

[*Whispers* Serjeant KITE.

Pear. So it seems that *Carolus* is three-and-twenty shillings and sixpence in Latin.

Apple. 'Tis the same thing in the Greek, for we are listed.

Pear. Flesh, but we an't, Tummas!—I desire to be carried before the Mayor, Captain.

Plume. [*Aside to* KITE.] 'Twill never do, Kite—your damned tricks will ruin me at last.—I won't lose the fellows though, if I can help it.—[*Aloud.*] Well, gentlemen, there must be some trick in this: my serjeant offers here to take his oath that you are fairly listed.

Apple. Why, Captain, we know that you soldiers have more liberty of conscience than other folks; but for me or neighbour Costar here to take such an oath, 'twould be a downright perjuration.

Plume. [*To* KITE.] Look'ee, you rascal! you villain! if I find that you have imposed upon these two honest fellows, I'll trample you to death, you dog! Come, how was't?

Apple. Nay, then, we will speak. Your sarjeant, as you say, is a rogue, begging your worship's pardon, and—

Pear. Nay, Tummas, let me speak; you know I can read.—And so, sir, he gave us those two pieces of money for pictures of the Queen, by way of a present.

Plume. How! by way of a present! The son of a whore! I'll teach him to abuse honest fellows like you!—Scoundrel, rogue, villain!

[*Beats off the* Serjeant, *and follows.*

Both. O brave noble Captain! Huzza! a brave captain, faith!

Pear. Now, Tummas, *Carolus* is Latin for a beating. This is the bravest captain I ever saw.—Wauns, I have a month's mind to go with him!

Re-enter PLUME.

Plume. A dog to abuse two such pretty fellows as you!—Look'ee, gentlemen, I love a pretty fellow: I come among you as an officer to list soldiers, not as a kidnapper, to steal slaves.

Pear. Mind that, Tummas.

Plume. I desire no man to go with me but as I went myself: I went a volunteer, as you, or you, may do; for a little time carried a musket, and now I command a company.

Apple. Mind that, Costar.—a sweet gentleman!

Plume. 'Tis true, gentlemen, I might take an advantage of you; the Queen's money was in your pockets, my serjeant was ready to take his oath you were listed; but I scorn to do a base thing, you are, both of you at your liberty.

Pear. Thank you, noble captain.—Ecod, I can't find in my heart to leave him, he talks so finely.

Apple. Ay, Costar, would he always hold in this mind.

Plume. Come, my lads, one thing more I'll tell you: you're both young tight fellows, and the army is the place to make you men for ever: every man has his lot, and you have yours. What think you now of a purse full of French gold out of a monsieur's pocket, after you have dashed out his brains with the butt of your firelock, eh?

Pear. Wauns! I'll have it, Captain—give me a shilling, I'll follow you to the end of the world.

Apple. Nay, dear Costar, duna; be advised.

Plume. Here, my hero, here are two guineas for thee, as earnest of what I'll do farther for thee.

Apple. Duna take it; duna, dear Costar!
                              [*Cries, and pulls back his arm.*

Pear. I wull! I wull!—Wauns, my mind gives me, that I shall be a captain myself.—I take your money, sir, and now I am a gentleman.

Plume. Give me thy hand, and now you and I will travel the world o'er, and command it wherever we tread. —[*Aside to* COSTAR PEARMAIN.] Bring your friend with you, if you can.

Pear. Well, Tummas, must we part?

Apple. No, Costar, I canno leave thee. — Come, Captain, I'll e'en go along too; and if you have two honester simpler lads in your company than we two been, I'll say no more.

Plume. Here, my lad.—[*Gives him money.*] Now, your name?

Apple. Tummas Appletree.[1]

Plume. And yours?

---

[1] For a curious anecdote of Pinkethman in the part of Appletree, see Davies, *Dramatic Miscellanies*, III., 87. Also Cibber's *Apology*, ed., Lowe, I., 153.

Pear. Costar Pearmain.

Plume. Born where?

Apple. Both in Herefordshire.

Plume. Very well; courage, my lads!—Now we'll sing, *Over the hills and far away.*   [*Sings.*

> *Courage, boys, 'tis one to ten,*
> *But we return all gentlemen, &c.*   [*Exeunt.* [1]

---

[1] So the scene ends in Q. 1 and Q. 2 and in the editions of 1710, 1714, Dublin 1775 and others. In the 1770 edition, followed wholly or in part by some later editions, it ends thus:

Plume. Courage, boys, 'tis one to ten.
> *But we return all gentlemen;*
> *While conquering colours we display*
> *Over the hills and far away.*

Kite, take care of 'em.

Enter KITE.

Kite. An't you a couple of pretty fellows now! Here you have complained to the captain, I am to be turned out, and one of you will be serjeant. Which of you is to have my halberd?

Both Recru. I.

Kite. So you shall—in your guts—march, you sons of whores.

[*Beats 'em off.*

ACT III

SCENE I.—*The Market-Place.*

Enter PLUME *and* WORTHY.

OR. I cannot forbear admiring the equality of our two fortunes. We love two ladies, they met us half way, and just as we were upon the point of leaping into their arms, fortune drops into their laps, pride possesses their hearts, a maggot fills their heads, madness takes 'em by the tails; they snort, kick up their heels, and away they run.

Plume. And leave us here to mourn upon the shore —a couple of poor melancholy monsters.—What shall we do?

Wor. I have a trick for mine; the letter, you know, and the fortune-teller.

Plume. And I have a trick of mine.

Wor. What is't?

Plume. I'll never think of her again.

Wor. No!

Plume. No; I think myself above administering to the pride of any woman, were she worth twelve thousand a year, and I han't the vanity to believe I shall ever gain a lady worth twelve hundred. The generous

good-natured Silvia in her smock I admire, but the
haughty scornful Silvia, with her fortune, I despise.[1]
What, sneak out of town, and not so much as a word, a
line, a compliment ! 'Sdeath, how far off does she
live ? I'll go and break her windows.

Wor. Ha, ha, ha, ay, and the window-bars too, to
come at her. Come, come, friend, no more of your
rough military airs.

Enter KITE.

Kite. Captain ! sir ! look yonder, she's a-coming this
way : 'tis the prettiest, cleanest little tit !

Plume. Now, Worthy, to show you how much I am in
love.—Here she comes ; and what is that great country
fellow with her ?

Kite. I can't tell, sir.

Enter ROSE *and her brother* BULLOCK,[2] ROSE *with
a basket on her arm, crying chickens.*

Rose. Buy chickens ! young and tender ! young and
tender chickens !

[1] In Q. 1 the following song is introduced here :

> Come, fair one, be kind ;
> You never shall find
> A fellow so fit for a lover ;
> The world shall view
> My passion for you,
> But never your passion discover.
>
> I still will complain
> Of your frowns and disdain,
> Though I revel through all your charms :
> The world shall declare
> That I die with despair,
> When I only die in your arms.
>
> I still will adore,
> And love more and more,
> But, by Jove, if you chance to prove cruel,
> I'll get me a miss
> That freely will kiss,
> Though I afterwards drink water-gruel.

It is omitted in Q. 2 and is obviously detrimental to the scene.

[2] In the indications of dialect, Q. 1 is almost always followed.

Plume. Here, you chickens !

Rose. Who calls ?

Plume. Come hither, pretty maid.

Rose. Will you please to buy, sir ?

Wor. Yes, child, we'll both buy.

Plume. Nay, Worthy, that's not fair, market for your-self.—Come, child, I'll buy all you have.

Rose. Then all I have is at your service.   [*Curtsies.*

Wor. Then I must shift for myself, I find.   [*Exit.*

Plume. Let me see ; young and tender you say ?

[*Chucks her under the chin.*

Rose. As ever you tasted in your life, sir.

Plume. Come, I must examine your basket to the bottom, my dear.

Rose, Nay, for that matter, put in your hand; feel, sir ; I warrant my ware as good as any in the market.

Plume. And I'll buy it all, child, were it ten times more.

Rose. Sir, I can furnish you.

Plume. Come, then, we won't quarrel about the price, they're fine birds.—Pray what's your name, pretty creature ?

Rose. Rose, sir.   My father is a farmer within three short mile o' the town ; we keep this market ; I sell chickens, eggs and butter, and my brother Bullock there sells corn.

Bull. Come, sister, hast ye, we shall be liate a whome.

[*All this while* BULLOCK *whistles about the stage.*

Plume. Kite !—[*Tips him the wink, he returns it.*]
Pretty Mrs Rose — you have, let me see — how many ?

Rose. A dozen, sir, and they are richly worth a crawn.

Bull. Come, Ruose, Ruose ! I sold fifty stracke o' barley to-day in half this time ; but you will higgle and higgle for a penny more than the commodity is worth.

Rose. What's that to you, oaf? I can make as much out of a groat as you can out of fourpence, I'm sure. The gentleman bids fair, and when I meet with a chapman I know how to make the best on him.—And so, sir, I say, for a crawn-piece, the bargain's yours.

Plume. Here's a guinea, my dear.

Rose. I can't change your money, sir.

Plume. Indeed, indeed, but you can : my lodging is hard by, chicken, and we'll make change there.[1]

[*Goes off, she follows him.*

Kite. So, sir, as I was telling you, I have seen one of these hussars eat up a ravelin for his breakfast, and afterwards pick his teeth with a palisado.

Bull. Ay, you soldiers see very strange things. But pray, sir, what is a ravelin ?

Kite. Why, 'tis like a modern minced pie, but the crust is confounded hard, and the plums are somewhat hard of digestion.

Bull. Then your palisado, pray what may he be ?—Come, Ruose, pray ha' done.

Kite. Your palisado is a pretty sort of bodkin, about the thickness of my leg.

Bull. [*Aside.*] That's a fib, I believe.—[*Aloud.*] Eh ! where's Ruose ? Ruose ! Ruose ! 'sflesh, where's Ruose gone ?

Kite. She's gone with the captain.

Bull. The captain ! Wauns, there's no pressing of women, surely ?

Kite. But there is, sir.

Bull. If the captain should press Ruose I should be ruined ! Which way went she ? Oh, the devil take your rablins and your palisaders ! [*Exit.*

Kite. You shall be better acquainted with them, honest Bullock, or I shall miss of my aim.

[1] Q. 1. "My lodging is hard by, you shall bring home the chickens," &c.

Re-enter WORTHY.

Wor. Why, thou art the most useful fellow in nature to your captain ; admirable in your way, I find.

Kite. Yes, sir, I understand my business, I will say it.—You must know, sir, I was born a gipsy, and bred among that crew till I was ten year old. There I learned canting and lying. I was bought from my mother, Cleopatra, by a certain nobleman for three pistoles ; who, liking my beauty, made me his page ; there I learned impudence and pimping. I was turned off for wearing my lord's linen, and drinking my lady's ratafia, and then turned bailiff's follower : there I learned bullying and swearing. I at last got into the army, and there I learned whoring and drinking : so that if your worship pleases to cast up the whole sum, viz., canting, lying, impudence, pimping, bullying, swearing, whoring, drinking, and a halberd, you will find the sum total will amount to a recruiting serjeant.

Wor. And pray what induced you to turn soldier ?

Kite. Hunger and ambition. The fears of starving, the hopes of a truncheon, led me along to a gentleman with a fair tongue and fair periwig, who loaded me with promises ; but, egad, it was the lightest load that ever I felt in my life. He promised to advance me, and indeed he did so—to a garret in the Savoy. I asked him why he put me in prison ; he called me lying dog, and said I was in garrison ; and indeed 'tis a garrison that may hold out till doomsday before I should desire to take it again.   But here comes Justice Balance.

Enter BALANCE *and* BULLOCK.

Bal. Here, you serjeant, where's your captain ? Here's a poor foolish fellow comes clamouring to me with a complaint that your captain has pressed his sister.—Do you know anything of this matter, Worthy ?

Wor. Ha, ha, ha ! I know his sister is gone with Plume to his lodging, to sell him some chickens.

Bal. Is that all? The fellow's a fool.

Bull. I know that, an't please you ; but if your worship pleases to grant me a warrant to bring her before you, for fear o' th' worst.

Bal. Thou'rt mad, fellow ; thy sister's safe enough.

Kite. [*Aside.*] I hope so too.

Wor. Hast thou no more sense, fellow, than to believe that the captain can list women ?

Bull. I know not whether they list them, or what they do with them, but, I am sure, they carry as many women as men with them out of the country.

Bal. But how came you not to go along with your sister?

Bull. Luord, sir, I thought no more of her going than I do of the day I shall die ; but this gentleman here, not suspecting any hurt neither, I believe—[*To* KITE.] You thought no harm, friend, did ye ?

Kite. Lackaday, sir, not I !—[*Aside.*] Only that I believe I shall marry her to-morrow.

Bal. I begin to smell powder.—Well, friend, but what did that gentleman with you ?

Bull. Why, sir, he entertained me with a fine story of a great fight between the Hungarians, I think it was, and the Irish ; and so, sir, while we were in the heat of the battle—the Captain carried off the baggage.

Bal. Serjeant, go along with this fellow to your Captain, give him my humble service, and desire [1] him to discharge the wench, though he has listed her.

Bull. Ay, and if he ben't free for that, he shall have another man in her place.

Kite. Come, honest friend.—[*Aside.*] You shall go to my quarters instead of the Captain's.

[*Exit with* BULLOCK.

Bal. We must get this mad captain his complement

Q. 1. "I desire."

of men, and send him a-packing, else he'll overrun the country.

Wor. You see, sir, how little he values your daughter's disdain.

Bal. I like him the better; I was just such another fellow at his age. I never set my heart upon any woman so much as to make myself uneasy at the disappointment; but what was very surprising both to myself and friends, I changed o' th' sudden from the most fickle lover to the most constant husband in the world. But how goes your affair with Melinda?

Wor. Very slowly. Cupid had formerly wings, but I think, in this age, he goes upon crutches; or, I fancy Venus has been dallying with her cripple Vulcan when my amour commenced, which has made it go on so lamely. My mistress has got a captain too, but such a captain! As I live, yonder he comes?

Bal. Who? that bluff fellow in the sash! I don't know him.

Wor. But I engage he knows you, and everybody, at first sight: his impudence were a prodigy were not his ignorance proportionable. He has the most universal acquaintance of any man living; for he won't be alone, and nobody will keep him company twice. Then he's a Cæsar among the women, *Veni, vidi, vici*, that's all: if he has but talked with the maid, he swears he has lain with the mistress. But the most surprising part of his character is his memory, which is the most prodigious and the most trifling in the world.

Bal. I have met with such men; and I take this good-for-nothing memory to proceed from a certain contexture of the brain, which is purely adapted to impertinencies, and there they lodge secure, the owner having no thoughts of his own to disturb them. I have known a man as perfect as a chronologer as to the day and year of most important transactions, but be altogether ignorant of the causes or consequences [1] of any one thing of moment. I have known another acquire so much by travel as to tell you the names of most places in Europe, with their distances of miles, leagues, or hours, as punctually as a postboy; but for anything else, as ignorant as the horse that carries the mail.

Wor. This is your man, sir: add but the traveller's privilege of lying; and even that he abuses. This is the picture, behold the life.

Enter BRAZEN.

Braz. Mr Worthy, I am your servant, and so forth.— Hark'ee, my dear.

Wor. Whispering, sir, before company is not manners, and when nobody's by 'tis foolish.

Braz. Company! *Mort de ma vie!* I beg the gentleman's pardon; who is he?

Wor. Ask him.

Braz. So I will.—My dear, I am your servant, and so forth—your name, my dear?

Bal. Very laconic, sir!

Braz. Laconic! a very good name, truly; I have known several of the Laconics abroad.—Poor Jack Laconic! he was killed at the battle of Landen. I remember that he had a blue ribbon in his hat that very day, and after he fell we found a piece of neat's tongue in his pocket.

Bal. Pray, sir, did the French attack us, or we them, at Landen?

Braz. The French attack us! Oons, sir, are you a Jacobite?

Bal. Why that question?

Braz. Because none but a Jacobite could think that the French durst attack us. No, sir, we attacked them on the—I have reason to remember the time, for I had two-and-twenty horses killed under me that day.

[1] Q. 1, "causes, springs or consequences."

Wor. Then, sir, you must have rid mighty hard.

Bal. Or perhaps, sir, like my countryman, you rid upon half-a-dozen horses at once.

Braz. What do you mean, gentlemen? I tell you they were killed, all torn to pieces by cannon-shot, except six I staked to death upon the enemy's *chevaux-de-frise*.

Bal. Noble Captain, may I crave your name?

Braz. Brazen, at your service.

Bal. Oh, Brazen, a very good name; I have known several of the Brazens abroad.

Wor. Do you know Captain Plume, sir?

Braz. Is he anything related to Frank Plume in Northamptonshire?—Honest Frank! many, many a dry bottle have we cracked hand to fist. You must have known his brother Charles that was concerned in the India Company; he married the daughter of old Tonguepad, the Master in Chancery, a very pretty woman, only squinted a little. She died in childbed of her first child, but the child survived; 'twas a daughter, but whether 'twas called Margaret or Margery, upon my soul, I can't remember.—[*Looking on his watch.*] But, gentlemen, I must meet a lady, a twenty thousand pounder, presently, upon the walk by the water.— Worthy, your servant.—Laconic, yours.   [*Exit.*

Bal. If you can have so mean an opinion of Melinda as to be jealous of this fellow, I think she ought to give you cause to be so.

Wor. I don't think she encourages him so much for gaining herself a lover, as to set me up a rival. Were there any credit to be given to his words, I should believe Melinda had made him this assignation. I must go see; sir, you'll pardon me.

Bal. Ay, ay, sir, you're a man of business.—[*Exit* Mr WORTHY.] But what have we got here?

Re-enter ROSE, *singing.*

Rose. And I shall be a lady, a captain's lady, and ride

single upon a white horse with a star, upon a velvet side-saddle; and I shall go to London, and see the tombs, and the lions, and the Queen.—Sir, an please your worship, I have often seen your worship ride through our grounds a-hunting, begging your worship's pardon—pray what may this lace be worth a yard?

[*Showing some lace.*

Bal. Right Mechlin, by this light! Where did you get this lace, child?

Rose. No matter for that, sir; I come honestly by it.

Bal. I question it much.

Rose. And see here, sir, a fine Turkey-shell snuff-box and fine mangeree, see here.—[*Takes snuff affectedly.*] The captain learned me how to take it with an air.

Bal. Oho! the captain! now the murder's out. And so the captain taught you to take it with an air?

Rose. Yes, and give it with an air too.—Will your worship please to taste my snuff.

[*Offers the box affectedly.*

Bal. You are a very apt scholar, pretty maid. And pray, what did you give the captain for these fine things?

Rose. He's to have my brother for a soldier, and two or three sweethearts that I have in the country, they shall all go with the captain. Oh, he's the finest man, and the humblest withal! Would you believe it, sir, he carried me up with him to his own chamber, with as much familiarity [1] as if I had been the best lady in the land!

Bal. Oh! he's a mighty familiar gentleman, as can be. [2]

---

[1] The edition of 1770 (evidently from a theatrical prompt-book) prints this word "fam-mam-mill-yara-rality" and is followed, oddly enough, by Leigh Hunt and Ewald.

[2] In Q. 1 the text runs as follows, after "familiar gentleman as can be."—

Rose. But I must beg your worship's pardon, I must go seek out my brother Bullock.   [*Runs off singing.*

Bal. If all officers took the same method of recruiting with this

Re-enter PLUME, *singing.*

Plume.   But it is not so
   With those that go,
   Through frost and snow.
   Most apropos,
   My maid with the milking-pail.
       [*Takes hold of* ROSE.

—[*Aside.*] How, the Justice! then I'm arraigned, condemned, and executed.

Bal. Oh, my noble Captain!

Rose. And my noble Captain too, sir.

Plume. [*Aside to* ROSE.] 'Sdeath, child! are you mad?
—[*Aloud.*] Mr Balance, I am so full of business about my recruits, that I han't a moment's time to—I have just now three or four people to—

Bal. Nay, Captain, I must speak to you—

Rose. And so must I too, Captain.

Plume. Any other time, sir—I cannot for my life, sir—

Bal. Pray, sir—

Plume. Twenty thousand things—I would—but now, sir, pray—devil take me— I cannot—I must—

       [*Breaks away.*

Bal. Nay, I'll follow you.   [*Exit.*

Rose. And I too.   [*Exit.*

gentlemen, they might come in time to be fathers as well as captains of their companies.

Enter PLUME, *singing.*

Plume. But it is not so, &c.

The intention, though the stage-directions are imperfect, evidently was that Plume should meet Rose outside and bring her back with him. It was doubtless found more effective that Rose should not leave the stage, but that Plume should enter and embrace her, not at first observing Balance.

SCENE II.—*The Walk by the Severn side.*

Enter MELINDA *and* LUCY.

Mel. And pray was it a ring, or buckle, or pendants, or knots? or in what shape was the almighty gold transformed that has bribed you so much in his favour?

Lucy. Indeed, madam, the last bribe I had was from the captain, and that was only a small piece of Flanders edging for pinners.[1]

Mel. Ay, Flanders lace is as constant a present from officers to their women as something élse is from their women to them.   They every year bring over a cargo of lace, to cheat the Queen of her duty, and her subjects of their honesty.

Lucy. They only barter one sort of prohibited goods for another, madam.

Mel. Has any of 'em been bartering with you, Mrs Pert, that you talk so like a trader?

Lucy. Madam, you talk as peevishly to me as if it were my fault; the crime is none of mine, though I pretend to excuse it: though he should not see you this week, can I help it?   But as I was saying, madam—his friend, Captain Plume, has so taken him up these two days.

Mel. Psha! would his friend, the captain, were tied upon his back!   I warrant he has never been sober since that confounded captain came to town.   The devil take all officers, I say! they do the nation more harm by debauching us at home than they do good by defending us abroad.   No sooner a captain comes to town but all the young fellows flock about him, and we can't keep a man to ourselves.

Lucy. One would imagine, madam, by your concern for Worthy's absence, that you should use him better when he's with you.

---

[1] " A female headdress, having long flaps hanging down the sides of the cheeks."

Mel. Who told you, pray, that I was concerned for his absence ? I'm only vexed that I've had nothing said to me these two days. One may like the love and despise the lover, I hope; as one may love the treason and hate the traitor.—Oh, here comes another captain, and a rogue that has the confidence to make love to me ; but, indeed, I don't wonder at that, when he has the assurance to fancy himself a fine gentleman.

Lucy. [*Aside.*] If he should speak o' th' assignation I should be ruined.

Enter BRAZEN.

Braz. [*Aside.*] True to the touch, faith !—[*Aloud.*] Madam, I am your humble servant, and all that, madam. —A fine river, this same Severn.—Do you love fishing, madam ?

Mel. 'Tis a pretty, melancholy amusement for lovers.

Braz. I'll go buy hooks and lines presently; for you must know, madam, that I have served in Flanders against the French, in Hungary against the Turks, and in Tangier against the Moors, and I was never so much in love before; and split me, madam, in all the campaigns I ever made, I have not seen so fine a woman as your ladyship.

Mel. And from all the men I ever saw I never had so fine a compliment; but you soldiers are the best bred men, that we must allow.

Braz. Some of us, madam.—But there are brutes among us too, very sad brutes ; for my own part, I have always had the good luck to prove agreeable.—I have had very considerable offers, madam—I might have married a German princess, worth fifty thousand crowns a year, but her stove disgusted me.—The daughter of a Turkish bashaw fell in love with me too, when I was prisoner among the Infidels ; she offered to rob her father of his treasure, and make her escape with me ; but I don't know how, my time was not come. Hanging

and marriage, you know, go by destiny; Fate has reserved me for a Shropshire lady with twenty thousand
pounds.—Do you know any such person, madam?

Mel. [*Aside.*] Extravagant coxcomb!—[*Aloud.*] To
be sure, a great many ladies of that fortune would be
proud of the name of Mrs Brazen.

Braz. Nay, for that matter, madam, there are women
of very good quality of the name of Brazen.

Enter WORTHY.

Mel. [*Aside.*] Oh, are you there, gentlemen?—[*Aloud.*]
Come, Captain, we'll walk this way; give me your hand.

Braz. My hand, heart's blood, and guts are at your
service.—Mr Worthy, your servant, my dear.

　　　　　[*Exit, leading* MELINDA, LUCY *following.*

Wor. Death and fire, this is not to be borne!

Enter Captain PLUME.

Plume. No more it is, faith.

Wor. What?

Plume. The March beer at the Raven. I have been
doubly serving the Queen—raising men, and raising the
excise. Recruiting and elections are rare friends to the
excise.

Wor. You an't drunk?

Plume. No, no, whimsical only: I could be mighty
foolish, and fancy myself mighty witty. Reason still
keeps its throne, but it nods a little, that's all.

Wor. Then you're just fit for a frolic.

Plume As fit as close pinners for a punk in the pit.

Wor. There's your play, then—recover me that vessel
from that Tangerine.

Plume. She's well rigged, but how is she manned?

Wor. By Captain Brazen, that I told you of to-day.
She is called the Melinda, a first-rate, I can assure you;
she sheered off with him just now, on purpose to affront
me; but, according to your advice, I would take no

notice, because I would seem to be above a concern for her behaviour.—But have a care of a quarrel.

Plume. No, no, I never quarrel with anything in my cups, but an oyster wench, or a cookmaid; and if they ben't civil, I knock 'em down. But heark'ee, my friend, I'll make love, and I must make love. I tell you what, I'll make love like a platoon.

Wor. Platoon, how's that?

Plume. I'll kneel, stoop, and stand, faith; most ladies are gained by platooning.

Wor. Here they come; I must leave you. [*Exit.*

Plume. Soh! now must I look as sober and as demure as a whore at a christening.

Re-enter BRAZEN *and* MELINDA.

Braz. Who's that, madam?

Mel. A brother officer of yours, I suppose, sir.

Braz. Ay!—[*To* PLUME.] My dear!

Plume. My dear!　　　　　　　[*Run and embrace.*

Braz. My dear boy, how is't? Your name, my dear? If I be not mistaken, I have seen your face.

Plume. I never saw yours in my life, my dear.—But there's a face well known as the sun's, that shines on all and is by all adored.

Braz. Have you any pretensions, sir?

Plume. Pretensions!

Braz. That is, sir, have you ever served abroad?

Plume. I have served at home, sir, for ages served this cruel fair—and that will serve the turn, sir.

Mel. [*Aside.*] So, between the fool and the rake I shall bring a fine spot of work upon my hands!—I see Worthy yonder—I could be content to be friends with him, would he come this way.

Braz. Will you fight for the lady, sir?

Plume. No, sir, but I'll have her notwithstanding.

Thou peerless princess of Salopian plains,
Envied by nymphs, and worshipp'd by the swains!

Braz. Oons, sir, not fight for her!

Plume. Prithee be quiet—I shall be out—

Behold how humbly does the Severn glide
To greet thee, princess of the Severn side!

Braz. Don't mind him, madam.—If he were not so well dressed, I should take him for a poet.—But I'll show the difference presently.—Come, madam, we'll place you between us; and now the longest sword carries her.   [*Draws*, MELINDA *shrieks*.

Re-enter WORTHY.

Mel. Oh! Mr Worthy! save me from these madmen.
                                        [*Exit with* WORTHY.

Plume. Ha, ha, ha! why don't you follow, sir, and fight the bold ravisher?

Braz. No, sir, you are my man.

Plume. I don't like the wages, and I won't be your man.

Braz. Then you're not worth my sword.

Plume. No! pray what did it cost?

Braz. It cost me twenty pistoles in France, and my enemies thousands of lives in Flanders.

Plume. Then they had a dear bargain.

Enter SILVIA, *in man's apparel.*

Silv. Save ye, save ye, gentlemen!

Braz. My dear, I'm yours.

Plume. Do you know the gentleman?

Braz. No, but I will presently.—[*To* SILVIA.] Your name, my dear?

Silv. Wilful; Jack Wilful, at your service.

Braz. What, the Kentish Wilfuls, or those of Staffordshire?

Silv. Both, sir, both; I'm related to all the Wilfuls in Europe, and I'm head of the family at present.

Plume. Do you live in this country, sir?

Silv. Yes, sir, I live where I stand; I have neither home, house, nor habitation, beyond this spot of ground.

Braz. What are you, sir?

Silv. A rake.

Plume. In the army, I presume.

Silv. No, but I intend to list immediately.—Look'ee, gentlemen, he that bids me fairest shall have me.

Braz. Sir, I'll prefer you, I'll make you a corporal this minute.

Plume. Corporal! I'll make you my companion; you shall eat with me.

Braz. You shall drink with me.

Plume. You shall lie with me, you young rogue.

[*Kisses her.*

Braz. You shall receive your pay, and do no duty.

Silv. Then you must make me a field officer.

Plume. Pho! pho! I'll do more than all this; I'll make you a corporal, and give you a brevet for serjeant.

Braz. Can you read and write, sir?

Silv. Yes.

Braz. Then your business is done—I'll make you chaplain to the regiment.

Silv. Your promises are so equal, that I'm at a loss to choose. There is one Plume, that I hear much commended, in town; pray, which of you is Captain Plume?

Plume. I am Captain Plume.

Braz. No, no, I am Captain Plume.

Silv. Heyday!

Plume. Captain Plume! I'm your servant, my dear.

Braz. Captain Brazen! I am yours.—[*Aside.*] The fellow dare not fight.

Enter KITE.

Kite. [*Goes to whisper to* PLUME.] Sir, if you please—

Plume. No, no, there's your captain.—Captain Plume, your serjeant here has got so drunk, he mistakes me for you.

Braz. He's an incorrigible sot!—[*To* SILVIA.] Here, my Hector of Holborn, forty shillings for you.

Plume. I forbid the banns.—Look'ee, friend, you shall list with Captain Brazen.

Silv. I will see Captain Brazen hanged first! I will list with Captain Plume. I am a freeborn Englishman, and will be a slave my own way.—[*To* BRAZEN.] Look'ee sir, will you stand by me?

Braz. I warrant you, my lad.

Silv. [*To* PLUME.] Then I will tell you, Captain Brazen, that you are an ignorant, pretending, impudent coxcomb.

Braz. Ay, ay, a sad dog.

Silv. A very sad dog.—Give me the money, noble Captain Plume.

Plume. Then you won't list with Captain Brazen?

Silv. I won't.

Braz. Never mind him, child, I'll end the dispute presently.—Heark'ee my dear.

> [*Takes* PLUME *to one side of the stage, and entertains him in dumb show.*

Kite. Sir, he in the plain coat is Captain Plume, I am his serjeant, and will take my oath on't.

Silv. What! are you Serjeant Kite?

Kite. At your service.

Silv. Then I would not take your oath for a farthing.

Kite. A very understanding youth of his age!—Pray, sir, let me look you full in the face.

Silv. Well, sir, what have you to say to my face.

Kite. The very image and superscription of my brother; two bullets of the same caliver were never so like: sure it must be Charles, Charles!

Silv. What d'ye mean by Charles?

Kite. The voice too, only a little variation in Effa-ut [1]

---

[1] " The fuller name (F *fa ut*) of the note F which was sung to the syllable *fa* or *ut* according as it occurred in one or other of the Hexachords (imperfect scales) to which it could belong."—*N. E. D.*

flat.—My dear brother, for I must call you so, if you should have the fortune to enter into the most noble society of the sword, I bespeak you for a comrade.

Silv. No, sir, I'll be your captain's comrade, if anybody's.

Kite. Ambition there again ! Tis a noble passion for a soldier ; by that I gained this glorious halberd. Ambition ! I see a commission in his face already. Pray, noble captain, give me leave to salute you.

[Offers to kiss her.

Silv. What, men kiss one another !

Kite. We officers do : 'tis our way ; we live together like man and wife, always either kissing or fighting.— But I see a storm a-coming.

Silv. Now, serjeant, I shall see who is your captain by your knocking down the t'other.

Kite. My captain scorns assistance, sir.

Braz. How dare you contend for anything, and not dare to draw your sword ? But you're a young fellow, and have not been much abroad ; I excuse that, but prithee resign the man, prithee do ; you're a very honest fellow.

Plume. You lie ; and you are a son of a whore.

[Draws and makes up to BRAZEN.

Braz. Hold ! hold ! did not you refuse to fight for the lady?   [*Retiring.*

Plume. I always do—but for a man I'll fight knee deep ; so you lie again.

> [PLUME *and* BRAZEN *fight a traverse or two about the stage ;* SILVIA *draws, and is held by* KITE, *who sounds to arms with his mouth ; takes* SILVIA *in his arms, and carries her off.*

Braz. Hold ! where's the man ?

Plume. Gone.

Braz. Then what do you fight for?—[*Puts up.*] Now let's embrace, my dear.

Plume. With all my heart, my dear. [*Putting up.*]

I suppose Kite has listed him by this time.

[They embrace.

Braz. You are a brave fellow. I always fight with a man before I make him my friend ; and if once I find he will fight, I never quarrel with him afterwards. And now I'll tell you a secret, my dear friend ; that lady we frighted out of the walk just now I found in bed this morning—so beautiful, so inviting !—I presently locked the door—but I am a man of honour.—But I believe I shall marry her nevertheless ; her twenty thousand pound, you know, will be a pretty convenience.—I had an assignation with her here, but your coming spoiled my sport. Curse you, my dear, but don't do so again.

Plume. No, no, my dear, men are my business at present. *[Exeunt.*

ACT IV

SCENE I.—*The Walk by the Severn.*

Enter ROSE *and* BULLOCK, *meeting.*

OSE. Where have you been, you great booby? You're always out o' the way in the time of preferment.

Bull. Preferment! who should prefer me?

Rose. I would prefer you! Who should prefer a man but a woman? Come, throw away that great club, hold up your head, cock your hat, and look big.

Bull. Ah, Ruose, Ruose, I fear somebody will look big sooner than folk think of! This genteel breeding never comes into the country without a train of followers.—Here has been Cartwheel, your sweetheart; what will become o' him?

Rose. Look'ee, I'm a great woman, and will provide for my relations. I told the captain how finely he could play upon the tabor and pipe, so he has set him down for drum-major.

Bull. Nay, sister, why did not you keep that place for me! You know I always loved to be a-drumming, if it were but on a table or on a quart pot.

302

Enter SILVIA.

Silv. Had I but a commission in my pocket, I fancy my breeches would become me as well as any ranting fellow of 'em all ; for I take a bold step, a rakish toss, a smart cock, and an impudent air, to be the principal ingredients in the composition of a captain.—What's here : Rose ! my nurse's daughter !—I'll go and practise. —Come, child, kiss me at once.—[*Kisses* ROSE.] And her brother too !—[*To* BULLOCK.] Weli, honest dung-fork, do you know the difference between a horse-cart and a cart-horse, eh ?

Bull. I presume that your worship is a captain by your clothes and your courage.

Silv. Suppose I were, would you be contented to list, friend ?

Rose. No, no, though your worship be a handsome man, there be others as fine as you ; my brother is engaged to Captain Plume.

Silv. Plume ! do you know Captain Plume?

Rose. Yes, I do, and he knows me. He took the very ribbons out of his shirt-sleeves, and put 'em into my shoes. See there !—I can assure you that I can do anything with the captain.

Bull. That is, in a modest way, sir.—Have a care what you say, Ruose, don't shame your parentage.

Rose. Nay, for that matter, I am not so simple as to say that I can do anything with the captain but what I may do with anybody else.

Silv. So !—And pray what do you expect from this captain, child ?

Rose. I expect, sir—I expect—but he ordered me to tell nobody.—But suppose that he should promise to marry me ?

Silv. You should have a care, my dear, men will promise anything beforehand.

Rose. I know that, but he promised to marry me afterwards.

Bull. Wauns, Ruose, what have you said?

Silv. Afterwards! after what?

Rose. After I had sold him my chickens.—I hope there's no harm in that.[1]

Enter PLUME.

Plume. What, Mr Wilful, so close with my market-woman!

Silv. [*Aside.*] I'll try if he loves her.—[*Aloud.*] Close, sir! ay, and closer yet, sir.—Come, my pretty maid, you and I will withdraw a little—

Plume. No, no, friend, I han't done with her yet.

Silv. Nor have I begun with her, so I have as good right as you have.

Plume. Thou art a bloody impudent fellow.[2]

Silv. Sir, I would qualify myself for the service.

Plume. Hast thou really a mind to the service?

Silv. Yes, sir: so let her go.

Rose. Pray, gentlemen, don't be so violent.

Plume. Come, leave it to the girl's own choice.—Will you belong to me or to that gentleman?

[1] Q. 1 adds "tho' there be an ugly song of chickens and sparagus."

[2] In Q. 1 the following passage, down to "I have heard before, indeed, that your captains used to sell your men," does not appear. In its stead we have this dialogue :—

Plume. Thou art a bloody impudent fellow—let her go, I say.

Sil. Do you let her go.

Plume. Entendez vous Francois, mon petit Garson?

Sil. Ouy.

Plume. Si vous voulez donc vous enroller dans ma Companie, la damoiselle sera a vous.

Sil. Avez vous couché avec elle?

Plume. Non.

Sil. Assurément?

Plume. Ma foi.

Sil. Cest assez.—Je serai votre soldat.

Plume. La prenez donc.—I'll change a woman for a man at any time.

Rose. But I hope, Captain, you won't part with me. [*Cries.*] I have heard before, indeed, etc.

Rose. Let me consider: you are both very handsome.

Plume. [*Aside.*] Now the natural unconstancy of her sex begins to work.

Rose. Pray, sir, what will you give me?

Bull. Don't be angry, sir, that my sister should be mercenary, for she's but young.

Silv. Give thee, child! I'll set thee above scandal; you shall have a coach with six before and six behind, an equipage to make vice fashionable, and put virtue out of countenance.

Plume. Pho! that's easily done.—I'll do more for thee, child; I'll buy you a furbelow scarf, and give you a ticket to see a play.

Bull. A play! Wauns, Ruose, take the ticket, and let's see the show.

Silv. Look'ee, Captain, if you won't resign, I'll go list with Captain Brazen this minute.

Plume. Will you list with me if I give up my title?

Silv. I will.

Plume. Take her: I'll change a woman for a man at any time.

Rose. I have heard before, indeed, that you captains used to sell your men.

Bull. Pray, Captain, do not send Ruose to the West Indies. [*Cries.*

Plume. Ha, ha, ha! West Indies!—No, no, my honest lad, give me thy hand; nor you nor she shall move a step further than I do.—This gentleman is one of us, and will be kind to you, Mrs Rose.

Rose. But will you be so kind to me, sir, as the captain would?

Silv. I can't be altogether so kind to you, my circumstances are not so good as the captain's; but I'll take care of you, upon my word.

Plume. Ay, ay, we'll all take care of her; she shall live like a princess, and her brother here shall be— What would you be?

Bull. Oh, sir! if you had not promised the place of drum-major—

Plume. Ay, that is promised. But what think you of barrack-master? You are a person of understanding, and barrack-master you shall be.—But what's become of this same Cartwheel you told me of, my dear?

Rose. We'll go fetch him.—Come, brother barrack-master.—We shall find you at home, noble Captain?

Plume. Yes, yes.—[*Exeunt* ROSE *and* BULLOCK.] And now, sir, here are your forty shillings.

Silv. Captain Plume, I despise your listing money; if I do serve, 'tis purely for love—of that wench, I mean. For you must know that, among my other sallies, I have spent the best part of my fortune in search of a maid, and could never find one hitherto: so you may be assured I'd not sell my freedom under a less purchase than I did my estate. So, before I list, I must be certified that this girl is a virgin.

Plume. Mr Wilful, I can't tell you how you can be certified in that point till you try; but, upon my honour, she may be a vestal for aught that I know to the contrary. I gained her heart, indeed, by some trifling presents and promises, and, knowing that the best security for a woman's soul is her body, I would have made myself master of that too, had not the jealousy of my impertinent landlady interposed.

Silv. So you only want an opportunity for accomplishing your designs upon her?

Plume. Not at all; I have already gained my ends, which were only the drawing in one or two of her followers. The women, you know, are the loadstones everywhere; gain the wives, and you are caressed by the husbands; please the mistresses, and you are valued by the gallants; secure an interest with the finest women at court, and you procure the favour of the greatest men: so, kiss the prettiest country wenches, and you are sure of listing the lustiest fellows. Some people may call this artifice, but I term it stratagem, since it is so main a part of the service. Besides, the fatigue of recruiting is so intolerable, that unless we could make ourselves some pleasure amidst the pain, no mortal man would be able to bear it.

Silv. Well, sir, I am satisfied as to the point in debate. But now let me beg you to lay aside your recruiting airs, put on the man of honour, and tell me plainly what usage I must expect when I am under your command?

Plume. You must know, in the first place, then, that I hate to have gentlemen in my company; for they are always troublesome and expensive, sometimes dangerous; and 'tis a constant maxim amongst us, that those who know the least obey the best. Notwithstanding all this, I find something so agreeable about you, that engages me to court your company; and I can't tell how it is, but I should be uneasy to see you under the command of anybody else. Your usage will chiefly depend upon your behaviour; only this you must expect, that if you commit a small fault I will excuse it, if a great one I'll discharge you; for something tells me I shall not be able to punish you.

Silv. And something tells me, that if you do discharge me, 'twill be the greatest punishment you can inflict; for were we this moment to go upon the greatest dangers in your profession, they would be less terrible to me than to stay behind you.—And now your hand, this lists me—and now you are my Captain.

Plume. [*Kissing her.*] Your friend.—[*Aside.*] 'Sdeath! there's something in this fellow that charms me.

Silv. One favour I must beg. This affair will make some noise, and I have some friends that would censure my conduct if I threw myself into the circumstance of a private sentinel of my own head: I must therefore take care to be impressed by the Act of Parliament; you shall leave that to me.

Plume. What you please as to that.—Will you lodge at my quarters in the meantime? you shall have part of my bed.

Silv. O fy! lie with a common soldier! Would not you rather lie with a common woman?

Plume. No, faith, I'm not that rake that the world imagines; I have got an air of freedom, which people mistake for lewdness in me, as they mistake formality in others for religion. The world is all a cheat; only I take mine, which is undesigned, to be more excusable than theirs, which is hypocritical. I hurt nobody but myself, and they abuse all mankind.—Will you lie with me?

Silv. No, no, Captain, you forget Rose; she's to be my bedfellow, you know.

Plume. I had forgot; pray be kind to her.

[*Exeunt severally*

SCENE II.[1]—*The same.*

Enter MELINDA *and* LUCY.

Mel. [*Aside.*] 'Tis the greatest misfortune in nature for a woman to want a confidant! We are so weak that we can do nothing without assistance, and then a secret racks us worse than the colic. I am at this minute so sick of a secret, that I'm ready to faint away.—[*Aloud.*] Help me, Lucy!

Lucy. Bless me, madam! what's the matter?

Mel. Vapours only, I begin to recover.—[*Aside.*] If Silvia were in town, I could heartily forgive her faults for the ease of discovering my own.

Lucy. You're thoughtful, madam; am not I worthy to know the cause?

See note, p. 81.

Mel. You are a servant, and a secret would make you saucy.

Lucy. Not unless you should find fault without a cause, madam.

Mel. Cause or not cause, I must not lose the pleasure of chiding when I please ; women must discharge their vapours somewhere, and before we get husbands our servants must expect to bear with 'em.

Lucy. Then, madam, you had better raise me to a degree above a servant.   You know my family, and that five hundred pounds would set me upon the foot of a gentlewoman, and make me worthy the confidence of any lady in the land.   Besides, madam, 'twill extremely encourage me in the great design I now have in hand.

Mel. I don't find that your design can be of any great advantage to you.   'Twill please me, indeed, in the humour I have of being revenged on the fool for his vanity of making love to me, so I don't much care if I do promise you five hundred pound upon my day of marriage.

Lucy. That is the way, madam, to make me diligent in the vocation of a confidant, which I think is generally to bring people together.

Mel. O Lucy !   I can hold my secret no longer.   You must know, that hearing of the famous fortune-teller in town, I went disguised to satisfy a curiosity, which has cost me dear.   That fellow is certainly the devil, or one of his bosom favourites ; he has told me the most surprising things of my past life—

Lucy. Things past, madam, can hardly be reckoned surprising, because we know them already.   Did he tell you anything surprising that was to come?

Mel. One thing very surprising ; he said I should die a maid !

Lucy. Die a maid !   come into the world for nothing ! Dear madam, if you should believe him, it might come to pass, for the bare thought on't might kill one in four-

and-twenty hours. —And did you ask him any questions about me?

Mel. You! Why, I passed for you.

Lucy. So 'tis I that am to die a maid !—But the devil was a liar from the beginning ; he can't make me die a maid.—[*Aside.*] I have put it out of his power already.

Mel. I do but jest. I would have passed for you, and called myself Lucy ; but he presently told me my name, my quality, my fortune, and gave me the whole history of my life. He told me of a lover I had in this country, and described Worthy exactly, but in nothing so well as in his present indifference. I fled to him for refuge here to-day ; he never so much as encouraged me in my fright, but coldly told me that he was sorry for the accident, because it might give the town cause to censure my conduct; excused his not waiting on me home, made me a careless bow, and walked off. 'Sdeath ! I could have stabbed him, or myself, 'twas the same thing.—Yonder he comes—I will so use him !

Lucy. Don't exasperate him ; consider what the fortune-teller told you. Men are scarce, and, as times go, it is not impossible for a woman to die a maid.

Mel. No matter.

Enter WORTHY.

Wor [*Aside.*] I find she's warmed ; I must strike while the iron is hot.—[*Aloud.*] You have a great deal of courage, madam, to venture into the walks where you were so lately frighted.

Mel. And you have a quantity of impudence to appear before me, that you have so lately affronted.

Wor. I had no design to affront you, nor appear before you either, madam : I left you here, because I had business in another place, and came hither, thinking to meet another person.

Mel. Since you find yourself disappointed, I hope you'll withdraw to another part of the walk.

Wor. The walk is as free for me as you, madam, and broad enough for us both.—[*They walk by one another, he with his hat cocked, she fretting and tearing her fan.*] Will you please to take snuff, madam?

[*Offers her his box, she strikes it out of his hand; while he is gathering it up,*

Enter BRAZEN.

Braz. What, here before me, my dear!

[*Takes* MELINDA *round the waist.*

Mel. What means this insolence?

[*She cuffs him.*

Lucy. [*To* BRAZEN.] Are you mad? don't you see Mr Worthy?

Braz. No, no, I'm struck blind.—Worthy! odso! well turned!—My mistress has wit at her fingers' ends.— Madam, I ask your pardon, 'tis our way abroad.—Mr Worthy, you are the happy man.

Wor. I don't envy your happiness very much, if the lady can afford no other sort of favours but what she has bestowed upon you.

Mel. I am sorry the favour miscarried, for it was designed for you, Mr Worthy; and be assured, 'tis the last and only favour you must expect at my hands.—Captain, I ask your pardon.

Braz. I grant it.—[*Exeunt* MELINDA *and* LUCY.] You see, Mr Worthy, 'twas only a random shot; it might have taken off your head as well as mine. Courage, my dear! 'tis the fortune of war.—But the enemy has thought fit to withdraw, I think.

Wor. Withdraw! oons, sir! what d'ye mean by withdraw?

Braz. I'll show you. [*Exit.*

Wor. She's lost, irrecoverably lost, and Plume's advice has ruined me! 'Sdeath! why should I, that knew her haughty spirit, be ruled by a man that's a stranger to her pride?

Enter PLUME.

Plume. Ha, ha, ha! a battle-royal.   Don't frown so, man; she's your own, I tell you; I saw the fury of her love in the extremity of her passion : the wildness of her anger is a certain sign that she loves you to madness. That rogue Kite began the battle with abundance of conduct, and will bring you off victorious, my life on't; he plays his part admirably; she's to be with him again presently.

Wor. But what could be the meaning of Brazen's familiarity with her?

Plume. You are no logician, if you pretend to draw consequences from the actions of fools: there's no arguing by the rule of reason upon a science without principles, and such is their conduct.   Whim, unaccountable whim, hurries 'em on like a man drunk with brandy before ten o'clock in the morning.—But we lose our sport : Kite has opened above an hour ago; let's away.

[Exeunt.

SCENE III.—*A Chamber.*

KITE, *disguised in a strange habit, sitting at a table, with books and globes.*

Kite. [*Rising.*] By the position of the heavens, gained from my observation upon these celestial globes, I find that Luna was a tidewaiter, Sol a surveyor, Mercury a thief, Venus a whore, Saturn an alderman, Jupiter a rake, and Mars a serjeant of grenadiers ; and this is the system of Kite the conjurer.

Enter PLUME *and* WORTHY.

Plume. Well, what success ?

Kite. I have sent away a shoemaker and a tailor

already ; one's to be a captain of marines, and the other a major of dragoons: I am to manage them at night.— Have you seen the lady, Mr Worthy?

Wor. Ay, but it won't do. Have you showed her her name, that I tore off from the bottom of the letter?

Kite. No, sir, I reserve that for the last stroke.

Plume. What letter?

Wor. One that I would not let you see, for fear that you should break windows [1] in good earnest.

[*Knocking at the door.*

Kite. Officers, to your posts. [PLUME *and* WORTHY *conceal themselves behind a screen.*]—Mind the door. [2]

[Servant *opens the door.*

Enter a Smith.

Smith. Well, master, are you the cunning man?

Kite. I am the learned Copernicus.

Smith. Well, master, [3] I'm but a poor man, and I can't afford above a shilling for my fortune.

Kite. Perhaps that is more than 'tis worth.

Smith. Look'ee, doctor, let me have something that's good for my shilling, or I'll have my money again.

Kite. If there be faith in the stars, you shall have your shilling forty-fold.—Your hand, countryman.— You are by trade a smith.

Smith. How the devil should you know that?

Kite. Because the devil and you are brother-tradesmen—you were born under Forceps.

Smith. Forceps, what's that?

Kite. One of the signs. There's Leo, Sagittarius, Forceps, Furnes, Dixmude, Namur, Brussels, Charleroy, and so forth—twelve of 'em.—Let me see—did you ever make any bombs or cannon-bullets?

Smith. Not I.

[1] Q. 1, "Melinda's windows."
[2] Q. 1, "Tycho, mind the door."
[3] Q. 1, "Master Coppernose."

Kite. You either have or will. The stars have decreed that you shall be—I must have more money, sir, your fortune's great.

Smith. Faith, doctor, I have no more.

Kite. O sir, I'll trust you, and take it out of your arrears.

Smith. Arrears! what arrears?

Kite. The five hundred pound that's owing to you from the government.

Smith. Owing me?

Kite. Owing you, sir.—Let me see your t'other hand. —I beg your pardon, it will be owing to you: and the rogue of an agent will demand fifty per cent. for a fortnight's advance.

Smith. I'm in the clouds, doctor, all this while.

Kite. Sir, I am above 'em, among the stars.[1] In two years, three months, and two hours, you will be made captain of the forges to the grand train of artillery, and will have ten shillings a day, and two servants. 'Tis the decree of the stars, and of the fixed stars, that are as immovable as your anvil; strike, sir, while the iron is hot. Fly, sir! begone!

Smith. What, what would you have me do, doctor? I wish the stars would put me in a way for this fine place.

Kite. The stars do.—Let me see—ay, about an hour hence walk carelessly into the market-place, and you'll see a tall, slender gentleman, cheapening a penny-worth of apples, with a cane hanging upon his button. This gentleman will ask you what's o'clock. He's your man, and the maker of your fortune! Follow him, follow him.—And now go home, and take leave of your wife and children; an hour hence exactly is your time.

Smith. A tall slender gentleman, you say, with a cane? Pray, what sort of head has the cane?

Kite. An amber head with a black ribbon.

[1] Q. 1, "So am I, sir, among the stars."

Smith. And pray of what employment is the gentleman?

Kite. Let me see; he's either a collector of the excise, a plenipotentiary, or a captain of grenadiers, I can't tell exactly which. But he'll call you honest—your name is—

Smith. Thomas.

Kite. Right! He'll call you honest Tom.

Smith. But how the devil should he know my name?

Kite. Oh, there are several sorts of 'Toms! Tom 'o Lincoln, Tom-tit, Tom Tell-troth, Tom o' Bedlam, and Tom Fool.—[*Knocking at the door.*] Begone!—an hour hence precisely.

Smith. You say he'll ask me what's o'clock?

Kite. Most certainly.—And you'll answer you don't know:—and be sure you look at St Mary's dial; for the sun won't shine, and if it should, you won't be able to tell the figures.

Smith. I will, I will. [*Exit.*

Plume. [*Behind.*] Well done, conjurer! go on and prosper.

Kite. As you were!

Enter a Butcher.

[*Aside.*] What, my old friend Pluck the butcher! I offered the surly bull-dog five guineas this morning, and he refused it.

Butcher. So, Master Conjurer, here's half-a-crown.— And now you must understand—

Kite. Hold, friend, I know your business beforehand.

Butcher. You're devilish cunning then, for I don't well know it myself.

Kite. I know more than you, friend.—You have a foolish saying, that such a one knows no more than the man in the moon: I tell you, the man in the moon knows more than all the men under the sun. Don't the moon see all the world?

Butcher. All the world see the moon, I must confess.

Kite. Then she must see all the world, that's certain.
—Give me your hand.—You're by trade either a butcher
or a surgeon.

Butcher. True, I am a butcher.

Kite. And a surgeon you will be, the employments
differ only in the name : he that can cut up an ox, may
dissect a man ; and the same dexterity that cracks a
marrow-bone, will cut off a leg or an arm.

Butcher. What d'ye mean, doctor, what d'ye mean?

Kite. Patience, patience, Mr Surgeon-General; the
stars are great bodies, and move slowly.

Butcher. But what d'ye mean by surgeon-general,
doctor?

Kite. Nay, sir, if your worship won't have patience, I
must beg the favour of your worship's absence.

Butcher. My worship! my worship! but why my
worship?

Kite. Nay then, I have done.   [*Sits down.*

Butcher. Pray doctor—

Kite. Fire and fury, sir !—[*Rises in a passion.*]   Do
you think the stars will be hurried?   Do the stars owe
you any money, sir, that you dare to dun their lordships
at this rate?   Sir, I am porter to the stars, and I am
ordered to let no dun come near their doors.

Butcher. Dear doctor, I never had any dealings with
the stars, they don't owe me a penny.   But since you
are their porter, please to accept of this half-crown to
drink their healths, and don't be angry.

Kite. Let me see your hand then once more.—Here
has been gold—five guineas, my friend, in this very
hand this morning.

Butcher. Nay, then he is the devil !—Pray, doctor,
were you born of a woman? or did you come into the
world of your own head?

Kite. That's a secret.—This gold was offered you by
a proper handsome man, called Hawk, or Buzzard, or—

Butcher. Kite, you mean.

Kite. Ay, ay, Kite.

Butcher. As arrant a rogue as ever carried a halberd ! The impudent rascal would have decoyed me for a soldier !

Kite. A soldier ! a man of your substance for a soldier ! Your mother has a hundred pound in hard money, lying at this minute in the hands of a mercer, not forty yards from this place.

Butcher. Oons ! and so she has, but very few know so much.

Kite. I know it, and that rogue, what's his name, Kite, knew it, and offered you five guineas to list because he knew your poor mother would give the hundred for your discharge.

Butcher. There's a dog now !—'sflesh, doctor, I'll give you t'other half-crown, and tell me that this same Kite will be hanged.

Kite. He's in as much danger as any man in the county of Salop.

Butcher. There's your fee.—But you have forgot the surgeon-general all this while.

Kite. You put the stars in a passion.—[*Looks on his books.*] But now they are pacified again :—Let me see, did you never cut off a man's leg?

Butcher. No.

Kite. Recollect, pray.

Butcher. I say, no.

Kite. That's strange ! wonderful strange ! but nothing is strange to me, such wonderful changes have I seen.— The second, or third, ay, the third campaign that you make in Flanders, the leg of a great officer will be shattered by a great shot, you will be there accidentally, and with your cleaver chop off the limb at a blow : in short, the operation will be performed with so much dexterity, that with general applause you will be made surgeon-general of the whole army.

Butcher. Nay, for the matter of cutting off a limb, I'll

do't, I'll do't with any surgeon in Europe; but I have no thoughts of making a campaign.

Kite. You have no thoughts! what's matter for your thoughts? The stars have decreed it, and you must go.

Butcher. The stars decree it! Oons, sir, the justices can't press me!

Kite. Nay, friend, 'tis none of my business—I have done; only mind this, you'll know more an hour and a half hence—that's all, farewell!   [*Going.*

Butcher. Hold, hold, doctor!—Surgeon-general! what is the place worth, pray?

Kite. Five hundred pounds a year, besides guineas for claps.

Butcher. Five hundred pounds a year!—An hour and a half hence, you say?

Kite. Prithee, friend, be quiet, don't be so trouble-some. Here's such a work to make a booby butcher accept of five hundred pound a year!—But if you must hear it—I tell you in short, you'll be standing in your stall an hour and half hence, and a gentleman will come by with a snuff-box in his hand, and the tip of his handkerchief hanging out of his right pocket; he'll ask you the price of a loin of veal, and at the same time stroke your great dog upon the head, and call him Chopper.

Butcher. Mercy on us! Chopper is the dog's name.

Kite. Look'ee there—what I say is true—things that are to come must come to pass. Get you home, sell off your stock, don't mind the whining and the snivelling of your mother and your sister—women always hinder preferment—make what money you can, and follow that gentleman, his name begins with a P, mind that.—There will be the barber's daughter, too, that you promised marriage to—she will be pulling and hauling you to pieces.

Butcher. What! know Sally too? He's the devil,

and he needs must go that the devil drives.—[*Going.*]
The tip of his handkerchief out of his left pocket?

Kite. No, no, his right pocket; if it be the left, 'tis
none of the man.

Butcher. Well, well, I'll mind him. [*Exit.*

Plume. [*Behind, with his pocket book.*] The right
pocket, you say?

Kite. I hear the rustling of silks. [*Knocking at the
door.*] Fly, sir! 'tis Madam Melinda.

Enter MELINDA *and* LUCY.

Tycho, chairs for the ladies. [*Calls to* Servant.

Mel. Don't trouble yourself, we sha'n't stay, doctor.

Kite. Your ladyship is to stay much longer than you
imagine.

Mel. For what?

Kite. For a husband.—[*To* LUCY.] For your part,
madam, you won't stay for a husband.

Lucy. Pray, doctor, do you converse with the stars, or
the devil?

Kite. With both. When I have the destinies of men
in search, I consult the stars; when the affairs of women
come under my hands, I advise with my t'other friend.

Mel. And have you raised the devil upon my account?

Kite. Yes, madam, and he's now under the table.

Lucy. Oh, Heavens protect us! Dear madam, let's
be gone.

Kite. If you be afraid of him, why do you come to
consult him?

Mel. [*To* LUCY.] Don't fear, fool.—[*To* KITE.]
Do you think, sir, that because I am a woman, I'm to
be fooled out of my reason, or frighted out of my
senses? Come, show me this devil.

Kite. He's a little busy at present; but when he has
done, he shall wait on you.

Mel. What is he doing?

Kite. Writing your name in his pocket-book.

Mel. Ha, ha! my name! Pray, what have you or he to do with my name?

Kite. Look'ee, fair lady, the devil is a very modest person, he seeks nobody unless they seek him first; he's chained up like a mastiff, and can't stir unless he be let loose. You come to me to have your fortune told—do you think, madam, that I can answer you of my own head? No, madam, the affairs of women are so irregular, that nothing less than the devil can give any account of 'em. Now to convince you of your incredulity, I'll show you a trial of my skill.—Here, you *Cacodemo del Plumo* [1]—exert your power, draw me this lady's name, the word Melinda, in the proper letters and character of her own handwriting.—Do it at three motions—one—two—three—'tis done.—Now, madam, will you please to send your maid to fetch it?

Lucy. I fetch it! the devil fetch me if I do!

Mel. My name in my own handwriting! that would be convincing indeed.

Kite. Seeing's believing.—[*Goes to the table, lifts up the carpet.*] Here, Tre, Tre, poor Tre, give me the bone, sirrah. [2]—There's your name upon that square piece of paper—behold!

Mel. 'Tis wonderful! my very letters to a tittle!

Lucy. 'Tis like your hand, madam, but not so like

---

[1] Q. 1, "*Cacodemon del fuego.*"

[2] In Q. 1 there occurs at this point the following outrageously farcical passage, which was doubtless found ineffective, and therefore omitted in Q. 2. :

[*He puts his hand under the table,* PLUME *steals to the other side of the table and catches him by the hand.*] Oh! oh! the devil! the devil in good earnest! My hand! my hand! the devil! my hand!—[MELINDA *and* LUCY *shriek, and run to a corner of the stage.* KITE *discovers* PLUME, *and gets away his hand.*] A plague o' your pincers! he has fixed his nails in my very flesh.—O madam! you put the demon in such a passion with your scruples, that it has almost cost me my hand.

Mel. It has cost us our lives almost—but have you got the name?

Kite. Got it! ay, madam, I have got it here—I'm sure the blood comes. But there's your name upon the square piece of paper—behold!

your hand neither, and now I look nearer, tis not like your hand at all.

Kite. Here's a chambermaid now that will outlie the devil!

Lucy. Look'ee, madam, they sha'n't impose upon us; people can't remember their hands, no more than they can their faces.—Come, madam, let us be certain: write your name upon this paper, then we'll compare the two names.

[*Takes out a paper, and folds it.*

Kite. Anything for your satisfaction, madam—here's pen and ink.

[MELINDA *writes,* LUCY *holds the paper.*

Lucy. Let me see it, madam. 'Tis the same—the very same.—[*Aside.*] But I'll secure one copy for my own affairs.

Mel. This is demonstration.

Kite. 'Tis so, madam.—The word demonstration comes from Dæmon, the father of lies.

Mel. Well, doctor, I am convinced; and now, pray, what account can you give me of my future fortune?

Kite. Before the sun has made one course round this earthly globe, your fortune will be fixed for happiness or misery.

Mel. What! so near the crisis of my fate!

Kite. Let me see—about the hour of ten to-morrow morning you will be saluted by a gentleman, who will come to take his leave of you, being designed for travel; his intention of going abroad is sudden, and the occasion a woman. Your fortune and his are like the bullet and the barrel, one runs plump into the other. In short, if the gentleman travels, he will die abroad; and if he does you will die before he comes home.

Mel. What sort of man is he?

Kite. Madam, he's a fine gentleman and a lover, that is, a man of very good sense, and a very great fool.

Mel. How is that possible, doctor?

Kite. Because, madam—because it is so.—A woman's reason is the best for a man's being a fool.

Mel. Ten o'clock, you say?

Kite. Ten—about the hour of tea-drinking throughout the kingdom.

Mel. Here, doctor.—[*Gives money.*] Lucy, have you any questions to ask?

Lucy. O madam! a thousand.

Kite. I must beg your patience till another time; for I expect more company this minute; besides, I must discharge the gentleman under the table.

Lucy. Oh, pray, sir, discharge us first!

Kite. Tycho, wait on the ladies down stairs.

> [*Exeunt* MELINDA *and* LUCY.   PLUME *and*
> WORTHY *come forward.*[1]

Kite. Mr Worthy, you were pleased to wish me joy to-day, I hope to be able to return the compliment to-morrow.

Wor. I'll make it the best compliment to you that ever I made in my life [2] if you do.   But I must be a traveller, you say?

Kite. No farther than the chops of the Channel, I presume, sir.

Plume. That we have concerted already.—[*Loud knocking at the door.*] Heyday! you don't profess midwifery, doctor.

---

[1] At this point in Q. 1 occurs the following pendent to the passage excised on p. 320.   The disappearance of the one of course necessitated the omission of the other :—

> "*Enter* PLUME *and* WORTHY, *laughing.*

Kite. Ay, you may well laugh, gentlemen, not all the cannon of the French army could have frighted me so much as that gripe you gave me under the table.

Plume. I think, Mr Doctor, I out-conjured you that bout.

Kite. I was surprised, for I should not have taken a captain for a conjurer.

Plume. No more than I should a serjeant for a wit.

[2] Q. 1, "that you ever made in your life."

Kite. Away to your ambuscade!

[PLUME *and* WORTHY *retire as before.*

Enter BRAZEN.

Braz. Your servant, servant, my dear.

Kite. Stand off, I have my familiar already.

Braz. Are you bewitched, my dear?

Kite. Yes, my dear; but mine is a peaceable spirit, and hates gunpowder. Thus I fortify myself—[*Draws a circle round him.*] And now, Captain, have a care how you force my lines.

Braz. Lines! what dost talk of lines! You have something like a fishing-rod there, indeed; but I come to be acquainted with you, man.—What's your name, my dear?

Kite. Conundrum.

Braz. Conundrum! Rat me, I knew a famous doctor in London of your name!—Where were you born?

Kite. I was born in Algebra.

Braz. Algebra! 'tis no country in Christendom, I'm sure, unless it be some place[1] in the Highlands in Scotland.

Kite. Right! I told you I was bewitched.

Braz. So am I, my dear: I am going to be married. I have had two letters from a lady of fortune that loves me to madness, fits, colic, spleen, and vapours. Shall I marry her in four-and-twenty hours, ay, or no?

Kite. I must have the year and day of the month when these letters were dated.

Braz. Why, you old bitch, did you ever hear of love-letters dated with the year and day o' the month? Do you think billets-doux are like bank bills?

Kite. They are not so good.—But if they bear no date, I must examine the contents.

Braz. Contents! that you shall, old boy: here they be both. [*Pulls out two letters.*

[1] Q. I, " pitiful place."

Kite. Only the last you received, if you please.—
[*Takes one of the letters.*] Now, sir, if you please to let
me consult my books for a minute, I'll send this letter
inclosed to you with the determination of the stars upon
it, to your lodgings.

Braz. With all my heart—I must give him—[*Puts his
hands in his pocket.*] Algebra ! I fancy, doctor, 'tis hard
to calculate the place of your nativity?—Here.—[*Gives
him money.*] And if I succeed, I'll build a watch-tower
upon the top of the highest mountain in Wales for the
study of astrology, and the benefit of Conundrums.
        [*Exit.* PLUME *and* WORTHY *come forward.*

Wor. O doctor! that letter's worth a million. Let
me see it.—[*Takes the letter.*] And now I have it, I
am afraid to open it.

Plume. Pho ! let me see it.—[*Snatches the letter from*
WORTHY *and opens it.*] If she be a jilt—damn her, she
is one ! there's her name at the bottom on't.

Wor. How ! then I'll travel in good earnest.— [*Looking at the letter.*] By all my hopes, 'tis Lucy's hand !

Plume. Lucy's !

Wor. Certainly ; 'tis no more like Melinda's character
than black is to white.

Plume. Then 'tis certainly Lucy's contrivance to draw
in Brazen for a husband.—But are you sure 'tis not
Melinda's hand ?

Wor. You shall see.—[*To* KITE.] Where's the bit
of paper I gave you just now that the devil writ Melinda
upon ?

Kite. Here, sir.

Plume. 'Tis plain they're not the same. And is this the
malicious name that was subscribed to the letter, which
made Mr Balance send his daughter into the country ?

Wor. The very same : the other fragments I showed
you just now. [1]

---

[1] Q. 1 adds, " I once intended it for another use, but I think I have
turned it now to better advantage."

Plume. But 'twas barbarous to conceal this so long, and to continue me so many hours in the pernicious heresy of believing that angelic creature could change! —Poor Silvia !

Wor. Rich Silvia you mean, and poor captain, ha, ha, ha ! Come, come, friend, Melinda is true and shall be mine ; Silvia is constant, and may be yours.

Plume. No, she's above my hopes : but for her sake I'll recant my opinion of her sex.

> By some the sex is blamed without design,
> Light harmless censure, such as yours and mine,
> Sallies of wit, and vapours of our wine.
> Others the justice of the sex condemn,
> And wanting merit to create esteem,
> Would hide their own defects by censuring them.
> But they, secure in their all-conquering charms,
> Laugh at the vain efforts [1] of false alarms ;
> He magnifies their conquests who complains,
> For none would struggle were they not in chains.
>
> $\qquad$ [*Exeunt.*

[1] Query, " effects " ?

ACT V

SCENE I.[1]—*An Anteroom adjoining* SILVIA'S *Bedchamber ; A periwig, hat, and sword, upon the table.*

Enter SILVIA *in her nightcap.*

ILV. I have rested but indifferently, and I believe my bedfellow was as little pleased ; poor Rose! here 'she comes—

Enter ROSE.

Good morrow, my dear, how d'ye this morning ?

Rose. Just as I was last night, neither better nor worse for you.

Silv. What's the matter ? Did you not like your bedfellow ?

Rose. I don't know whether I had a bedfellow or not.

Silv. Did not I lie with you?

Rose. No——I wonder you could have the conscience to ruin a poor girl for nothing.

Silv. I have saved thee from ruin, child ; don't be melancholy, I can give you as many fine things as the captain can.

Rose. But you can't, I'm sure.

[*Knocking at the door.*

[1] This scene is wholly omitted in Q. 2.

326

Silv. Odso! my accoutrements.—[*Puts on her peri-wig, hat, and sword.*] Who's at the door?

Constable. [*Without.*] Open the door, or we'll break it down.

Silv. Patience a little—— [*Opens the door.*

Enter Constable *and* Mob.

Con. We have 'um, we have 'um! the duck and the mallard both in the decoy.

Silv. What means this riot? Stand off!—[*Draws.*] The man dies that comes within reach of my point.

Con. That is not the point, master; put up your sword or I shall knock you down; and so I command the Queen's peace.

Silv. You are some blockhead of a constable.

Con. I am so, and have a warrant to apprehend the bodies of you and your whore there.

Rose. Whore! Never was poor woman so abused.

Enter BULLOCK *unbuttoned.*

Bull. What's the matter now?—O Mr Bridewell! what brings you abroad so early?

Con. This, sir.—[*Lays hold of* BULLOCK.] you're the Queen's prisoner.

Bull. Wauns, you lie, sir! I'm the Queen's soldier.

Con. No matter for that, you shall go before Justice Balance.

Silv. Balance! 'tis what I wanted. — Here, Mr Constable, I resign my sword.

Rose. Can't you carry us before the captain, Mr Bridewell?

Con. Captain! han't you got your bellyfull of captains yet?—Come, come, make way there.

[*Exeunt.*

SCENE II.—Justice BALANCE'S *House.*

Enter BALANCE *and* SCALE.

Scale. I say 'tis not to be borne, Mr Balance!

Bal. Look'ee, Mr Scale, for my own part I shall be very tender in what regards the officers of the army; they expose their lives to so many dangers for us abroad, that we may give them some grain[1] of allowance at home.

Scale. Allowance! This poor girl's father is my tenant; and, if I mistake not, her mother nursed a child for you. Shall they debauch our daughters to our faces?

Bal. Consider, Mr Scale, that were it not for the bravery of these officers, we should have French dragoons among us, that would leave us neither liberty, property, wife, nor daughter. Come, Mr Scale, the gentlemen are vigorous and warm, and may they continue so; the same heat that stirs them up to love, spurs them on to battle; you never knew a great general in your life, that did not love a whore. This I only speak in reference to Captain Plume—for the other spark I know nothing of.

Scale. Nor can I hear of anybody that does.—Oh, here they come.

Enter SILVIA, BULLOCK, *and* ROSE, *prisoners;* Constable *and* Mob.

Con. May it please your worships we took them in the very act, *re infecta,* sir. The gentleman, indeed, behaved himself like a gentleman; for he drew his sword and swore, and afterwards laid it down and said nothing.

Bal. Give the gentleman his sword again—wait you

[1] Q. 1, "grains."

without.—[*Exeunt* Constable *and* Mob.] I'm sorry, sir,—[*To* SILVIA.] to know a gentleman upon such terms, that the occasion of our meeting should prevent the satisfaction of an acquaintance.

Silv. Sir, you need make no apology for your warrant, no more than I shall do for my behaviour: my innocence is upon an equal foot with your authority.

Scale. Innocence! Have not you seduced that young maid?

Silv. No, Mr Goosecap, she seduced me.

Bull. So she did, I'll swear—for she proposed marriage first.

Bal. What! then you are married, child?

[*To* ROSE.

Rose. Yes, sir, to my sorrow.

Bal. Who was witness?

Bull. That was I—I danced, threw the stocking, and spoke jokes by their bedside, I'm sure.

Bal. Who was the minister?

Bull. Minister! we are soldiers, and want no minister.[1] They were married by the Articles of War.

Bal. Hold thy prating, fool!—[*To* SILVIA.] Your appearance, sir, promises some understanding; pray what does this fellow mean?

Silv. He means marriage, I think—but that, you know, is so odd a thing, that hardly any two people under the sun agree in the ceremony; some make it a sacrament, others a convenience, and others make it a jest; but among soldiers 'tis most sacred. Our sword, you know, is our honour; that we lay down; the hero jumps over it first, and the amazon after— leap rogue, follow whore—the drum beats a ruff, and so to bed; that's all—the ceremony is concise.

Bull. And the prettiest ceremony, so full of pastime and prodigality!

[1] Q. 1, "ministers."

Bal. What! are you a soldier?

Bull. Ay, that I am. Will your worship lend me your cane, and I'll show you how I can exercise.

Bal. [*Striking him over the head.*] Take it.—[*To* SILVIA.] Pray, sir, what commission may you bear?

Silv. I'm called captain, sir, by all the coffeemen, drawers, whores, and groom-porters in London; for I wear a red coat, a sword, a hat *bien troussé*, a martial twist in my cravat, a fierce knot in my periwig, a cane upon my button, piquet in my head, and dice in my pocket.

Scale. Your name, pray, sir?

Silv. Captain Pinch: I cock my hat with a pinch, I take snuff with a pinch, pay my whores with a pinch. In short, I can do anything at a pinch, but fight and fill my belly.

Bal. And pray, sir, what brought you into Shropshire?

Silv. A pinch, sir: I knew you country gentlemen want wit, and you know that we town gentlemen want money, and so—

Bal. I understand you, sir.—Here, constable!

Re-enter Constable.

Take this gentleman into custody till farther orders.

Rose. Pray, your worship, don't be uncivil to him, for he did me no hurt; he's the most harmless man in the world, for all he talks so.

Scale. Come, come, child, I'll take care of you.

Silv. What, gentlemen! Rob me of my freedom, and my wife at once! 'Tis the first time they ever went together.

Bal. Heark'ee, constable !   [*Whispers him.*

Con. It shall be done, sir.—Come along, sir.

[*Exit with* BULLOCK, ROSE, *and* SILVIA.

Bal. Come, Mr Scale, we'll manage the spark presently.   [*Exeunt.*

SCENE III.—MELINDA'S *Apartment.*

Enter MELINDA *and* WORTHY.

Mel. [*Aside.*] So far the prediction is right, 'tis ten exactly.—[*Aloud.*] And pray, sir, how long have you been in this travelling humour?

Wor. 'Tis natural, madam, for us to avoid what disturbs our quiet.

Mel. Rather the love of change, which is more natural, may be the occasion of it.

Wor. To be sure, madam, there must be charms in variety, else neither you nor I should be so fond of it.

Mel. You mistake, Mr Worthy, I am not so fond of variety as to travel for't, nor do I think it prudence in you to run yourself into a certain expense and danger, in hopes of precarious pleasures, which at best never answer expectation; as 'tis evident from the example of most travellers, that long more to return to their own country than they did to go abroad.

Wor. What pleasures I may receive abroad are indeed uncertain; but this I am sure of, I shall meet with less cruelty among the most barbarous nations than I have found at home.

Mel. Come, sir, you and I have been jangling a great while; I fancy if we made up our accounts, we should the sooner come to an agreement.

Wor. Sure, madam, you won't dispute your being in my debt? My fears, sighs, vows, promises, assiduities, anxieties, jealousies, have run on for a whole year, without any payment.

Mel. A year! Oh, Mr Worthy! what you owe to me is not to be paid under a seven years' servitude. How did you use me the year before? when, taking the advantage of my innocence and necessity, you would have made me your mistress, that is, your slave. Remember the wicked insinuations, artful baits, deceitful arguments, cunning pretences; then your impudent behaviour, loose expressions, familiar letters, rude visits, —remember those! those, Mr Worthy!

Wor. [*Aside.*] I do remember, and am sorry I made no better use of 'em.—[*Aloud.*] But you may remember, madam, that—

Mel. Sir, I'll remember nothing—'tis your interest that I should forget: you have been barbarous to me, I have been cruel to you; put that and that together, and let one balance the other. Now if you will begin upon a new score, lay aside your adventuring airs, and behave yourself handsomely till Lent be over; here's my hand, I'll use you as a gentleman should be.

Wor. And if I don't use you as a gentlewoman should be, may this be my poison.   [*Kissing her hand.*

Enter Servant.

Ser. Madam, the coach is at the door.   [*Exit.*

Mel. I am going to Mr Balance's country-house to see my cousin Silvia; I have done her an injury, and can't be easy till I have asked her pardon.

Wor. I dare not hope for the honour of waiting on you.

Mel. My coach is full; but if you will be so gallant as to mount your own horses and follow us, we shall be glad to be overtaken; and if you bring Captain Plume with you, we sha'n't have the worse reception.

Wor. I'll endeavour it.   [*Exit, leading* MELINDA.

SCENE IV.—*The Market-Place.*

Enter PLUME *and* KITE.

Plume. A baker, a tailor, a smith, and a butcher—I believe the first colony planted in Virginia had not more trades in their company than I have in mine.

Kite. The butcher, sir, will have his hands full; for we have two sheep-stealers among us. I hear of a fellow, too, committed just now for stealing of horses.

Plume. We'll dispose of him among the dragoons. Have we ne'er a poulterer among us?

Kite. Yes, sir, the king of the gipsies is a very good one, he has an excellent hand at a goose or a turkey.— Here's Captain Brazen, sir; I must go look after the men. [*Exit.*

Enter BRAZEN, *reading a letter.*

Braz. Um, um, um, the canonical hour—Um, um, very well.—My dear Plume! give me a buss.

Plume. Half a score, if you will, my dear. What hast got in thy hand, child?

Braz. 'Tis a project for laying out a thousand pound.

Plume. Were it not requisite to project first how to get it in?

Braz. You can't imagine, my dear, that I want twenty thousand pound; I have spent twenty times as much in the service. Now, my dear, pray advise me, my head runs much upon architecture; shall I build a privateer or a playhouse?

Plume. An odd question—a privateer or a playhouse! 'Twill require some consideration.—Faith, I'm for a privateer.

Braz. I'm not of your opinion, my dear.—For in the first place a privateer may be ill built.

Plume. And so may a playhouse.

Braz. But a privateer may be ill manned.

Plume. And so may a playhouse.

Braz. But a privateer may run upon the shallows.

Plume. Not so often as a playhouse.

Braz. But you know a privateer may spring a leak.

Plume. And I know that a playhouse may spring a great many.

Braz. But suppose the privateer come home with a rich booty, we should never agree about our shares.

Plume. 'Tis just so in a playhouse :—so, by my advice, you shall fix upon the privateer.

Braz. Agreed!—But if this twenty thousand should not be in specie—

Plume. What twenty thousand?

Braz. Heark'ee. [*Whispers.*

Plume. Married!

Braz. Presently, we're to meet about half a mile out of town at the water-side—and so forth.—[*Reads.*] *For fear I should be known by any of Worthy's friends, you must give me leave to wear my mask till after the ceremony, which will make me for ever yours.*—Look'ee there, my dear dog. [*Shows the bottom of the letter to* PLUME.

Plume. Melinda!—and by this light, her own hand! —Once more, if you please, my dear.—Her hand exactly!—Just now, you say?

Braz. This minute I must be gone.

Plume. Have a little patience, and I'll go with you.

Braz. No, no, I see a gentleman coming this way, that may be inquisitive; 'tis Worthy, do you know him?

Plume. By sight only.

Braz. Have a care, the very eyes discover secrets.
[*Exit.*

Enter WORTHY.

Wor. To boot and saddle, Captain! you must mount.

Plume. Whip and spur, Worthy, or you won't mount.

Wor. But I shall: Melinda and I are agreed, she's gone to visit Silvia, we are to mount and follow; and could we carry a parson with us, who knows what might be done for us both?

Plume. Don't trouble your head; Melinda has secured a parson already.

Wor. Already! Do you know more than I?

Plume. Yes, I saw it under her hand.—Brazen and

she are to meet half a mile hence at the water-side, there
to take boat, I suppose to be ferried over to the Elysian
fields, if there be any such thing in matrimony.

Wor. I parted with Melinda just now; she assured
me she hated Brazen, and that she resolved to discard
Lucy for daring to write letters to him in her name.

Plume. Nay, nay, there's nothing of Lucy in this—I
tell ye, I saw Melinda's hand, as surely as this is mine.

Wor. But I tell you she's gone this minute to Justice
Balance's country-house.

Plume. But I tell you she's gone this minute to the
water-side.

Enter SERVANT.

Ser. [*To* WORTHY.] Madam Melinda has sent word
that you need not trouble yourself to follow her, because
her journey to Justice Balance's is put off, and she's gone
to take the air another way.

Wor. How! her journey put off!

Plume. That is, her journey was a put-off to you.

Wor. 'Tis plain, plain!—But how, where, when is she
to meet Brazen?

Plume. Just now, I tell you, half a mile hence, at the
water-side.

Wor. Up or down the water?

Plume. That I don't know.

Wor. I'm glad my horses are ready.—Jack, get 'em
out. [*Exit* Servant.

Plume. Shall I go with you?

Wor. Not an inch; I shall return presently.

Plume. You'll find me at the hall; the justices are
sitting by this time, and I must attend them.

[*Exeunt severally.*

SCENE V.—*A Court of Justice.*[1]

BALANCE, SCALE *and* SCRUPLE *upon the bench;* KITE, Constable, *and* Mob. KITE *and* Constable *advance forward.*[2]

Kite. Pray, who are those honourable gentlemen upon the bench?

Con. He in the middle is Justice Balance, he on the right is Justice Scale, and he on the left is Justice Scruple; and I am Mr Constable:—four very honest gentlemen.

Kite. O dear Sir! I am your most obedient servant.— [*Saluting him.*] I fancy, sir, that your employment and mine are much the same; for my business is to keep people in order, and if they disobey, to knock 'em down; and then we are both staff-officers.

Con. Nay, I'm a serjeant myself—of the militia. Come, brother, you shall see me exercise. Suppose this a musket now: now I am shouldered.

[*Puts his staff on his right shoulder.*

Kite. Ay, you are shouldered pretty well for a constable's staff; but for a musket, you must put it on t'other shoulder, my dear.

[1] This scene, and indeed the whole play, form a commentary on the Mutiny and Impressment Acts (1 Anne, c. 16; 2 and 3 Anne c. 16 and c. 19) called forth by the pressure of the War of the Spanish Succession. By these Acts debtors and even convicted felons might be released from prison on condition that they should serve in the army or navy; and justices of the peace were empowered " to raise and levy such able-bodied men as have not any lawful calling or employment, or visible means for their maintenance and livelihood, to serve as soldiers." " The regular officers of the army," says J. H. Burton, "were excluded from acting as justices for the enrolment, and the Mutiny Acts and Articles of War were to be read over to the recruit before he was sworn and enrolled." It would appear, then, that there is a touch of satire in the Justice's invitation to Plume to sit beside them on the bench, as showing that the restrictions of the Act were observed in the letter rather than in the spirit.

[2] So in Q. 2. In Q. 1, "*advance to the front of the stage.*"

Con. Adso! that's true.—Come, now give the word of command.

Kite. Silence!

Con. Ay, ay, so we will—we will be silent.

Kite. Silence, you dog, silence!

[*Strikes him over the head with his halberd.*

Con. That's the way to silence a man with a witness! What d'ye mean, friend?

Kite. Only to exercise you, sir.

Con. Your exercise differs so from ours, that we shall ne'er agree about it. If my own captain had given me such a rap, I had taken the law of him.

Enter PLUME.

Bal. Captain, you're welcome.

Plume. Gentlemen, I thank you.

Scrup. Come, honest Captain, sit by me.—[PLUME *ascends and sits upon the bench.*] Now produce your prisoners.—Here, that fellow there—set him up.—[1] Mr Constable, what have you to say against this man?

Con. I have nothing to say against him, an please you.

Bal. No! What made you bring him hither?

Con. I don't know, an please your worship.

Scale. Did not the contents of your warrant direct you what sort of men to take up?

Con. I can't tell, an please ye; I can't read.

Scrup. A very pretty constable truly!—I find we have no business here.

Kite. May it please the worshipful bench, I desire to be heard in this case, as being counsel for the Queen.

Bal. Come, serjeant, you shall be heard, since

[1] The stage-directions in this scene are very imperfect. Evidently several Rustics have been forcibly brought before the Justices for enrolment. Two of them are among the "Mob," while others (as we shall see presently) have slipped through the Constable's fingers.

nobody else will speak; we won't come here for nothing.

Kite. This man is but one man; the country may spare him, and the army wants him; besides, he's cut out by nature for a grenadier; he's five foot ten inches high; he shall box, wrestle, or dance the Cheshire Round with any man in the county; he gets drunk every sabbath day, and he beats his wife.

Wife. You lie, sirrah! you lie!—An please your worship, he's the best-natur'dst, pains-taking'st man in the parish, witness my five poor children.

Scrup. A wife and five children!—You, constable, you rogue, how durst you impress a man that has a wife and five children?

Scale. Discharge him! discharge him!

Bal. Hold, gentlemen!—Hark'ee, friend, how do you maintain your wife and children?

Plume.[1] They live upon wildfowl and venison, sir; the husband keeps a gun, and kills all the hares and partridges within five miles round.

Bal. A gun! nay, if he be so good at gunning, he shall have enough on't. He may be of use against the French, for he shoots flying, to be sure.

Scrup. But his wife and children, Mr Balance!

Wife. Ay, ay, that's the reason you would send him away; you know I have a child every year, and you are afraid they should come upon the parish at last.

Plume. Look'ee there, gentlemen, the honest woman has spoke it at once; the parish had better maintain five children this year, than six or seven the next. That fellow, upon his high feeding, may get you two or three beggars at a birth.

Wife. Look'ee, Mr Captain, the parish shall get nothing by sending him away, for I won't lose my teeming-time, if there be a man left in the parish.

---

[1] This speech is assigned to Plume in all editions; but surely it belongs to Kite.

Bal. Send that woman to the house of correction—and the man—

Kite. I'll take care o' him, if you please.

[*Takes him down.*

Scale. Here, you constable, the next:—set up that black-faced fellow, he has a gunpowder look. What can you say against this man, constable?

Con. Nothing, but that he is a very honest man.

Plume. Pray, gentlemen, let me have one honest man in my company, for the novelty's sake.

Bal. What are you, friend?

Mob. A collier; I work in the coal-pits.

Scrup. Look'ee, gentlemen, this fellow has a trade, and the act of parliament here expresses, that we are to impress no man that has any visible means of a livelihood.[1]

Kite. May it please your worships, this man has no visible means of livelihood, for he works underground.

Plume. Well said, Kite! Besides, the army wants miners.

Bal. Right, and had we an order of government for't, we could raise you in this, and the neighbouring county of Stafford, five hundred colliers, that would run you underground like moles, and do more service in a siege than all the miners in the army.

Scrup. Well, friend, what have you to say for yourself?

Mob. I'm married.

Kite. Lack-a-day, so am I!

Mob. Here's my wife, poor woman.

Bal. Are you married, good woman?

Wom. I'm married in conscience.

Kite. May it please your worship, she's with child in conscience.

Scale. Who married you, mistress?

Wom. My husband—we agreed that I should call

[1] *See* note, p. 336.

him husband to avoid passing for a whore, and that he should call me wife, to shun going for a soldier.

Scrup. A very pretty couple! Pray, captain, will you take 'em both?

Plume. What say you, Mr Kite? will you take care of the woman?

Kite. Yes, sir; she shall go with us to the seaside, and there, if she has a mind to drown herself, we'll take care that nobody shall hinder her.

Bal. Here, constable, bring in my man. — [*Exit* Constable.] Now, Captain, I'll fit you with a man, such as you ne'er listed in your life.

Re-enter Constable *with* SILVIA.

Oh! my friend Pinch, I'm very glad to see you.

Silv. Well, sir, and what then?

Scale. What then! is that your respect to the bench?

Silv. Sir, I don't care a farthing for you nor your bench neither.

Scrup. Look'ee, gentlemen, that's enough: he's a very impudent fellow, and fit for a soldier.

Scale. A notorious rogue, I say, and very fit for a soldier.

Con. A whoremaster, I say, and therefore fit to go.

Bal. What think you, captain?

Plume. I think he's a very pretty fellow, and therefore fit to serve.

Silv. Me for a soldier! Send your own lazy, lubberly sons at home, fellows that hazard their necks every day in pursuit of a fox, yet dare not peep abroad to look an enemy in the face.

Con. May it please your worships, I have a woman at the door to swear a rape against this rogue.

Silv. Is it your wife or daughter, booby? I ravished 'em both yesterday.

Bal. Pray, captain, read the Articles of War, we'll see him listed immediately.

Plume. [Reads.] *Articles of War against mutiny and desertion—* [1]

Silv. Hold, sir !—Once more, gentlemen, have a care what you do, for you shall severely smart for any violence you offer to me ; and you, Mr Balance, I speak to you particularly, you shall heartily repent it.

Plume. Look'ee, young spark, say but one word more, and I'll build a horse for you as high as the ceiling, and make you ride the most tiresome journey that ever you made in your life.

Silv. You have made a fine speech, good Captain Huffcap, but you had better be quiet ; I shall find a way to cool your courage.

Plume. Pray, gentlemen, don't mind him, he's distracted.

Silv. 'Tis false ! I am descended of as good a family as any in your country ; my father is as good a man as any upon your bench, and I am heir to twelve hundred pound a year.

Bal. He's certainly mad !—Pray, Captain, read the Articles of War.

Silv. Hold once more !—Pray, Mr Balance, to you I speak : suppose I were your child, would you use me at this rate ?

Bal. No, faith, were you mine, I would send you to Bedlam first, and into the army afterwards.

Silv. But consider my father, sir : he's as good, as generous, as brave, as just a man as ever served his country ; I'm his only child, perhaps the loss of me may break his heart.

Bal. He's a very great fool if it does.—Captain, if you don't list him this minute, I'll leave the court.

Plume. Kite, do you distribute the levy-money to the men while I read.

[1] *See* note, p. 336. In both Q. 1 and Q. 2 this line appears as a stage-direction. "*Plume reads Articles of War against Mutiny and Desertion.*" The above emendation, manifestly right, is due to an eighteenth-century editor.

Kite. Ay, sir.—Silence, gentlemen!

[PLUME *reads the Articles of War.*

Bal. Very well; now, Captain, let me beg the favour of you, not to discharge this fellow upon any account whatsoever.—Bring in the rest.

Con There are no more, an't please your worship.

Bal. No more! there were five two hours ago.

Silv. 'Tis true, sir; but this rogue of a constable let the rest escape for a bribe of eleven shillings a man; because he said the act allowed him but ten, so the odd shilling was clear gains.

Justices. How!

Silv. Gentlemen, he offered to let me get away for two guineas, but I had not so much about me. This is truth, and I'm ready to swear it.

Kite. And I'll swear it; give me the book, 'tis for the good of the service.

Mob. May it please your worship, I gave him half-a-crown to say that I was an honest man; but now, since that your worships have made me a rogue, I hope I shall have my money again.

Bal. 'Tis my opinion that this constable be put into the captain's hands, and if his friends don't bring four good men for his ransom by to-morrow night—Captain, you shall carry him to Flanders.

Scale. Scrup. Agreed! agreed!

Plume. Mr Kite, take the constable into custody.

Kite. Ay, ay, sir.—[*To* Constable.] Will you please to have your office taken from you? or will you handsomely lay down your staff, as your betters have done before you?   [Constable *drops his staff.*

Bal. Come, gentlemen, there needs no great ceremony in adjourning this court.—Captain, you shall dine with me.

Kite. [*To* Constable.] Come, Mr Militia Serjeant, I shall silence you now, I believe, without your taking the law of me.   [*Exeunt omnes.*

SCENE VI.—*The Fields.*

Enter BRAZEN *leading in* LUCY, *masked.*

Braz. The boat is just below here.

Enter WORTHY *with a case of pistols under his arm.*

Wor. Here, sir, take your choice.

[*Going between them, and offering the pistols.*

Braz. What! pistols! Are they charged, my dear?

Wor. With a brace of bullets each.

Braz. But I'm a foot-officer, my dear, and never use pistols. The sword is my way—and I won't be put out of my road to please any man.

Wor. Nor I neither ; so have at you.

[*Cocks one pistol.*

Braz. Look'ee, my dear, I don't care for pistols.— Pray, oblige me, and let us have a bout at sharps ; damn it, there's no parrying these bullets !

Wor. Sir, if you han't your bellyfull of these, the swords shall come in for second course.

Braz. Why, then, fire and fury! I have eaten smoke from the mouth of a cannon, sir ; don't think I fear powder, for I live upon't. Let me see—[*Takes one.*] And now, sir, how many paces distant shall we fire ?

Wor. Fire you when you please, I'll reserve my shot till I'm sure of you.

Braz. Come. where's your cloak ?

Wor. Cloak ! what d'ye mean ?

Braz. To fight upon ; I always fight upon a cloak, tis our way abroad.

Lucy. Come, gentlemen, I'll end the strife.

[*Unmasks.*

Wor. Lucy !—take her.

Braz. The devil take me if I do ! Huzza !—[*Fires his pistol.*] D'ye hear, d'ye hear, you plaguy harridan, how those bullets whistle ! Suppose they had been lodged in my gizzard now !

Lucy. Pray, sir, pardon me.

Braz. I can't tell, child, till I know whether my money be safe.—[*Searching his pockets.*] Yes, yes, I do pardon you, but if I had you in the Rose Tavern, [1] Covent Garden, with three or four hearty rakes, and three or four smart napkins, I would tell you another story, my dear.   [*Exit.*

Wor. And was Melinda privy to this ?

Lucy. No, sir, she wrote her name upon a piece of paper at the fortune-teller's last night, which I put in my pocket, and so writ above it to the captain.

Wor. And how came Melinda's journey put off ?

Lucy. At the town's end she met Mr Balance's steward, who told her that Mrs Silvia was gone from her father's, and nobody could tell whither.

Wor. Silvia gone from her father's !   This will be news to Plume.—Go home, and tell your lady how near I was being shot for her.   [*Exeunt severally.*

SCENE VII.—Justice BALANCE'S *House.*

Enter BALANCE, *with a napkin in his hand, as risen from dinner, and* Steward.

Stew. We did not miss her till the evening, sir ; and then, searching for her in the chamber that was my young master's, we found her clothes there ; but the suit that your son left in the press, when he went to London, was gone.

Bal. The white trimmed with silver?

Stew. The same.

Bal. You han't told that circumstance to anybody ?

[1] See ante, p. 133.

Stew. To none but your worship.

Bal. And be sure you don't. Go into the dining-room and tell Captain Plume that I beg to speak with him.

Stew. I shall. [*Exit.*

Bal. Was ever man so imposed upon! I had her promise, indeed, that she should never dispose of herself without my consent. I have consented with a witness, given her away as my act and deed. And this, I warrant, the captain thinks will pass! No, I shall never pardon him the villainy, first of robbing me of my daughter, and then the mean opinion he must have of me, to think that I could be so wretchedly imposed upon. Her extravagant passion might encourage her in the attempt, but the contrivance must be his. I'll know the truth presently.

Enter PLUME.

Pray, Captain, what have you done with your young gentleman soldier?

Plume. He's at my quarters, I suppose, with the rest of my men.

Bal. Does he keep company with the common soldiers?

Plume. No, he's generally with me.

Bal. He lies with you, I presume!

Plume. No, faith, I offered him part of my bed; but the young rogue fell in love with Rose, and has lain with her, I think, since he came to town.

Bal. So that, between you both, Rose has been finely managed.

Plume. Upon my honour, sir, she had no harm from me.

Bal. [*Aside.*] All's safe, I find!—[*Aloud.*] Now, Captain, you must know that the young fellow's impudence in court was well grounded; he said I should heartily repent his being listed, and so I do from my soul.

Plume. Ay ! For what reason ?

Bal. Because he is no less than what he said he was, born of as good a family as any in this county, and is heir to twelve hundred pound a year.

Plume. I'm very glad to hear it—for I wanted but a man of that quality to make my company a perfect representative of the whole commons of England.

Bal. Won't you discharge him ?

Plume. Not under a hundred pound sterling.

Bal. You shall have it, for his father is my intimate friend.

Plume. Then you shall have him for nothing.

Bal. Nay, sir, you shall have your price.

Plume. Not a penny, sir; I value an obligation to you much above a hundred pound.

Bal. Perhaps, sir, you sha'n't repent your generosity. —Will you please to write his discharge in my pocket-book ? —[*Gives his book.*] In the meantime, we'll send for the gentleman—Who waits there?

Enter Servant.

Go to the captain's lodging and inquire for Mr Wilful; tell him his captain wants him here immediately.

Ser. Sir, the gentleman's below at the door, inquiring for the captain.

Plume. Bid him come up.—[*Exit* Servant.] Here's the discharge, sir.

Bal. Sir, I thank you.—[*Aside.*] 'Tis plain he had no hand in't.

Enter SILVIA.

Silv. I think, Captain, you might have used me better than to leave me yonder among your swearing drunken crew. And you, Mr Justice, might have been so civil as to have invited me to dinner, for I have eaten with as good a man as your worship.

Plume. Sir, you must charge our want of respect upon

our ignorance of your quality.—But now you are at
liberty—I have discharged you.

Silv. Discharged me!

Bal. Yes, sir, and you must once more go home to
your father.

Silv. My father! then I am discovered.—O sir!
[*Kneeling.*] I expect no pardon.

Bal. Pardon! No, no, child, your crime shall be your
punishment.—Here, Captain, I deliver her over to the
conjugal power for her chastisement; since she will be
a wife, be you a husband, a very husband. When she
tells you of her love, upbraid her with her folly; be
modishly ungrateful, because she has been unfashion-
ably kind, and use her worse than you would anybody
else, because you can't use her so well as she deserves.

Plume. And are you Silvia, in good earnest?

Silv. Earnest! I have gone too far to make it a jest, sir.

Plume. And do you give her to me in good earnest?

Bal. If you please to take her, sir.

Plume. Why then I have saved my legs and arms, and
lost my liberty; secure from wounds, I am prepared for
the gout; farewell subsistence, and welcome taxes!—
Sir, my liberty, and hopes of being a general, are much
dearer to me than your twelve hundred pound a year.—
But to your love, madam, I resign my freedom, and to
your beauty my ambition: greater in obeying at your
feet, than commanding at the head of an army.

Enter WORTHY.

Wor. I am sorry to hear, Mr Balance, that your
daughter is lost.

Bal. So am not I, sir, since an honest gentleman has
found her.

Enter MELINDA.

Mel. Pray, Mr Balance, what's become of my cousin
Silvia?

Bal. Your cousin Silvia is talking yonder with your cousin Plume.

Mel. and *Wor.* How!

Silv. Do you think it strange, cousin, that a woman should change! But, I hope you'll excuse a change that has proceeded from constancy. I altered my outside, because I was the same within, and only laid by the woman to make sure of my man ; that's my history.

Mel. Your history is a little romantic, cousin ; but since success has crowned your adventures, you will have the world o' your side, and I shall be willing to go with the tide, provided you'll pardon an injury I offered you in the letter to your father.

Plume. That injury, madam, was done to me, and the reparation I expect shall be made to my friend : make Mr Worthy happy, and I shall be satisfied.

Mel. A good example, sir, will go a long way ; when my cousin is pleased to surrender, 'tis probable I sha'n't hold out much longer.

Enter BRAZEN.

Braz. Gentlemen, I am yours.—Madam, I am not yours.

Mel. I'm glad on't, sir.

Braz. So am I.—You have got a pretty house here, Mr Laconic.

Bal. 'Tis time to right all mistakes.—My name, sir, is Balance.

Braz. Balance! Sir, I am your most obedient!—I know your whole generation. Had not you an uncle that was governor of the Leeward Islands some years ago?

Bal. Did you know him?

Braz. Intimately, sir. He played at billiards to a miracle. You had a brother, too, that was captain of a fireship—poor Dick—he had the most engaging way with him—of making punch—and then his cabin was

so neat—but his boy Jack was the most comical bastard
—ha, ha, ha, ha! a pickled dog, I shall never forget him.

Plume. Well, Captain, are you fixed in your project
yet? are you still for the privateer?

Braz. No, no, I had enough of a privateer just now;
I had like to have been picked up by a cruiser under
false colours, and a French pickaroon for aught I
know.

Plume. But have you got your recruits, my dear?

Braz. Not a stick, my dear.

Plume. Probably I shall furnish you.

Enter ROSE *and* BULLOCK.

Rose. Captain, Captain, I have got loose once more,
and have persuaded my sweetheart Cartwheel to go with
us; but you must promise not to part with me again.

Silv. I find Mrs Rose has not been pleased with her
bedfellow.

Rose. Bedfellow! I don't know whether I had a bedfellow or not.

Silv. Don't be in a passion, child; I was as little
pleased with your company as you could be with mine.

Bull. Pray, sir, dunna be offended at my sister, she's
something underbred; but if you please, I'll lie with
you in her stead.

Plume. I have promised, madam, to provide for this
girl; now will you be pleased to let her wait upon you?
or shall I take care of her?

Silv. She shall be my charge, sir; you may find it
business enough to take care of me.

Bull. Ay, and of me, Captain; for wauns! if ever you
lift your hand against me, I'll desart—

Plume. Captain Brazen shall take care o' that.—[*To*
BRAZEN.] My dear, instead of the twenty thousand
pound you talked of, you shall have the twenty brave
recruits that I have raised, at the rate they cost me.—
My commission I lay down, to be taken up by some

braver fellow, that has more merit and less good
fortune ; whilst I endeavour, by the example of this
worthy gentleman, to serve my Queen and country at
home.

> With some regret I quit the active field,
> Where glory full reward for life does yield ;
> But the recruiting trade, with all its train
> Of lasting plague, fatigue, and endless pain,
> I gladly quit, with my fair spouse to stay,
> And raise recruits the matrimonial way.

[*Exeunt.*

EPILOGUE

LL ladies and gentlemen that are willing to see the comedy, called *The Recruiting Officer*, let them repair to-morrow night, by six o'clock, to the sign of the Theatre Royal in Drury Lane, and they shall be kindly entertained.

We scorn the vulgar ways to bid you come,
Whole Europe now obeys the call of drum.
The soldier, not the poet, here appears,
And beats up for a corps of volunteers :
He finds that music chiefly does delight ye,
And therefore chooses music to invite ye.

Beat the Grenadier March. — Row, row, tow!— Gentlemen, this piece of music, called *An Overture to a Battle*, was composed by a famous Italian master, and was performed with wonderful success at the great operas of Vigo, Schellenberg, and Blenheim [1]—it came off with the applause of all Europe, excepting France; the French found it a little too rough for their *delicatesse*.

Some that have acted on those glorious stages,
Are here to witness to succeeding ages,
That [2] no music like the grenadier's engages.

---

[1] On Vigo, see note, p. 169. On Blenheim see note p. 266. The battle of Schellenberg, in which Marlborough and Prince Louis of Baden defeated the Elector of Bavaria, shortly preceded Blenheim.

[2] Though Farquhar was no great metrist, one would fain hope that he did not write this superfluous " That.'

Ladies, we must own, that this music of ours is not altogether so soft as Bononcini's ;[1] yet, we dare affirm, that it has laid more people asleep than all the *Camillas* in the world; and you'll condescend to own that it keeps one awake better than any opera that ever was acted.

The Grenadier March seems to be a composure excellently adapted to the genius of the English, for no music was ever followed so far by us, nor with so much alacrity; and, with all deference to the present subscription, we must say, that the Grenadier March has been subscribed for by the whole Grand Alliance; and we presume to inform the ladies that it always has the pre-eminence abroad, and is constantly heard by the tallest, handsomest men in the whole army. In short, to gratify the present taste, our author is now adapting some words to the Grenadier March, which he intends to have performed to-morrow, if the lady who is to sing it should not happen to be sick.

> This he concludes to be the surest way
> To draw you hither; for you'll all obey
> Soft music's call, though you should damn his play.

[1] Marc Antonio Bononcini, brother of Giovanni Bononcini, the rival of Handel, composed the music of *Camilla*, the libretto being translated from the Italian of Silvio Stampiglio, and adapted to Bononcini's music, by Owen MacSwiney or Swiney. The opera, described by Genest as "contemptible," was produced at D.L., March 30, 1706, *The Recruiting Officer* following on April 8. Mr W. J. Lawrence writes: "All operas were produced at that period by subscription, and, the theatre not being particularly concerned in their success, Farquhar was at liberty to gird at *Camilla*." Hence also the allusion below to "the present subscription."

THE

BEAUX STRATAGEM.

A

COMEDY

As it is Acted at the

QUEEN's THEATRE

IN THE

HAY - MARKET.

BY

Her MAJESTY's Sworn Comedians.

Written by Mr Farquhar, *Author of the* Recruiting-Officer.

LONDON:

Printed for BERNARD LINTOTT, at the *Cross Keys* next
Nando's Coffee-House in *Fleetstreet.*

As to the date of this comedy (1707) and the circumstances attending its production, *see* Introduction, p. 13. It is the only one of Farquhar's plays (except *The Stage Coach*) not produced at Drury Lane. It was first acted at the Haymarket, where the leading members of the former Drury Lane company were appearing under Swiney's management. It rivalled, and probably surpassed, *The Recruiting Officer* in popularity. Archer was played by Ryan, by Garrick (it was one of his favourite parts), by Smith, by Elliston, by Charles Kemble and many other actors. Sullen was played by Quin, and Scrub by Macklin, Garrick (for a benefit), Shuter, Quick, Liston and Keeley. Oddly enough, Scrub was occasionally acted by women—notably by Mrs Abington for her benefit in 1786. Almost all the leading actresses of the 18th century, except Miss Siddons, were frequently seen in the part of Mrs Sullen—for instance, Mrs Pritchard, Mrs Woffington, Mrs Barry, Mrs Abington, Miss Farren, Mrs Jordan. The charming part of Cherry, too, was naturally a favourite. It included among its representatives Mrs Clive, Miss Pope and Miss Mellon. The last revival took place under Miss Litton's management at the Imperial Theatre, on September 22, 1879, when Miss Litton played Mrs Sullen, Mrs Stirling Lady Bountiful, Miss Carlotta Addison Cherry, William Farren Archer, John Ryder Sullen, Fred Everill Boniface, Kyrle Bellew Gibbet, and Lionel Brough Scrub.

ADVERTISEMENT.

THE reader may find some faults in this play, which my illness prevented the amending of ; but there is great amends made in the representation, which cannot be matched, no more than the friendly and indefatigable care of Mr Wilks, to whom I chiefly owe the success of the play.

GEORGE FARQUHAR.

PROLOGUE

SPOKEN BY MR WILKS.

HEN strife disturbs, or sloth
    corrupts an age,
Keen satire is the business of
    the stage.
When the Plain-Dealer [1] writ,
    he lash'd those crimes,
Which then infested most the
modish times :
But now, when faction sleeps, and sloth is fled,
And all our youth in active fields are bred;
When, through Great Britain's fair extensive round,
The trumps of fame the notes of UNION sound; [2]
When Anna's sceptre points the laws their course,
And her example gives her precepts force :
There scarce is room for satire; all our lays
Must be, or songs of triumph, or of praise.
But as in grounds best cultivated, tares
And poppies rise among the golden ears,
Our products so, fit for the field or school,
Must mix with Nature's favourite plant—a fool :
A weed that has to twenty summers ran,
Shoots up in stalk, and vegetates to man.
Simpling our author goes from field to field,
And culls such fools as may diversion yield;
And, thanks to Nature, there's no want of those,

[1] Wycherley.
[2] The Act of Union between England and Scotland received the Royal assent, March 6, 1707, two days before this comedy was produced.

For, rain or shine, the thriving coxcomb grows,
Follies to-night we show ne'er lash'd before,
Yet such as Nature shows you every hour ;
Nor can the pictures give a just offence,
For fools are made for jests to men of sense.

DRAMATIS PERSONÆ

MEN

AIMWELL, ⎧ two Gentlemen of broken ⎫ Mr MILLS.
ARCHER, ⎨ Fortunes, the first as Master, ⎬ Mr WILKS.
⎩ and the second as Servant, ⎭

COUNT BELLAIR, a French Officer,
   Prisoner at Lichfield .   .   . Mr BOWMAN.

SULLEN, a Country Blockhead, brutal to
   his Wife   .   .   . Mr VERBRUGGEN.

FREEMAN, a Gentleman from London . Mr KEEN

FOIGARD, a Priest, Chaplain to the French
   Officers   .   .   . . Mr BOWEN.

GIBBET, a Highwayman .   . . Mr CIBBER.

HOUNSLOW, ⎫ his Companions.
BAGSHOT, ⎭

BONIFACE, Landlord of the Inn .   . Mr BULLOCK.

SCRUB, servant to Mr Sullen   . . Mr NORRIS.

WOMEN

LADY BOUNTIFUL, an old, civil, Country ⎫
   Gentlewoman, that cures all her ⎬ Mrs POWELL.
   Neighbours of all distempers, and ⎪
   foolishly fond of her Son, SULLEN. ⎭

DORINDA, LADY BOUNTIFUL'S daughter. Mrs BRADSHAW

Mrs SULLEN, her Daughter-in-Law   . Mrs OLDFIELD.

GIPSY, Maid to the Ladies   . . Mrs MILLS.

CHERRY, the Landlord's Daughter in the
   Inn   .   .   .   . . Mrs BIGNAL.

[Tapster, Coach-passengers, Countryman, Countrywoman,
   and Servants.]

SCENE—LICHFIELD.

ACT I

SCENE I.—*An Inn.*

Enter BONIFACE *running.*

BON. Chamberlain ! maid ! Cherry ! daughter Cherry ! all asleep ? all dead ?

Enter CHERRY *running.*

Cher. Here ! here ! Why d'ye bawl so, father ? d'ye think we have no ears ?

Bon. You deserve to have none, you young minx ! The company of the Warrington coach has stood in the hall this hour, and nobody to show them to their chambers.

Cher. And let 'em wait, father; there's neither redcoat in the coach, nor footman behind it.

Bon. But they threaten to go to another inn to-night.

Cher. That they dare not, for fear the coachman should overturn them to-morrow.—Coming ! coming ! —Here's the London coach arrived.

Enter several People with trunks, bandboxes, and other luggage, and cross the stage.

Bon. Welcome, ladies !

Cher. Very welcome, gentlemen ! — Chamberlain, show the Lion and the Rose.   [*Exit with the company.*

359

Enter AIMWELL *in riding habit,* ARCHER *as Footman carrying a portmantle.*

Bon. This way, this way, gentlemen !

Aim. [*To* ARCHER.] Set down the things ; go to the stable, and see my horses well rubbed.

Arch. I shall, sir.   [*Exit.*

Aim. You're my landlord, I suppose ?

Bon. Yes, sir ; I'm old Will Boniface, pretty well known upon this road, as the saying is.

Aim. O Mr Boniface, your servant !

Bon. O sir !—What will your honour please to drink, as the saying is.

Aim. I have heard your town of Lichfield much famed for ale ; I think I'll taste that.

Bo. Sir, I have now in my cellar ten tun of the best ale in Staffordshire ; 'tis smooth as oil, sweet as milk, clear as amber, and strong as brandy ; and will be just fourteen year old the fifth day of next March, old style.

Aim. You're very exact, I find, in the age of your ale.

Bon. As punctual, sir, as I am in the age of my children.   I'll show you such ale !—Here, tapster, broach number 1706, as the saying is.—Sir, you shall taste my *Anno Domini.*—I have lived in Lichfield, man and boy, above eight-and-fifty years, and, I believe, have not consumed eight-and-fifty ounces of meat.

Aim. At a meal, you mean, if one may guess your sense by your bulk.

Bon. Not in my life, sir.   I have fed purely upon ale. I have eat my ale, drank my ale, and I always sleep upon ale.

[*Enter* Tapster *with a bottle and glass,*[1] *and exit.*]

---

[1] So all editions ; but it is evident from what follows that the tapster brings two glasses ; and the stage-direction, *Filling it out* (for which modern editors substitute *Pouring out a glass*), really means that Boniface pours for himself as well as for his guest. Compare *The Twin-Rivals*, Act. 1, Sc. 1, where Balderdash and Benjamin Wouldbe drink together in the same way.

Now, sir, you shall see!—[*Filling it out.*]   Your
worship's health.—Ha! delicious, delicious! fancy it
burgundy, only fancy it, and 'tis worth ten shillings a
quart.

Aim. [*Drinks.*] 'Tis confounded strong!

Bon. Strong! It must be so, or how should we be
strong that drink it?

Aim. And have you lived so long upon this ale,
landlord?

Bon. Eight-and-fifty years, upon my credit, sir—but
it killed my wife, poor woman, as the saying is.

Aim. How came that to pass?

Bon. I don't know how, sir; she would not let the
ale take its natural course, sir; she was for qualifying
it every now and then with a dram, as the saying is;
and an honest gentleman that came this way from
Ireland made her a present of a dozen bottles of
usquebaugh — but the poor woman was never well
after. But, howe'er, I was obliged to the gentleman,
you know.

Aim. Why, was it the usquebaugh that killed her?

Bon. My Lady Bountiful said so. She, good lady.
did what could be done; she cured her of three
tympanies, but the fourth carried her off. But she's
happy, and I'm contented, as the saying is.

Aim. Who's that Lady Bountiful you mentioned?

Bon. Od's my life, sir, we'll drink her health.—
[*Drinks.*] My Lady Bountiful is one of the best of
women. Her last husband, Sir Charles Bountiful, left
her worth a thousand pound a year; and, I believe, she
lays out one-half on't in charitable uses for the good of
her neighbours. She cures rheumatisms, ruptures, and
broken shins in men; green-sickness, obstructions, and
fits of the mother,[1] in women; the king's evil, chin-
cough,[2] and chilblains, in children. In short, she has
cured more people in and about Lichfield within ten

---

[1] Hysterics.   [2] Whooping-cough.

years than the doctors have killed in twenty; and that's a bold word.

Aim. Has the lady been any other way useful in her generation?

Bon. Yes, sir; she has a daughter by Sir Charles, the finest woman in all our country, and the greatest fortune. She has a son too, by her first husband, Squire Sullen, who married a fine lady from London t'other day; if you please, sir, we'll drink his health.

Aim. What sort of a man is he?

Bon. Why, sir, the man's well enough; says little, thinks less, and does—nothing at all, faith. But he's a man of great estate, and values nobody.

Aim. A sportsman, I suppose?

Bon. Yes, sir, he's a man of pleasure; he plays at whisk and smokes his pipe eighty-and-forty hours together sometimes.

Aim. And married, you say?

Bon. Ay, and to a curious woman, sir. But he's a —he wants it; here, sir.   [*Pointing to his forehead.*

Aim. He has it there, you mean?

Bon. That's none of my business; he's my landlord, and so a man, you know, would not——But—ecod, he's no better than — Sir, my humble service to you.— [*Drinks.*] Though I value not a farthing what he can do to me; I pay him his rent at quarter-day, I have a good running trade, I have but one daughter, and I can give her—but no matter for that.

Aim. You're very happy, Mr Boniface. Pray, what other company have you in town?

Bon. A power of fine ladies; and then we have the French officers.

Aim. Oh, that's right, you have a good many of those gentlemen. Pray, how do you like their company?

Bon. So well, as the saying is, that I could wish we had as many more of 'em; they're full of money, and pay double for everything they have. They know, sir,

that we paid good round taxes for the taking of 'em, and so they are willing to reimburse us a little. One of 'em lodges in my house.

Re-enter ARCHER.

Arch. Landlord, there are some French gentlemen below that ask for you.

Bon. I'll wait on 'em.—[*Aside to* ARCHER.] Does your master stay long in town, as the saying is?

Arch. I can't tell, as the saying is.

Bon. Come from London?

Arch. No.

Bon. Going to London, mayhap?

Arch. No.

Bon. [*Aside.*] An odd fellow this. — [*To* AIMWELL.] I beg your worship's pardon, I'll wait on you in half a minute.   [*Exit.*

Aim. The coast's clear, I see.—Now, my dear Archer, welcome to Lichfield.

Arch. I thank thee, my dear brother in iniquity.

Aim. Iniquity! prithee, leave canting; you need not change your style with your dress.

Arch. Don't mistake me, Aimwell, for 'tis still my maxim, that there is no scandal like rags, nor any crime so shameful as poverty.

Aim. The world confesses it every day in its practice, though men won't own it for their opinion. Who did that worthy lord, my brother, single out of the side-box to sup with him t'other night?

Arch. Jack Handycraft, a handsome, well-dressed, mannerly, sharping rogue, who keeps the best company in town.

Aim. Right!   And, pray, who married my Lady Manslaughter t'other day, the great fortune?

Arch. Why, Nick Marrabone, a professed pick-pocket, and a good bowler; but he makes a handsome

figure, and rides in his coach, that he formerly used to ride behind.

Aim. But did you observe poor Jack Generous in the Park last week?

Arch. Yes, with his autumnal periwig, shading his melancholy face, his coat older than anything but its fashion, with one hand idle in his pocket, and with the other picking his useless teeth; and, though the Mall was crowded with company, yet was poor Jack as single and solitary as a lion in a desert.

Aim. And as much avoided, for no crime upon earth but the want of money.

Arch. And that's enough. Men must not be poor; idleness is the root of all evil; the world's wide enough, let 'em bustle. Fortune has taken the weak under her protection, but men of sense are left to their industry.

Aim. Upon which topic we proceed, and I think luckily hitherto. Would not any man swear, now, that I am a man of quality, and you my servant; when if our intrinsic value were known—

Arch. Come, come, we are the men of intrinsic value, who can strike our fortunes out of ourselves, whose worth is independent of accidents in life, or revolutions in government; we have heads to get money and hearts to spend it.

Aim. As to our hearts, I grant ye, they are as willing tits as any within twenty degrees; but I can have no great opinion of our heads from the service they have done us hitherto, unless it be that they have brought us from London hither to Lichfield, made me a lord, and you my servant.

Arch. That's more than you could expect already But what money have we left?

Aim. But two hundred pound.

Arch. And our horses, clothes, rings, &c.—Why, we have very good fortunes now for moderate people; and, let me tell you besides, that this two hundred pound,

with the experience that we are now masters of, is a better estate than the ten thousand we have spent.[1] Our friends, indeed, began to suspect that our pockets were low; but we came off with flying colours, showed no signs of want either in word or deed—

Aim. Ay, and our going to Brussels was a good pretence enough for our sudden disappearing; and, I warrant you, our friends imagine that we are gone a-volunteering.

Arch. Why, faith, if this prospect fails, it must e'en come to that. I am for venturing one of the hundreds, if you will, upon this knight-errantry; but, in case it should fail, we'll reserve the t'other to carry us to some counterscarp, where we may die, as we lived, in a blaze.

Aim. With all my heart; and we have lived justly, Archer; we can't say that we have spent our fortunes, but that we have enjoyed 'em.

Arch. Right! So much pleasure for so much money, we have had our pennyworths; and, had I millions, I would go to the same market again.—Oh London! London!—Well, we have had our share, and let us be thankful: past pleasures, for aught I know, are best, such as we are sure of; those to come may disappoint us.

Aim. It has often grieved the heart of me to see how some inhuman wretches murther their kind fortunes; those that, by sacrificing all to one appetite, shall starve all the rest. You shall have some that live only in their palates, and in their sense of tasting shall drown the

---

[1] In Q. 1, this passage runs: "and let me tell you, besides Thousand, that this Two hundred Pound, with the experience that we are now Masters of, is a better Estate than the Ten we have spent." Editors have been content simply to drop out the unintelligible words "besides Thousand." But "the ten we have spent" (implying, of course, "ten hundred pound") is a feeble and almost impossible phrase. It seems manifest to me that Farquhar wrote as above, and that the word "thousand" was somehow misplaced by the printers. At any rate, my emendation is less sweeping than the silent deletion of two words.

other four.   Others are only epicures in appearances, such who shall starve their nights to make a figure a-days, and famish their own to feed the eyes of others. A contrary sort confine their pleasures to the dark, and contract their spacious acres to the circuit of a muff-string.

Arch. Right ; but they find the Indies in that spot where they consume 'em.   And I think your kind keepers have much the best on't ; for they indulge the most senses by one expense.   There's the seeing, hearing, and feeling, amply gratified ; and some philosophers will tell you that from such a commerce there arises a sixth sense, that gives infinitely more pleasure than the other five put together.

Aim. And to pass to the other extremity, of all keepers I think those the worst that keep their money.

Arch. Those are the most miserable wights in being : they destroy the rights of nature, and disappoint the blessings of Providence.   Give me a man that keeps his five senses keen and bright as his sword ; that has 'em always drawn out in their just order and strength, with his reason as commander at the head of 'em ; that detaches 'em by turns upon whatever party of pleasure agreeably offers, and commands 'em to retreat upon the least appearance of disadvantage or danger !   For my part, I can stick to my bottle while my wine, my company, and my reason, holds good ; I can be charmed with Sappho's singing without falling in love with her face ; I love hunting, but would not, like Actæon, be eaten up by my own dogs ; I love a fine house, but let another keep it ; and just so I love a fine woman.

Aim. In that last particular you have the better of me.

Arch. Ay, you're such an amorous puppy, that I'm afraid you'll spoil our sport ; you can't counterfeit the passion without feeling it.

Aim. Though the whining part be out of doors in town, 'tis still in force with the country ladies : and let

me tell you, Frank, the fool in that passion shall outdo the knave at any time.

Arch. Well, I won't dispute it now; you command for the day, and so I submit: at Nottingham, you know, I am to be master.

Aim. And at Lincoln, I again.

Arch. Then, at Norwich I mount, which, I think, shall be our last stage; for, if we fail there, we'll embark for Holland, bid adieu to Venus, and welcome Mars.

Aim. A match!—Mum!

Re-enter BONIFACE.

Bon. What will your worship please to have for supper?

Aim. What have you got?

Bon. Sir, we have a delicate piece of beef in the pot, and a pig at the fire.

Aim. Good supper-meat, I must confess. I can't eat beef, landlord.

Arch. And I hate pig.

Aim. Hold your prating, sirrah! Do you know who you are?

Bon. Please to bespeak something else; I have everything in the house.

Aim. Have you any veal?

Bon. Veal, sir! We had a delicate loin of veal on Wednesday last.

Aim. Have you got any fish or wildfowl?

Bon. As for fish, truly, sir, we are an inland town and indifferently provided with fish, that's the truth on't; and then for wildfowl—we have a delicate couple of rabbits.

Aim. Get me the rabbits fricasseed.

Bon. Fricasseed! Lard, sir, they'll eat much better smothered with onions.

Arch. Psha! damn your onions!

Aim. Again, sirrah!—Well, landlord, what you please. But hold—I have a small charge of money, and your

house is so full of strangers, that I believe it may be safer in your custody than mine; for when this fellow of mine gets drunk he minds nothing.—Here, sirrah, reach me the strong-box.

Arch. Yes, sir.—[*Aside.*] This will give us a reputation.   [*Gives* AIMWELL *a box.*

Aim. Here, landlord; the locks are sealed down both for your security and mine; it holds somewhat above two hundred pound; if you doubt it, I'll count it to you after supper. But be sure you lay it where I may have it at a minute's warning; for my affairs are a little dubious at present; perhaps I may be gone in half an hour, perhaps I may be your guest till the best part of that be spent; and pray order your ostler to keep my horses always saddled. But one thing above the rest I must beg, that you would let this fellow have none of your *Anno Domini*, as you call it; for he's the most insufferable sot.—Here, sirrah, light me to my chamber.

                    [*Exit, lighted by* ARCHER.

Bon. Cherry! daughter Cherry!

Re-enter CHERRY.

Cher. D'ye call, father?

Bon. Ay, child, you must lay by this box for the gentleman; 'tis full of money.

Cher. Money! all that money! why, sure, father, the gentleman comes to be chosen parliament-man. Who is he?

Bon. I don't know what to make of him; he talks of keeping his horses ready saddled, and of going perhaps at a minute's warning, or of staying perhaps till the best part of this be spent.

Cher. Ay, ten to one, father, he's a highwayman.

Bon. A highwayman! upon my life, girl, you have hit it, and this box is some new-purchased booty. Now, could we find him out, the money were ours.

Cher. He don't belong to our gang.

Bon. What horses have they?

Cher. The master rides upon a black.

Bon. A black! ten to one the man upon the black mare! And since he don't belong to our fraternity, we may betray him with a safe conscience; I don't think it lawful to harbour any rogues but my own. Look'ee, child, as the saying is, we must go cunningly to work: proofs we must have. The gentleman's servant loves drink, I'll ply him that way; and ten to one loves a wench—you must work him t'other way.

Cher. Father, would you have me give my secret for his?

Bon. Consider, child, there's two hundred pound to boot.—[*Ringing without.*] Coming!—coming!— Child, mind your business. [*Exit.*

Cher. What a rogue is my father! My father! I deny it. My mother was a good, generous, free-hearted woman, and I can't tell how far her good-nature might have extended for the good of her children. This landlord of mine, for I think I can call him no more, would betray his guest, and debauch his daughter into the bargain—by a footman too!

Re-enter ARCHER.

Arch. What footman, pray, mistress, is so happy as to be the subject of your contemplation?

Cher. Whoever he is, friend, he'll be but little the better for't.

Arch. I hope so, for I'm sure you did not think of me.

Cher. Suppose I had?

Arch. Why then you're but even with me; for the minute I came in, I was a-considering in what manner I should make love to you.

Cher. Love to me, friend!

Arch. Yes, child.

Cher. Child! manners!—If you kept a little more distance, friend, it would become you much better.

Arch. Distance! Good-night, sauce-box.   [*Going.*

Cher. [*Aside.*] A pretty fellow! I like his pride. —[*Aloud.*] Sir, pray, sir, you see, sir, [ARCHER *returns.*] I have the credit to be entrusted with your master's fortune here, which sets me a degree above his footman ; I hope, sir, you an't affronted?

Arch. Let me look you full in the face, and I'll tell you whether you can affront me or no.—'Sdeath, child, you have a pair of delicate eyes, and you don't know what to do with 'em!

Cher. Why, sir, don't I see everybody?

Arch. Ay, but if some women had 'em, they would kill everybody.—Prithee, instruct me, I would fain make love to you, but I don't know what to say.

Cher. Why, did you never make love to anybody before?

Arch. Never to a person of your figure, I can assure you, madam. My addresses have been always confined to people within my own sphere ; I never aspired as high before.   [*Sings.*

    But you look so bright,[1]
    And are dress'd so tight,
    That a man would swear you're right,
As arm was e'er laid over.
    Such an air
    You freely wear
    To ensnare,
As makes each guest a lover!

Since then, my dear, I'm your guest,
    Prithee give me of the best
    Of what is ready drest :
Since then, my dear, etc.

    [1] Only the first two lines of this song are given in the first edition.

Cher. [*Aside.*] What can I think of this man?—
[*Aloud.*] Will you give me that song, sir?

Arch. Ay, my dear, take it while 'tis warm.—[*Kisses her.*] Death and fire! her lips are honeycombs.

Cher. And I wish there had been bees too, to have stung you for your impudence.

Arch. There's a swarm of Cupids, my little Venus, that has done the business much better.

Cher. [*Aside.*] This fellow is misbegotten as well as I.—[*Aloud.*] What's your name, sir?

Arch. [*Aside.*] Name! egad, I have forgot it.— [*Aloud.*] Oh! Martin.

Cher. Where were you born?

Arch. In St Martin's parish.

Cher. What was your father?

Arch. St Martin's parish.

Cher. Then, friend, good night.

Arch. I hope not.

Cher. You may depend upon't.

Arch. Upon what?

Cher. That you're very impudent.

Arch. That you're very handsome.

Cher. That you're a footman.

Arch. That you're an angel.

Cher. I shall be rude.

Arch. So shall I.   [*Seizes her hand*

Cher. Let go my hand.

Arch. Give me a kiss.   [*Kisses her*

Bon. [*Without.*] Cherry! Cherry!

Cher. I'mm [1]——my father calls; you plaguy devil, how durst you stop my breath so? Offer to follow me one step, if you dare.   [*Exit.*

Arch. A fair challenge, by this light! This is a pretty fair opening of an adventure; but we are knight-errants, and so Fortune be our guide.   [*Exit.*

[1] So in Q. 1.—evidently indicating her struggle to say "My father," while Archer kisses her. The "I'm" of later editions is meaningless.

ACT II

SCENE I.—*A Gallery in* Lady BOUNTIFUL's *House.*

Mrs SULLEN *and* DORINDA, *meeting.*

OR. Morrow, my dear sister; are you for church this morning?

Mrs. Sul. Anywhere to pray; for Heaven alone can help me. But I think, Dorinda, there's no form of prayer in the liturgy against bad husbands.

Dor. But there's a form of law in Doctors-Commons; and I swear, sister Sullen, rather than see you thus continually discontented, I would advise you to apply to that: for besides the part that I bear in your vexatious brolis, as being sister to the husband, and friend to the wife, your example gives me such an impression of matrimony, that I shall be apt to condemn my person to a long vacation all its life. But supposing, madam, that you brought it to a case of separation, what can you urge against your husband? My brother is, first, the most constant man alive.

Mrs Sul. The most constant husband, I grant ye.

Dor. He never sleeps from you.

Mrs Sul. No; he always sleeps with me.

Dor. He allows you a maintenance suitable to your quality.

Mrs Sul. A maintenance! do you take me, madam, for an hospital child, that I must sit down, and bless my benefactors for meat, drink, and clothes? As I take it, madam, I brought your brother ten thousand pounds, out of which I might expect some pretty things, called pleasures.

Dor. You share in all the pleasures that the country affords.

Mrs Sul. Country pleasures! racks and torments! Dost think, child, that my limbs were made for leaping of ditches, and clambering over stiles? or that my parents, wisely foreseeing my future happiness in country pleasures, had early instructed me in the rural accomplishments of drinking fat ale, playing at whisk, and smoking tobacco with my husband? or of spreading of plasters, brewing of diet-drinks, and stilling rosemary-water, with the good old gentlewoman my mother-in-law?

Dor. I'm sorry, madam, that it is not more in our power to divert you; I could wish, indeed, that our entertainments were a little more polite, or your taste a little less refined. But, pray, madam, how came the poets and philosophers, that laboured so much in hunting after pleasure, to place it at last in a country life?

Mrs Sul. Because they wanted money, child, to find out the pleasures of the town. Did you ever see a poet or philosopher worth ten thousand pound? If you can show me such a man, I'll lay you fifty pound you'll find him somewhere within the weekly bills.[1] Not that I disapprove rural pleasures, as the poets have painted them; in their landscape, every Phillis has her Corydon, every murmuring stream, and every flowery mead, gives fresh alarms to love. Besides, you'll find that their couples were never married.— But yonder I see my Corydon, and a sweet swain it is,

[1] The Weekly Bills of Mortality for London.

Heaven knows! Come, Dorinda, don't be angry; he's my husband, and your brother; and between both, is he not a sad brute?

Dor. I have nothing to say to your part of him—you're the best judge.

Mrs Sul. O sister, sister! if ever you marry, beware of a sullen, silent sot, one that's always musing, but never thinks. There's some diversion in a talking blockhead; and since a woman must wear chains, I would have the pleasure of hearing 'em rattle a little. Now you shall see—but take this by the way: he came home this morning at his usual hour of four, wakened me out of a sweet dream of something else, by tumbling over the tea-table, which he broke all to pieces; after his man and he had rolled about the room, like sick passengers in a storm, he comes flounce into bed, dead as a salmon into a fishmonger's basket; his feet cold as ice, his breath hot as a furnace, and his hands and his face as greasy as his flannel nightcap. O matrimony! He tosses up the clothes with a barbarous swing over his shoulders, disorders the whole economy of my bed, leaves me half naked, and my whole night's comfort is the tuneable serenade of that wakeful nightingale, his nose! Oh, the pleasure of counting the melancholy clock by a snoring husband! But now, sister, you shall see how handsomely, being a well-bred man, he will beg my pardon.

Enter SULLEN.

Squire Sul. My head aches consumedly.

Mrs Sul. Will you be pleased, my dear, to drink tea with us this morning? It may do your head good.

Squire Sul. No.

Dor. Coffee, brother?

Squire Sul. Psha!

Mrs Sul. Will you please to dress, and go to church with me? The air may help you.

Squire Sul. Scrub !   [*Calls.*

Enter SCRUB.

Scrub. Sir !

Squire Sul. What day o' th' week is this?

Scrub. Sunday, an't please your worship.

Squire Sul. Sunday ! Bring me a dram ; and d'ye hear, set out the venison-pasty, and a tankard of strong beer upon the hall-table ; I'll go to breakfast.   [*Going.*

Dor. Stay, stay, brother, you sha'n't get off so ; you were very naughty last night, and must make your wife reparation ; come, come, brother, won't you ask pardon ?

Squire Sul. For what?

Dor. For being drunk last night.

Squire Sul. I can afford it, can't I ?

Mrs Sul. But I can't, sir.

Squire Sul. Then you may let it alone.

Mrs Sul. But I must tell you, sir, that this is not to be borne.

Squire Sul. I'm glad on't.

Mrs Sul. What is the reason, sir, that you use me thus inhumanly?

Squire Sul. Scrub !

Scrub. Sir !

Squire Sul. Get things ready to shave my head.

[*Exit*, SCRUB *following.*

Mrs Sul. Have a care of coming near his temples, Scrub, for fear you meet something there that may turn the edge of your razor.—Inveterate stupidity ! Did you ever know so hard, so obstinate, a spleen as his? O sister, sister ! I shall never ha' good of the beast till I get him to town ; London, dear London, is the place for managing and breaking a husband.

Dor. And has not a husband the same opportunities there for humbling a wife?

Mrs Sul. No, no, child ; 'tis a standing maxim in conjugal discipline, that when a man would enslave his

wife, he hurries her into the country; and when a lady would be arbitrary with her husband, she wheedles her booby up to town.—A man dare not play the tyrant in London, because there are so many examples to encourage the subject to rebel. O Dorinda! Dorinda! a fine woman may do anything in London: o' my conscience, she may raise an army of forty thousand men.

Dor. I fancy, sister, you have a mind to be trying your power that way here in Lichfield; you have drawn the French Count to your colours already.

Mrs Sul. The French are a people that can't live without their gallantries.

Dor. And some English that I know, sister, are not averse to such amusements.

Mrs Sul. Well, sister, since the truth must out, it may do as well now as hereafter: I think one way to rouse my lethargic, sottish husband is to give him a rival. Security begets negligence in all people, and men must be alarmed to make 'em alert in their duty. Women are like pictures, of no value in the hands of a fool, till he hears men of sense bid high for the purchase.

Dor. This might do, sister, if my brother's understanding were to be convinced into a passion for you; but I fancy, there's a natural aversion of his side; and I fancy, sister, that you don't come much behind him, if you dealt fairly.

Mrs Sul. I own it, we are united contradictions, fire and water: but I could be contented, with a great many other wives, to humour the censorious mob, and give the world an appearance of living well with my husband, could I bring him but to dissemble a little kindness to keep me in countenance.

Dor. But how do you know, sister, but that, instead of rousing your husband by this artifice to a counterfeit kindness, he should awake in a real fury?

Mrs Sul. Let him: if I can't entice him to the one, I would provoke him to the other.

Dor. But how must I behave myself between ye?

Mrs Sul. You must assist me.

Dor. What, against my own brother?

Mrs Sul. He's but half a brother, and I'm your entire friend. If I go a step beyond the bounds of honour, leave me; till then, I expect you should go along with me in everything; while I trust my honour in your hands, you may trust your brother's in mine. The Count is to dine here to-day.

Dor. 'Tis a strange thing, sister, that I can't like that man.

Mrs Sul. You like nothing; your time is not come; love and death have their fatalities, and strike home one time or other. You'll pay for all one day, I warrant ye. But come, my lady's tea is ready, and 'tis almost church time. [*Exeunt.*

SCENE II.—*The Inn.*

Enter AIMWELL *dressed, and* ARCHER.

Aim. And was she the daughter of the house?

Arch. The landlord is so blind as to think so; but I dare swear she has better blood in her veins.

Aim. Why dost think so?

Arch. Because the baggage has a pert *je ne sais quoi;* she reads plays, keeps a monkey, and is troubled with vapours.

Aim. By which discoveries I guess that you know more of her.

Arch. Not yet, faith; the lady gives herself airs; forsooth, nothing under a gentleman!

Aim. Let me take her in hand.

Arch. Say one word more o' that, and I'll declare

myself, spoil your sport there, and everywhere else; look ye, Aimwell, every man in his own sphere.

Aim. Right; and therefore you must pimp for your master.

Arch. In the usual forms, good sir—after I have served myself.—But to our business. You are so well dressed, Tom, and make so handsome a figure, that I fancy you may do execution in a country church; the exterior part strikes first, and you're in the right to make that impression favourable.

Aim. There's something in that which may turn to advantage. The appearance of a stranger in a country church draws as many gazers as a blazing star; no sooner he comes into the cathedral, but a train of whispers runs buzzing round the congregation in a moment: *Who is he? Whence comes he? Do you know him?* Then I, sir, tips me the verger with half-a-crown; he pockets the simony, and inducts me into the best pew in the church. I pull out my snuff-box, turn myself round, bow to the bishop or the dean, if he be the commanding officer; single out a beauty, rivet both my eyes to hers, set my nose a-bleeding by the strength of imagination, and show the whole church my concern, by my endeavouring to hide it. After the sermon, the whole town gives me to her for a lover; and by persuading the lady that I am a-dying for her, the tables are turned, and she in good earnest falls in love with me.

Arch. There's nothing in this, Tom, without a precedent; but instead of riveting your eyes to a beauty, try and fix 'em upon a fortune; that's our business at present.

Aim. Psha! no woman can be a beauty without a fortune. Let me alone, for I am a marksman.

Arch. Tom!

Aim. Ay.

Arch. When were you at church before, pray?

Aim. Um—I was there at the coronation.

Arch. And how can you expect a blessing by going to church now?

Aim. Blessing! nay, Frank, I ask but for a wife.

[Exit.

Arch. Truly, the man is not very unreasonable in his demands. *[Exit at the opposite door.*

SCENE III.—*Another Room in the same.*[1]

Enter BONIFACE *and* CHERRY.

Bon. Well, daughter, as the saying is, have you brought Martin to confess?

Cher. Pray, father, don't put me upon getting anything out of a man; I'm but young, you know, father, and I don't understand wheedling.

Bon. Young! why, you jade, as the saying is, can any woman wheedle that is not young? Your mother was useless at five-and-twenty. Not wheedle! would you make your mother a whore, and me a cuckold, as the saying is? I tell you, his silence confesses it; and his master spends his money so freely, and is so much a gentleman every manner of way, that he must be a highwayman.

Enter GIBBET, *in a cloak.*

Gib. Landlord, landlord, is the coast clear?

Bon. O Mr Gibbet, what's the news?

Gib. No matter, ask no questions, all fair and honourable.—Here, my dear Cherry.—[*Gives her a bag.*] Two hundred sterling pounds, as good as any that ever hanged or saved a rogue; lay 'em by with the rest; and here—three wedding or mourning rings, 'tis much the

' Leigh Hunt is apparently responsible for this change of scene. It is not indicated in early editions and is quite unnecessary.

same, you know—here, two silver-hilted swords; I took
those from fellows that never show any part of their
swords but the hilts—here is a diamond necklace which
the lady hid in the privatest place in the coach, but I
found it out—this gold watch I took from a pawn-
broker's wife; it was left in her hands by a person of
quality, there's the arms upon the case.

Cher. But who had you the money from?

Gib. Ah! poor woman! I pitied her;—from a poor
lady just eloped from her husband. She had made up
her cargo, and was bound for Ireland, as hard as she
could drive; she told me of her husband's barbarous
usage, and so I left her half-a-crown. But I had almost
forgot, my dear Cherry, I have a present for you.

Cher. What is't?

Gib. A pot of ceruse, my child, that I took out of a
lady's under-pocket.

Cher. What, Mr Gibbet, do you think that I paint?

Gib. Why, you jade, your betters do; I'm sure the
lady that I took it from had a coronet upon her
handkerchief. Here, take my cloak, and go, secure the
premises.[1]

Cher. I will secure 'em.   [*Exit.*

Bon. But, heark'ee, where's Hounslow and Bagshot?

Gib. They'll be here to-night.

Bon. D'ye know of any other gentlemen o' the pad on
this road?

Gib. No.

Bon. I fancy that I have two that lodge in the house
just now.

Gib. The devil! How d'ye smoke 'em?

Bon. Why, the one is gone to church.

Gib. That's suspicious, I must confess.

Bon. And the other is now in his master's chamber;
he pretends to be servant to the other. We'll call him
out and pump him a little.

[1] The articles before mentioned.

Gib. With all my heart.

Bon. Mr Martin, Mr Martin! [*Calls.*

Enter ARCHER, *combing a periwig and singing.*

Gib. The roads are consumed deep, I'm as dirty as old Brentford at Christmas.—A good pretty fellow that. Whose servant are you, friend?

Arch. My master's.

Gib. Really!

Arch. Really.

Gib. That's much.—The fellow has been at the bar, by his evasions.—But, pray, sir, what is your master's name?

Arch. Tall, all, dall!—[*Sings and combs the periwig.*] This is the most obstinate curl—

Gib. I ask you his name?

Arch. Name, sir—tall, all, dall!—I never asked him his name in my life.—Tall, all, dall!

Bon. What think you now? [*Aside to* GIBBET.

Gib. [*Aside to* BONIFACE.] Plain, plain; he talks now as if he were before a judge.—[*To* ARCHER.] But pray, friend, which way does your master travel?

Arch. A-horseback.

Gib. [*Aside.*] Very well again, an old offender, right. —[*To* ARCHER.] But, I mean, does he go upwards or downwards?

Arch. Downwards, I fear, sir.—Tall, all!

Gib. I'm afraid my fate will be a contrary way.

Bon. Ha, ha, ha! Mr Martin, you're very arch. This gentleman is only travelling towards Chester, and would be glad of your company, that's all.—Come, Captain, you'll stay to-night, I suppose? I'll show you a chamber—come, Captain.

Gib. Farewell, friend!

Arch. Captain, your servant.—[*Exeunt* BONIFACE *and* GIBBET.] Captain! a pretty fellow! 'Sdeath, I wonder

that the officers of the army don't conspire to beat all
scoundrels in red but their own.

Re-enter CHERRY.

Cher. [*Aside.*] Gone! and Martin here! I hope he
did not listen; I would have the merit of the discovery
all my own, because I would oblige him to love me.—
[*Aloud.*] Mr Martin, who was that man with my
father?

Arch. Some recruiting serjeant, or whipped-out
trooper, I suppose.

Cher. All's safe, I find.   [*Aside.*

Arch. Come, my dear, have you conned over the
catechise I taught you last night?

Cher. Come, question me.

Arch. What is love?

Cher. Love is I know not what, it comes I know not
how, and goes I know not when.

Arch. Very well, an apt scholar.—[*Chucks her under
the chin.*] Where does love enter?

Cher. Into the eyes.

Arch. And where go out?

Cher. I won't tell ye.

Arch. What are the objects of that passion?

Cher. Youth, beauty, and clean linen.

Arch. The reason?

Cher. The two first are fashionable in nature, and the
third at court.

Arch. That's my dear.—What are the signs and
tokens of that passion?

Cher. A stealing look, a stammering tongue, words
improbable, designs impossible, and actions impractic-
able.

Arch. That's my good child, kiss me.—What must a
lover do to obtain his mistress?

Cher. He must adore the person that disdains him,
he must bribe the chambermaid that betrays him, and

court the footman that laughs at him. He must—he must—

Arch. Nay, child, I must whip you if you don't mind your lesson ; he must treat his—

Cher. O ay!—he must treat his enemies with respect, his friends with indifference, and all the world with contempt ; he must suffer much, and fear more ; he must desire much, and hope little ; in short, he must embrace his ruin, and throw himself away.

Arch. Had ever man so hopeful a pupil as mine!— Come, my dear, why is love called a riddle?

Cher. Because, being blind, he leads those that see, and, though a child, he governs a man.

Arch. Mighty well!—And why is Love pictured blind?

Cher. Because the painters out of the weakness or privilege of their art chose to hide those eyes that they could not draw.

Arch. That's my dear little scholar, kiss me again.— And why should Love, that's a child, govern a man?

Cher. Because that a child is the end of love.

Arch. And so ends Love's catechism.—And now, my dear, we'll go in and make my master's bed.

Cher. Hold, hold, Mr Martin! You have taken a great deal of pains to instruct me, and, what d'ye think I have learned by it?

Arch. What?

Cher. That your discourse and your habit are contradictions, and it would be nonsense in me to believe you a footman any longer.

Arch. 'Oons, what a witch it is!

Cher. Depend upon this, sir, nothing in this garb shall ever tempt me ; for, though I was born to servitude, I hate it. Own your condition, swear you love me, and then—

Arch. And then we shall go make the bed?

Cher. Yes.

Arch. You must know then, that I am born a gentleman, my education was liberal; but I went to London, a younger brother, fell into the hands of sharpers, who stripped me of my money, my friends disowned me, and now my necessity brings me to what you see.

Cher. Then take my hand—promise to marry me before you sleep, and I'll make you master of two thousand pounds.

Arch. How!

Cher. Two thousand pounds that I have this minute in my own custody; so, throw off your livery this instant, and I'll go find a parson.

Arch. What said you? a parson!

Cher. What! do you scruple?

Arch. Scruple! no, no, but—Two thousand pound, you say?

Cher. And better.

Arch. [*Aside.*] 'Sdeath, what shall I do?—[*Aloud.*] But heark'ee, child, what need you make me master of yourself and money, when you may have the same pleasure out of me, and still keep your fortune in your hands.

Cher. Then you won't marry me?

Arch. I would marry you, but—

Cher. O, sweet sir, I'm your humble servant, you're fairly caught! Would you persuade me that any gentleman who could bear the scandal of wearing a livery would refuse two thousand pound, let the condition be what it would? No, no, sir. But I hope you'll pardon the freedom I have taken, since it was only to inform myself of the respect that I ought to pay you.

Arch. [*Aside.*] Fairly bit, by Jupiter!—[*Aloud.*] Hold! hold!—And have you actually two thousand pounds?

Cher. Sir, I have my secrets as well as you; when you please to be more open I shall be more free; and be assured that I have discoveries that will match yours,

be what they will. In the meanwhile, be satisfied that
no discovery I make shall ever hurt you; but beware of
my father!   [*Exit.*

Arch. So! we're like to have as many adventures in
our inn as Don Quixote had in his. Let me see—two
thousand pounds!—If the wench would promise to die
when the money were spent, egad, one would marry her;
but the fortune may go off in a year or two, and the wife
may live—Lord knows how long. Then an innkeeper's
daughter; ay, that's the devil—there my pride brings me
off.

> For whatsoe'er the sages charge on pride,
> The angels' fall, and twenty faults beside,
> On earth, I'm sure, 'mong us of mortal calling,
> Pride saves man oft, and woman too, from falling.
>   [*Exit.*

ACT III

SCENE I.—*The Gallery in* Lady BOUNTIFUL'S *House.*

Enter Mrs SULLEN *and* DORINDA.

RS SUL. Ha, ha, ha! my dear sister, let me embrace thee! Now we are friends indeed; for I shall have a secret of yours as a pledge for mine— now you'll be good for something, I shall have you conversable in the subjects of the sex.

Dor. But do you think that I am so weak as to fall in love with a fellow at first sight?

Mrs Sul. Psha! now you spoil all; why should not we be as free in our friendships as the men? I warrant you the gentleman has got to his confidant already, has avowed his passion, toasted your health, called you ten thousand angels, has run over your lips, eyes, neck, shape, air, and everything in a description that warms their mirth [1] to a second enjoyment.

Dor. You hand, sister, I an't well.

Mrs Sul. So—she's breeding already! Come, child, up with it—hem a little—so—now tell me, don't you like the gentleman that we saw at church just now?

Dor. The man's well enough.

[1] Query " mind "?

Mrs Sul. Well enough! is he not a demigod, a Narcissus, a star, the man i' the moon?

Dor. O sister, I'm extremely ill!

Mrs Sul. Shall I send to your mother, child, for a little of her cephalic plaster to put to the soles of your feet, or shall I send to the gentleman for something for you? Come, unlace your stays, unbosom yourself. The man is perfectly a pretty fellow, I saw him when he first came into church.

Dor. I saw him too, sister, and with an air that shone, methought, like rays about his person.

Mrs Sul. Well said, up with it!

Dor. No forward coquette behaviour, no airs to set him off, no studied looks nor artful posture,—but nature did it all—

Mrs Sul. Better and better!—one touch more—come!

Dor. But then his looks—did you observe his eyes?

Mrs Sul. Yes, yes, I did—his eyes—well, what of his eyes?

Dor. Sprightly, but not wandering; they seemed to view, but never gazed on anything but me.—And then his looks so humble were, and yet so noble, that they aimed to tell me that he could with pride die at my feet, though he scorned slavery anywhere else.

Mrs Sul. The physic works purely!—How d'ye find yourself now, my dear?

Dor. Hem! much better, my dear.—Oh, here comes our Mercury!

Enter SCRUB.

Well, Scrub, what news of the gentleman?

Scrub. Madam, I have brought you a packet of news.

Dor. Open it quickly, come.

Scrub. In the first place I inquired who the gentleman was; they told me he was a stranger. Secondly, I asked what the gentleman was; they answered and said, that

they never saw him before. Thirdly, I inquired what countryman he was; they replied, 'twas more than they knew. Fourthly, I demanded whence he came; their answer was, they could not tell. And fifthly, I asked whither he went; and they replied, they knew nothing of the matter,—and this is all I could learn.

Mrs Sul. But what do the people say? can't they guess?

Scrub. Why, some think he's a spy, some guess he's a mountebank, some say one thing, some another; but for my own part, I believe he's a Jesuit.

Dor. A Jesuit! why a Jesuit?

Scrub. Because he keeps his horses always ready saddled, and his footman talks French.

Mrs Sul. His footman!

Scrub. Ay, he and the Count's footman were gabbering French like two intriguing ducks in a mill-pond; and I believe they talked of me, for they laughed consumedly.

Dor. What sort of livery has the footman?

Scrub. Livery! Lord, madam, I took him for a captain, he's so bedizened with lace! And then he has tops on his shoes up to his mid leg, a silver-headed cane dangling at his knuckles; he carries his hands in his pockets just so—[*Walks in the French air.*] and has a fine long periwig tied up in a bag.—Lord, madam, he's clear another sort of man than I!

Mrs Sul. That may easily be.—But what shall we do now, sister?

Dor. I have it—this fellow has a world of simplicity, and some cunning; the first hides the latter by abundance.—Scrub!

Scrub. Madam!

Dor. We have a great mind to know who this gentleman is, only for our satisfaction.

Scrub. Yes, madam, it would be a satisfaction no doubt.

Dor. You must go and get acquainted with his footman, and invite him hither to drink a bottle of your ale, because you're butler to-day.

Scrub. Yes, madam, I am butler every Sunday.

Mrs Sul. O brave! Sister, o' my conscience, you understand the mathematics already. 'Tis the best plot in the world; your mother, you know, will be gone to church, my spouse will be got to the ale-house with his scoundrels, and the house will be our own—so we drop in by accident, and ask the fellow some questions ourselves. In the country, you know, any stranger, is company, and we're glad to take up with the butler in a country dance, and happy if he'll do us the favour.

Scrub. O madam, you wrong me! I never refused your ladyship the favour in my life.

Enter GIPSY.

Gip. Ladies, dinner's upon table.

Dor. Scrub, we'll excuse your waiting—go where we ordered you.

Scrub. I shall.   [*Exeunt.*

SCENE II.—*The Inn.*

Enter AIMWELL *and* ARCHER.

Arch. Well, Tom, I find you're a marksman.

Aim. A marksman! who so blind could be, as not discern a swan among the ravens?

Arch. Well, but hark'ee, Aimwell—

Aim. Aimwell! call me Oroondates, Cesario, Amadis all that romance can in a lover paint, and then I'll answer. O Archer! I read her thousands in her looks, she looked like Ceres in her harvest: corn, wine and oil, milk and honey, gardens, groves, and purling streams, played on her plenteous face.

Arch. Her face! her pocket, you mean; the corn, wine and oil, lies there. In short, she has ten thousand pound, that's the English on't.

Aim. Her eyes—

Arch. Are demi-cannons, to be sure; so I won't stand their battery. [*Going.*

Aim. Pray excuse me, my passion must have vent.

Arch. Passion! what a plague, d'ye think these romantic airs will do our business? Were my temper as extravagant as yours, my adventures have something more romantic by half.

Aim. Your adventures!

Arch. Yes,
The nymph that with her twice ten hundred pounds,
With brazen engine hot, and quoif clear starched,
Can fire the guest in warming of the bed—
There's a touch of sublime Milton for you, and the subject but an inn-keeper's daughter! I can play with a girl as an angler does with his fish; he keeps it at the end of his line, runs it up the stream, and down the stream, till at last he brings it to hand, tickles the trout, and so whips it into his basket.

Enter BONIFACE.

Bon. Mr Martin, as the saying is—yonder's an honest fellow below, my Lady Bountiful's butler, who begs the honour that you would go home with him and see his cellar.

Arch. Do my *baise-mains* to the gentleman, and tell him I will do myself the honour to wait on him immediately. [*Exit* BONIFACE.

Aim. What do I hear?
Soft Orpheus play, and fair Toftida [1] sing!

Arch. Psha! damn your raptures; I tell you, here's a pump going to be put into the vessel, and the ship

---

[1] Katherine Tofts, a famous soprano. Retired from the stage, 1709.

will get into harbour, my life on't. You say, there's another lady very handsome there?

Aim. Yes, faith.

Arch. I'm in love with her already.

Aim. Can't you give me a bill upon Cherry in the meantime?

Arch. No, no, friend, all her corn, wine and oil, is ingrossed to my market. And once more I warn you to keep your anchorage clear of mine ; for if you fall foul of me, by this light you shall go to the bottom ! What ! make prize of my little frigate, while I am upon the cruise for you !—

Aim. Well, well, I won't.— [*Exit* ARCHER.

Re-enter BONIFACE.

Landlord, have you any tolerable company in the house ? I don't care for dining alone.

Bon. Yes, sir, there's a captain below, as the saying is, that arrived about an hour ago.

Aim. Gentlemen of his coat are welcome everywhere ; will you make him a compliment from me, and tell him I should be glad of his company?

Bon. Who shall I tell him, sir, would—

Aim. [*Aside.*] Ha ! that stroke was well thrown in ! —[*Aloud.*] I'm only a traveller like himself, and would be glad of his company, that's all.

Bon. I obey your commands, as the saying is.

[*Exit.*

Re-enter ARCHER.

Arch. 'Sdeath ! I had forgot : what title will you give yourself ?

Aim. My brother's, to be sure ; he would never give me anything else, so I'll make bold with his honour this bout !—You know the rest of your cue.

Arch. Ay, ay. [*Exit.*

Enter GIBBET.

Gib. Sir, I'm yours.

Aim. 'Tis more than I deserve, sir, for I don't know you.

Gib. I don't wonder at that, sir, for you never saw me before.—[*Aside.*] I hope.

Aim. And pray, sir, how came I by the honour of seeing you now?

Gib. Sir, I scorn to intrude upon any gentleman—but my landlord—

Aim. O sir, I ask your pardon; you're the captain he told me of?

Gib. At your service, sir.

Aim. What regiment, may I be so bold?

Gib. A marching regiment, sir, an old corps.

Aim. [*Aside.*] Very old, if your coat be regimental.— [*Aloud.*] You have served abroad, sir?

Gib. Yes, sir, in the plantations; 'twas my lot to be sent into the worst service. I would have quitted it indeed, but a man of honour, you know——Besides, 'twas for the good of my country that I should be abroad:—anything for the good of one's country—I'm a Roman for that.

Aim. [*Aside.*] One of the first, I'll lay my life. [*Aloud.*] You found the West Indies very hot, sir?

Gib. Ay, sir, too hot for me.

Aim. Pray, sir, han't I seen your face at Will's coffee-house?

Gib. Yes, sir, and at White's too.

Aim. And where is your company now, Captain?

Gib. They an't come yet.

Aim. Why, d'ye expect 'em here?

Gib. They'll be here to-night, sir.

Aim. Which way do they march?

Gib. Across the country.—[*Aside.*] The devil's in't, if I han't said enough to encourage him to declare! But I'm afraid he's not right, I must tack about.

Aim. Is your company to quarter in Lichfield?

Gib. In this house, sir.

Aim. What! all?

Gib. My company's but thin, ha, ha, ha! we are but three, ha, ha, ha!

Aim. You're merry, sir.

Gib. Ay, sir, you must excuse me, sir, I understand the world, especially the art of travelling: I don't care, sir, for answering questions directly upon the road—for I generally ride with a charge about me.

Aim. [*Aside.*] Three or four, I believe.

Gib. I am credibly informed there are highwaymen upon this quarter. Not, sir, that I could suspect a gentleman of your figure—but truly, sir, I have got such a way of evasion upon the road, that I don't care for speaking truth to any man.

Aim. Your caution may be necessary.—Then I presume you're no captain?

Gib. Not I, sir. Captain is a good travelling name, and so I take it; it stops a great many foolish inquiries that are generally made about gentlemen that travel, it gives a man an air of something, and makes the drawers obedient:—and thus far I am a captain, and no farther.

Aim. And pray, sir, what is your true profession?

Gib. O sir, you must excuse me!—upon my word, sir, I don't think it safe to tell ye.

Aim. Ha, ha, ha! upon my word, I commend you.

Re-enter BONIFACE.

Well, Mr Boniface, what's the news?

Bon. There's another gentleman below, as the saying is, that hearing you were but two, would be glad to make the third man, if you would give him leave.

Aim. What is he?

Bon. A clergyman, as the saying is.

Aim. A clergyman! Is he really a clergyman? or is it only his travelling name, as my friend the captain has it?

Bon. O sir, he's a priest, and chaplain to the French officers in town.

Aim. Is he a Frenchman?

Bon. Yes, sir, born at Brussels.

Gib. A Frenchman, and a priest! I won't be seen in his company, sir; I have a value for my reputation, sir.

Aim. Nay, but, Captain, since we are by ourselves— Can he speak English, landlord?

Bon. Very well, sir; you may know him, as the saying is, to be a foreigner by his accent, and that's all.

Aim. Then he has been in England before?

Bon. Never, sir; but he's a master of languages, as the saying is; he talks Latin—it does me good to hear him talk Latin.

Aim. Then you understand Latin, Mr Boniface?

Bon. Not I, sir, as the saying is; but he talks it so very fast, that I'm sure it must be good.

Aim. Pray, desire him to walk up.

Bon. Here he is, as the saying is.

Enter FOIGARD.

Foi. Save you, gentlemens, both.

Aim. [*Aside.*] A Frenchman!—[*To* FOIGARD.] Sir, your most humble servant.

Foi. Och, dear joy, I am your most faithful shervant, and yours alsho.   ·

Gib. Doctor, you talk very good English, but you have a mighty twang of the foreigner.

Foi. My English is very vell for the vords, but we foreigners, you know, cannot bring our tongues about the pronunciation so soon.

Aim. [*Aside.*] A foreigner! a downright Teague,[1] by this light!—[*Aloud.*] Were you born in France, doctor?

Foi. I was educated in France, but I was borned at Brussels; I am a subject of the King of Spain, joy.

[1] *See* note, p. 190.

Gib. What King of Spain, sir? speak! [1]

Foi. Upon my shoul, joy, I cannot tell you as yet.

Aim. Nay, Captain, that was too hard upon the doctor; he's a stranger.

Foi. Oh, let him alone, dear joy, I am of a nation that is not easily put out of countenance.

Aim. Come, gentlemen, I'll end the dispute.—Here, landlord, is dinner ready?

Bon. Upon the table, as the saying is.

Aim. Gentlemen—pray—that door—

Foi. No, no, fait, the captain must lead.

Aim. No, doctor, the church is our guide.

Gib. Ay, ay, so it is—   [*Exit foremost, they follow*

SCENE III.—*The Gallery in* Lady BOUNTIFUL'S *House.*

Enter ARCHER *and* SCRUB *singing, and hugging one another,* SCRUB *with a tankard in his hand.* GIPSY *listening at a distance.*

Scrub. Tall, all, dall!—Come, my dear boy, let's have that song once more.

Arch. No, no, we shall disturb the family.— But will you be sure to keep the secret?

Scrub. Pho! upon my honour, as I'm a gentleman.

Arch. 'Tis enough. You must know then, that my master is the Lord Viscount Aimwell; he fought a duel t'other day in London, wounded his man so dangerously, that he thinks fit to withdraw till he hears whether the gentleman's wounds be mortal or not. He never was in this part of England before, so he chose to retire to this place—that's all.

---

[1] It will be remembered that the War of the Spanish Succession was now in progress.

Gip. [*Aside.*] And that's enough for me.   [*Exit.*

Scrub. And where were you when your master fought?

Arch. We never know of our masters' quarrels.

Scrub. No! If our masters in the country here receive a challenge, the first thing they do is to tell their wives; the wife tells the servants, the servants alarm the tenants, and in half an hour you shall have the whole county in arms.

Arch. To hinder two men from doing what they have no mind for.—But if you should chance to talk now of my business?

Scrub. Talk! ay, sir, had I not learned the knack of holding my tongue, I had never lived so long in a great family.

Arch. Ay, ay, to be sure there are secrets in all families.

Scrub. Secrets! ay;—but I'll say no more. Come, sit down, we'll make an end of our tankard: here—

        [*Gives* ARCHER *the tankard.*

Arch. With all my heart; who knows but you and I may come to be better acquainted, eh? Here's your ladies' healths; you have three, I think, and to be sure there must be secrets among 'em.

Scrub. Secrets! ay, friend. — I wish I had a friend—

Arch. Am not I your friend? Come, you and I will be sworn brothers.

Scrub. Shall we?

Arch. From this minute. Give me a kiss:—and now, brother Scrub—

Scrub. And now, brother Martin, I will tell you a secret that will make your hair stand on end. You must know that I am consumedly in love.

Arch. That's a terrible secret, that's the truth on't.

Scrub. That jade, Gipsy, that was with us just now in the cellar, is the arrantest whore that ever wore a petticoat; and I'm dying for love of her.

Arch. Ha, ha, ha!—Are you in love with her person or her virtue, brother Scrub?

Scrub. I should like virtue best, because it is more durable than beauty; for virtue holds good with some women long, and many a day after they have lost it.

Arch. In the country, I grant ye, where no woman's virtue is lost till a bastard be found.

Scrub. Ay, could I bring her to a bastard, I should have her all to myself; but I dare not put it upon that lay, for fear of being sent for a soldier. Pray, brother, how do you gentlemen in London like that same Pressing Act?[1]

Arch. Very ill, brother Scrub; 'tis the worst that ever was made for us. Formerly I remember the good days, when we could dun our masters for our wages, and if they refused to pay us, we could have a warrant to carry 'em before a justice: but now if we talk of eating, they have a warrant for us, and carry us before three justices.

Scrub. And to be sure we go, if we talk of eating; for the justices won't give their own servants a bad example. Now this is my misfortune—I dare not speak in the house, while that jade Gipsy dings about like a fury.—Once I had the better end of the staff.

Arch. And how comes the change now?

Scrub. Why, the mother of all this mischief is a priest!

Arch. A priest!

Scrub. Ay, a damned son of a whore of Babylon, that came over hither to say grace to the French officers, and eat up our provisions. There's not a day goes over his head without dinner or supper in this house.

Arch. How came he so familiar in the family?

[1] As to the Impressment Acts, *see* note p. 336.

Scrub. Because he speaks English as if he had lived here all his life, and tells lies as if he had been a traveller from his cradle.

Arch. And this priest, I'm afraid, has converted the affections of your Gipsy.

Scrub. Converted! ay, and perverted, my dear friend: for, I'm afraid, he has made her a whore and a papist! But this is not all; there's the French Count and Mrs Sullen, they're in the confederacy, and for some private ends of their own, to be sure.

Arch. A very hopeful family yours, brother Scrub! I suppose the maiden lady has her lover too?

Scrub. Not that I know. She's the best on 'em, that's the truth on't. But they take care to prevent my curiosity, by giving me so much business, that I'm a perfect slave. What d'ye think is my place in this family?

Arch. Butler, I suppose.

Scrub. Ah, Lord help you! I'll tell you. Of a Monday I drive the coach; of a Tuesday I drive the plough; on Wednesday I follow the hounds; a Thursday I dun the tenants; on Friday I go to market; on Saturday I draw warrants; and a Sunday I draw beer.

Arch. Ha, ha, ha! if variety be a pleasure in life, you have enough on't, my dear brother.

Enter Mrs SULLEN *and* DORINDA.

But what ladies are those?

Scrub. Ours, ours; that upon the right hand is Mrs Sullen, and the other is Mrs Dorinda. Don't mind 'em, sit still, man.

Mrs Sul. I have heard my brother talk of my Lord Aimwell; but they say that his brother is the finer gentleman.

Dor. That's impossible, sister.

Mrs Sul. He's vastly rich, but very close, they say.

Dor. No matter for that; if I can creep into his heart, I'll open his breast, I warrant him. I have heard say, that people may be guessed at by the behaviour of their servants; I could wish we might talk to that fellow.

Mrs Sul. So do I; for I think he's a very pretty fellow. Come this way, I'll throw out a lure for him presently.

[*They walk towards the opposite side of the stage.*

Arch. [*Aside.*] Corn, wine, and oil indeed! — But I think the wife has the greatest plenty of flesh and blood; she should be my choice.—Ay, ay, say you so! —[Mrs SULLEN *drops her glove,* ARCHER *runs, takes it up, and gives it to her.*] Madam—your ladyship's glove.

Mrs Sul. O sir, I thank you!—[*To* DORINDA.] What a handsome bow the fellow has!

Dor. Bow! why I have known several footmen come down from London set up here for dancing-masters, and carry off the best fortunes in the country.

Arch. [*Aside.*] That project, for aught I know, had been better than ours.—[*To* SCRUB.] Brother Scrub, why don't you introduce me?

Scrub. Ladies, this is the strange gentleman's servant that you see at church to-day; I understood he came from London, and so I invited him to the cellar, that he might show me the newest flourish in whetting my knives.

Dor. And I hope you have made much of him?

Arch. O yes, madam; but the strength of your ladyship's liquor is a little too potent for the constitution of your humble servant.

Mrs Sul. What! then you don't usually drink ale?

Arch. No, madam; my constant drink is tea, or a little wine and water. 'Tis prescribed me by the physician for a remedy against the spleen.

Scrub. O la ! O la ! a footman have the spleen !

Mrs Sul. I thought that distemper had been only proper to people of quality?

Arch. Madam, like all other fashions it wears out, and so descends to their servants; though in a great many of us, I believe, it proceeds from some melancholy particles in the blood, occasioned by the stagnation of wages.

Dor. [*Aside to* Mrs SULLEN.] How affectedly the fellow talks !—[*To* ARCHER.] How long, pray, have you served your present master?

Arch. Not long; my life has been mostly spent in the service of the ladies.

Mrs Sul. And pray, which service do you like best?

Arch. Madam, the ladies pay best; the honour of serving them is sufficient wages; there is a charm in their looks that delivers a pleasure with their commands, and gives our duty the wings of inclination.

Mrs Sul. [*Aside.*] That flight was above the pitch of a livery.—[*Aloud.*] And, sir, would not you be satisfied to serve a lady again?

Arch. As a groom of the chamber, madam, but not as a footman.

Mrs Sul. I suppose you served as footman before?

Arch. For that reason I would not serve in that post again; for my memory is too weak for the load of messages that the ladies lay upon their servants in London. My Lady Howd'ye, the last mistress I served, called me up one morning, and told me: Martin, go to my Lady Allnight with my humble service; tell her I was to wait on her ladyship yesterday, and left word with Mrs Rebecca, that the preliminaries of the affair she knows of are stopped till we know the concurrence of the person that I know of, for which there are circumstances wanting which we shall accommodate at the old place; but that in the meantime there is a person about her ladyship, that, from several hints and

surmises, was accessory at a certain time to the disappointments that naturally attend things, that to her knowledge are of more importance—

Mrs Sul. and Dor. Ha, ha, ha! where are you going, sir?

Arch. Why, I han't half done!—The whole howd'ye was about half an hour long; so I happened to misplace two syllables, and was turned off, and rendered incapable.

Dor. [*Aside to* Mrs SULLEN.] The pleasantest fellow, sister, I ever saw!—[*To* ARCHER.] But, friend, if your master be married, I presume you still serve a lady?

Arch. No, madam, I take care never to come into a married family; the commands of the master and mistress are always so contrary, that 'tis impossible to please both.

Dor. [*Aside.*] There's a main point gained: my lord is not married, I find.

Mrs Sul. But I wonder, friend, that in so many good services, you had not a better provision made for you.

Arch. I don't know how, madam. I had a lieutenancy offered me three or four times; but that is not bread, madam—I live much better as I do.

Scrub. Madam, he sings rarely! I was thought to do pretty well here in the country till he came; but alack a day, I'm nothing to my brother Martin!

Dor. Does he?—Pray, sir, will you oblige us with a song?

Arch. Are you for passion or humour?

Scrub. O la! he has the purest ballad about a trifle—

Mrs Sul. A trifle! pray, sir, let's have it.

Arch. I'm ashamed to offer you a trifle, madam; but since you command me—

> [*Sings to the tune of* "Sir Simon the King." [1]

---

[1] A popular tune, said to take its name from one Simon Wadloe, master of the Devil Tavern, frequented by Ben Jonson. Only the first two lines of the song appear in Q. 1.

A trifling song you shall hear,
Begun with a trifle and ended:
All trifling people draw near,
And I shall be nobly attended.

Were it not for trifles, a few,
That lately have come into play,
The men would want something to do,
And the women want something to say.

What makes men trifle in dressing?
Because the ladies (they know)
Admire, by often possessing,
That eminent trifle a beau.

When the lover his moments has trifled,
The trifle of trifles to gain,
No sooner the virgin is rifled,
But a trifle shall part 'em again.

What mortal man would be able
At White's half-an-hour to sit,
Or who could bear a tea-table,
Without talking of trifles for wit?

The Court is from trifles secure,
Gold keys are no trifles, we see!
White rods are no trifles, I'm sure,
Whatever their bearers may be.

But if you will go to the place,
Where trifles abundantly breed,
The levee will show you his Grace
Makes promises trifles indeed.[1]

A coach with six footmen behind,
I count neither trifle nor sin:
But, ye gods! how oft do we find
A scandalous trifle within.

[1] This verse is thought to be an allusion to the Duke of Ormond's failure to fulfil a promise to Farquhar. *See* Introduction, p. 13.

A flask of champagne, people think it
A trifle, or something as bad :
But if you'll contrive how to drink it,
You'll find it no trifle, egad !

A parson's a trifle at sea,
A widow's a trifle in sorrow :
A peace is a trifle to-day :
Who knows what may happen to-morrow !

A black coat a trifle may cloke,
Or to hide it the red may endeavour :
But if once the army is broke,
We shall have more trifles than ever.

The stage is a trifle, they say,
The reason, pray carry along,
Because at every new play,
The house they with trifles so throng.

But with people's malice to trifle,
And to set us all on a foot :
The author of this is a trifle,
And his song is a trifle to boot.

Mrs Sul. Very well, sir, we're obliged to you.—
Something for a pair of gloves.   [*Offering him money.*

Arch. I humbly beg leave to be excused : my master,
madam, pays me ; nor dare I take money from any
other hand, without injuring his honour, and disobey-
ing his commands.   [*Exit with* SCRUB.

Dor. This is surprising ! Did you ever see so pretty
a well-bred fellow ?

Mrs Sul. The devil take him for wearing that livery !

Dor. I fancy, sister, he may be some gentleman, a
friend of my lord's, that his lordship has pitched upon
for his courage, fidelity, and discretion, to bear him
company in this dress—and who, ten to one, was his
second too.

Mrs. Sul. It is so, must be so, and it shall be so!—for I like him.

Dor. What! better than the Count?

Mrs Sul. The Count happened to be the most agreeable man upon the place; and so I chose him to serve me in my design upon my husband. But I should like this fellow better in a design upon myself.

Dor. But now, sister, for an interview with this lord and this gentleman; how shall we bring that about?

Mrs Sul. Patience! you country ladies give no quarter if once you be entered. Would you prevent their desires, and give the fellows no wishing-time? Look'ee, Dorinda, if my Lord Aimwell loves you or deserves you, he'll find a way to see you, and there we must leave it.—My business comes now upon the tapis. Have you prepared your brother?

Dor. Yes, yes.

Mrs Sul. And how did he relish it?

Dor. He said little, mumbled something to himself, promised to be guided by me—but here he comes.

Enter SULLEN.

Squire Sul. What singing was that I heard just now?

Mrs Sul. The singing in your head, my dear; you complained of it all day.

Squire Sul. You're impertinent.

Mrs Sul. I was ever so, since I became one flesh with you.

Squire Sul. One flesh! rather two carcasses joined unnaturally together.

Mrs Sul. Or rather a living soul coupled to a dead body.

Dor. So, this is fine encouragement for me!

Squire Sul. Yes, my wife shows you what you must do.

Mrs Sul. And my husband shows you what you must suffer.

Squire Sul. 'Sdeath, why can't you be silent?

Mrs Sul. 'Sdeath, why can't you talk?

Squire Sul. Do you talk to any purpose?

Mrs Sul. Do you think to any purpose?

Squire Sul. Sister, heark'ye!—[*Whispers to* DORINDA; *then aloud.*] I shan't be home till it be late. [*Exit.*

Mrs Sul. What did he whisper to ye?

Dor. That he would go round the back way, come into the closet, and listen as I directed him. But let me beg you once more, dear sister, to drop this project; for as I told you before, instead of awaking him to kindness, you may provoke him to a rage; and then who knows how far his brutality may carry him?

Mrs Sul. I'm provided to receive him, I warrant you. But here comes the Count, vanish! [*Exit* DORINDA.

Enter Count BELLAIR.[1]

Don't you wonder, Monsieur le Comte, that I was not at church this afternoon?

Count Bel. I more wonder, madam, that you go dere at all, or how you dare to lift those eyes to heaven that are guilty of so much killing.

Mrs Sul. If Heaven, sir, has given to my eyes, with the power of killing, the virtue of making a cure, I hope the one may atone for the other.

Count Bel. Oh, largely, madam, would your ladyship be as ready to apply the remedy as to give the wound. Consider, madam, I am doubly a prisoner; first to the arms of your general, then to your more conquering eyes. My first chains are easy, there a ransom may redeem me; but from your fetters I never shall get free.

Mrs Sul. Alas, sir! why should you complain to me

[1] Note in edition of 1736: "This scene . . . with the entire part of the Count, was cut out by the author after the first night's representation; and where he should enter in the last scene of the fifth act, it is added to the part of Foigard."

of your captivity, who am in chains myself? You know, sir, that I am bound, nay, must be tied up in that particular that might give you ease. I am like you, a prisoner of war,—of war, indeed! I have given my parole of honour; would you break yours to gain your liberty?

Count Bel. Most certainly I would, were I a prisoner among the Turks; dis is your case; you're a slave, madam, slave to the worst of Turks, a husband.

Mrs Sul. There lies my foible, I confess; no fortifications, no courage, conduct, nor vigilancy, can pretend to defend a place, where the cruelty of the governor forces the garrison to mutiny.

Count Bel. And where de besieger is resolved to die before de place.—Here will I fix;—[*Kneels*] with tears, vows, and prayers assault your heart, and never rise till you surrender; or if I must storm—Love and St Michael!—And so I begin the attack——

Mrs Sul. Stand off!—[*Aside.*] Sure he hears me not! —And I could almost wish he—did not!—The fellow makes love very prettily.—[*Aloud.*] But, sir, why should you put such a value upon my person, when you see it despised by one that knows it so much better?

Count Bel. He knows it not, though he possesses it; if he but knew the value of the jewel he is master of, he would always wear it next his heart, and sleep with it in his arms.

Mrs Sul. But since he throws me unregarded from him—

Count Bel. And one that knows your value well comes by and takes you up, is not justice?

[*Goes to lay hold on her.*

Enter SULLEN *with his sword drawn.*

Squire Sul. Hold, villain, hold!

Mrs Sul. [*Presenting a pistol.*] Do you hold!

Squire Sul. What! murther your husband, to defend your bully!

Mrs Sul. Bully! for shame, Mr Sullen! Bullies wear long swords, the gentleman has none, he's a prisoner, you know. I was aware of your outrage, and prepared this to receive your violence; and, if occasion were, to preserve myself against the force of this other gentleman.

Count Bel. O madam, your eyes be bettre firearms than your pistol; they nevre miss.

Squire Sul. What! court my wife to my face!

Mrs Sul. Pray, Mr Sullen, put up; suspend your fury for a minute.

Squire Sul. To give you time to invent an excuse!

Mrs Sul. I need none.

Squire Sul. No, for I heard every syllable of your discourse.

Count Bel. Ay! and begar, I tink the dialogue was vera pretty.

Mrs Sul. Then I suppose, sir, you heard something of your own barbarity?

Squire Sul. Barbarity! Oons, what does the woman call barbarity? Do I ever meddle with you?

Mrs Sul. No.

Squire Sul. As for you, sir, I shall take another time.

Count Bel. Ah, begar, and so must I.

Squire Sul. Look'ee, madam, don't think that my anger proceeds from any concern I have for your honour, but for my own; and if you can contrive any way of being a whore without making me a cuckold, do it and welcome.

Mrs Sul. Sir, I thank you kindly: you would allow me the sin but rob me of the pleasure. No, no, I'm resolved never to venture upon the crime without the satisfaction of seeing you punished for't.

Squire Sul. Then will you grant me this, my dear? Let anybody else do you the favour but that Frenchman, for I mortally hate his whole generation. [*Exit.*

Count Bel. Ah, sir, that be ungrateful, for begar, I love some of yours.   Madam—   [*Approaching her.*
Mrs Sul. No, sir.
Count Bel. No, sir! Garzoon, madam, I am not your husband.
Mrs Sul. 'Tis time to undeceive you, sir.   I believed your addresses to me were no more than an amusement, and I hope you will think the same of my complaisance; and to convince you that you ought, you must know that I brought you hither only to make you instrumental in setting me right with my husband, for he was planted to listen by my appointment.
Count Bel. By your appointment?
Mrs Sul. Certainly.
Count Bel. And so, madam, while I was telling twenty stories to part you from your husband, begar, I was bringing you together all the while?
Mrs Sul. I ask your pardon, sir, but I hope this will give you a taste of the virtue of the English ladies.
Count Bel. Begar, madam, your virtue be vera great, but garzoon, your honeste be vera little.

Re-enter DORINDA.

Mrs Sul. Nay, now, you're angry, sir.
Count Bel. Angry!—*Fair Dorinda* [*Sings* DORINDA *the Opera Tune, and addresses to* DORINDA.] Madam, when your ladyship want a fool, send for me.   *Fair Dorinda, Revenge, &c.*[1]   [*Exit singing.*

---

[1] I have not succeeded in identifying this song. Dorinda is one of the characters introduced by Dryden and Davenant into their perversion of *The Tempest*; but no such song occurs in the text as it appears in Dryden's works. The heroine of the opera *Camilla*, referred to by Farquhar in the Epilogue to *The Recruiting Officer*, (*see* p. 352) assumed in the course of the action the name of Dorinda; but no song beginning "Fair Dorinda revenge" was addressed to her. In Act. iii. Sc. 1, she herself sings a song containing these lines :—

My wrongs aloud for vengeance crave !
Revenge ! Revenge ! I summon !
Revenge is all my care.

Mrs Sul. There goes the true humour of his nation—resentment with good manners, and the height of anger in a song! Well, sister, you must be judge, for you have heard the trial.

Dor. And I bring in my brother guilty.

Mrs Sul. But I must bear the punishment. 'Tis hard, sister.

Dor. I own it; but you must have patience.

Mrs Sul. Patience! the cant of custom—Providence sends no evil without a remedy. Should I lie groaning under a yoke I can shake off, I were accessary to my ruin, and my patience were no better than self-murder.

Dor. But how can you shake off the yoke? Your divisions don't come within the reach of the law for a divorce.

Mrs Sul. Law! what law can search into the remote abyss of nature? What evidence can prove the un-accountable disaffections of wedlock? Can a jury sum up the endless aversions that are rooted in our souls, or can a bench give judgment upon antipathies?

Dor. They never pretended, sister; they never meddle, but in case of uncleanness.

Mrs Sul. Uncleanness! O sister! casual violation is a transient injury, and may possibly be repaired; but can radical hatreds be ever reconciled? No, no, sister; Nature is the first lawgiver; and when she has set tempers opposite, not all the golden links of wedlock, nor iron manacles of law, can keep 'em fast.

> Wedlock we own ordained by Heaven's decree,
> But such as Heaven ordained it first to be;—
> Concurring tempers in the man and wife
> As mutual helps to draw the load of life.
> View all the works of Providence above:
> The stars with harmony and concord move;
> View all the works of Providence below:
> The fire, the water, earth and air, we know,

All in one plant agree to make it grow.
Must man, the chiefest work of art divine,
Be doomed in endless discord to repine?
No, we should injure Heaven by that surmise:
Omnipotence is just, were man but wise.

[Exeunt.

ACT IV

SCENE I.— *The Gallery in* Lady BOUNTIFUL's *House.*

Enter Mrs SULLEN.

RS SUL. Were I born an humble Turk, where women have no soul nor property, there I must sit contented. But in England, a country whose women are its glory, must women be abused? Where women rule, must women be enslaved? Nay, cheated into slavery, mocked by a promise of comfortable society into a wilderness of solitude! I dare not keep the thought about me. Oh, here comes something to divert me.

Enter a Countrywoman.

Wom. I come, an't please your ladyship—you're my Lady Bountiful, an't ye?

Mrs Sul. Well, good woman, go on.

Wom. I come seventeen long mail to have a cure for my husband's sore leg.

Mrs Sul. Your husband! what, woman, cure your husband!

Wom. Ay, poor man, for his sore leg won't let him stir from home.

Mrs Sul. There, I confess, you have given me a reason. Well, good woman, I'll tell you what you must do. You must lay your husband's leg upon a table, and with a chopping-knife you must lay it open as broad as you can ; then you must take out the bone, and beat the flesh soundly with a rolling-pin ; then take salt, pepper, cloves, mace and ginger, some sweet herbs, and season it very well ; then roll it up like brawn, and put it into the oven for two hours.

Wom. Heavens reward your ladyship! I have two little babies too that are piteous bad with the graips, an't please ye.

Mrs Sul. Put a little pepper and salt in their bellies, good woman.

Enter Lady BOUNTIFUL.

I beg your ladyship's pardon for taking your business out of your hands ; I have been a-tampering here a little with one of your patients.

Lady Boun. Come, good woman, don't mind this mad creature ; I am the person that you want, I suppose. What would you have, woman?

Mrs Sul. She wants something for her husband's sore leg.

Lady Boun. What's the matter with his leg, goody?

Wom. It come first, as one might say, with a sort of dizziness in his foot, then he had a kind of laziness in his joints, and then his leg broke out, and then it swelled, and then it closed again, and then it broke out again, and then it festered, and then it grew better, and then it grew worse again.

Mrs Sul. Ha, ha, ha !

Lady Boun. How can you be merry with the misfortunes of other people?

Mrs Sul. Because my own make me sad, madam.

Lady Boun. The worst reason in the world, daughter ;

your own misfortunes should teach you to pity others.

Mrs Sul. But the woman's misfortunes and mine are nothing alike; her husband is sick, and mine, alas! is in health.

Lady Boun. What! would you wish your husband sick?

Mrs Sul. Not of a sore leg, of all things.

Lady Boun. Well, good woman, go to the pantry, get your bellyful of victuals, then I'll give you a receipt of diet-drink for your husband. But d'ye hear, goody, you must not let your husband move too much.

Wom. No, no, madam, the poor man's inclinable enough to lie still. [*Exit.*

Lady Boun. Well, daughter Sullen, though you laugh, I have done miracles about the country here with my receipts.

Mrs Sul. Miracles indeed, if they have cured anybody; but I believe, madam, the patient's faith goes farther toward the miracle than your prescription.

Lady Boun. Fancy helps in some cases; but there's your husband, who has as little fancy as anybody, I brought him from death's door.

Mrs Sul. I suppose, madam, you made him drink plentifully of ass's milk.

Enter DORINDA, *runs to* Mrs SULLEN.

Dor. News, dear sister! news! news!

Enter ARCHER, *running.*

Arch. Where, where is my Lady Bountiful?—Pray, which is the old lady of you three?

Lady Boun. I am.

Arch. O madam, the fame of your ladyship's charity, goodness, benevolence, skill and ability, have drawn me hither to implore your ladyship's help in behalf of

my unfortunate master, who is this moment breathing his last.

Lady Boun. Your master! where is he?

Arch. At your gate, madam. Drawn by the appearance of your handsome house to view it nearer, and walking up the avenue within five paces of the courtyard, he was taken ill of a sudden with a sort of I know not what, but down he fell, and there he lies.

Lady Boun. Here, Scrub, Gipsy, all run, get my easy-chair downstairs, put the gentleman in it, and bring him in quickly! quickly!

Arch. Heaven will reward your ladyship for this charitable act.

Lady Boun. Is your master used to these fits?

Arch. O yes, madam, frequently: I have known him have five or six of a night.

Lady Boun. What's his name?

Arch. Lord, madam, he's a-dying! a minute's care or neglect may save or destroy his life.

Lady Boun. Ah, poor gentleman!—Come, friend, show me the way; I'll see him brought in myself.

[*Exit with* ARCHER.

Dor. O sister, my heart flutters about strangely! I can hardly forbear running to his assistance.

Mrs Sul. And I'll lay my life he deserves your assistance more than he wants it. Did not I tell you that my lord would find a way to come at you? Love's his distemper, and you must be the physician; put on all your charms, summon all your fire into your eyes, plant the whole artillery of your looks against his breast, and down with him.

Dor. O sister! I'm but a young gunner; I shall be afraid to shoot, for fear the piece should recoil, and hurt myself.

Mrs Sul. Never fear! You shall see me shoot before you, if you will.

Dor. No, no, dear sister; you have missed your

mark so unfortunately, that I sha'n't care for being instructed by you.

Enter AIMWELL, *in a chair, carried by* ARCHER *and* SCRUB: Lady BOUNTIFUL *and* GIPSY *following.* AIMWELL *counterfeiting a swoon.*

Lady Boun. Here, here, let's see the hartshorn drops.—Gipsy, a glass of fair water! His fit's very strong.—Bless me, how his hands are clenched!

Arch. For shame, ladies, what d'ye do? why don't you help us?—[*To* DORINDA.] Pray, madam, take his hand, and open it, if you can, whilst I hold his head.   [DORINDA *takes his hand.*

Dor. Poor gentleman!—Oh!—he has got my hand within his, and he squeezes it unmercifully—

Lady Boun. 'Tis the violence of his convulsion, child.

Arch. Oh, madam, he's perfectly possessed in these cases—he'll bite if you don't have a care.

Dor. Oh, my hand! my hand!

Lady Boun. What's the matter with the foolish girl? I have got this hand open you see with a great deal of ease.

Arch. Ay, but, madam, your daughter's hand is somewhat warmer than your ladyship's, and the heat of it draws the force of the spirits that way.

Mrs Sul. I find, friend, you're very learned in these sorts of fits.

Arch. 'Tis no wonder, madam, for I'm often troubled with them myself; I find myself extremely ill at this minute.   [*Looking hard at* Mrs SULLEN

Mrs Sul. [*Aside.*] I fancy I could find a way to cure you.

Lady Boun. His fit holds him very long.

Arch. Longer than usual, madam.—Pray, young lady, open his breast, and give him air.

Lady Boun. Where did his illness take him first, pray?

Arch. To-day, at church, madam.

Lady Boun. In what manner was he taken?

Arch. Very strangely, my lady. He was of a sudden touched with something in his eyes, which, at the first, he only felt, but could not tell whether 'twas pain or pleasure.

Lady Boun. Wind, nothing but wind!

Arch. By soft degrees it grew and mounted to his brain; there his fancy caught it, there formed it so beautiful, and dressed it up in such gay, pleasing colours, that his transported appetite seized the fair idea, and straight conveyed it to his heart. That hospitable seat of life sent all its sanguine spirits forth to meet, and opened all its sluicy gates to take the stranger in.

Lady Boun. Your master should never go without a bottle to smell to.—Oh,—he recovers!—The lavender water—some feathers to burn under his nose—Hungary water to rub his temples.—Oh, he comes to himself!— Hem a little, sir, hem.—Gipsy! bring the cordial-water.

　　　　　[AIMWELL *seems to awake in amaze.*

Dor. How d'ye, sir?

Aim. Where am I?　　　　　　　　　　[*Rising.*

　　Sure I have pass'd the gulf of silent death,
　　And now I land on the Elysian shore!—
　　Behold the goddess of those happy plains,
　　Fair Proserpine—
　　Let me adore thy bright divinity.

　　　　　[*Kneels to* DORINDA, *and kisses her hand.*

Mrs Sui. So, so, so! I knew where the fit would end!

Aim. Eurydice perhaps—
　　How could thy Orpheus keep his word,
　　And not look back upon thee?
　　No treasure but thyself could sure have bribed him
　　To look one minute off thee.

Lady Boun. Delirious, poor gentleman!

Arch. Very delirious, madam, very delirious.

Aim. Martin's voice, I think.

Arch. Yes, my lord.—How does your lordship?

Lady Boun. [*Aside to* Mrs SULLEN *and* DORINDA.] Lord! did you mind that, girls?

Aim. Where am I?

Arch. In very good hands, sir. You were taken just now with one of your old fits, under the trees, just by this good lady's house; her ladyship had you taken in, and has miraculously brought you to yourself, as you see—

Aim. I am so confounded with shame, madam, that I can now only beg pardon, and refer my acknowledgments for your ladyship's care till an opportunity offers of making some amends. I dare be no longer troublesome.—-Martin, give two guineas to the servants. [*Going.*

Dor. Sir, you may catch cold by going so soon into the air; you don't look, sir, as if you were perfectly recovered.

[*Here* ARCHER *talks to* Lady BOUNTIFUL *in dumb show.*

Aim. That I shall never be, madam; my present illness is so rooted that I must expect to carry it to my grave.

Mrs Sul. Don't despair, sir; I have known several in your distemper shake it off with a fortnight's physic.

Lady Boun. Come, sir, your servant has been telling me that you're apt to relapse if you go into the air: your good manners sha'n't get the better of ours—you shall sit down again, sir. Come, sir, we don't mind ceremonies in the country. Here, sir, my service t'ye.— You shall taste my water; 'tis a cordial I can assure you, and of my own making—drink it off, sir.— [AIMWELL *drinks.*] And how d'ye find yourself now, sir?

Aim. Somewhat better—though very faint still.

Lady Boun. Ay, ay, people are always faint after

these fits.—Come, girls, you shall show the gentleman the house.—'Tis but an old family building, sir;
but you had better walk about, and cool by degrees,
than venture immediately into the air. You'll find
some tolerable pictures.—Dorinda, show the gentleman
the way. I must go to the poor woman below. [*Exit.*

Dor. This way, sir.

Aim. Ladies, shall I beg leave for my servant to wait
on you, for he understands pictures very well?

Mrs Sul. Sir, we understand originals as well as he
does pictures, so he may come along.

[*Exeunt all but* SCRUB, AIMWELL *leading* DORINDA.

Enter FOIGARD.

Foi. Save you, Master Scrub!

Scrub. Sir, I won't be saved your way—I hate a
priest, I abhor the French, and I defy the devil. Sir,
I'm a bold Briton, and will spill the last drop of my
blood to keep out popery and slavery.

Foi. Master Scrub, you would put me down in
politics, and so I would be speaking with Mrs
Shipsy.

Scrub. Good Mr Priest, you can't speak with her;
she's sick, sir, she's gone abroad, sir, she's—dead two
months ago, sir.

Re-enter GIPSY.

Gip. How now, impudence! how dare you talk so
saucily to the doctor?—Pray, sir, don't take it ill; for
the common people of England are not so civil to
strangers, as—

Scrub. You lie! you lie! 'tis the common people that
are civillest to strangers.

Gip. Sirrah, I have a good mind to—get you out,
I say!

Scrub. I won't.

Gip. You won't, sauce-box! — Pray, doctor, what is the captain's name that came to your inn last night?

Scrub. [*Aside.*] The captain! ah, the devil, there she hampers me again; the captain has me on one side, and the priest on t'other: so between the gown and the sword, I have a fine time on't—But, *Cedunt arma togæ.* [*Going.*

Gip. What, sirrah, won't you march?

Scrub. No, my dear, I won't march—but I'll walk.— [*Aside.*] And I'll make bold to listen a little too.

[*Goes behind the side-scene, and listens.*

Gip. Indeed, doctor, the Count has been barbarously treated, that's the truth on't.

Foi. Ah, Mrs Gipsy, upon my shoul, now, gra, his complainings would mollify the marrow in your bones, and move the bowels of your commiseration! He veeps, and he dances, and he fistles, and he swears, and he laughs, and he stamps, and he sings: in conclusion, joy, he's afflicted *à la Fransçaise*, and a stranger would not know whider to cry or to laugh with him.

Gip. What would you have me do, doctor?

Foi. Noting, joy, but only hide the Count in Mrs Sullen's closet when it is dark.

Gip. Nothing! is that nothing? It would be both a sin and a shame, doctor.

Foi. Here is twenty Lewidores, joy, for your shame; and I will give you an absolution for the shin.

Gip. But won't that money look like a bribe?

Foi. Dat is according as you shall tauk it. If you receive the money beforehand, 'twill be, *logice*, a bribe; but if you stay till afterwards, 'twill be only a gratification.

Gip. Well, doctor, I'll take it *logice*. But what must I do with my conscience, sir?

Foi. Leave dat wid me, joy; I am your priest, gra; and your conscience is under my hands.

Gip. But should I put the Count into the closet—

Foi. Vel, is dere any shin for a man's being in a closhet? One may go to prayers in a closhet.

Gip. But if the lady should come into her chamber, and go to bed?

Foi. Vel, and is dere any shin in going to bed, joy?

Gip. Ay, but if the parties should meet, doctor?

Foi. Vel den—the parties must be responsable. Do you be after putting the Count in the closhet, and leave the shins wid themselves. I will come with the Count to instruct you in your chamber.

Gip. Well, doctor, your religion is so pure! Methinks I'm so easy after an absolution, and can sin afresh with so much security, that I'm resolved to die a martyr to't. Here's the key of the garden door, come in the back way when 'tis late, I'll be ready to receive you; but don't so much as whisper, only take hold of my hand; I'll lead you, and do you lead the Count, and follow me.   [*Exeunt.*

Scrub. [*Coming forward.*]   What witchcraft now have these two imps of the devil been a-hatching here? There's twenty Lewidores; I heard that, and saw the purse.—But I must give room to my betters.   [*Exit.*

Re-enter AIMWELL, *leading* DORINDA, *and making love in dumb show;* Mrs SULLEN *and* ARCHER.

Mrs Sul. [*To* ARCHER.] Pray, sir, how d'ye like that piece?

Arch. Oh, 'tis Leda! You find, madam, how Jupiter comes disguised to make love—

Mrs Sul. But what think you there of Alexander's battles?[1]

Arch. We want only a Le Brun, madam, to draw greater battles, and a greater general of our own. The

[1] Le Brun's famous pictures of the battles of Alexander the Great.

Danube, madam, would make a greater figure in a picture than the Granicus; and we have our Ramilies to match their Arbela.

Mrs Sul. Pray, sir, what head is that in the corner there?

Arch. O madam, 'tis poor Ovid in his exile.

Mrs Sul. What was he banished for?

Arch. His ambitious love, madam.—[*Bowing.*] His misfortune touches me.

Mrs Sul. Was he successful in his amours?

Arch. There he has left us in the dark.—He was too much a gentleman to tell.

Mrs Sul. If he were secret, I pity him.

Arch. And if he were successful, I envy him.

Mrs Sul. How d'ye like that Venus over the chimney?

Arch. Venus! I protest, madam, I took it for your picture; but now I look again, 'tis not handsome enough.

Mrs Sul. Oh, what a charm is flattery! If you would see my picture, there it is, over that cabinet. How d'ye like it?

Arch. I must admire anything, madam, that has the least resemblance of you. But, methinks, madam—[*He looks at the picture and* Mrs SULLEN *three or four times, by turns.*] Pray, madam, who drew it?

Mrs Sul. A famous hand, sir.

[*Here* AIMWELL *and* DORINDA *go off.*

Arch. A famous hand, madam!—Your eyes, indeed, are featured there; but where's the sparkling moisture, shining fluid, in which they swim? The picture, indeed, has your dimples; but where's the swarm of killing Cupids that should ambush there? The lips too are figured out; but where's the carnation dew, the pouting ripeness, that tempts the taste in the original?

Mrs Sul. [*Aside.*] Had it been my lot to have matched with such a man!

Arch. Your breasts too—presumptuous man! what, paint Heaven!—Apropos, madam, in the very next

picture is Salmoneus, that was struck dead with lightning, for offering to imitate Jove's thunder; I hope you served the painter so, madam?

Mrs Sul. Had my eyes the power of thunder, they should employ their lightning better.

Arch. There's the finest bed in that room, madam! I suppose 'tis your ladyship's bedchamber.

Mrs Sul. And what then, sir?

Arch. I think the quilt is the richest that ever I saw. I can't at this distance, madam, distinguish the figures of the embroidery; will you give me leave, madam——?
                                                    [*Goes into the chamber.*

Mrs Sul. The devil take his impudence!—Sure, if I gave him an opportunity, he durst not offer it?—I have a great mind to try.—[*Going in, returns.*] 'Sdeath, what am I doing?—And alone, too!—Sister! sister!
                                                    [*Runs out.*

Arch. [*Coming out.*] I'll follow her close—
For where a Frenchman durst attempt to storm,
A Briton sure may well the work perform.   [*Going.*

                    Re-enter SCRUB.

Scrub. Martin! brother Martin!

Arch. O brother Scrub, I beg your pardon, I was not a-going: here's a guinea my master ordered you.

Scrub. A guinea! hi! hi! hi! a guinea! eh—by this light it is a guinea! But I suppose you expect one and twenty shillings in change?

Arch. Not at all; I have another for Gipsy.

Scrub. A guinea for her! Faggot and fire for the witch! Sir, give me that guinea, and I'll discover a plot.

Arch. A plot!

Scrub. Ay, sir, a plot, and a horrid plot! First, it must be a plot, because there's a woman in't: secondly, it must be a plot, because there's a priest in't: thirdly, it must be a plot, because there's French gold in't: and

fourthly, it must be a plot, because I don't know what to make on't.

Arch. Nor anybody else, I'm afraid, brother Scrub.

Scrub. Truly, I'm afraid so too; for where there's a priest and a woman, there's always a mystery and a riddle. This I know, that here has been the doctor with a temptation in one hand and an absolution in the other, and Gipsy has sold herself to the devil; I saw the price paid down, my eyes shall take their oath on't.

Arch. And is all this bustle about Gipsy?

Scrub. That's not all; I could hear but a word here and there; but I remember they mentioned a Count, a closet, a back-door, and a key.

Arch. The Count!—Did you hear nothing of Mrs Sullen?

Scrub. I did hear some word that sounded that way; but whether it was Sullen or Dorinda, I could not distinguish.

Arch. You have told this matter to nobody, brother?

Scrub. Told! no, sir, I thank you for that; I'm resolved never to speak one word, *pro* nor *con*, till we have a peace.

Arch. You're i' the right, brother Scrub. Here's a treaty a-foot between the Count and the lady: the priest and the chambermaid are the plenipotentiaries. It shall go hard but I find a way to be included in the treaty.— Where's the doctor now?

Scrub. He and Gipsy are this moment devouring my lady's marmalade in the closet.

Aim. [*Without.*] Martin! Martin!

Arch. I come, sir, I come.

Scrub. But you forgot the other guinea, brother Martin.

Arch. Here, I give it with all my heart.

Scrub. And I take it with all my soul.—[*Exit* ARCHER.] Ecod, I'll spoil your plotting, Mrs Gipsy! and if you should set the captain upon me, these two guineas will buy me off. [*Exit.*

Re-enter Mrs SULLEN *and* DORINDA, *meeting.*

Mrs Sul. Well, sister!

Dor. And well, sister!

Mrs Sul. What's become of my lord?

Dor. What's become of his servant?

Mrs Sul. Servant! he's a prettier fellow, and a finer gentleman by fifty degrees, than his master.

Dor. O' my conscience, I fancy you could beg that fellow at the gallows-foot!

Mrs Sul. O' my conscience I could, provided I could put a friend of yours in his room.

Dor. You desired me, sister, to leave you when you transgressed the bounds of honour.

Mrs Sul. Thou dear censorious country girl! what dost mean? You can't think of the man without the bedfellow, I find.

Dor. I don't find anything unnatural in that thought: while the mind is conversant with flesh and blood, it must conform to the humours of the company.

Mrs Sul. How a little love and good company improves a woman! Why, child, you begin to live—you never spoke before.

Dor. Because I was never spoke to.—My lord has told me that I have more wit and beauty than any of my sex; and truly I begin to think the man is sincere.

Mrs Sul. You're in the right, Dorinda; pride is the life of a woman, and flattery is our daily bread; and she's a fool that won't believe a man there, as much as she that believes him in anything else. But I'll lay you a guinea that I had finer things said to me than you had.

Dor. Done! What did your fellow say to ye?

Mrs Sul. My fellow took the picture of Venus for mine.

Dor. But my lover took me for Venus herself.

Mrs Sul. Common cant! Had my spark called me

a Venus directly, I should have believed him a footman
in good earnest.

Dor. But my lover was upon his knees to me.

Mrs Sul. And mine was upon his tiptoes to me.

Dor. Mine vowed to die for me.

Mrs Sul. Mine swore to die with me.

Dor. Mine spoke the softest moving things.

Mrs .Sul. Mine had his moving things too.

Dor. Mine kissed my hand ten thousand times.

Mrs Sul. Mine has all that pleasure to come.

Dor. Mine offered marriage.

Mrs Sul. O Lard! d'ye call that a moving thing?

Dor. The sharpest arrow in his quiver, my dear
sister!   Why, my ten thousand pounds may lie brooding
here this seven years, and hatch nothing at last but some
ill-natured clown like yours!   Whereas, if I marry my
Lord Aimwell, there will be title, place, and precedence,
the Park, the play, and the drawing-room, splendour,
equipage, noise, and flambeaux.—*Hey, my Lady Aimwell's servants there!—Lights, lights to the stairs!—
My Lady Aimwell's coach put forward!—Stand by, make
room for her ladyship!*—Are not these things moving?—
What! melancholy of a sudden?

Mrs Sul. Happy, happy sister! your angel has been
watchful for your happiness, whilst mine has slept,
regardless of his charge.   Long smiling years of circling
joys for you, but not one hour for me!   [*Weeps.*

Dor. Come, my dear, we'll talk of something else.

Mrs Sul. O Dorinda! I own myself a woman, full of
my sex ; a gentle, generous soul, easy and yielding to
soft desires; a spacious heart, where love and all his
train might lodge.   And must the fair apartment of my
breast be made a stable for a brute to lie in?

Dor. Meaning your husband, I suppose?

Mrs Sul. Husband! no; even husband is too soft a
name for him.—But, come, I expect my brother here
to-night or to-morrow; he was abroad when my father

married me; perhaps he'll find a way to make me easy.

Dor. Will you promise not to make yourself easy in the meantime, with my lord's friend?

Mrs Sul. You mistake me, sister. It happens with us as among the men, the greatest talkers are the greatest cowards; and there's a reason for it; those spirits evaporate in prattle, which might do more mischief if they took another course. — Though, to confess the truth, I do love that fellow;—and if I met him dressed as he should be, and I undressed as I should be— look'ye, sister, I have no supernatural gifts—I can't swear I could resist the temptation; though I can safely promise to avoid it; and that's as much as the best of us can do.   [*Exeunt.*

SCENE II.—*The Inn.*

Enter AIMWELL *and* ARCHER, *laughing.*

Arch. And the awkward kindness of the good motherly old gentlewoman—

Aim. And the coming easiness of the young one— Sdeath, 'tis pity to deceive her!

Arch. Nay, if you adhere to those principles, stop where you are.

Aim. I can't stop; for I love her to distraction.

Arch. 'Sdeath, if you love her a hair's breadth beyond discretion, you must go no farther.

Aim. Well, well, anything to deliver us from saun- tering away our idle evenings at White's, Tom's or Will's, and be stinted to bare looking at our old ac- quaintance, the cards, because our impotent pockets can't afford us a guinea for the mercenary drabs.

Arch. Or be obliged to some purse-proud coxcomb for a scandalous bottle, where we must not pretend to our share of the discourse, because we can't pay our club o' th' reckoning.—Damn it, I had rather spunge upon Morris, and sup upon a dish of bohea scored behind the door !

Aim. And there expose our want of sense by talking criticisms, as we should our want of money by railing at the government.

Arch. Or be obliged to sneak into the side-box, and between both houses steal two acts of a play, and because we han't money to see the other three, we come away discontented, and damn the whole five.[1]

Aim. And ten thousand such rascally tricks—had we outlived our fortunes among our acquaintance.—But now—

Arch. Ay, now is the time to prevent all this :—strike while the iron is hot.—This priest is the luckiest part of our adventure ; he shall marry you, and pimp for me.

Aim. But I should not like a woman that can be so fond of a Frenchman.

Arch. Alas, sir, necessity has no law. The lady may be in distress ; perhaps she has a confounded husband, and her revenge may carry her farther than her love. Egad, I have so good an opinion of her, and of myself, that I begin to fancy strange things ; and we must say this for the honour of our women, and indeed of ourselves, that they do stick to their men as they do to their *Magna charta*. If the plot lies as I suspect, I must put on the gentleman. — But here comes the doctor—I shall be ready.   [*Exit.*

Enter FOIGARD.

Foi. Sauve you, noble friend.

---

[1] One of the frequent allusions to the fact that playgoers could see one act of a play for nothing, their money not being collected unless they stayed to see another act.

Aim. O, sir, your servant! Pray, doctor, may I crave your name?

Foi. Fat naam is upon me! My naam is Foigard, joy.

Aim. Foigard! A very good name for a clergyman. Pray, Doctor Foigard, were you ever in Ireland?

Foi. Ireland! No, joy. Fat sort of plaace is dat saam Ireland? Dey say de people are catched dere when dey are young.

Aim. And some of 'em when they're old:—as for example.—[*Takes* FOIGARD *by the shoulder.*] Sir, I arrest you as a traitor against the government; you're a subject of England, and this morning showed me a commission, by which you served as chaplain in the French army. This is death by our law, and your reverence must hang for't.

Foi. Upon my shoul, noble friend, dis is strange news you tell me! Fader Foigard a subject of England! de son of a burgomaster of Brussels a subject of England! Ubooboo—

Aim. The son of a bog-trotter in Ireland! Sir, your tongue will condemn you before any bench in the kingdom.

Foi. And is my tongue all your evidensh, joy?

Aim. That's enough.

Foi. No, no, joy, for I vil never spake English no more.

Aim. Sir, I have other evidence.—Here, Martin!

Re-enter ARCHER.

You know this fellow?

Arch. [*In a brogue.*] Saave you, my dear cussen, how does your health.

Foi. [*Aside.*] Ah! upon my shoul dere is my country-man, and his brogue will hang mine.—[*To* ARCHER.] *Mynheer, Ick wet neat watt hey zacht, Ick universton ewe neat, sacramant!*

Aim. Altering your language won't do, sir; this fellow knows your person, and will swear to your face.

Foi. Faash! fey, is dere a brogue upon my faash too?

Arch. Upon my soulvation, dere ish, joy!—But cussen Mackshane, vil you not put a remembrance upon me?

Foi. [*Aside.*] Mackshane! by St Paatrick, dat ish naame [1] sure enough.

Aim. [*Aside* to ARCHER.] I fancy, Archer, you have it.

Foi. The devil hang you, joy! by fat acquaintance are you my cussen?

Arch. Oh, de devil hang yourshelf, joy! you know we were little boys togeder upon de school, and your foster-moder's son was married upon my nurse's chister, joy, and so we are Irish cussens.

Foi. De devil taak de relation! Vel, joy, and fat school was it?

Arch. I tinks it vas—aay,—'twas Tipperary.

Foi. No, no, joy; it vas Kilkenny.

Aim. That's enough for us—self-confession. Come, sir, we must deliver you into the hands of the next magistrate.

Arch. He sends you to jail, you're tried next assizes, and away you go swing into purgatory.

Foi. And is it so wid you, cussen?

Arch. It vil be sho wid you, cussen, if you don't immediately confess the secret between you and Mrs Gipsy. Look'ee, sir, the gallows or the secret, take your choice.

Foi. The gallows! upon my shoul I hate that saame gallow, for it is a diseash dat is fatal to our family. Vel den, dere is nothing, shentlemens, but Mrs Shullen would spaak wid the Count in her chamber at midnight and dere is no haarm, joy, for I am to conduct the Count to the plash myshelf.

[1] Query " my name "

Arch. As I guessed.—Have you communicated the matter to the Count?

Foi. I have not sheen him since.

Arch. Right again! Why then, doctor—you shall conduct me to the lady instead of the Count.

Foi. Fat, my cussen to the lady! upon my shoul, gra, dat is too much upon the brogue.

Arch. Come, come, doctor; consider we have got a rope about your neck, and if you offer to squeak, we'll stop your windpipe, most certainly. We shall have another job for you in a day or two, I hope.

Aim. Here's company coming this way; let's into my chamber, and there concert our affair farther.

Arch. Come, my dear cussen, come along.   [*Exeunt.*

Enter BONIFACE, HOUNSLOW *and* BAGSHOT *at one door*, GIBBET *at the opposite*.

Gib. Well, gentlemen, 'tis a fine night for our enterprise.

Houn. Dark as hell.

Bag. And blows like the devil; our landlord here has showed us the window where we must break in, and tells us the plate stands in the wainscot cupboard in the parlour.

Bon. Ay, ay, Mr Bagshot, as the saying is, knives and forks, and cups and cans, and tumblers and tankards. There's one tankard, as the saying is, that's near upon as big as me; it was a present to the squire from his godmother, and smells of nutmeg and toast like an East-India ship.

Houn. Then you say we must divide at the stair-head?

Bon. Yes, Mr Hounslow, as the saying is. At one end of that gallery lies my Lady Bountiful and her daughter, and at the other Mrs Sullen. As for the squire—

Gib. He's safe enough, I have fairly entered him, and

he's more than half seas over already. But such a parcel of scoundrels are got about him now, that, egad, I was ashamed to be seen in their company.

Bon. 'Tis now twelve, as the saying is—gentlemen, you must set out at one.

Gib. Hounslow, do you and Bagshot see our arms fixed, and I'll come to you presently.

Houn. and Bag. We will. 　　　　　　[*Exeunt.*

Gib. Well, my dear Bonny, you assure me that Scrub is a coward?

Bon. A chicken, as the saying is. You'll have no creature to deal with but the ladies.

Gib. And I can assure you, friend, there's a great deal of address and good manners in robbing a lady; I am the most a gentleman that way that ever travelled the road.—But, my dear Bonny, this prize will be a galleon, a Vigo business. [1]—I warrant you we shall bring off three or four thousand pound.

Bon. In plate, jewels, and money, as the saying is, you may.

Gib. Why then, Tyburn, I defy thee! I'll get up to town, sell off my horse and arms, buy myself some pretty employment in the household, and be as snug and as honest as any courtier of 'em all.

Bon. And what think you then of my daughter Cherry for a wife?

Gib. Look'ee, my dear Bonny—Cherry *is the Goddess I adore*, as the song goes; but it is a maxim that man and wife should never have it in their power to hang one another; for if they should, the Lord have mercy on 'um both! 　　　　　　[*Exeunt.*

---

[1] In Sir George Rooke's action off Vigo, 12th October 1702, "abundance of plate and other valuables fell into the hands of the conquerors."

ACT V

SCENE I.—*The Inn.*

Knocking without, enter BONIFACE.

ON. Coming! coming!—A coach and six foaming horses at this time o'night! Some great man, as the saying is, for he scorns to travel with other people.

Enter Sir CHARLES FREEMAN.

Sir Chas. What, fellow! a public house, and abed when other people sleep!

Bon. Sir, I an't abed, as the saying is.

Sir Chas. Is Mr Sullen's family abed, think'ee?

Bon. All but the squire himself, sir, as the saying is ——he's in the house.

Sir Chas. What company has he?

Bon. Why, sir, there's the constable, Mr Gage the exciseman, the hunchbacked barber, and two or three other gentlemen.

Sir Chas. [*Aside.*] I find my sister's letters gave me the true picture of her spouse.

Enter SULLEN, *drunk.*

Bon. Sir, here's the squire.

432

Squire Sul. The puppies left me asleep—Sir !

Sir Chas. Well, sir.

Squire Sul. Sir, I'm an unfortunate man—I have three thousand pound a year, and I can't get a man to drink a cup of ale with me.

Sir Chas. That's very hard.

Squire Sul. Ay, sir; and unless you have pity upon me, and smoke one pipe with me, I must e'en go home to my wife, and I'd rather go to the devil by half.

Sir Chas. But I presume, sir, you won't see your wife to-night ; she'll be gone to bed.   You don't use to lie with your wife in that pickle ?

Squire Sul. What ! not lie with my wife !   Why, sir, do you take me for an atheist or a rake ?

Sir Chas. If you hate her, sir, I think you had better lie from her.

Squire Sul. I think so too, friend.   But I'm a justice of peace, and must do nothing against the law.

Sir Chas. Law ! As I take it, Mr Justice, nobody observes law for law's sake, only for the good of those for whom it was made.

Squire Sul. But, if the law orders me to send you to jail, you must lie there, my friend.

Sir Chas. Not unless I commit a crime to deserve it.

Squire Sul. A crime ! oons, an't I married ?

Sir Chas. Nay, sir, if you call marriage a crime, you must disown it for a law.

Squire Sul. Eh ! I must be acquainted with you, sir. —But, sir, I should be very glad to know the truth of this matter.

Sir Chas. Truth, sir, is a profound sea, and few there be that dare wade deep enough to find out the bottom on't.   Besides, sir, I'm afraid the line of your understanding mayn't be long enough.

Squire Sul. Look'ee, sir, I have nothing to say to your sea of truth, but if a good parcel of land can entitle a

man to a little truth, I have as much as any he in the country.

Bon. I never heard your worship, as the saying is, talk so much before.

Squire Sul. Because I never met with a man that I liked before.

Bon. Pray, sir, as the saying is, let me ask you one question : are not man and wife one flesh ?

Sir Chas. You and your wife, Mr Guts, may be one flesh, because ye are nothing else ; but rational creatures have minds that must be united.

Squire Sul. Minds !

Sir Chas. Ay, minds, sir : don't you think that the mind takes place of the body ?

Squire Sul. In some people.

Sir Chas. Then the interest of the master must be consulted before that of his servant.

Squire Sul. Sir, you shall dine with me to-morrow !— Oons, I always thought that we were naturally one.

Sir Chas. Sir, I know that my two hands are naturally one, because they love one another, kiss one another, help one another in all the actions of life ; but I could not say so much if they were always at cuffs.

Squire Sul. Then 'tis plain that we are two.

Sir Chas. Why don't you part with her, sir ?

Squire Sul. Will you take her, sir ?

Sir Chas. With all my heart.

Squire Sul. You shall have her to-morrow morning, and a venison-pasty into the bargain.

Sir Chas. You'll let me have her fortune too ?

Squire Sul. Fortune ! why, sir, I have no quarrel at her fortune : I only hate the woman, sir, and none but the woman shall go.

Sir Chas. But her fortune, sir—

Squire Sul. Can you play at whisk, sir ?

Sir Chas. No, truly, sir.

Squire Sul. Nor at all-fours?

Sir Chas. Neither.

Squire Sul. [*Aside.*] Oons! where was this man bred?—[*Aloud.*] Burn me, sir! I can't go home, 'tis but two a clock.

Sir Chas. For half an hour, sir, if you please; but you must consider 'tis late.

Squire Sul. Late! that's the reason I can't go to bed —Come, sir!   [*Exeunt.*

SCENE II [1].—*The Lobby before* AIMWELL'S *Chamber in the same.*

Enter CHERRY, *runs across the stage, and knocks at* AIMWELL'S *chamber-door. Enter* AIMWELL *in his nightcap and gown.*

Aim. What's the matter? You tremble, child, you're frighted.

Cher. No wonder, sir.—But, in short, sir, this very minute a gang of rogues are gone to rob my Lady Bountiful's house.

Aim. How!

Cher. I dogged 'em to the very door, and left 'em breaking in.

Aim. Have you alarmed anybody else with the news?

Cher. No, no, sir, I wanted to have discovered the whole plot, and twenty other things, to your man Martin; but I have searched the whole house, and can't find him! Where is he?

Aim. No matter, child; will you guide me immediately to the house?

Cher. With all my heart, sir; my Lady Bountiful is my godmother, and I love Mrs Dorinda so well—

[1] Change of scene not indicated in early editions, and unnecessary.

Aim. Dorinda ! the name inspires me ! The glory and the danger shall be all my own.—Come, my life, let me but get my sword.   [*Exeunt.*

SCENE III.—*A Bedchamber in* Lady BOUNTIFUL'S
House.

Mrs SULLEN *and* DORINDA *discovered.*[1]

Dor. 'Tis very late, sister—no news of your spouse yet ?

Mrs Sul. No, I'm condemned to be alone till towards four, and then perhaps I may be executed with his company.

Dor. Well, my dear, I'll leave you to your rest. You'll go directly to bed, I suppose ?

Mrs Sul. I don't know what to do.—Heigh-ho !

Dor. That's a desiring sigh, sister.

Mrs Sul. This is a languishing hour, sister.

Dor. And might prove a critical minute, if the pretty fellow were here.

Mrs Sul. Here ! what, in my bedchamber at two o'clock o' th' morning, I undressed, the family asleep my hated husband abroad, and my lovely fellow at my feet !—O 'gad, sister !

Dor. Thoughts are free, sister, and them I allow you.—So, my dear, good night.

Mrs Sul. A good rest to my dear Dorinda !—[*Exit* DORINDA.] Thoughts free ! are they so ? Why, then, suppose him here, dressed like a youthful, gay, and burning bridegroom,
     Here ARCHER *steals out of the closet.*
with tongue enchanting, eyes bewitching, knees implor-

[1] First edition : "*Enter* Mrs SUL., DOR. *undress'd, a Table and Lights.*"

ing.—[*Turns a little o' one side and sees* ARCHER *in the posture she describes.*]—Ah !—[*Shrieks and runs to the other side of the stage.*] Have my thoughts raised a spirit?—What are you, sir?—a man or a devil?

Arch. A man, a man, madam.   [*Rising.*

Mrs Sul. How shall I be sure of it?

Arch. Madam, I'll give you demonstration this minute.   [*Takes her hand.*

Mrs Sul. What, sir ! do you intend to be rude?

Arch. Yes, madam, if you please.

Mrs Sul. In the name of wonder, whence came ye?

Arch. From the skies, madam—I'm a Jupiter in love, and you shall be my Alcmena.

Mrs Sul. How came you in?

Arch. I flew in at the window, madam ; your cousin Cupid lent me his wings, and your sister Venus opened the casement.

Mrs Sul. I'm struck dumb with admiration !

Arch. And I—with wonder.

                              [*Looks passionately at her.*

Mrs Sul. What will become of me?

Arch. How beautiful she looks !—The teeming jolly Spring smiles in her blooming face, and, when she was conceived, her mother smelt to roses, looked on lilies—

Lilies unfold their white, their fragrant charms,

When the warm sun thus darts into their arms.

                                        [*Runs to her.*

Mrs Sul. Ah !   [*Shrieks.*

Arch. Oons, madam, what d'ye mean? you'll raise the house.

Mrs Sul. Sir, I'll wake the dead before I bear this ! —What ! approach me with the freedoms of a keeper ! I'm glad on't, your impudence has cured me.

Arch. If this be impudence,—[*Kneels.*] I leave to your partial self; no panting pilgrim, after a tedious, painful voyage, e'er bowed before his saint with more devotion.

Mrs Sul. [*Aside.*] Now, now, I'm ruined if he kneels !

—[*Aloud.*] Rise, thou prostrate engineer, not all thy undermining skill shall reach my heart.—Rise, and know, I am a woman without my sex; I can love to all the tenderness of wishes, sighs, and tears—but go no farther. Still, to convince you that I'm more than woman, I can speak my frailty, confess my weakness even for you—but—

Arch. For me!   [*Going to lay hold on her.*

Mrs Sul. Hold, sir! build not upon that; for my most mortal hatred follows if you disobey what I command you now.—Leave me this minute.—[*Aside.*] If he denies I'm lost.

Arch. Then you'll promise—

Mrs Sul. Anything another time.

Arch. When shall I come?

Mrs Sul. To-morrow—when you will.

Arch. Your lips must seal the promise.

Mrs Sul. Psha!

Arch. They must! they must!—[*Kisses her.*] Raptures and paradise!—And why not now, my angel? the time, the place, silence, and secrecy, all conspire—And the now conscious stars have preordained this moment for my happiness.   [*Takes her in his arms.*

Mrs Sul. You will not! cannot, sure!

Arch. If the sun rides fast, and disappoints not mortals of to-morrow's dawn, this night shall crown my joys.

Mrs Sul. My sex's pride assist me!

Arch. My sex's strength help me!

Mrs Sul. You shall kill me first!

Arch. I'll die with you.   [*Carrying her off.*

Mrs Sul. Thieves! thieves! murther!—

Enter SCRUB *in his breeches and one shoe.*

Scrub. Thieves! thieves! murder! popery!

Arch. Ha! the very timorous stag will kill in rutting time.   [*Draws, and offers to stab* SCRUB.

Scrub. [*Kneeling.*] O pray, sir, spare all I have, and take my life !

Mrs Sul. [*Holding* ARCHER'S *hand.*] What does the fellow mean ?

Scrub. O madam, down upon your knees, you marrowbones !—he's one of 'um.

Arch. Of whom ?

Scrub. One of the rogues—I beg your pardon, sir,—of the honest gentlemen that just now are broke into the house.

Arch. How !

Mrs Sul. I hope you did not come to rob me ?

Arch. Indeed I did, madam, but I would have taken nothing but what you might ha' spared ; but your crying " Thieves " has waked this dreaming fool, and so he takes 'em for granted.

Scrub. Granted ! 'tis granted, sir, take all we have.

Mrs Sul. The fellow looks as if he were broke out of Bedlam.

Scrub. Oons, madam, they're broke into the house with fire and sword ! I saw them, heard them, they'll be here this minute.

Arch. What, thieves ?

Scrub. Under favour, sir, I think so.

Mrs Sul. What shall we do, sir ?

Arch. Madam, I wish your ladyship a good night.

Mrs Sul. Will you leave me ?

Arch. Leave you ! Lord, madam, did not you command me to be gone just now, upon pain of your immortal hatred ?

Mrs Sul. Nay, but pray, sir— [*Takes hold of him.*

Arch. Ha, ha, ha ! now comes my turn to be ravished. —You see now, madam, you must use men one way or other ; but take this by the way, good madam, that none but a fool will give you the benefit of his courage, unless you'll take his love along with it.—How are they armed, friend ?

Scrub. With sword and pistol, sir.

Arch. Hush!—I see a dark lantern coming through the gallery.—Madam, be assured I will protect you, or lose my life.

Mrs Sul. Your life! no, sir, they can rob me of nothing that I value half so much; therefore, now, sir, let me entreat you to be gone.

Arch. No, madam, I'll consult my own safety for the sake of yours; I'll work by stratagem. Have you courage enough to stand the appearance of 'em!

Mrs Sul. Yes, yes, since I have 'scaped your hands, I can face anything.

Arch. Come hither, brother Scrub! don't you know me?

Scrub. Eh, my dear brother, let me kiss thee.

[Kisses ARCHER.

Arch. This way—here—

[ARCHER and SCRUB hide behind the bed.

Enter GIBBET, *with a dark lantern in one hand, and a pistol in t'other.*

Gib. Ay, ay, this is the chamber, and the lady alone.

Mrs Sul. Who are you, sir? what would you have? d'ye come to rob me?

Gib. Rob you! alack a day, madam, I'm only a younger brother, madam; and so, madam, if you make a noise, I'll shoot you through the head; but don't be afraid, madam.—[*Laying his lantern and pistol upon the table.*] These rings, madam—don't be concerned, madam, I have a profound respect for you, madam! Your keys, madam—don't be frighted, madam, I'm the most of a gentleman.—[*Searching her pockets.*] This necklace, madam—I never was rude to a lady;—I have a veneration—for this necklace—

[Here ARCHER having come round and seized the pistol, takes GIBBET by the collar, trips up his heels, and claps the pistol to his breast.

Arch. Hold, profane villain, and take the reward of thy sacrilege!

Gib. Oh! pray, sir, don't kill me; I an't prepared.

Arch. How many is there of 'em, Scrub?

Scrub. Five-and-forty, sir.

Arch. Then I must kill the villain, to have him out of the way.

Gib. Hold, hold, sir; we are but three, upon my honour.

Arch. Scrub, will you undertake to secure him?

Scrub. Not I, sir; kill him, kill him!

Arch. Run to Gipsy's chamber, there you'll find the doctor; bring him hither presently.—[*Exit* SCRUB, *running.*] Come, rogue, if you have a short prayer, say it.

Gib. Sir, I have no prayer at all; the government has provided a chaplain to say prayers for us on these occasions.

Mrs Sul. Pray, sir, don't kill him; you fright me as much as him.

Arch. The dog shall die, madam, for being the occasion of my disappointment.—Sirrah, this moment is your last.

Gib. Sir, I'll give you two hundred pound to spare my life.

Arch. Have you no more, rascal?

Gib. Yes, sir, I can command four hundred, but I must reserve two of 'em to save my life at the sessions.

Re-enter SCRUB *with* FOIGARD.

Arch. Here, doctor—I suppose Scrub and you between you may manage him. Lay hold of him, doctor. [FOIGARD *lays hold of* GIBBET.

Gib. What! turned over to the priest already!— Look'ye, doctor, you come before your time; I an't condemned yet, I thank ye.

Foi. Come, my dear joy, I vill secure your body and your shoul too; I vill make you a good catholic, and give you an absolution.

Gib. Absolution! can you procure me a pardon, doctor.

Foi. No, joy.

Gib. Then you and your absolution may go to the devil!

Arch. Convey him into the cellar, there bind him :—take the pistol, and if he offers to resist, shoot him through the head—and come back to us with all the speed you can.

Scrub. Ay, ay; come, doctor—do you hold him fast, and I'll guard him.

[*Exit* FOIGARD *with* GIBBET, SCRUB *following.*

Mr Sul. But how came the doctor.

Arch. In short, madam—[*Shrieking without.*] 'Sdeath! the rogues are at work with the other ladies—I'm vexed I parted with the pistol; but I must fly to their assistance.—Will you stay here, madam, or venture yourself with me?

Mrs Sul. [*Taking him by the arm.*] Oh, with you, dear sir, with you.   [*Exeunt.*

SCENE IV.

Another Apartment in the same House.

Enter HOUNSLOW *dragging in* Lady BOUNTIFUL, *and* BAGSHOT *haling in* DORINDA; *the rogues with swords drawn.*

Houn. Come, come, your jewels, mistress!

Bag. Yonr keys, your keys, old gentlewoman!

Enter AIMWELL *and* CHERRY.

Aim. Turn this way, villains! I durst engage an army in such a cause.   [*He engages 'em both.*

Dor. O madam, had I but a sword to help the brave man!

Lady Boun. There's three or four hanging up in the hall; but they won't draw. I'll go fetch one, however.
                                        [*Exit.*

Enter ARCHER *and* Mrs SULLEN.

Arch. Hold, hold, my lord! every man his bird, pray.   [*They engage man to man, the rogues are thrown and disarmed.*

Cher. [*Aside.*] What! the rogues taken! then they'll impeach my father; I must give him timely notice.   [*Runs out.*

Arch. Shall we kill the rogues?

Aim. No, no, we'll bind them.

Arch. Ay, Ay.—[*To* Mrs SULLEN *who stands by him.*] Here, madam, lend me your garter.

Mrs Sul. [*Aside.*] The devil's in this fellow! he fights, loves, and banters, all in a breath.—[*Aloud.*] Here's a cord that the rogues brought with 'em, I suppose.

Arch. Right, right, the rogue's destiny, a rope to hang himself.—Come, my lord—this is but a scandalous sort of an office, [*Binding the Rogues together.*] if our adventures should end in this sort of hangman-work; but I hope there is something in prospect, that—

Enter SCRUB.

Well, Scrub, have you secured your Tartar?

Scrub. Yes, sir, I left the priest and him disputing about religion.

Aim. And pray carry these gentlemen to reap the benefit of the controversy.   [*Delivers the prisoners to* SCRUB, *who leads 'em out.*

Mrs Sul. Pray, sister, how came my lord here?

Dor. And pray how came the gentleman here?

Mrs Sul. I'll tell you the greatest piece of villainy—   [*They talk in dumb show.*

Aim. I fancy, Archer, you have been more successful in your adventures than the housebreakers.

Arch. No matter for my adventure, yours is the principal.—Press her this minute to marry you—now

while she's hurried between the palpitation of her fear
and the joy of her deliverance, now, while the tide of her
spirits are at high-flood—throw yourself at her feet,
speak some romantic nonsense or other—address her
like Alexander in the height of his victory, confound her
senses, bear down her reason, and away with her.—The
priest is now in the cellar, and dare not refuse to do the
work.

Re-enter Lady BOUNTIFUL.

Aim. But how shall I get off without being observed?

Arch. You a lover, and not find a way to get off !—
Let me see—

Aim. You bleed, Archer.

Arch. 'Sdeath, I'm glad on't; this wound will do the
business. I'll amuse the old lady and Mrs Sullen about
dressing my wound, while you carry off Dorinda.

Lady Boun. Gentlemen, could we understand how you
would be gratified for the services—

Arch. Come, come, my lady, this is no time for com-
pliments; I'm wounded, madam.

Lady Boun. and Mrs Sul. How! wounded!

Dor. I hope, sir, you have received no hurt.

Aim. None but what you may cure—

[*Makes love in dumb show.*

Lady Boun. Let me see your arm, sir—I must have
some powder-sugar to stop the blood.—O me! an ugly
gash, upon my word, sir! You must go into bed.

Arch. Ay, my lady, a bed would do very well.—[*To
Mrs* SULLEN.] Madam, will you do me the favour to
conduct me to a chamber?

Lady Boun. Do, do, daughter—while I get the lint
and the probe and the plaster ready.

[*Runs out one way,* AIMWELL *carries
off* DORINDA *another.*

Arch. Come, madam, why don't you obey your
mother's commands?

Mrs Sul. How can you, after what is passed, have the confidence to ask me?

Arch. And if you go to that, how can you, after what is passed, have the confidence to deny me? Was not this blood shed in your defence, and my life exposed for your protection? Look'ye, madam, I'm none of your romantic fools, that fight giants and monsters for nothing; my valour is downright Swiss; I'm a soldier of fortune, and must be paid.

Mrs Sul. 'Tis ungenerous in you, sir, to upbraid me with your services!

Arch. 'Tis ungenerous in you, madam, not to reward 'em.

Mrs Sul. How! at the expense of my honour?

Arch. Honour! can honour consist with ingratitude? If you would deal like a woman of honour, do like a man of honour. D'ye think I would deny you in such a case?

Enter a Servant.

Ser. Madam, my lady ordered me to tell you that your brother is below at the gate.   [*Exit.*

Mrs Sul. My brother! Heavens be praised!—Sir, he shall thank you for your services, he has it in his power.

Arch. Who is your brother, madam?

Mrs Sul. Sir Charles Freeman.—You'll excuse me, sir; I must go and receive him.   [*Exit.*

Arch. Sir Charles Freeman! 'sdeath and hell! my old acquaintance! Now unless Aimwell has made good use of his time, all our fair machine goes souse into the sea like the Eddystone. [1]   [*Exit.*

---

[1] "The first lighthouse was commenced under Mr Winstanley in 1696; finished in 1699; and destroyed in the dreadful tempest of 27th November 1703, when Mr Winstanley and others perished."

SCENE V.—*The Gallery in the same.*

Enter AIMWELL *and* DORINDA.

Dor. Well, well, my lord, you have conquered; your
late generous action will, I hope, plead for my easy
yielding; though I must own, your lordship had a friend
in the fort before.

Aim. The sweets of Hybla dwell upon her tongue!—
Here, doctor—

Enter FOIGARD, *with a book.*

Foi. Are you prepared boat?

Dor. I'm ready. But first, my lord, one word—I
have a frightful example of a hasty marriage in my own
family; when I reflect upon't, it shocks me. Pray, my
lord, consider a little—

Aim. Consider! do you doubt my honour or my love?

Dor. Neither: I do believe you equally just as brave :
and were your whole sex drawn out for me to choose, I
should not cast a look upon the multitude if you were
absent. But, my lord, I'm a woman; colours, conceal-
ments may hide a thousand faults in me—therefore
know me better first. I hardly dare affirm I know myself, in anything except my love.

Aim. [*Aside.*] Such goodness who could injure! I
find myself unequal to the task of villain; she has
gained my soul, and made it honest like her own—I
cannot, cannot hurt her.—[*Aloud.*] Doctor, retire.—
[*Exit* FOIGARD.] Madam, behold your lover and your
proselyte, and judge of my passion by my conversion!—
I'm all a lie, nor dare I give a fiction to your arms; I'm
all counterfeit, except my passion.

Dor. Forbid it, Heaven! a counterfeit!

Aim. I am no lord, but a poor needy man, come with
a mean, a scandalous design to prey upon your fortune;
but the beauties of your mind and person have so won

me from myself, that, like a trusty servant, I prefer the interest of my mistress to my own.

Dor. Sure I have had the dream of some poor mariner, a sleepy image of a welcome port, and wake involved in storms !—Pray, sir, who are you?

Aim. Brother to the man whose title I usurped, but stranger to his honour or his fortune.

Dor. Matchless honesty !—Once I was proud, sir, of your wealth and title, but now am prouder that you want it: now I can show my love was justly levelled, and had no aim but love.—Doctor, come in.

Enter Foigard *at one door,* Gipsy *at another, who whispers* Dorinda.

[*To* Foigard.] Your pardon, sir, we shannot want you now.—[*To* Aimwell.] Sir, you must excuse me—I'll wait on you presently.   [*Exit with* Gipsy.

Foi. Upon my shoul, now, dis is foolish.   [*Exit.*

Aim. Gone! and bid the priest depart!—It has an ominous look.

Enter Archer.

Arch. Courage, Tom !—Shall I wish you joy?

Aim. No.

Arch. Oons, man, what ha' you been doing?

Aim. O Archer! my honesty, I fear, has ruined me.

Arch. How!

Aim. I have discovered myself.

Arch. Discovered! and without my consent? What! have I embarked my small remains in the same bottom with yours, and you dispose of all without my partnership?

Aim. O Archer! I own my fault.

Arch. After conviction—'tis then too late for pardon. —You may remember, Mr Aimwell, that you proposed this folly: as you begun, so end it. Henceforth I'll hunt my fortune single—so farewell!

Aim. Stay, my dear Archer, but a minute.

Arch. Stay! what, to be despised, exposed, and laughed at! No, I would sooner change conditions with the worst of the rogues we just now bound, than bear one scornful smile from the proud knight that once I treated as my equal.

Aim. What knight?

Arch. Sir Charles Freeman, brother to the lady that I had almost—but no matter for that, 'tis a cursed night's work, and so I leave you to make the best on't. [*Going.*

Aim. Freeman!—One word, Archer. Still I have hopes; methought she received my confession with pleasure.

Arch. 'Sdeath, who doubts it?

Aim. She consented after to the match; and still I dare believe she will be just.

Arch. To herself, I warrant her, as you should have been.

Aim. By all my hopes, she comes, and smiling comes!

Re-enter DORINDA *mighty gay.*

Dor. Come, my dear lord—I fly with impatience to your arms—the minutes of my absence was a tedious year. Where's this tedious priest?

Re-enter FOIGARD.

Arch. Oons, a brave girl!

Dor. I suppose, my lord, this gentleman is privy to our affairs?

Arch. Yes, yes, madam; I'm to be your father.

Dor. Come, priest, do your office.

Arch. Make haste, make haste, couple 'em any way. —[*Takes* AIMWELL's *hand.*] Come, madam, I'm to give you—

Dor. My mind's altered; I won't.

Arch. Eh!—

Aim. I'm confounded!

Foi. Upon my shoul, and sho is myshelf.

Arch. What's the matter now, madam?

Dor. Look'ye, sir, one generous action deserves another.—This gentleman's honour obliged him to hide nothing from me; my justice engages me to conceal nothing from him. In short, sir, you are the person that you thought you counterfeited; you are the true Lord Viscount Aimwell, and I wish your lordship joy.— Now, priest, you may be gone; if my lord is pleased now with the match, let his lordship marry me in the the face of the world.

Aim. and Arch. What does she mean?

Dor. Here's a witness for my truth.

Enter Sir CHARLES FREEMAN *and* Mrs SULLEN.

Sir Chas. My dear Lord Aimwell, I wish you joy.

Aim. Of what?

Sir Chas. Of your honour and estate. Your brother died the day before I left London; and all your friends have writ after you to Brussels;—among the rest I did myself the honour.

Arch. Heark'ye, sir knight, don't you banter now?

Sir Chas. 'Tis truth, upon my honour.

Aim. Thanks to the pregnant stars that formed this accident!

Arch. Thanks to the womb of time that brought it forth!—away with it!

Aim. Thanks to my guardian angel that led me to the prize! [*Taking* DORINDA'S *hand.*

Arch. And double thanks to the noble Sir Charles Freeman.—My lord, I wish you joy.—My lady, I wish you joy.—Egad, Sir Freeman, you're the honestest fellow living!—'Sdeath, I'm grown strange airy upon this matter.—My lord, how d'ye?—A word, my lord; don't you remember something of a previous agreement, that entitles me to the moiety of this lady's

fortune, which I think will amount to five thousand
pound?

Aim. Not a penny, Archer; you would ha' cut my
throat just now, because I would not deceive this lady.

Arch. Ay, and I'll cut your throat again, if you should
deceive her now.

Aim. That's what I expected; and to end the dispute, the lady's fortune is ten thousand pounds, we'll
divide stakes: take the ten thousand pounds or the
lady.

Dor. How! is your lordship so indifferent?

Arch. No, no, no, madam! his lordship knows very
well that I'll take the money; I leave you to his lordship, and so we're both provided for.

Enter Count BELLAIR.[1]

Count Bel. *Mesdames et Messieurs*, I am your servant
trice humble! I hear you be rob here.

Aim. The ladies have been in some danger, sir.

Count Bel. And, begar, our inn be rob too!

Aim. Our inn! by whom?

Count Bel. By the landlord, begar!—Garzoon, he has
rob himself, and run away?

Arch. Robbed himself!

Count Bel. Ay, begar,, and me too of a hundre
pound.

Arch. A hundred pound?

Count Bel. Yes, that I owed him.

Aim. Our money's gone, Frank.

Arch. Rot the money! my wench is gone.—[*To*
Count BELLAIR.] *Savez-vous quelquechose de Mademoiselle
Cherry?*

Enter a Fellow with a strong box and a letter.

Fell. Is there one Martin here?

Arch. Ay, ay—who wants him?

Fell. I have a box here, and letter for him.

[*Gives the box and letter to* ARCHER *and exit.*

Arch. Ha, ha, ha! what's here? Legerdemain!—By this light, my lord, our money again!—But this unfolds the riddle.—[*Opening the letter, reads.*] Hum, hum, hum!—Oh, 'tis for the public good, and must be communicated to the company.   [*Reads.*

> *Mr Martin,*
>
> *My father being afraid of an impeachment by the rogues that are taken to-night, is gone off; but if you can procure him a pardon, he will make great discoveries that may be useful to the country. Could I have met you instead of your master to-night, I would have delivered myself into your hands, with a sum that much exceeds that in your strong-box, which I have sent you, with an assurance to my dear Martin that I shall ever be his most faithful friend till death.* CHERRY BONIFACE.

There's a billet-doux for you! As for the father, I think he ought to be encouraged; and for the daughter —pray, my lord, persuade your bride to take her into her service instead of Gipsy.

Aim. I can assure you, madam, your deliverance was owing to her discovery.

Dor. Your command, my lord, will do without the obligation. I'll take care of her.

Sir Chas. This good company meets opportunely in favour of a design I have in behalf of my unfortunate sister. I intend to part her from her husband—gentlemen, will you assist me?

Arch. Assist you! 'sdeath, who would not?

Count Bel. Assist! garzoon, we all assist!

Enter SULLEN *and* SCRUB.

Squire Sul. What's all this? They tell me, spouse, that you had like to have been robbed.

Mrs Sul. Truly, spouse, I was pretty near it—had not these two gentlemen interposed.

Squire Sul. How came these gentlemen here?

Mrs Sul. That's his way of returning thanks, you must know.

Count Bel. Garzoon, the question be apropos for all dat.

Sir Chas. You promised last night, sir, that you would deliver your lady to me this morning.

Squire Sul. Humph!

Arch. Humph! what do you mean by humph? Sir, you shall deliver her! In short, sir, we have saved you and your family; and if you are not civil, we'll unbind the rogues, join with 'um, and set fire to your house. What does the man mean? not part with his wife!

Count Bel. Ay, garzoon, de man no understan common justice.

Mrs Sul. Hold, gentlemen! All things here must move by consent; compulsion would spoil us. Let my dear and I talk the matter over, and you shall judge it between us.

Squire Sul. Let me know first who are to be our judges. Pray, sir, who are you?

Sir Chas. I am Sir Charles Freeman, come to take away your wife.

Squire Sul. And you, good sir?

Aim. Charles, Viscount Aimwell, come to take away your sister.

Squire Sul. And you, pray, sir?

Arch. Francis Archer, esquire, come—

Squire Sul. To take away my mother, I hope. Gentlemen, you're heartily welcome; I never met with three more obliging people since I was born!—And now, my dear, if you please, you shall have the first word.

Arch. And the last, for five pound!

Mrs Sul. Spouse!

Squire Sul. Rib!

Mrs Sul. How long have we been married?

Squire Sul. By the almanac, fourteen months; but by my account, fourteen years.

Mrs Sul. 'Tis thereabout by my reckoning.

Count Bel. Garzoon, their account will agree.

Mrs Sul. Pray, spouse, what did you marry for?

Squire Sul. To get an heir to my estate.

Sir Chas. And have you succeeded?

Squire Sul. No.

Arch. The condition fails of his side.—Pray, madam, what did you marry for?

Mrs Sul. To support the weakness of my sex by the strength of his, and to enjoy the pleasures of an agreeable society.

Sir Chas. Are your expectations answered?

Mrs Sul. No.

Count Bel. A clear case! a clear case!

Sir Chas. What are the bars to your mutual contentment?

Mrs Sul. In the first place, I can't drink ale with him.

Squire Sul. Nor can I drink tea with her.

Mrs Sul. I can't hunt with you.

Squire Sul. Nor can I dance with you.

Mrs Sul. I hate cocking and racing.

Squire Sul. And I abhor ombre and piquet.

Mrs Sul. Your silence is intolerable.

Squire Sul. Your prating is worse.

Mrs Sul. Have we not been a perpetual offence to each other? a gnawing vulture at the heart?

Squire Sul. A frightful goblin to the sight?

Mrs Sul. A porcupine to the feeling?

Squire Sul. Perpetual wormwood to the taste?

Mrs Sul. Is there on earth a thing we could agree in?

Squire Sul. Yes—to part.

Mrs Sul. With all my heart.

Squire Sul. Your hand.

Mrs Sul. Here.

Squire Sul. These hands joined us, these shall part us.—Away !

Mrs Sul. North.

Squire Sul. South.

Mrs Sul. East.

Squire Sul. West—far as the poles asunder.

Count Bel. Begar, the ceremony be vera pretty.

Sir Chas. Now, Mr Sullen, there wants only my sister's fortune to make us easy.

Squire Sul. Sir Charles, you love your sister and I love her fortune ; every one to his fancy.

Arch. Then you won't refund ?

Squire Sul. Not a stiver.

Arch. Then I find, madam, you must e'en go to your prison again.

Count Bel. What is the portion ?

Sir Chas. Ten thousand pound, sir.

Count Bel. Garzoon, I'll pay it, and she shall go home wid me.

Arch. Ha, ha, ha ! French all over.—Do you know, sir, what ten thousand pound English is ?

Count Bel. No, begar, not justement.

Arch. Why, sir, 'tis a hundred thousand livres.

Count Bel. A hundre tousand livres ! A garzoon, me canno' do't ! Your beauties and their fortunes are both too much for me.

Arch. Then I will.—This night's adventure has proved strangely lucky to us all—for Captain Gibbet in his walk had made bold, Mr Sullen, with your study and escritoir, and had taken out all the writings of your estate, all the articles of marriage with your lady, bills, bonds, leases, receipts to an infinite value ; I took 'em from him, and I deliver 'em to Sir Charles.

[*Gives* Sir CHARLES FREEMAN *a parcel of papers and parchments.*

Squire Sul. How, my writings !—my head aches con-

sumedly.—Well, gentlemen, you shall have her fortune, but I can't talk. If you have a mind, Sir Charles, to be merry, and celebrate my sister's wedding and my divorce, you may command my house—but my head aches consumedly.—Scrub, bring me a dram.

Arch. [*To* Mrs SULLEN.] Madam, there's a country dance to the trifle that I sung to-day; your hand, and we'll lead it up.

Here a Dance.

Arch. 'Twould be hard to guess which of these parties is the better pleased, the couple joined, or the couple parted: the one rejoicing in hopes of an untasted happiness, and the other in their deliverance from an experienced misery.

Both happy in their several states we find,
Those parted by consent, and those conjoined.
Consent, if mutual, saves the lawyer's fee—
Consent is law enough to set you free.

EPILOGUE

DESIGNED TO BE SPOKE IN THE " BEAUX'
STRATAGEM."

F to our play your judgment can't be
kind,
Let its expiring author pity find :
Survey his mournful case with melt-
ing eyes,
Nor let the bard be damned before
he dies.
Forbear, you fair, on his last scene to frown,
But his true exit with a plaudit crown ;
Then shall the dying poet cease to fear
The dreadful knell, while your applause he hears.
At Leuctra so the conquering Theban died,
Claimed his friends' praises, but their tears denied :
Pleased in the pangs of death, he greatly thought
Conquest with loss of life but cheaply bought.
The difference this,—the Greek was one would fight,
As brave, though not so gay, as Serjeant Kite ;
Ye sons of Will's,[1] what's that to those who write ?
To Thebes alone the Grecian owed his bays ;
You may the bard above the hero raise,
Since yours is greater than Athenian praise.

[1] Frequenters of Will's coffee-house : poets, men of letters.

Lightning Source UK Ltd.
Milton Keynes UK
UKOW04f1929210715

255602UK00001B/87/P